CRITICAL ACCLAIM
FOR *A WOMAN'S WORLD*

"Whether it's trekking through remote Bhutan, congregating at a well in Cameroon or piling into a minivan fro an annual trip to an outlet mall in Eastern Tennessee, women approach travel with a unique sense of discovery and appreciation for other cultures. *A Woman's World* is another excellent addition to the *Travelers' Tales* series. I wanted to meet all of these women."

— Carol Pucci, *The Seattle Times*

"A Woman's World is a wondrous journey into the heart of womanhood and a hard book to put down. I felt a true sisterhood with the writers as they shared their laughter and pain, and was awed by the adventures they chose to tackle. More than entertaining, this moving collection of personal tales is certain to encourage and inspire women in their search for the true meaning of life."

— Barbara Harris, Editor-in-Chief, *Shape Magazine*

"Women do travel differently than men, and as I read *A Woman's World* I found myself admiring their insight, their determination and their courage. Marybeth Bond has put together a wonderful collection of stories that shape a fascinating perspective of women on the go and the places they visit."

— Jay Clarke, Travel Editor, *The Miami Herald*

"This is not just a book for 'Everywoman'…It's also a book for 'Everyman.' It shows how women travel through the world and how the world relates to them."

— Everett Potter, *The New York Times*

"I chose *A Woman's World* as required reading for my class because here I see very positive experiences of women taking risks to make change in their lives. There is an important message here: don't get discouraged, don't get scared."

— Mary Beth Halsey, 10th grade English teacher, Santa Rosa, California

"My top pick for travel books this year is *A Woman's World*—56 short stories written by the world's finest female travel writers. You'll be taken on every kind of adventure: walking, hiking, fishing, diving…and discover why women make some of the best travelers. Well-written, insightful, and even humorous at times, these stories will touch your heart and get you planning and packing for your next adventure."

— Linda Frahm, Managing Editor, *Walking Magazine*

TRAVELERS' TALES BOOKS

Country and Regional Guides
America, Australia, Brazil, Central America, Cuba, France, Greece,
India, Ireland, Italy, Japan, Mexico, Nepal, Spain, Thailand, Tibet,
Turkey; American Southwest, Grand Canyon, Hawai'i,
Hong Kong, Paris, Provence, San Francisco, Tuscany

Women's Travel
Her Fork in the Road, A Woman's Path, A Woman's
Passion for Travel, A Woman's World, Women in the Wild,
A Mother's World, Safety and Security for Women
Who Travel, Gutsy Women, Gutsy Mamas

Body & Soul
The Spiritual Gifts of Travel, The Road Within,
Love & Romance, Food, The Fearless Diner, The Adventure
of Food, The Ultimate Journey, Pilgrimage

Special Interest
Not So Funny When It Happened,
The Gift of Rivers, Shitting Pretty, Testosterone Planet,
Danger!, The Fearless Shopper, The Penny Pincher's
Passport to Luxury Travel, The Gift of Birds, Family Travel,
A Dog's World, There's No Toilet Paper on the Road
Less Traveled, The Gift of Travel, 365 Travel,
Adventures in Wine, Sand in My Bra and Other Misadventures

Footsteps
Kite Strings of the Southern Cross, The Sword of Heaven,
Storm, Take Me With You, Last Trout in Venice, The Way of
the Wanderer, One Year Off, The Fire Never Dies

Classics
The Royal Road to Romance,
Unbeaten Tracks in Japan, The Rivers Ran East,
Coast to Coast, Trader Horn

TRAVELERS' TALES

A WOMAN'S WORLD

TRUE STORIES OF WORLD TRAVEL

TRAVELERS' TALES

A WOMAN'S
WORLD

TRUE STORIES OF WORLD TRAVEL

Edited by
MARYBETH BOND

Series Editors
JAMES O'REILLY AND LARRY HABEGGER

TRAVELERS' TALES
SAN FRANCISCO

Art Direction: Michele Wetherbee
Interior design: Kathryn Heflin and Susan Bailey
Spot Illustrations: David White
Part Opener Illustrations: Nina Stewart
Cover photograph: Marybeth bond at the summit of 20,305-foot Island Peak in Nepal
Page layout: Cynthia Lamb and Patty Holden using the fonts Bembo and Boulevard

Distributed by: Publishers Group West, 1700 Fourth Street, Berkeley, California 94710.

Library of Congress Cataloguing-in-Publication Data

Available upon request

First Edition

Printed in the United States

10 9 8 7 6 5 4 3 2 1

I wish that every human life might be pure transparent freedom.

—SIMONE DE BEAUVOIR,
The Blood of Others

Table of Contents

Part Two
SOME THINGS TO DO

Part Four
IN THE SHADOWS

Part Five
THE LAST WORD

Preface

TRAVELERS' TALES

"Of all the gifts that people can give to one another, the most meaningful and long lasting are strong but simple love and the gift of story."
> — Clarissa Pinkola Estés, Ph.D., *The Gift of Story:*
> *A Wise Tale About What is Enough*

Years ago two simple magazine articles appeared in *Outside* and *Self* magazines about my solo travels in Asia and Africa. They generated an amazing response from female readers. Although my story intrigued them, my intuition told me that what they really wanted was support and encouragement to make their own escapes. Hence this book, which now appears in this updated edition.

As I became aware of other women's travel experiences, I also began to be aware that women travel quite differently than men do, that we look for different things, we stop for different reasons, our goals and styles are different, and what we take from our travels is different. I also noticed that while more and more women of all ages and means are taking to the road, the majority of travel books are by men and geared to men and their view of our small blue universe. And no matter how egalitarian the writer, there are often things missing for the woman traveler and reader.

The moment we step out of the door, we are aware of the footsteps behind us. We are more concerned for our personal safety than men, and with good reason. We are haunted by different fears.

When we travel, we pause more to listen, assimilate, to move in and out of the lives of those we meet on the way. Where women go, relationships follow, from encounters with nature or special moments of connection and friendship with others.

I am reminded of a trek I took in the Himalayas, traveling with a group of men and women. When hiking through local villages, most of the men focused their cameras, snapped their pictures, and, intent on reaching their goal, hiked quickly on. The women, on the other hand, lingered, moved in closer, made eye contact (most often with other women), sometimes cooing over a child or going as far as rocking a baby.

Most women travelers I know try to learn enough words in the local language to say not just "How much?" or "How far?" but "Nice home. Beautiful jewelry," or ask "How many children? Boys or girls? How old?" Silent bonds develop through smiles and gestures. Women easily play the fool to bring laughter to groups of children or adults with puppets, wind-up toys, or dancing the Hokey Pokey.

Women love to talk. But we also love to listen to each other's experiences, joys, and heartbreaks. And we love to do it whether we're on the road or at home, gathered at the well, in a café, or on the telephone sharing a good story. In *A Woman's World,* I've gathered contemporary stories that describe the inner and outer panoramas of women's journeys.

In this anthology women relate their most intimate travel experiences, from the absurd to the sublime. They range from a villa in Acapulco to a village in Cameroon, a haircut in Beijing to a bus ride through the American West. In one story, a pilgrim has a spiritual awakening at the sanctuary of the Mother Goddess in France, in another a woman fishes for marlin in memory of her father, in another a woman struggles with menopause in a Borneo jungle.

The authors come from many walks of life. They are writers, doctors, teachers, nurses, athletes, young and old, mothers and grandmothers, novice and well-seasoned travelers, women traveling alone, in a couple, in a group. But whatever their background or mode of travel, in each story a female voice resonates: a ten-year-old gives her perspective of a plane ride to Europe, an arthritic senior shoots the rapids in the Grand Canyon with her daughter, a young woman swims the Bering Strait on the very edge of life.

The reader response has been enthusiastic and passionate.

"Sometimes in the frenetic pace of my everyday world, I lose that part of me that is so uniquely female," one reader wrote. "*A Woman's World* reawakened that wonderful place inside of me—and reminded me that I share it with every other woman out there. *A Woman's World* made me feel good about being a woman."

Another letter read, "This was more than a book about travel for me—it was a book about living, about feeling, about learning, about loving. There are times in our lives when we all feel alone. I was at one of those places in my life when I read your book. What wonderful therapy! I came away still feeling alone, but feeling my strength in being a woman alone—and loving it."

A school librarian in Dyersburg, Tennessee lent the book to a friend who read one story a day to her dying mother. She wrote that her friend found the stories were both healing and life-affirming.

A high school English teacher used the book with her students to contrast with *Lord of the Flies*, in which there are no female characters. The teacher wrote, "Thank you for providing young women with confident, capable, adventurous role models as they move through a period of upheaval in their lives, the teenage years."

Such heartfelt words inspired us to release this updated edition with a few minor changes. My new contributions to *A Woman's World* reflect my evolving life journeys, from two years of solo travel around the world when I was in my late twenties (which was at a time of remarkable intellectual and personal freedom), to my recent travels with my husband, children, and girlfriends.

After I appeared, with my book *Gutsy Women,* on *The Oprah Winfrey Show* on a segment about "Sabbaticals for the Soul," I renewed my efforts to urge women to take time off to revive themselves. As demonstrated throughout this book, many women use travel as the cocoon stage in which to grow, discover themselves, and make changes that would be harder to make at home.

As women, our voices, our words, and our stories help us understand and celebrate our collective experience and individual strengths. In these pages we share our stories of success and vulnerability, thereby sharing vital knowledge, encouragement, and confidence—even, yes, wisdom.

Whether you read one or all the stories in this book, may something in these voices touch you, inspire you, and open a door.

MARYBETH BOND

A Woman's World: An Introduction

BY DERVLA MURPHY

Travelers' Tales: A Woman's World records a piquant variety of experiences: probing a mother-daughter relationship in Guatemala; finding the answer to "some deep nostalgia" in Bhutan; being absorbed into a New Delhi family; coming to terms with a major emotional crisis on the Great Barrier Reef; learning from the attitudes of fellow patients in a rural Javanese hospital; self-testing, on several levels, during a long-distance bus journey through America; fighting depression by camping out alone in below-freezing temperatures.... What next? Eagerly one turns the pages to find out. And gradually a tendency to use travel as therapy emerges.

In times past, women also used travel as therapy—but less self-consciously. For centuries traveling abroad was the only acceptable form of rebellion available to the nicely-brought-up woman. Well, *fairly* acceptable; it did mark her as eccentric but not actually immoral. Or at least not provably so, for who could know what she might get up—or down—to in far-flung places.... The relief of escaping from their conventional domestic role is palpable in the writings of Lady Mary Wortley Montagu, Margaret Fountaine, Lucy Duff Gordon, Isabelle Eberhardt, Lady Anne Blunt, Alexandra David-Neel, Isabella Bird, and very many others less well-known but no less enterprising.

During the imperial/colonial era women's insouciant adaptability to unfamiliar, and often disconcerting, cultures and climates showed up the essential timidity of most of their male contemporaries. On the whole, men had to impose *their* way of life on a territory before they could feel at ease; they sought to dominate, convert, exploit, "improve." The average woman traveler was—

and, as this book proves, still is—much more responsive to the individuals met en route, more interested in the minutiae of their daily
lives, in local social problems, in the subtle nuances of family life as
it has been variously molded by different religions and economic
or climatic conditions.

Nowadays the only restraints put on women's rovings are self-
imposed; they no longer have to rebel before taking off for Far-
Flungery. Yet I often get letters, from women of all ages, plaintively
admitting, "I would love to do what you do but I haven't got the
courage." This greatly bothers me, as a measure of how unliberated
some women remain. (From men I get letters saying, "I'm going to
do what you did, please can you advise me on X, Y, or Z.")

The notion that women traveling alone are more at risk than
men is difficult to dislodge from our mass-consciousness. I, however, believe the reverse to be true, in places as yet uncorrupted by
tourists. The solo woman traveler—there is a nice irony here—
brings out the best in the male chauvinists who populate remote
regions. At home she is seen as a model of "liberation": independent, innovative, resourceful, self-assured. Away out in the wilds,
where no one has ever heard of feminism and would spit if they
had, she is safe not because she is resourceful and self-assured but
because she is seen as a member of the weaker sex, needing protection. In areas where the lone male might arouse suspicions of their
motive for being there, and/or covetousness of his few possessions,
the lone female need not worry. Perceived as vulnerable, she won't
be hurt.

But what about rape? Many of my unknown correspondents,
living in societies so shattered that rape has become a hobby, give
that as their reason for fearing to travel. Some register incredulity
when told that in unshattered rural societies, bound by tradition,
rape is not a hobby and solitary women are not fair game. They
may be approached by hopeful men who fancy them, but that is no
threat. Having politely to decline sexual advances in Baltistan,
Coorg, or Ecuador is no more stressful than having politely to decline them in San Francisco, London, or Paris. In my experience
the only exceptions to the above are Eastern Turkey and the adja-

cent northwestern corner of Iran. There you must exert yourself to avoid rape; bring a heavy stick and don't hesitate to wield it with vigour.

As a sexagenarian, approaching the end of a lifetime of travel, I am alarmed by a new hazard in the way of the itchy-footed young. Moving around the world has become so easy, and organized tourism is so pervasive that it is hard to be a genuine traveler rather than a tourist. Hard but not impossible. And the effort is well worthwhile, especially for women who like to go it alone.

Each individual has to devise her own adventure, sitting at home poring over the atlas, being personally ignited by the notion of *here* or *there*. Real travel is not a consumer item, it is a private, idiosyncratic thing, the traveler feeling the urge to go forth, un-protected, to confront the unfamiliar, and being happy to accept modifications—hitherto unimaginable—of the standards and prej-udices with which she left home. That unprotected confrontation of the unfamiliar, implying trust of one's fellow beings, is what makes traveling a mutually enriching experience. "Primitive" peo-ple are not just there to be photographed. They have much to teach us citizens of the over-developed West. Unlike us, they are still plugged in to the physical, mental, and emotional realities of ordinary human existence. By insisting on bringing our own world with us, by refusing to share in their daily lives, we waste our journeys. If organized tourism becomes the norm, our omi-nous disconnectedness from others (and at the deepest level from ourselves) will be aggravated.

However, as this book makes plain, women travelers are less prone to disconnectedness than men. In her Preface, Marybeth Bond notes: "Where women go, relationships follow…" She quotes a telling example from one of her own lengthy journeys through the Himalayas, an example which suggests that the shared experi-ence of nurturing creates a peculiarly strong link between women, however dissimilar their backgrounds may be. *A Woman's World* illustrates this attentiveness to others through an astounding range of experiences from the apparently trivial to the profound, from the suspenseful to the soothing, from the melodramatic to the comic. Marybeth Bond mentions the importance of her mother, who taught her to believe in herself. The contrasting experiences recorded in this book have the potential to help thousands of women believe in themselves *as travelers.*

Dervla Murphy is the award-winning author of numerous books and is considered the "Grand Dame of Women's Travel Literature." Since 1964, when she rode her bicycle from her home in Ireland to India, she has been writing about her intrepid journeys—on foot, mule, and bicycle—to remote areas of the world. Her books include: In Ethiopia with a Mule, Eight Feet in the Andes *(in which Dervla and her young daughter walked 1300 miles through the Andes),* Where the Indus is Young, *and* Full Tilt.

Think of Jan Back Packing around the world
and you going to Baja
and "Galoping Birds" an the Trip!

PART ONE

ESSENCE OF TRAVEL

JO BROYLES YOHAY

* * *

Five Pounds of Almonds

Delivering a gift leads to sharing
a woman's life in India.

FOR SEVERAL WEEKS, ACROSS THREE-QUARTERS OF INDIA, I HAD lugged five pounds of almonds. I had agreed to deliver them, in Delhi, to the brother of a New York friend. Almonds, critical to north Indian cuisine, are obscenely expensive when bought locally.

I was in India for the first time—alone. I had left my husband and two teen-aged sons to fend for themselves for six weeks while I went on a midlife, self-confrontational adventure. I needed to test a childhood vision of myself that I was, at heart, an explorer. I had to do something bold—on my own and for myself.

Pulsating, riveting, difficult India was everything I wanted it to be. My senses were bombarded: cold water poured from buckets served as my morning shower; ceiling fans stirred hot dust; acrid smoke of dung fire burned my eyes. The ancient villages, the artistry of the people, the exotic colors, sounds, and smells were exactly what I had come for.

With one exception: people stared. On buses, in restaurants, people eyed me with undisguised interest, sometimes discussing me as if I weren't there. I found it unnerving.

In Delhi, cheered by the prospect of reducing the weight of my backpack, I unfolded myself from the rickshaw and walked

3

through an iron gate toward a white stucco house, its narrow garden crowded with sprawling trees, noisy with birds.

The door opened on a man with kind, dark eyes, tall and regal in full beard and aquamarine turban, two exuberant teen-aged girls—and Meera. Lovely in the colorful pants and tunic of north Indian women, thick black hair braided in a single plait down her back, Meera smiled shyly and led me inside. The living room, furnished with worn Western-style sofa and chairs, had two focal points: a large, black-and-white TV and a refrigerator. Both proclaimed to visitors that this forward-thinking household could afford such amenities.

Amrit pumped my hand; the girls questioned me about their uncle. The entire family spoke the King's English. Clearly I was more to them than an envoy bearing nuts. True, I came endorsed by an emigrant brother. But beyond that, I sensed the unadorned excitement of "having company" that is practically gone from the overscheduled, Type-A West. From their viewpoint, our relationship was sealed: I would move in with them for the duration of my stay in Delhi.

Perfect. I would have a chance to see family life firsthand. And I would have a respite from the stares. Unbelievable, long, greedy stares. Stares that left me feeling exposed, disapproved of, vulgar.

At first I had thought it was my clothes. American skirts showed spans of leg. Slacks revealed the forbidden zone veiled by saris: the joining of female thighs to torso. So I had bought a *salvar-kamiz*, a loose knee-length tunic worn over baggy trousers, two yards wide at the top and gathered with a drawstring. You could be pregnant for months before anyone noticed. When I draped the veil, or *dupatta*, a filmy scarf, around my shoulders, my "Punjabi pants suit" effectively hid all curves pertaining to the female form. Curves I had spent many sweaty gym hours preserving.

I had left the shop feeling blessedly invisible and boarded a bus. Silent faces turned toward me, staring unabashedly, like carnival goers at a side show watching the flame-eater or the two-headed cow.

Questions finally set me straight: "Where is your husband?" "Why has your son let you come here by yourself?" A woman without a male guardian? Unthinkable.

No wonder male heads of families stepped in to order my tea at roadside bus stops, telling me what to eat, where to wash—their code of conduct stating that any woman not your wife must be viewed as a sister. And—obviously—any sister alone needs help.

I realized now why I rarely saw Indian women alone. The seclusion of *purdah*, after all, is not so far in India's past. For more than a thousand years, women literally were sequestered. On the rare occasions when they went out, they were covered head to toe by a heavy veil, shielded from the eyes of men. Theory had it that a man would be unable to control his desires should he look upon the naked face of a woman. In fact, rape of unmarried women— as the *Raj Quartet* shows—was quite common. If a woman were dishonored, her male relatives had to avenge the deed. Infinitely easier, to keep the women out of sight.

The physical veil is gone from most of India, but the remnants linger: outdoors, village women huddle in clusters, tails of saris pulled up to cover head and face. Even in bustling commercial centers, where privileged women often become doctors, teachers, or government employees, the women still remain relatively clois- tered in public and rarely do they walk. In markets, vendors bring baskets of produce to their car windows.

If I had come to India to redefine myself as a woman, I had picked a laboratory of paradox to do it in. India: one of the world's first governments to elect a woman as its leader; a country which had accepted women physicians before the West had; and a culture which until recent times forced a widow to throw herself on the burning funeral pyre of her husband.

Five pounds of almonds opened the door on a remarkable friendship with Meera. Our interest in each other was magnetic. She was full of curiosity about America, where she expected to emigrate soon, and I was ever the amateur anthropologist. Quickly, we became fast friends. We told each other stories endlessly, like fourteen-year-olds at a sleepover.

Meera had seen Amrit only once before their marriage, in a room crowded with her family and an "inspection team" from the groom's house. "I served him tea," she told me. "I was so nervous I couldn't look at him. Afterward, my father asked if I would marry him. I said yes."

From my reading I knew that the future bride or groom normally has refusal rights after the first visit. But since a lot of groundwork has preceded the initial meeting, family pressure discourages rejecting more than two or three prospects.

The next time Meera saw Amrit was at their wedding. That day she left her place as adored daughter, sheltered by the family that made the major decisions of her life, and moved miles away to become the wife of a stranger—who would now make her decisions. "The first years were horrible," she said. "My husband was short tempered." (As custom dictates, she never calls him by name.) "Since he's in the Air Force, we moved a lot, far from my family. I was so unhappy. But finally things got better. When a child is born, parents put away their quarrels and work for the tranquility of the family. He became more patient."

Although love matches do occur across caste and religion (disasters in the eyes of most families), the system of arranged marriages has not been seriously challenged; freedom of contact between the sexes is rigourously proscribed and in many areas college students lead segregated lives and there is no mixing among the young in public.

Women are still seriously hampered at all levels except at the very top by their subordinate and dependent status.

—Una Flett, "Lonely You Come?"
Women Travel: A Rough Guide
Special edited by Natania Jansz and Miranda Davies, et. al.

One afternoon Meera and I read "matrimonial" ads together and she talked about arranging marriages for her daughters when they finished school. Entire pages of national newspapers are filled by hopeful parents:

WANTED: Extremely beautiful bride for smart, handsome, Punjabi USA immigrant boy... Only families of status need apply.

Highly educated, well-placed match for girl, 163 cms., personal income over 2,500 per month, slim, beautiful, very fair complexion, South Delhi millionaire family.

Where on earth would I be today, I wondered, if my parents had advertised for a husband for me? "Well mannered, cheerful, industrious. Likes children and dogs." Would they also have added: "Severe case of wanderlust, apparent genetic condition passed through paternal grandmother who read maps instead of novels, filled her house with *National Geographic* and *Arizona Highway*, and spent Sunday afternoons at Huntsville Airport watching airplanes take off and land. Longs to uncover hidden strengths. Needs strong husband, sure enough of himself to appreciate spirited, insecure bride unendingly—through her grouchy phases, explosions, explorations."

I summoned my courage to ask a too-personal question, inevitable to my Western mind: "Do you love each other?"

"Oh, yes!" she said, then blushed and looked away.

Meera and I spent several days indoors, chatting. She asked the now familiar, inevitable eastern question: "Why did you choose to travel alone?"

The roots lie, I began, in the small-town South of the 1950s where I grew up—groomed, in a sense, for perpetual childhood. Become a teacher, learn to type, they said. So you can support yourself until a man comes along to take care of you. I had fled the predictability of the Deep South for New York, married, had children, built a career.

I paused. I felt as close to Meera as I ever had to another woman. The last thing I wanted was to put distance between us. But I didn't know how to negotiate the cultural gulf. I was trying to describe what felt to me like a life-or-death need for self-definition. Over eighteen years, some part of me had gotten lost in the tangle of a household. I had felt anesthetized. Something *had* to change. In Meera's culture, individual definition barely existed; the family was paramount. The difference in our options was staggering. I had come 12,000 miles to reclaim myself. Yet, Meera's brother had to come by train to fetch her when she visited her parents in the next state. How could I explain to her that I loved my family, but that I also needed to be independent and self-sufficient? Her life, modern by Indian standards, seemed as insular as the one I had fled in Alabama thirty years before.

Meera lured me on with questions. "Did your husband mind your coming here?"

"He knew it was something I had to do," I said. "He was a little bewildered because he doesn't have the same need. But he never tried to stop me; in fact, he encouraged me to come."

I wasn't sure what Meera made of all this until one afternoon I returned from a day-trip to the Taj Mahal; the whole family was deep in conversation. Meera brought me a cup of tea. Then, flushed and excited, she announced that the next afternoon she would take me out sightseeing. There was electricity in the air that I didn't understand, as if something were going over my head. Then I recalled our afternoons indoors, remembering the day I had suggested to Meera that we go for a walk. She had looked embarrassed. "When my husband comes home, we will go for a drive," she had answered. Startled, I realized that in the three years they had lived in Delhi, Meera had never left the house without her husband. Until now. What had happened?

Oh, my God, I thought. Have I waltzed through the door with a bag of almonds and started something? How does Amrit feel? I couldn't tell.

Meera planned our trip meticulously, asking her husband the names of the streets she did not know. He supplied them readily. We would go to old Delhi, she said, traveling by autorickshaw because it cost less than a taxi, was more comfortable than a bus. An afternoon's outing with a new-found friend had taken on huge proportions.

The next day, we strolled arm-in-arm through the Red Fort, Meera offering details of its history, remembered from school. We made our way through the hopelessly congested shopping street, Chandni Chowk, around huge, hump-backed cows and bullock carts, honking trucks, bicycles, peacocks, and never-ending crowds on foot. In a gift shop, we showed each other which jewelry we liked and which we did not. We sipped cool, carbonated Limca in the hot afternoon. At a puppet shop, she hid me while she went inside to bargain for a sultan in rich green robes. "If they see a foreigner, the price will be six times more," she cautioned.

Wandering with a friend, after so many days alone, felt wonderful. Still India had her say. At the mosque, Jami Masjid, a sign proclaimed that women are allowed in the turrets only if accompanied by "the responsible male relatives." Two women had to content themselves with the view from the gate.

When I saw a boy staring at us, I laughed. "People don't stare like that in America," I said. I was getting used to it—another cultural phenomenon. Maybe we are the odd ones, I thought, taught not to stare, peeking from the corners of our eyes when we want to examine others.

The best was yet to come. Starting home, we hailed an autorickshaw—a noisy, three-wheeled motor scooter with a small cab for passengers tacked on behind. Both machine and operator had seen better days. In grimy white shirt and head cloth, the scrawny driver gunned the motor furiously to keep us moving;

Autorickshaw

still, on the slightest incline the scooter coughed and inched its way toward the crest. Meera and I started to giggle. The engine was hopeless. The next hill was steeper and our hilarity heightened. Meera tried to keep her mouth closed when she laughed. Failing that, she veiled it with her hands, then with her scarf. Was frank laughter unseemly? Finally, on the highest hill, near home, we crawled at such a pace that a pedestrian came from behind and passed us. We laughed, helpless and unencumbered, our cheeks drenched with tears, Meera's scarf forgotten, our cultural gulf dissolved.

At home, over dinner, high with accomplishment, Meera recounted every detail of our afternoon. "I'm so glad you had fun," Amrit said simply. His pride was so obvious, so tender, that my eyes filled with tears. Meera's husband, like mine, had not held her back. Our histories, each in its cultural context, had woven veils around us. But one day, the time had come to do something bold. I traveled to India; Meera took me out sightseeing. We both stepped toward our autonomy.

"I will never forget it," she told me as she started to laugh again. I knew we would both retell our stories for months to come, remembering how well we had managed outside on our own, watching our adventures change us—reliving an autorickshaw ride with a friend on a hot afternoon.

Manhattan-based writer Jo Broyles Yohay often travels alone. She first felt the call of the road while a child in small-town Alabama, where missionaries came back on home leave and told stories of their exploits in exotic reaches of the globe. A ten-year-old explorer budded. Jo stashed her allowance in a sock drawer: travel funds, a commitment to herself. She was going places.

★

I have found that most travelers to remote destinations are deeply touched by the people they've met and places they've seen and are inspired to help them. There are many ways to give something back, either on the spot or upon your return.

Years ago, on a trip to Nepal, one of our Sherpa guides, Ringee, joined us around the fire in the evening. Even though he was painfully shy, he forced himself to speak to us because he wanted to learn English. We eventually learned that his dream was to pursue university-level studies. Only one thing prevented this dream from materializing: "a lack of ru-

pees." Over the course of our trek, we decided to support him. We created a "Ringee Scholarship Fund" and made donations for the next three
years.

Mary Lu, an editor from Texas, sent him books. Penny, our guide, who
lived in Kathmandu, checked up on him and reviewed all his report cards.
I was in Kathmandu the month he graduated and presented him with a
down coat as a token of our praise. He landed a good job as an accountant in a trekking agency. When I asked him what he would do with his
first pay check, I was surprised by his answer. I thought he would buy a
motor scooter, the symbol of status and upward mobility in Kathmandu.
Instead Ringee told me, "I will send the money home to my father (a
widower) so he can use it for a good dowry for my sister. Then he can
find her a good husband who will treat her well."

—MBB

JAN HAAG

✦ ✦ ✦

Mission Walk

Traveling through history on a California pilgrimage.

I HAD FIVE EXTRA DAYS, SO I DECIDED TO WALK DOWN CALIFORNIA'S Salinas Valley. I started at the Soledad Mission, walked down the blazing summer valley, and spent the first night atop Pine Canyon in the crystal-clear night air.

At the side of the road just behind a private gate high above King City, I laid out my sleeping equipment—two emergency blankets that fold into three inch squares. It was the first night I had ever slept by myself, all alone, beneath the stars. It was a night of ecstatic pleasure in sights and sounds: the lights of the valley miles below me, the leaves rustling in the slightest breeze, the noises of nocturnal animals, and the road was so hard that I probably didn't sleep more than twenty minutes.

The owner of the private gate, wearing a ten-gallon hat and cowboy boots, discovered me in the dark on his property. "You scared my wife!" he said. Then, finding I was just a harmless grey-haired lady, he told me how to find the road that would lead me down to Mission San Antonio which lies in the middle of the Hunter-Liggett military base.

In the morning as I finished packing my sleeping gear, my host drove up again in his pickup with some water. I had asked him in the night where to find water in the morning and he gave me directions so complicated that I was sure I'd never find the spring. Thankful, I drank and drank from his huge canteen and filled my plastic water bottle. Then he pointed me down the road which led directly into Hunter-Liggett, along which, he cautioned, I would find 100 unmarked dirt roads built for practice maneuvers, where the army could prepare for war.

"Stay to the right," he said, "every time you come to a main crossroads. Once down in the valley, go left, the mission is south."

I thanked him profusely and walked away into the dawn.

The top of the road was flat and ran through thick pines, then it began a steep decline. It went down and down and down and down and down and down for, perhaps, ten miles. Having taken off my sandals, as I often do in India, what a joy it was to walk effortlessly downhill, alone, through the silk-soft dirt. The trees changed to sycamores; narrow dirt roads disappeared in all directions, over every mound and around many trees. There was not a single person or habitation to be seen. One huge commercial plane passed overhead, going north, so high I could barely hear its sound. Farther along I came to an old corral with a wooden water tank, dry, cracked, and askew on its high stilts. The vegetation became sparser as I approached the valley floor where the baked dust and rocks fairly shimmered with the heat. I drank more thirstily of my gift-given water.

At the main crossroad on the valley floor, I turned left, but I had no idea how far away the mission lay. I walked for another hour. A single car came by on that dirt road, going north. The woman driving, who was not at all surprised to see me, assured me the mission was in the direction I was going—she didn't know how far. It was as if she often saw straw-hatted women with small orange backpacks ambling along her route.

"Is there any water between here and there?"

"I don't know." As the car moved slowly up the road, puffs of dust rose behind her tires. "Good luck," she called.

Noon approached. The heat grew more intense. My water was almost gone. Men, I had already begun to learn, weren't so insou-

ciant about water. The next day I was to be repeatedly warned by
men from passing cars that I was walking in the worst heat wave
the Salinas Valley had ever known, and several would insist on
transporting me from shade point to shade point. But that was
later.

At the moment, how confident it made me feel *not* to be
warned by the woman driver about the possible dire consequences
of my walk. The Spanish had traversed the unmarked land in the
17th century, and she and I saw nothing odd about a walk along
known roads in the 20th.

As I continued, nothing but acres of sage and bits of chaparral
met my gaze. The dazzle of the bone dry air made me squint and
filled me with delight. Could I make my water last? I watched this
interesting thought turn from a movie-like image of prospectors
lost in the desert, to amusement, to wonder, to concern, to worry.
Then I began to take deep breaths as it touched, ever so slightly,
on uncivilized fear. For it seemed no matter what judiciously bird-
like sips I took, the water disappeared as if I were boiling it on a
high flame. Nor did my sparing efforts allow me even once to
slake my thirst. The sun rose higher and turned white. I was wearing my sandals now, for the hard dirt was too hot to touch with
my bare feet.

Then, as if in answer to my requirement for a miracle, taller and
taller, almost bamboo-like trees began to appear on my left. I saw
a cow.

Trees? Cow? There must be water.

I quickened my pace. A little farther on I stepped off the road.
Within minutes I found a running stream. It not only supplied me
with water to drink, but a cool bath and a gourmet lunch of fresh
watercress. I rinsed my blue neckerchief blouse, and put it on dripping wet to set off again for the mission.

Another half-hour down the road I met a man jogging in the
noon day heat. How could anyone jog in such weather? He must,
I guessed, be a soldier not far from home. God himself, I decided,
must be keeping an eye on this particular sparrow, for already I'd
drunk half my new bottle of stream water, and the heat had began

to patina my legs with white powder. It was as if the water in my system were evaporating so fast that it left salt on my surface. The jogger assured me, without slacking his pace, that my goal was just ahead.

Across a bridge over a dry course and beyond some platinum-colored grassy mounds lay one of California's most beautiful missions. I approached its dusty, creamy stucco exterior as if I had arrived at the gates of heaven. Huge carved doors opened into a high-vaulted church which was dark, deserted, and very cool. It was like plunging into a secret pool deep within the earth which seemed to hold only the darkness, the coolness, and the friendly, if ghostly, flickering of votive candles.

Slowly my eyes adjusted. I gazed for a long time at the aged pigments of the altar, the designs along the walls that the Indians had painted. Though I had heard nothing but my own footsteps and the call of a bird or two most of the morning, still I was entranced by the utter silence the church offered, and grateful for shelter from the blazing sun. I speculated on how soon I would be able to walk on in the heat, how far I would get that day. After all, it was just past noon. Then I closed my eyes and allowed myself to dream.

Longingly I thought, Oh, if only these were the old days. If only I were a real pilgrim during the time the California missions had flourished. If only I were a traveler of

Mission San Antonio

200 years ago—with news from Soledad or San Francisco, the Presidio, maybe, or from Spain—how they would welcome me, how they would rejoice at my coming, as people still do in parts of Asia. For in many countries, to this day, the guest is considered to be God. Any guest or stranger's coming is looked upon as a rare and wonderful event. In the old days the missionaries would have offered me hospitality, a bed, food. They would have urged me to stay, urged me to talk. I would have told them such stories!

More than 150 years ago, Father Junipero Serra and a group of Franciscan missionaries founded a chain of 21 Spanish missions that ran much of the length of California. The simple yet beautiful adobe structures represent part of the expansion of the Spanish Empire along the Pacific Coast. Today visiting the missions is a special way of experiencing California history.

—MBB

After awhile I stepped from the cool darkness of the sanctuary into the courtyard. The sun poured its white, hot light down on a central rose garden enclosed by a columned and roofed arcade. A fountain, to which spoked paths led, splashed in the middle. I chose a shaded wooden bench and put down my pack. From it I took my needlepoint and began to stitch. I always carry a piece of needlepoint; it is my form of meditation. I use them as diaries, incorporating into their designs patterns I find along the way. The finished works, which resemble small Oriental rugs, remind me of my earthly and spiritual journeys.

In the shade it was just a little more than pleasantly warm. I stitched, working a blue-and-brown border around a central motif of the Tibetan *Kundalini* symbol. In the garden, a young man worked around the base of the roses, cultivating, weeding, snipping the withered blooms. His movement was the only movement in the breathless heat. After a while a woman came to sit on another wooden bench under the shade of the arcade some distance from me.

When the young man finished his work with the roses, he gathered the clippings, put away his tools, and paused to speak to the other woman. Then he walked soundlessly toward me down the terra-cotta tiles of the arcade. He was dressed in blue jeans and a blue shirt; his hair was blond. He stopped beside my bench and looked at me. His eyes were dark, yet reflected the blue of the sky and, even before he spoke, I was awed by the depth of their compassion. He said to me as if he were continuing a conversation, "And where have you come from?"

I said rather breathlessly, perhaps a little proudly, and certainly feeling like the impostor of a pilgrim: "I just walked over from the Soledad Mission." (In case you are not familiar with the terrain, there is a distance of about 30 miles between each of the 21 missions; they were one day's ride by horse from each other along El Camino Real from San Diego to Sonoma. Years later, now, when I have more humor, I find myself smiling. I realize what an amazing statement that must have been from a middle-aged woman in the 100-degree heat in the courtyard of the remotest mission of them all, where, very probably, no one had walked in from a neighboring mission in the last 100 years.)

"Oh, you must be tired," this kind young man said with total, unquestioning belief and enormous sympathy. "Would you like a shower?"

"Oh yes!" I fairly gasped.

He smiled. "Would you like to stay the night?"

"Oh yes!"

My ability to believe in miracles took a quantum leap.

It turned out—a fact I had not known—that Mission San Antonio was a functioning mission run by the Franciscans. The young man in the blue jeans with the dark eyes bluer than the heavens, bluer than Michelangelo's cerulean blue skies, was a Franciscan brother. He showed me to a small cell in the women's cloisters and invited me to supper in the refectory. The room held a narrow bed, a desk, a chair, a small old-fashioned wardrobe, and a casement window embedded in the two-foot thick walls. This window looked out on the platinum-and-gold fields, studded here and there with live oaks, a landscape so beautiful one could not doubt it was designed by God for his padres. I washed the clothes I had been wearing and showered in the women's bathroom. I rested, read a little, and put in a few more stitches.

There are moments when a sudden, unexpected connection is made somewhere in the world, powerful and undeniable. When the energy is exactly right, it doesn't matter where you are. Things just happen as they should.

—Paula McDonald,
"A Waltz at the End of Earth"

At supper, the food was abundant, but not my kind of fare: boiled cabbage, ham, potatoes, with applesauce for desert. And I was not, as I never am when I walk, very hungry. I carried only dried figs and almonds, and ate along the road only what I could glean: wild berries, a tomato left in the harvested fields, one green pepper—nothing I felt that anyone would begrudge me.

There were several brothers at the table, and the old priest—Irish, I guessed—who had a florid complexion, was gracious, and talked of all the worldly subjects about which I could not—living as I was that evening in the richness of the miraculous—utter a single word. The young man with the loving eyes was dressed now, like the others, in a brown and cowled homespun robe. He asked me my story, how I happened to be walking from the Soledad Mission to San Antonio. I hesitantly spoke of my interest in pilgrimage, how it was my desire to walk around the world. I did not tell them my practice and religious interest at that time was mostly in Eastern meditation, the Hindu tradition. They invited me to attend early morning Mass in the small chapel. I said I had to start walking very early in the morning because it would get too hot soon after sunrise, but I would come to Mass if I could. They reminded me that San Miguel was the next stop down on the mission trail.

Looking out at the stars that gleamed beyond the window embedded in the deep, thick walls, I rested that night in the delight of a wish granted. Rising early, I packed and went, even before Mass, to leave a little gift of some figs and almonds on the kitchen table. I attended Mass and left as quickly as I could, but not quickly enough to avoid a kindly invitation to breakfast, which I declined. I stepped into the dark church, left a coin, and lighted a votive candle. My heart was almost breaking with bliss for the sweetness of the miracle that had granted me my pilgrim's wish when I had first sat in the darkened church. Then I stepped out the great front doors.

There, to meet me on the steps, was the young brother in his brown robes, again inviting me to breakfast. Again I declined, saying I must go because already it was getting hot. It was nearly nine o'clock. I could feel in the heat the promise of a blistering day.

Then, to my heart-stopping astonishment, the young Franciscan, whom I had learned from the other woman was called Brother Joachim, knelt. Extending a tender and gentle hand, he touched my feet, saying, "But your feet are blistered."

Which was true. I was wearing rubber zoris and great pockets of fluid had formed on the insides of my big toes. But the blisters did not hurt. I felt them not at all. However, I had, late yesterday afternoon, mentioned them to the other woman. She must have mentioned them to the brother.

"But they do not hurt at all," I assured him, "And truly, I must be going or it will be too hot to walk."

He touched my feet again. I felt it as a blessing. As he stood up, he said, "What can I give you? I must give you something." Out of a few moments search of his habit, he found a St. Christopher medal of red plastic. "Take this," he said.

I did. I walked away as a pilgrim who had been blessed.

Nowhere in all my spiritual pilgrimage have I ever again seen eyes so full of grace and love as those of the young Franciscan, Brother Joachim.

Jan Haag is a writer, musician, and textile artist, and former Director of National Production Programs for the American Film Institute. She has lived and studied in India, China, Thailand, Nepal, Russia, and Mexico. She is currently living in Seattle and her travel-inspired needlepoint designs are on exhibit at the Seattle Asian Art Museum.

✳

We read the same books as children—Kipling,
Haggard, Stevenson—and dreamt adventure,
but they went off, the boys, to munch on sago
grubs with cannibals, be rocked to sleep

in a hold where rats and roaches rustled
under the slap of a moon-starched sail
and on the volcano's steaming lip, pose
for the camera, their calves fringed with leeches.

Coming to adventure late I'm not sure
I'd savor grubs. I didn't join my Burmese
bus companions when they dined with their
right hands. On a tramp off Sumatra's coast,

I held a scream, a bobbing bathtub toy
in my throat, as two-inch roaches filed
above my head. My bones ached to the marrow
scrambling up to fourteen thousand feet.

I envy the acceptance that accrues to cocks.
They are the universal, catholic sex.
Witch doctors don't ask wives why they've allowed
their husbands out to roam the world alone.

Green with begrudging as a young rice field,
I'm a prurient curiosity,
in my unorthodox sex, to the local men
in foreign towns who hope, or else assume.
They're shoals to navigate with care as I
tack Malacca's strait, round Java's head
sails spread and bellying to cross the shadow
line, gathering my way before the salty wind.

> —Karen Swenson, "What Does a Woman Want?"
> *The Landlady in Bangkok*

ALISON DAROSA

★ ★ ★

I Dream of Fishing

Marlin fishing in Mexico fulfills a family legacy.

IF I'D BEEN BORN MALE, I WOULDN'T BE WRITING ABOUT FISHING for marlin off Los Cabos.

I'd be somewhere in the western Pacific, fishing for a living. There's no doubt in my mind that I'd be one of the best commercial tuna skippers in the world.

Because fishing is in my blood.

My great-grandfather was a whaler when he lived in the Azores in the mid-Atlantic. When he came to the United States, he fished for cod in a small wooden dory off Provincetown, Massachusetts.

My grandfather fished for tuna off San Diego in the '20s and '30s. He worked from the stern of a wooden boat, hauling in 200-pound yellowfin with a bamboo pole.

Marlin

My father started fishing for a living when he was 17. By 31, he was skipper of his own tuna boat. As far back as I can remember, he was one of the top two or

21

three producers for San Diego canneries, which then kept the world stocked with tuna.

Dad taught me to fish. He rigged poles for me off the stern of his docked tuna boat. He taught me to hold the line between my thumb and forefinger; to be still when I got a nibble; and to yank hard, setting the hook, when I got a bite.

ishing has long been an escape for me, and of course, escape is complicated. Escape is good when it means freeing oneself from the weight of an obscure and explosive father or the constant grating of a mind embattled by memory. Escape is bad when it means ignoring the kinds of memories powerful enough to turn a life into a fortress, a man into stone. Few images of lessons fondly passed from father to daughter linger in my memory. I never fly fished with my father. We spun no stories together. No line connected us in silence. No metronome. He never knew the meter of his own life, or mine. But he inhabits my fishing life. His image rises like a rainbow to disappear elusively or be hooked and tangled with.

—Holly Morris, "Homewaters of the Mind," *Another Wilderness: New Outdoor Writing by Women,* edited by Susan Fox Rogers

"I got a fi-ish," I'd sing up to him when I landed one. One afternoon I sang the song 28 times.

When I graduated from eighth grade at St. Agnes School in San Diego, the other girls in my class wanted stereos. I asked for a fishing rod. I still have it.

My father taught my sisters to fish, too. But I was the best. (At least that's how I remember it.) I was the oldest, after all. According to Portuguese family tradition, I was the one who would join my father on his tuna boat as soon as I finished high school—maybe sooner. When he was ready to retire, I would take over as skipper.

But I was born female.

Fishing was in my blood; it was not to be my future.

I went grudgingly to college instead of to sea. But I never quite lost the need to prove—to my father and to myself—that I could catch the biggest, toughest fish of all. When I read Hemingway's *Old Man and the Sea*, I knew the fish I wanted.

Fishing for marlin is utterly satisfying as a sport, a living, a spectacle, and a form of exercise, Hemingway told his friends.

I went to Los Cabos, the so-called marlin capital of the world, to test his theory—and myself.

"Of course you can do it," a grizzled San Diego fisherman admonished before I left. "Hell, little kids do it."

"They strap you into a chair; the pole's locked into a holster," he said. "If you need more help than that, they'll help you."

It was 8:07 a.m. when we pulled out of the marina at Cabo San Lucas. I was staying at Hotel Twin Dolphin and had chartered a 31-foot cruiser from the Dolphin fleet.

We stopped at a small skiff in the harbor to buy ten live fish for bait. The fish are called *caballitos*, little horses, because of their strength. They were as big as some of the fish I caught from the stern of my father's tuna boat.

We were just past the mouth of Cabo San Lucas harbor, just beyond the arched rock that marks the southernmost tip of Baja California, when we ran into a school of porpoise. Within seconds we had our first strike.

Tuna.

Within a few more seconds, we lost it.

Just as well, I thought. I didn't want to waste marlin-fishing time.

The skipper, Jose Luis Cossio Cota, explained that we would be heading about 90 minutes east, up the Gulf of California. That's where the big fish were swimming today.

His first mate (and only crewman), Juan Edwardo Galindo, rigged big colorful lures on three lines that hid hooks. Around 10 a.m., Jose Luis slowed the boat to eight knots; Juan threw the lines into the water.

The lures danced along in the wake of the boat, close to the surface, but at varying distances from the stern. To marlin, the lures were supposed to look like a school of tasty fish.

Jose Luis warned me that we'd only get to keep one marlin.

Strict policy, he said: all but one marlin a day must be released. Some charter fleets lay off skippers who break the rule.

Sure, one's fine, I thought. The thought of "just one" made me giddy. I started fantasizing about how many we'd hook.

But by 10:30 a.m. we weren't even seeing any porpoise. The sea was flat and shone like high-gloss linoleum. It was violet-blue, the color of the India ink I remember my mother used to address flour sacks that she packed with clothes and sent to needy relatives in Portugal.

There's time—and space—for such reminiscences when you're trolling for marlin. My mind wandered from Portugal to Robinson Creek, northeast of Yosemite, where my father had baited our hooks with iridescent pink salmon eggs.

The scythelike spike jabbed me back to reality. It was the tail of a marlin feeding on the surface about twenty feet away.

Jose Luis had seen it, too. He gunned the engine, circled the marlin, chased it, played hot-rod waiter with the boat—all but stuffing the baited hook into the marlin's mouth.

But this fish wasn't interested.

"He went down fast," Jose Luis said.

By this time, Cabo San Lucas was little more than a faint smudge on the horizon. It disappeared as we continued northeast, across the Tropic of Cancer, toward Los Frailes, where other boats radioed in reports of billfish feeding on the surface.

It was 11:09 a.m. when the marlin hit.

The reel sizzled with a ratcheting whir that triggered every muscle in my body. My heart raced as fast as the line that disappeared into the sea.

Jose Luis gunned the engine. The boat sprang forward, driving the hook into the big fish.

I was on my feet, aching to grab a rod. Behind my sunglasses there were tears—laughing and crying tears—emotional tears. I was finally going to catch my big fish.

I made sure none of the tears slipped beyond the edge of my sunglasses. Real fishermen don't cry.

Juan raced from one rod to another. He was as frantic as I was.

But not for the same reason. The whirring clatter had stopped. The marlin was gone.

It was more than three hours before we got another taste of marlin. This time it was a jumper, about 50 feet from our boat. It flashed silver in the sun, leaping three times. Magnificent. Marlin foreplay, I thought. It only made me want to get closer.

"Sorry, missus," Jose Luis said. "Not today."

It was 3:15 p.m. when Juan reeled in the lines. He estimated we'd be back in Cabo San Lucas by 4:30 p.m. I'd spent $350 and eight hours and hadn't even touched a fishing rod.

I was disappointed, big time. I remembered those silly Portuguese superstitions about women being bad luck on fishing boats. I wondered whether any other boats had caught marlin. I pondered what you tip a crew that hasn't caught any fish. But mostly, I thought about trying again.

That night, I called Ozzie Marquez, the skipper who was scheduled to take me on his 23-foot skifflike *panga*, *El Tapir*, for a half-day outing in two days. We were supposed to go fishing for tuna and small game fish.

I begged him to take me marlin fishing instead. And I begged him to take me out the next morning and to stay out until we caught one, even if it took the entire two days left of my Cabo trip.

Marquez had another customer the next morning; we'd go out as originally planned, he said.

"It's far, for marlin," he added. Too far, in his *panga*.

But then he softened. By the time I hung up, he had promised we'd stay out until we caught fish or I had to catch my flight home.

"Marlin, maybe," he said. "It's possible."

I met Ozzie at 6:30 a.m., bleary eyed but awake enough to refuse coffee; I remembered there's no bathroom on the *panga*.

I liked Ozzie immediately. And I liked Rolando, his seventeen-year-old first mate. Rolando has fishing in his blood, too. He is Ozzie's son.

As we headed east toward Gordo Bank, I pumped Ozzie for

fishing stories. He started hunting marlin off Los Cabos 31 years ago, when there were fewer than 20 boats based here. Now there are more than 400.

His happiest client might have been a guy named George from San Diego. "He went home with a bruised gut—and a 1,110-pound blue marlin," Ozzie said.

Actor John Wayne was a client in 1961: "He fought a swordfish for six hours, but it broke off the line at the last minute."

By 8:20 a.m., we were thirteen miles from the cape. No sign of marlin.

"Sometimes they don't bite in the morning," Ozzie said. "Sometimes they bite later."

Sometimes they don't bite at all, I thought.

But so what? This wasn't so bad. Hemingway wrote in *The Old Man and the Sea* that it was considered a virtue not to talk unnecessarily at sea.

I leaned up against the windbreak and rode the swells with the *panga* and a school of porpoise. I tasted the cool, salty breeze that softened the heat of the morning sun. I studied the prisms of sunlight that sank deep into the sea. I searched for flying fish with set wings skimming the surface, a good sign for marlin fishing. Most of all, I relished the excitement of not knowing what the day held.

> *Aye, I recall the time when on an all-day fishing trip using flies, I could land 50 trout, no trouble at all.*
>
> —Hannah Hauxwell with Barry Cockcroft, *Hannah's North Country*

"Sometimes I don't say anything because I'm looking for fish," Ozzie said. "Just looking. Looking. All the time, I'm looking."

"And sometimes, praying, inside—to find the fish."

We were 25 miles from Cabo San Lucas, two miles off Gordo Bank, when all three of us got our prayers answered.

We had a strike. We had two. Three.

We had mayhem—glorious mayhem. From every direction came the staccato whir of lines racing out.

Rolando had one of the rods; Ozzie handed me another and took the third for himself. Nobody was driving the boat.

As my line raced out, I just gripped with both hands and all my strength. There was no fancy chair to be strapped into, no holster for the rod. This was fishing, real fishing off the back of the boat. Me against my big fish. The childhood fantasy, playing out.

Ozzie worked the third rod long enough to release the marlin on that line. Before he went back to the wheel, he wrapped a plastic fishing apron around my waist; the rod fit in a swiveling socket on the apron.

When my line stopped sizzling out, I started reeling it in. Slowly. I'd gain a few yards; the marlin would take them back. But I was gaining more than I was losing. We battled one another silently, ferociously.

"See your fish," Ozzie said.

For the first time, I took my eyes off the reel.

My marlin was in the air, leaping, crashing down, leaping again, dancing atop the water.

I couldn't believe it. Not just its powerful beauty. I couldn't believe how far away it still was.

Ozzie laughed. "When it comes out of the water, it's getting tired," he said.

But with a surge of strength, the marlin raced away, taking yards and yards of hard-earned line with it.

"There's nothing you can do," Ozzie said. "Just relax. Let it go. Enjoy it."

While the marlin took more line, Ozzie slipped my arms through a jacketlike harness. He twisted a pair of straps until they were short enough to team with my short arms. Then he hooked the straps to the fishing reel. It relieved the pressure on my arms, shifting some of the work to my back.

"If the rod goes now," Ozzie said, "you're going with it."

He told me I'd been fighting the marlin for about fifteen minutes. "Only about an hour more," he said.

"And this one's waiting for you," Rolando said. He still had the second marlin on his line.

Ozzie taught me to shake out my left arm to relieve the burning muscles that held the weight of the fish. He sat me down and hauled over an ice chest so that I could brace my feet as I pulled up on the rod, before reeling fast on the downward motion.

I was drenched in sweat.

But by this time, I could distinguish the lavender-blue stripes on my marlin when it leaped.

As Rolando and I pulled our two fish closer to the *panga*, the fighting got wilder. We wrestled one another as the two marlins crossed paths—then crossed back again.

"Almost, almost," Ozzie shouted. "Just a little bit more."

Those last few yards and the seconds that followed were a whirlwind: I had the marlin at the boat, Ozzie gaffed it. Rolando and I switched rods. They hauled my fish aboard.

I don't remember fighting that second marlin at all. I had my fish.

When we got the second marlin to the boat, we removed the hook and released it. It took off, fast as light, pectoral fins set wide like wings. It made me wish we'd released my fish, too.

"No, I don't feel bad," Ozzie said. "I'm going to eat it. You're going to eat it. God made fish for us to eat."

It was 11:40 a.m. when we were ready to head back to Cabo San Lucas. It had taken me 35 minutes to land my marlin. "Very, very good," Ozzie said, and we toasted one another with cans of Diet 7-Up. Then Ozzie radioed in our success.

On our way back to Cabo San Lucas, we talked about fishing—how you get to be really good at it. The muscles in my right hand were too shaky to hold a pen; I couldn't write what he said. The memory chambers in my brain were on overload.

We stopped once, when a yellowfin tuna took one of the lures we were trolling. I could hardly reel the shivering line; my muscles had quit. But I wanted a tuna for my dad. I got it.

Just outside the Cabo San Lucas marina, Ozzie raised two blue flags and a white one atop the *panga's* mast. It was a signal that we had caught two marlin and a tuna.

At the marina, I posed with my marlin. Heck, I hugged the fish. Tourists took pictures; they asked for details. Ozzie and Rolando joined in.

My fish weighed 140 pounds. Ozzie took home half of it; I packed most of my half in an ice chest I'd brought from home. What wouldn't fit, I saved for dinner.

I joined three women who had shared a cab with me to the marina that morning. They had caught 36 tuna.

We went to the Trailer Park restaurant, where the chef cooked my marlin.

Soon other fishers joined our table. Men, mostly. We drank Mexican beer, ate marlin, and told fish stories. It was the stuff of Hemingway.

And when I came home and told my father about my marlin, it was the stuff of family, tradition, and love.

Alison DaRosa grew up in a Portuguese-American fishing household in San Diego. In 1977 she joined the San Diego Evening Tribune *as a reporter and eventually became a daily city columnist. When the* Tribune *and the* San Diego Union *merged in 1992, she became the travel editor of the* San Diego Union-Tribune.

✳

Women catch disproportionately more fish than men. It's a fact. Some people claim salmon are attracted by the smell of the hormones women produce. I think that's a load of hooey. Women are just a lot more patient than men. It's crucial to be patient. Often I'll tell a man to stand in a certain place, but I'll come back an hour later and he's left because he hasn't caught anything. Women take a much more relaxed approach to things. They keep put. And what do you know, they catch more fish than their husbands do. This infuriates men so much that they often end up not speaking to their wives.

Another tip men should take from their wives is not to cast so far. Women catch more fish partly because they're covering closer water instead of trying to show off by casting their lines to Kingdom-come. With just a delicate flick of their wrists, they out-fish their macho husbands.

—Jim Tritton, as interviewed by Mark Jenkins, "Two Qualities
Make a Good Angler," Condé Nast Traveler

MEG LUKENS NOONAN

✦ ✦ ✦

Dangerous Isles

A woman takes a different approach to diving than
her male companions in the South Pacific.

IT FIGURES THAT ON MY FIRST DIVE IN RANGIROA I WOULD GET in the same boat as a Dutch rail traffic controller with a suicide fixation. I was already nervous enough without having him tell me how every day in Amsterdam people kill themselves by belly-flopping onto the train tracks.

I spit into my face mask. That's what you are supposed to do before you dive, spit into your face mask.

"At least three people a day," he said.

"Really," I said and rubbed the saliva around on the glass.

"It's why they built the hospitals next to the tracks," he said, leaning closer. "Three...people...every...day."

All right already. I got the picture. And it was not the picture I wanted in my head at that particular moment. I was, after all, in tropical gaga land—smack in the popsicle blue heart of French Polynesia. I wanted to concentrate on the way the coconut palms arched over the edge of the limpid lagoon, the way our rubber boat seemed airborne as it headed out to the reef, the way the funny yellow fish gathered under us the instant the engine was cut. Mostly I wanted to concentrate on remembering how to breathe.

It had been a long time since I had gone scuba diving. I told

Didier, the dive master, that it had been five years, but when I stopped to think about it, I realized it was really more like eight. Still, I jumped at the chance to join a scouting trip to this remote atoll in the Tuamotu Archipelago, about an hour's flight from Tahiti. I was with a group of dive shop owners and dive magazine publishers—all men, all highly experienced divers, and all half-crazed at the prospect of diving such pristine waters.

Americans rarely visit the Tuamotus—and when they do it is often by accident. Also known as the "Dangerous Islands," the sparsely populated chain of low coral atolls is notorious among yachtsmen for its treacherous reefs and shallow waters. But those very hazards are what make this region so enticing to divers. Because the islands are flat, the water is not clouded by runoff from higher ground, and because tourism and development are minimal, the reefs thrive, and fish—including manta rays, barracudas, jacks, groupers, pompanos, surgeonfish, and a huge population of grey and hammerhead sharks—fill the lens-clear water.

From the air Rangiroa is a dazzling broken necklace of palm-studded islets, or *motu*, surrounding a vast azure lagoon. The biggest *motu*, called Avatoru, sits between the only two navigable passes in the atoll. Only a few miles long, it has a tiny thatched-hut airport, a small village, and a couple of resorts catering to divers.

While my traveling companions headed out to dive the Tiputa Pass, I planned to spend my first morning getting my diving legs back with a low-key lagoon dive.

I couldn't have asked for a gentler reintroduction to diving. We were anchored just a few minutes offshore. The sky was clear, the water was barely ruffled by a breeze, and Virginia, the instructor, was patient, earnest, and pleasantly French.

When she gave the command, I put my hand over my mask, tucked my chin, and rolled backward into the water. I released the air from my buoyancy vest, and slowly sinking, saw the world turn blue. Settling down onto a patch of sand, I listened to myself breathe and watched the little mushroom clouds of bubbles rise toward the light.

It was working. I was underwater and I was breathing. This was going to be okay. I let my hands drift to my side and started to do a little flutter kick.

*D*iving won't really erase wrinkles, smooth out cellulite, or do for the abs what 50 crunches a day will, but it feels as if it does. It lifts the spirit, soothes the soul, and puts the diver temporarily into a very special, timeless, and rejuvenating world.

—Claire Walter,
"The Scuba Solution"

And just like that, I was cruising the coral heads, buzzing schools of sashaying jacks. I saw fish under every ledge, behind every waving fan. A flick of my finger sent a couple of parrotfish finning off into the blue; a wave of my hand scattered a group of iridescently striped something-or-others. I hung motionless over a knot of coral and watched the balletlike fluttering of a fringed sea anemone, and the delicate nibbling mouths of trumpetfish searching for food. I'd forgotten how magnificent this world was—and what a privilege it was to be granted a visitor's pass.

When we got back to the resort, the rest of my group was sitting wild-eyed in the open bar, chugging pineapple juice, and talking a million miles an hour. They'd been to 120 feet. They'd seen sharks. Tons of sharks. Big ones that streaked straight for their video cameras then turned at the last second. Little ones that grazed the divers' flippers like misfired bullets. At one point they had backed into an underwater grotto and let the sharks go whooshing by on the swift current, as if the big fish were surly drivers bearing down on them in the passing lane.

"You should have come," they said. "It was fantastic." "Unbelievable." "You would have been blown away." Then Jerry, a laconic pony-tailed dive shop owner from Georgia, leaned my way and said, "It's a good thing you didn't do it; you would have freaked."

And I knew he was right. I wasn't ready for shark gridlock. Not yet.

All through our lunch of crab-stuffed avocados, curried mahi-mahi, and poached pears, they talked about their dive. They let me look at their videos so I could see the sharks. Then somebody asked me if I was going to go with them on their afternoon dive. Go deep, you know, really see something; some mantas or some hammerheads.

I told them I'd pass.

Instead, I took a boat across the channel to the village of Tiputa, where I walked a chalky road which fronted neat lime-stone houses and a stark white church. I greeted the people I encountered, and most of them smiled and said, "*Bonjour.*" I came to a graveyard where the bleached headstones were draped with flower leis, and I walked out onto an empty beach and looked for cowrie shells. When I felt light-headed from the heat I sat down and stuck my feet in a tide pool.

On my way back through town, a couple of wiry brown dogs trotted at my heels for a few minutes, then gave up and flopped down in the shadow of an old pickup truck.

Back at the dock, I bought a Coke and sat under an enormous tree next to half-a-dozen local women in flowered *pareus.* A cargo ship was being unloaded,

I am reminded of the advice of a Texan diver at the bar of the Palau Pacific Hotel.

"Honey, dive deep, grab the reef wall, and hold on for dear life because the current is hell. There you'll see the really big ones. Yep, those sharks will streak right by and look you in the eye. After that you can go home. It doesn't get any better."

At margarita time every night, he and his buddies compared stories and dive videos of their shark encounters.

He was right; the size, number, and proximity of the sharks we saw on the reef was impressive, at times, even frightening. But my husband and I didn't search for bigger sharks every day. Sitting on the ocean floor, just ten feet from the surface, amid a dervish of rain-bow-colored fish, in the decaying seat of a Japanese Zero fighter plane bombed down in World War II, was my most vivid memory. Deeper isn't necessarily better.

—MBB

and it seemed that most of the village had come down to the dock. Some were there to load up their bicycles with cartons of Pampers and pineapples; others were there to comment on how well the Pampers and pineapples were being loaded.

Over dinner that night my traveling buddies told me all about their afternoon dive. It had been disappointing. Not as many sharks, not much big stuff at all. And they were kind of irritated. They had wanted to go deeper and wander off on their own a bit, but the dive master had insisted they stick together. They hadn't had enough time on the reef, either, because they'd been made to take an extra-long decompression stop on the way up. They were going to have a talk with the dive master. After all, they said, "Americans won't come here if they can't have their freedom."

In the morning they all left for another deep pass dive—and I joined the boatload heading out into the lagoon. As we motored to the reef, I was feeling confident—cocky, even. My tan was coming along nicely. I knew how to clear my mask. I went so far as to assure the nervous Polish med student sitting next to me that he wouldn't need to wear neoprene gloves. And when it was time, I rolled eagerly backward into the azure sea and it was all there again, like switching on the Discovery Channel—and finding yourself behind the screen.

There were fish everywhere and pretty whorled blobs of coral. A bank of fluorescent blue eyes looked out from a bone-white fluted shell. I peered into one dark hole and saw something looking back at me. I chased a translucent sea horsey thing and touched a sea cucumber the size of a dachshund. I even scraped my leg on some coral and didn't mind at all; it was kind of like getting a tattoo.

In fact, I was feeling so good that I decided to accompany the guys on their afternoon open-ocean dive. They were "only" going to 60 or 70 feet, and Virginia assured me she would help me through it.

We motored out into the huge swells surging through the channel. I smiled at Peter, a soft-spoken Canadian who had made it his personal crusade to see me make this dive. I knew the others were glad I had come. They couldn't wait for me to see what they had seen, to feel that rush.

When we reached the dive site, we rolled out of the boat. I spent a couple of clumsy minutes in the water struggling to get my ears cleared. Virginia was dragging me down by my vest and my group was disappearing beneath my fins and my right ear was still killing me. I couldn't get it clear. I couldn't do this. I shook my head at Virginia and she motioned for me to get back into the boat. But before I started up, I saw two dark shark-shapes pass under me—beautiful daggers slicing through the blue.

Later, in the steamy calm of dusk we all gathered in the bar and drank cold Hinano beer and talked about the dive. It had been a good one, they all said, not a great one. If they had been able to go a little deeper, explore a little farther...

"At least you gave it a shot," Jerry said to me.

"Ear trouble," Peter said. "Well, anybody can have ear trouble."

"Too bad," somebody else said. "It would have given you something to write about."

After dinner I walked over the dock, sat down, and dangled my feet above the water. They were kind of sweet, those dive guys. They thought I needed cheering up, but they were wrong. After all, I had seen clouds of little clown-faced fish and that shimmying sea horse thing and a pair of fat-lipped groupers. I had even seen the shadow of sharks.

I leaned forward, and a red hibiscus fluttered down into the dark water. I had forgotten it was behind my ear. I could hear the voices of some of the fellows in my group. They had moved to the bar, and they were getting riled up again about the long decompression stops. They sounded unhappy. I listened to them for awhile and watched my flower drift away. Then I stood up and headed back to my bungalow, grateful for the gift of inexperience.

Meg Lukens Noonan is a correspondent for Outside *magazine and co-author of* Albatross: The True Story of a Woman's Survival at Sea. *She lives in New Hampshire with her husband and two children.*

*

I touched a whale. Imagine.

Imagine actually petting a whale that welcomes our human touch. Not at Sea World; in the wild. Picture yourself leaning over the side of a small wooden boat in an isolated Pacific lagoon, stroking one of the world's living giants. This 45-foot, 50-ton mammal then rolls over, ever so gently, to have it's tummy rubbed like an enormous, gentle puppy.

It loves having it's lips rubbed and lies perfectly still on its side while I stroke and croon and tell it how beautiful it is.

Tell *her* how beautiful *she* is, because she is definitely a female.

Her lips are longer than my little boat. They feel like cool, smooth, wet surfboards. I scratch and tickle and cluck like a mother hen, fretting over the cruel barnacles, but she is really the mother hen. Bigger than my house, with a shy baby peeking up through the surface twenty feet away, a baby bigger than my living room.

I have been here for days—on this vast lagoon filled with breeding wild whales who will soon leave for the Arctic—cooing, cheering, crying at times, overcome with the overwhelming emotion of the connection.

Emotion is what this is all about. At this moment in time, a frontier has been crossed, perhaps the ultimate frontier. I have touched a whale, again and again and again, and it is a thrill beyond belief; an exhilarating, uplifting, emotional connection with another species, another world.

I touched a whale. And it was her idea.

—Paula McDonald, "I Touched a Whale"

PAM HOUSTON

✶ ✶ ✶

A Blizzard under Blue Sky

Winter camping proves to be better than Prozac.

THE DOCTOR SAID I WAS CLINICALLY DEPRESSED. IT WAS FEBRUARY, the month in which depression runs rampant in the inversion-cloaked Salt Lake Valley and the city dwellers escape to Park City, where the snow is fresh and the sun is shining and everybody is happy, except me. In truth, my life was on the verge of more spectacular and satisfying discoveries than I had ever imagined, but of course I couldn't see that far ahead. What I saw was work that wasn't getting done, bills that weren't getting paid, and a man I'd given my heart to weekending in the desert with his ex.

The doctor said, "I can give you drugs."

I said, "No way."

She said, "The machine that drives you is broken. You need something to help you get it fixed."

I said, "Winter camping."

She said, "Whatever floats your boat."

One of the things I love most about the natural world is the way it gives you what's good for you even if you don't know it at the time. I had never been winter camping before, at least not in the high country, and the weekend I chose to try and fix my machine

37

was the same weekend the air mass they called the Alaska Clipper showed up. It was 32 degrees below zero in town on the night I spent in my snow cave. I don't know how cold it was out on Beaver Creek. I had listened to the weather forecast and to the advice of my housemate, Alex, who was an experienced winter camper.

"I don't know what you think you're going to prove by freezing to death," Alex said, "but if you've got to, take my bivvy sack; it's warmer than anything you have."

"Thanks," I said.

"If you mix Kool-Aid with your water it won't freeze up," he said, "and don't forget lighting paste for your stove."

"Okay," I said.

"I hope it turns out to be worth it," he said, "because you are going to freeze your butt."

When everything in your life is uncertain, there's nothing quite like the clarity and precision of fresh snow and blue sky. That was the first thought I had on Saturday morning as I stepped away from the warmth of my truck and let my skis slap the snow in front of me. There was no wind and no clouds that morning, just still air and cold sunshine. The hair in my nostrils froze almost immediately. When I took a deep breath, my lungs only filled up halfway.

I opened the tailgate to excited whines and whimpers. I never go skiing without Jackson and Hailey: my two best friends, my yin and yang of dogs. Some of you might know Jackson. He's the oversized sheepdog-and-something-else with the great big nose and the bark that will shatter glass. He gets out and about more than I do. People I've never seen before come by my house daily and call him by name. He's all grace, and he's tireless; he won't go skiing with me unless I let him lead. Hailey is not so graceful, and her body seems in constant indecision when she runs. When we ski she stays behind me, and on the downhills she tries to sneak rides on my skis.

The dogs ran circles in the chest-high snow while I inventoried my backpack one more time to make sure I had everything I needed. My sleeping bag, my Thermarest, my stove, Alex's bivvy sack, matches, lighting paste, flashlight, knife. I brought three pairs of long underwear—tops and bottoms—so I could change once before I went to bed and once again in the morning, so I wouldn't get chilled by my own sweat. I brought paper and pen, and Kool-Aid to mix with my water. I brought Mountain House chicken stew and some freeze-dried green peas, some peanut butter and honey, lots of dried apricots, coffee, and Carnation Instant Breakfast for morning.

Jackson stood very still while I adjusted his backpack. He carries the dog food and enough water for all of us. He takes himself very seriously when he's got his pack on. He won't step off the trail for any reason, not even to chase rabbits, and he gets nervous and angry if I do. That morning he was impatient with me. "Miles to go, Mom," he said over his shoulder. I snapped my boots into my skis and we were off.

There are not too many good things you can say about temperatures that dip past twenty below zero, except this: they turn the landscape into a crystal palace and they turn your vision into Superman's. In the cold thin morning air the trees and mountains, even the twigs and shadows, seemed to leap out of the background like a 3-D movie, only it was better than 3-D because I could feel the sharpness of the air.

I have a friend in Moab who swears that Utah is the center of the fourth dimension, and although I know he has in mind something different and more complicated than subzero weather, it was there, on that ice-edged morning, that I felt on the verge of seeing something more than depth perception in the brutal clarity of the morning sun.

As I kicked along the first couple of miles, I noticed the sun crawling higher in the sky, and yet the day wasn't really warming, and I wondered if I should have brought another vest, another layer to put between me and the cold night ahead.

It was utterly quiet out there, and what minimal noise we made intruded on the morning like a brass band: the squeaking of my bindings, the slosh of the water in Jackson's pack, the whoosh of nylon, the jangle of dog tags. It was the bass line and percussion to some primal song, and I kept wanting to sing to it, but I didn't know the words.

Jackson and I crested the top of a hill and stopped to wait for Hailey. The trail stretched out as far as we could see into the meadow below us and beyond, a double track and pole plants carving through softer trails of rabbit and deer.

"Nice place," I said to Jackson, and his tail thumped the snow underneath him without sound.

We stopped for lunch near something that looked like it could be a lake in its other life, or maybe just a womb-shaped meadow. I made peanut butter and honey sandwiches for all of us, and we opened the apricots.

"It's fabulous here," I told the dogs. "But so far it's not working."

There had never been anything wrong with my life that a few good days in the wilderness wouldn't cure, but there I sat in the middle of all those crystal-coated trees, all that diamond-studded sunshine, and I didn't feel any better. Apparently, clinical depression was not like having a bad day, it wasn't even like having a lot of bad days, it was more like a house of mirrors, it was like being in a room full of one-way glass.

"Come on, Mom," Jackson said. "Ski harder, go faster, climb higher."

Hailey turned her belly to the sun and groaned.

"He's right," I told her. "It's all we can do."

After lunch the sun had moved behind our backs, throwing a whole different light on the path ahead of us. The snow we moved through stopped being simply white and became translucent, hinting at other colors, reflections of blues and purples and grays. I thought of Moby Dick, you know, the whiteness of the whale, where white is really the absence of all color, and whiteness equals truth, and Ahab's search is finally futile, as he finds nothing but his own reflection.

"Put your mind where your skis are," Jackson said, and we made considerably better time after that.

The sun was getting quite low in the sky when I asked Jackson if he thought we should stop to build the snow cave, and he said he'd look for the next good bank. About 100 yards down the trail we found it, a gentle slope with eastern exposure that didn't look like it would cave in under any circumstances. Jackson started to dig first.

Let me make one thing clear. I knew only slightly more about building snow caves than Jackson, having never built one, and all my knowledge coming from disaster tales of winter camping fatalities. I knew several things *not* to do when building a snow cave, but I was having a hard time knowing what exactly to do. But Jackson helped, and Hailey supervised, and before too long we had a little cave built, just big enough for three. We ate dinner quite pleased with our accomplishments and set the bivvy sack up inside the cave just as the sun slipped away and dusk came over Beaver Creek.

White is the color of the new, the pure, the pristine. It is also the color of the soul free of the body, of spirit unencumbered by the physical. It is the color of the essential nourishment, mother's milk. Conversely it is the color of the dead, of things which have lost their rosiness, their flush of vitality. When there is white, everything is, for the moment, tabula rasa, *unwritten upon. White is a promise that there is nourishment enough for things to begin anew.*

—Clarissa Pinkola Estés, Ph.D.,
Women Who Run With the Wolves: Myths & Stories of the Wild Woman Archetype

The temperature, which hadn't exactly soared during the day, dropped twenty degrees in as many minutes, and suddenly it didn't seem like such a great idea to change my long underwear. The original plan was to sleep with the dogs inside the bivvy sack but outside the sleeping bag, which was okay with Jackson the super-metabolizer, but not so with Hailey, the couch potato. She whined and wriggled and managed to stuff her entire fat body down inside my mummy bag, and Jackson stretched out full-length on top.

One of the unfortunate things about winter camping is that it has to happen when the days are so short. Fourteen hours is a long time to lie in a snow cave under the most perfect of circumstances. And when it's 32 below, or 40, fourteen hours seems like weeks.

I wish I could tell you I dropped right off to sleep. In truth, fear crept up my spine with the cold and I never closed my eyes.

Cuddled there, amid my dogs and water bottles, I spent half of the night chastising myself for thinking I was Wonder Woman, not only risking my own life but the lives of my dogs, and the other half trying to keep the numbness in my feet from crawling up to my knees. When I did doze off, I'd come back to my senses wondering if I had frozen to death, but the alternating pain and numbness that started in my extremities and worked its way into my bones convinced me I must still be alive.

It was a clear night, and every now and again I would poke my head out of its nest of down and nylon to watch the progress of the moon across the sky. There is no doubt that it was the longest and most uncomfortable night of my life.

But then the sky began to get gray, and then it began to get pink, and before too long the sun was on my bivvy sack, not warm, exactly, but holding the promise of warmth later in the day. And I ate apricots and drank Kool-Aid flavored coffee and celebrated the rebirth of my fingers and toes, and the survival of many more important parts of my body. I sang "Rocky Mountain High" and "If I Had a Hammer," and yodeled and whistled, and even danced the two-step with Jackson and let him lick my face. And when Hailey finally emerged from the sleeping bag a full hour after I did, we shared a peanut butter and honey sandwich and she said nothing ever tasted so good.

We broke camp and packed up and kicked in the snow cave with something resembling glee.

I was five miles down the trail before I realized what had happened. Not once in that fourteen-hour night did I think about deadlines, or bills, or the man in the desert. For the first time in many months I was happy to see a day beginning. The morning sunshine was like a present from the gods. What really happened, of course, is that I remembered about joy.

I know that one night out at 32 below doesn't sound like much to those of you who have climbed Everest or run the Iditarod or kayaked to Antarctica, and I won't try to convince you that my life was like the movies where depression goes away in one weekend, and all of life's problems vanish with a moment's clear sight. The simple truth of the matter is this: on Sunday I had a glimpse out-side of the house of mirrors, on Saturday I couldn't have seen my way out of a paper bag. And while I was skiing back toward the truck that morning, a wind came up behind us and swirled the snow around our bodies like a blizzard under blue sky. And I was struck by the simple perfection of the snowflakes, and startled by the hopefulness of sun on frozen trees.

Pam Houston is the author of two collections of short stories, Waltzing the Cat *and* Cowboys Are My Weakness, *which is a work of fiction but for this one story. A licensed river guide and horsewoman, she has edited a collection of fiction, nonfiction, and poetry called* Women on Hunting, *and she is at work on a novel called* Sighthound. *She lives in Colorado, 9,000 feet above sea level near the headwaters of the Rio Grande.*

✳

This earth owns me, for I have borrowed the matter from which I'm made from her sticks and grasses and clouds. Someday, she will reclaim this form, as she reclaims the fallen tree in the hemlock grove.

I know, too, all that is powerful and holy is here—breath and wind, stone and sky, trees, and life. Here is God, the "Great I Am." If I flee this moment or fill it with fear and anxiety, I dishonor it, and miss a sweet touch of eternity. I will linger in this place for some timeless time, re-peating the prayer, feeling the solid earth beneath my back and breathing the gentle incense of the woods.

The time comes for Abbey [my German Shepherd] and me to return to our house and our feline housemate. Abbey leads the way, and I follow. The West has worked her magic; the Earth has healed her creature.

—Karen Monk, "Spirit Walk," *Another Wilderness: New Outdoor Writing by Women,* edited by Susan Fox Rogers

SHARON DIRLAM

*　✦　*

Stranded in Volos

*An unexpected friendship found in an unlikely
place leads to an unusual conclusion.*

IDEALLY, I WOULD PREFER NEVER HAVING TO TRAVEL ON A RIGID
schedule. But then, I wouldn't have met Rita.

I met Rita late one rainy night in a bus line in the industrial city
of Volos, on the northeastern coast of Greece. Few tourists have
visited Volos. Most who do go there are budget travelers on their
way to the Sporades Islands in the far northern Aegean Sea.

After two weeks in the Sporades I needed to get back to Athens
to catch a plane home. But the night before I was scheduled to
leave the island of Skiathos on a small commuter plane, a storm
moved in and hung over the island. In the morning, the dark skies
opened and drenched the ground with rain, then blasted it with
cold wind and drenched it again, like a heavenly fury of spring
cleaning. This was on a Saturday at the beginning of the Greek
Easter week.

I sat in a crowded travel office for hours, along with dozens of
island residents surrounded by their children, heavy suitcases, and
baskets of food. But it was finally announced in the late afternoon
that all flights were canceled until Sunday at the earliest. In Greek
money, I only had fifteen hundred drachmas left, worth a little

more than ten dollars. On a Saturday in Skiathos, there was no place to change money.

My plane back to the United States was due to leave Athens Monday night. My choices were to wait and hope that planes could fly off the island the next day—and I could get a seat on one—or take the ferry to the mainland city of Volos and try to catch a bus or train from there to Athens.

In spite of the wind whipping across Skiathos and the rain flying past in cold, wet gusts, I decided to take my chances on the ferry. The clerk handed me a ticket and said the departure time was 4:45 p.m.

"But it's already five o'clock," I cried.

"No problem," she replied. "It's raining, so the ferry is probably late."

I raced to the wharf, following the rest of the crowd, my heart pounding. I was afraid of missing the boat and apprehensive about catching it.

The ferry was big and old. As it lumbered away from Skiathos—its bottom smacked against the water and its sides shuddered and creaked. It plowed a zigzag eastward course through mountainous swells rolling down from the north. Grim-faced Greek women clutched the rails at the windows of the boat and stared directly out to the sea, their children hanging onto their coats. Men sat at tables in the middle of the ferry, smoking cigarettes and drinking beer. They were silent and dour and kept their hands wrapped around their beer bottles.

After two hours, the ferry finally bumped against the dock in Volos. The passengers surged toward the exits, dragging their children and their luggage, eager to reach the security of solid land. It was still raining heavily and the gray light of evening had turned to pitch black.

Only one taxi was waiting at the dock, and I was the only one interested in it. The other passengers disappeared into the dark night, down side streets, some onto an old trolley car that clattered away on an ancient track, others on a bus headed another way. I had no idea where Volos was, exactly, let alone how far the down-town was from the waterfront.

The taxi driver was worse than useless. He drove me around in circles while I tried to communicate with him in my few Greek words. He seemed not to understand the words for "city" or "hotel" or "train station." He seemed only to know that I was a foreigner from whom he could extract some money at some point. He drove and muttered and shrugged, smoked cigarettes, and twid-dled with the radio dial. After several minutes of circling, I noticed a neon sign at the end of a street and demanded that he let me out. I shoved a few drachmas at him, grabbed my bag out of the back seat, and hurried down the street toward the light. I had not pro-gressed more than a stone's throw from the dock.

The neon sign hung over the entrance to a shabby hotel, not a place I would willingly stay, but I was getting desperate. I hadn't eaten for hours and I was tired and lost. I thought if I could get a room for the night, I'd be better able to cope with things in the morning.

But the night clerk wouldn't give me a room! I didn't have enough drachmas.

I showed him U.S. dollars. I showed him credit cards. I showed him traveler's checks. None of these would do. Greek cash or nothing. He turned his back and refused to reconsider. I went back outside. The rain had settled into a steady drizzle. I stood on the empty street with my suitcase, not knowing what to do. I walked to the other end of the street and noticed another neon sign in the distance. It was the Volos train station. At last, I thought, my luck was changing.

But the station was virtually empty; there was no train out until the next morning, and the clerk at the ticket window refused to sell me a ticket for that departure because I didn't have enough Greek money to pay for it. Again, he refused to consider U.S. dol-lars or credit cards or even traveler's checks. However, he pointed out the way to the bus station, a few blocks away.

There were a few people waiting in the ticket line at the bus station, a brightly lighted little place in the middle of a very run-down neighborhood. I recognized some of the people in line; they had been on the ferry. By then it was nine p.m. I joined the line, counting out my Greek money, which after paying the taxi driver had dwindled to about eight dollars worth. I wondered if it would be enough for a bus ticket to Athens.

"You are American," said a heavily accented voice. I looked up at the woman in front of me in line. She was about 35 and had the black hair and heavy features characteristic of many Greek women, but she was wearing tight-fitting jeans and a man's leather jacket—not something I'd seen on a Greek woman before. And she was traveling alone.

"Hello!" I said eagerly, happy to hear a familiar word for the first time in hours. I explained that I was counting my money to see if I had enough to buy a bus ticket. She smiled and shrugged. She arrived at the head of the line and bought her ticket, then took a seat in the small waiting room.

U nless you're one of those travellers who unplug themselves from their earphones and novels only to take photographs of donkeys, then you'll want to meet the Greeks. Although the massive influx of foreign visitors in recent years has had an inevitable numbing effect on the traditional hospitality offered to strangers, you will find that almost everyone you meet is friendly and gracious, and the older islanders— especially in the small villages— full of wonderful stories.

—Dana Facaros,
Cadogan Guides: Greek Islands

The night bus was scheduled to depart for Athens in one hour and arrive at five a.m. By this time, I would have been glad for any escape from Volos, but I found myself in the same frustrating situation I had been in at the hotel and the train station—not quite enough Greek money. I showed twenty-dollar bills to the woman behind the ticket window. I was willing to pay double the price, triple, or more, if only she would take dollars. But she waved me away.

Saturday night, stranded in Volos. I left the ticket window and sank onto a chair, expecting to spend the night in the bus station and try to figure out what to do in the morning. I closed my eyes.

The next minute, the woman in the leather jacket was standing in front of me, waving a ticket in my face.

"Athens! Forty-five minutes!"

"What? I don't understand."

"I buy you bus ticket. Athens! Forty-five minutes!" She said, enunciating carefully, as though talking to a stupid child. Her face was close to mine and her black eyes stared into my eyes. She had incredibly long eyelashes and dark brows. She smiled, showing an even row of large cigarette-stained teeth.

Relief washed over me. "What? My God! Wow! That's wonderful," I stammered, as she pressed the bus ticket into my hand. "You must have heard...you're the first person...."

I reached for my money belt. "Oh, here's twenty dollars. I'm sure that'll more than cover it and you'll have no trouble changing money in Athens. How can I ever thank you?"

"No thanks," she said. "I buy you bus ticket."

"Oh, I can't let you pay for my ticket," I protested. "You don't even know me. I do have money. It's just that I didn't have drachmas."

"No problem," she said, and started to walk away.

"Wait!" I said. "Are you hungry? Is there anyplace around here to eat? I'll buy you dinner."

She turned back toward me and flashed her big smile again. "There is one place. Open to midnight. I show you."

We grabbed our bags, and she took me firmly by the elbow and led me into the rainy night and around the corner to a tiny restaurant that consisted of two booths, a formica bar, and six stools.

We were the only customers. The food was good and cheap and my remaining Greek money would more than pay for it. We sat in a booth and ate grilled chicken and fried potatoes and drank cool, dark beer. She told me her name was Rita and she had two children, a boy and a girl, who lived with her mother in a suburb of Athens. She was going to visit them. Rita said she was one of only a few women in all of Greece who work as crew members on cargo freighters.

"I get this job from my husband. My husband is dead. He was killed in accident on his ship. We have two babies. I tell his captain I need money to support my children. This captain, he gives me the job of my husband." Rita leaned back and tilted her head to one side, smiling with pride. She lit a thin brown cigarette and inhaled deeply. "I work hard," she said. "I travel around the world. One time I go to San Diego, California. I like that city very much."

We finished our beers and I reached for the bill, but Rita pushed my hand away.

"I pay. You save your money," she said.

I protested. "You bought my ticket. At least let me buy you dinner."

"No. I pay. Americans are nice to me. I am nice to you."

Rita's insistence on paying the bill was just as stubborn and determined as the three clerks had been in refusing to take my money. I thought my will was strong, but hers was stronger. The bus pulled in to the station as we walked back. The rain had stopped and the wet pavement glistened in the glow of a few dim streetlights. I thanked her several times for her generosity, having given up on trying to explain that I didn't need her hard-earned money.

The big, modern bus pulled out of Volos around eleven p.m., with twenty or so passengers. As the bus made its way through the mountains toward Athens, Rita and I talked about our children, our mothers, our husbands. We grew sleepy and were quiet. When I woke up, the sky was black and full of stars. Rita slept with her head on my shoulder, her hands tucked around my arm.

The sun rose on a newly washed landscape, and the air around Athens was unusually clear and clean. Shortly before we reached the downtown Athens bus station, Rita asked if I had a paper and pen. I handed her my notebook. In big block letters, she wrote her name, Rita Handopolous, and her address, and closed the notebook and handed it back to me.

"This is me. Do not forget me," she ordered.

I promised I would remember her and gave her my business card and said to call me if she came to California again. I told her I would write to her when I got home.

"I am your friend," she said. "Do not forget. Do not send money. If you send money, you will forget me."

I promised I would not send money and I would not forget her.

Later, when I wrote my travel article about the island, I mentioned the problem with the bus ticket and the kind Greek woman who had helped me. I mailed the article to Rita, to show her my appreciation, thinking she would enjoy reading about herself.

Weeks later, I got a card in the mail from Rita, addressed in her careful block printing. It was the only time I ever heard from her. She wrote:

> "Dear Sharon. I am your friend Rita. I have your newspaper article. My mother and friends read this article and they say the kind Greek woman is not me. My name is not in the article.
>
>   Yours truly, Rita Handopolous."

She underlined her name three times.

Sharon Dirlam was a staff writer for the Travel Section of the Los Angeles Times *for eight years, and is the author of* Two Years Beyond Siberia, *an account of her Peace Corps service. She has worked in China and the Czech Republic as a teacher and journalist. In between planes, trains, and ports, she and her husband, John McCafferty, live in Santa Barbara, California.*

★

Out traveling I have met some of the most wonderful, friendly people in the world. Like musical notes, they sounded in my life with unutterable beauty and left a great poignancy when they were gone. I have learned as much from an acquaintance of nine minutes as I have learned from other relationships of nine years.

Yet there is a sadness that lingers from travel. All those good-byes to old friends, to new friends, to five-minute friends, to two-day friends. Travel, as life, is always full of good-byes. I used to cry coming back from the airport when I was a settled, normal, worker-of-the-world, for I was in a profession where it seemed at least once or twice a week I was driving a friend or colleague out to the airport and crying on the way home. But travel itself has mellowed my life and let me loosen my hold on others. It has taught me to let my hand open for the swans to come and feed and also to fly away.

—Jan Haag, "Last Minute Terror"

* * *

Excess Baggage

*Women must learn to carry their own luggage,
emotional and physical, before they can
truly venture out.*

YEARS AGO I JOURNEYED TO EUROPE AND TOOK WITH ME EXCESS baggage. Among my material excesses were assorted electrical appliances I'd never use, high heels that made no sense on cobblestone streets, dozens of pleated skirts and sweaters of high school vintage, weighty guidebooks I abandoned on trains, jackets for all weathers, and all those innumerable items called accessories, as if they were accomplices in crime. Along with heavy bags I carried a heavy heart. My inner baggage—a desire to be taken care of, an endless search for love, and excessive needs—weighed me down. I spent much of my journey standing in train stations and bus terminals waiting for a porter or some other man to come to my aid.

Excess baggage is a symptom of something we are missing on the inside—a fear that we won't be accepted for what we are, as if our selves are not enough. We bring too much of our past experience, the clutter of our emotions. These things get in the way and keep us from getting close to others. Then we are left with the task of having to find someone else to carry it, whether it is our luggage or our loneliness.

It was my friend Carol who taught me the value of lightness. A few years ago I went to Peru, where she was living. I had just ended a long relationship and I overpacked because I wanted men to admire me so I would feel better about myself. I arrived in a bad mood. We flew to Lake Titicaca and hired a boat to take us to the island of Taquili. En route we encountered a storm. Arriving four hours late, in pitch darkness, drenched to the skin, we still had an hour's hike up a steep incline and then down again to get to the village. Everything in life looked grim as I crawled up the slope.

A small duffel slung over her shoulder, Carol scrambled up the hill like a mountain goat while I dragged myself and my possessions over rocks and mud. Carol had had some difficult times lately as well, but she was able to put them behind her. She was annoyed with me, but finally she took pity. Grabbing one of my bags, she said, "I'll help you this trip, but next time, lighten up," referring to my entire being.

In the end I would have no choice. On the journey from Peru to Mexico the airlines lost my bags. What I had left were the clothes on my back and a carry-on with a pair of jeans, t-shirts, a sweater. At first I was obsessed by my missing things, as if I'd lost a part of myself. I wanted to stay in Mexico City and await their return, but I was meeting a friend in San Miguel. I went straight to San Miguel, but my friend hadn't arrived and that night I had nothing—no possessions, no people—to distract me from myself. I spent a dark and anxious night, troubled by memories and a concern for what lay ahead. In the morning, the Mexican light streamed in like a blessing.

I went to the market, where I was struck by the colors and smells. Fresh mangoes and gladiolas, raw meat, flowers and grains, burlap sacks of lentils and beans.

I bought an avocado, some cheese, tortillas and beer, put them in my small pack and walked down the road heading out of town. I walked through hills covered with cactus and wildflowers until I reached a lake, and there I sat, in the heat of the day, having a picnic with myself.

I forgot about my luggage and all the other baggage I carried with me. I settled into the freedom that lightness brings. I wandered the hills. Unencumbered I moved for several days from place to place. When my bags were finally located, having spent some time in Honolulu, I wondered why I thought I'd needed all that stuff in the first place.

The women referred to by 19th-century writers as "traveling ladies" were often romantic dreamers, going off into the wilds or in search of "the spirit of the East." Women who were explorers in the early 20th century were a different breed—goal-oriented, directed toward scientific inquiry.

The women of my generation are also explorers, although our field work is of a different sort. We pioneer in uncharted emotional terrain—entering new professions, living with or without husbands, bringing up children alone, choosing a career and the single life. Or any combination of the above.

What we bring with us as we forge ahead tells a lot about who we are. A large part of independence is learning to carry our own weight. As long as women ask others to take care of their physical or psychic luggage, we will always be searching for emotional porters, not the equals we say we desire.

Through an arduous process, over many years and via many mistakes, I have tried to shed luggage as a snake sheds skin. With each journey I bring less. I gain more. In clothing I have acquired the layered look. And inside of me I have tried to undo the layers.

I was never the type for a huge backpack, but last year managed to get around the world with a small suitcase on wheels. I move less burdened by the weight of self—the self I had opted to journey with. And I've learned what every traveler needs to know along the way: to scream if you must, smile when you can, and travel light.

Mary Morris is the author of eight books, including Nothing to Declare: Memoirs of a Woman Traveling Alone *and she is co-editor of* Maiden Voyages: Writings of Women Travelers. *She has written numerous travel stories which have appeared in major U.S. magazines and she lives in Brooklyn, New York, with her husband and daughter.*

★

We two ladies…have found out and will maintain that ladies *alone* get on travelling much better than with gentlemen: they set about things in a quieter manner, and always have their own way; while men are sure to get into passions and make rows, if things are not right immediately. Should ladies have no escort with them, then everyone is so civil, and trying of what use they can be; while, when there is a gentleman of the party, no one thinks of interfering, but all take it for granted they are well provided for.

The only use of a gentleman in travelling is to look after the luggage, and we take care to have no luggage. "The Unprotected" should never go beyond one portable carpet-bag. This, if properly managed, will contain a complete change of everything; and what is the use of more in a country where dress and finery would be in the worst taste?

—Emily Love, *Unprotected Females in Norway* (1857)

CATHY N. DAVIDSON

* * *

A Typical Japanese Woman

A foreigner wins new friends in
a traditional Japanese bath.

As soon as I arrive in Shirahama with the members of the Japanese Women's Studies Society, I realize that this is not going to be a typical three-day vacation by the sea. Instead of being shown to my room, I'm shown to *our* room, a gigantic tatami room. Except when we're at the beach, I'm told, this is where we will be meeting during the day and sleeping at night, all fifteen of us. Now we need to hurry to take our bath together because our dinner will be served in this room in an hour and a half.

"You've had a Japanese-style bath before, haven't you?" Kazue-san asks a little nervously as we head down the hall to the women's bath.

"Oh, of course," I shrug off her comment.

Of course I haven't but I'm not about to give that away. I know the basics from the guidebooks: wash thoroughly *before* you get into the bath; make sure never to do anything to spoil the communal, clean bath water. I figure I can wing it on the details.

We undress in a small anteroom and fold our clothes neatly into baskets on the shelves. We walk into the bath with our tiny white terry washcloths. Along one wall is a row of faucets for washing, with drains in the sloping tiled floors. On the other side is the mosaic-tiled bath, as blue as the sea, beneath a cascade of tropical plants.

I've seen naked women before in showers in various gyms in America, but the mood in this Japanese bath is entirely different. I've never seen people more comfortable with their bodies. There are 25 or 30 women in the room, our group plus a group of *obasan* (grandmothers) here on vacation from the countryside and some members of an Osaka teachers' association having an annual meeting. The oldest woman is probably close to ninety; the youngest is three. The mood is quietly happy, utterly relaxed.

We sit naked on low wooden stools, soaping ourselves with the terry washcloths, rinsing with red buckets filled from the taps and poured over the body. The conversation is lulled, languid, like the water, like the steamy air.

I finish washing my entire body and notice that most of the women from my group are still soaping a first arm. I slow down, going back again over my entire body, washing and washing, the soapy cloth, the warm water, the joking talking laughing atmosphere, the bodies. The women in my group are now washing a second arm. I slow down again, deciding I will try to do it right this time, Japanese-style, concentrating on a leg. I baby each toe, each toenail, each fold of flesh, noticing for the first time in years the small scar on the inside of my ankle, a muffler burn from a motorcycle when I was a teenager. I'm fascinated by this ritual attention to the body, so different from the brisk Western morning wake-up shower. When I finish (again) and go to shampoo my hair, I see that most of the women in my group are still scrubbing. I give up. It must take practice. I have never seen such luxuriant pampering of bodies.

The bath is a revelation for another reason. I read once that a one-hour bath has the same physiological effect as four hours of sleep. Maybe this is how the Japanese do it, I think, a ritual stop in the otherwise frenetic day.

As I watch these women soaping their bodies with such slow concentration, it is almost impossible for me to remember what they are like most of the time, raising families, working full-time,

responsible for all of the household chores and the household fi-
nances, as busy as any American woman I have ever met.

I tell this to my friend, Kazue-san.

"It's hard to be busy when you're naked," she says smiling. "It
looks too silly!"

I find myself laughing. Everywhere around me are the bodies of
typical Japanese women, every one different, every one alike.

"May I help you wash your hair?" Kazue-san asks, as I struggle
to pour some water over my hair from the little red plastic bucket.

"Please let me!" interjects one of the *obasan* who has been
watching me for several minutes. She is very old, probably in her
seventies or even eighties. Standing, her face comes even with
mine as I sit on the tiny stool. Her body is bent over, almost par-
allel to the ground. Kazue-san says she's probably crippled from
malnutrition during the War years and the chronic lack of calcium
in the traditional Japanese diet as well as from bending to plant and
harvest the rice crop every year.

"I bet she still works in the fields," Kazue-san whispers in
English, and I smile back into the old woman's smiling face. Her
hair is pure white, her face covered with spidery lines, but her eyes
are absolutely clear, sparkling. The old woman introduces herself,
bowing even more deeply. Her name is Keiko Doi. I'm too self-
conscious to stand up so I introduce myself sheepishly, trying to
bow as low and respectfully as I can without getting up from my
little stool. The other old ladies in the bath are watching us. They
seem abashed by Doi-san's forwardness, but they also look thoroughly delighted. One of the old ladies says you can never tell
what Doi-san will do next. She is their ringleader, a real character.

"She has no shame!" one of the grandmothers says half criti-
cally, half affectionately of the mischievous Doi-san.

"Too old for shame!" Doi-san retorts, and the other old lady
starts laughing so hard I'm afraid she might hurt herself. She pulls
up a stool and sits down next to us, watching intently, still unable
to stifle her laughter.

Doi-san squeezes shampoo into her hand and then rubs her
palms together briskly. She's a pro. She massages the shampoo into

my hair, the thick pads of her fingers making circles against my scalp. Then she lays one hand on my head, making a sound like castanets as she works her hands over my head. It feels great. After about ten minutes, she chops with the sides of her hands over my head, my neck, and my shoulders, a kind of shiatsu massage.

I think I could die at this moment with no regrets. I feel about four years old and totally at home, this tiny grandmother massaging my back and shoulders, my scalp and forehead. "Do you like this?" she keeps asking. "Is this comfortable?"

Yes, yes.

The other ladies are cutting up, making jokes, and Doi-san douses one of them with a bucket of water. The woman douses back, and someone else flips at Doi-san with a washcloth. Kazue-san says we've run into a group of 80-year-old juvenile delinquents. She's never seen anything like this in her life, and she tells Doi-san, jokingly but admiringly, that she's the most outrageous old lady of them all. In English, I start calling Doi-san the "Leader of the Pack."

"Shuuush!" Doi-san admonishes us to stop talking English to one another. She hands me a cloth to put over my eyes and motions to her friends. Each fills her bucket and comes to stand in a circle around me. They take turns; one pours a full bucket over my head like a waterfall. I take a breath, then the next bucket comes. The water is exactly the right temperature.

The body is a multilingual being. It speaks through its color and its temperature, the flush of recognition, the glow of love, the ash of pain, the heat of arousal, the coldness of nonconviction. It speaks through its constant tiny dance, sometimes swaying, sometimes a-jitter, sometimes trembling. It speaks through the leaping of the heart, the falling of the spirit, the pit at the center, and rising hope.

The body remembers, the bones remember, the joints remember, even the little finger remembers. Memory is lodged in pictures and feelings in the cells themselves. Like a sponge filled with water, anywhere the flesh is pressed, wrung, even touched lightly, a memory may flow out in a stream.

—Clarissa Pinkola Estés, Ph.D., *Women Who Run With the Wolves: Myths & Stories of the Wild Woman Archetype*

When they finish, I just sit there for a while, feeling cleaner than I've ever felt in my life.

The old ladies can't stop laughing, and several of them are slapping Doi-san on the back, chiding her for her outrageousness, but also beamingly proud of their brazen friend.

I ask Doi-san if I may wash her hair but she refuses. Now, she commands, I must soak in the bath. It's time for me to relax.

I say that I can't take water as hot as most Japanese, and one of the strangers already in the bath motions me to a place beside her where the water, she says, is coolest. I lower myself slowly, allowing my body to adjust to the heat.

When I look around, Doi-san has disappeared. The rogue and her octogenarian gang from the countryside have all departed. A new group of bathers is coming in. They look startled at first to see me, a *gaijin*, but then go about their business. They are probably high school or junior high school girls, many of them still at the last stages of chubby adolescence, utterly unself-conscious about their nakedness.

"That was her," Kazue-san whispers, absolutely deadpan, as she slips into the water beside me.

"Who? What do you mean?" I ask, puzzled at first, then skeptical as Kazue-san smiles impishly.

"Why, the typical Japanese woman," she teases. "Doi-san. I think you finally found her."

Cathy N. Davidson has written and edited seven books, among them 36 Views of Mount Fuji, *from which this story was excerpted. Cathy first went to Japan to teach English and began a deep fascination with the culture and people. She is currently a professor of English at Duke University in North Carolina.*

★

There is a 300-year-old Turkish bath on an Istanbul back street: Cagaloglu Hamami, a palace of marble and mist, steam and serenity. There you can become a child again. "The works," for a few dollars, allows you to enter an ancient world of tradition and ritual and become part of Turkish life for awhile in a way Westerners rarely glimpse.

At Cagaloglu, enormously fat, pale, pale, pale women, with skin so white and smooth they seem like huge rubber dolls, wash, scrub and massage those of us who put ourselves in their hands. Oddly, these female versions of the classic sumo wrestler all wear black bikini underpants, nothing more. We are led naked to lounge on warm ledges and sit under marble fountains where the women slowly pour warm water over us, wash our hair, scrub inside our ears, lay us on their slippery, wet marble daises and scour us briskly with luffas, then massage us with lotions and potions and marvelous mysterious things.

A Westerner, not understanding the murmured chatter, soon drifts and nods into a state of simple sensual beingness. You are there, being attended to like a toddler at bath time, flipped, flopped, slid here and there across the slick marble slabs. The regulars exchange soft words, quiet laughter at this, their weekly ritual. In the United States, people have standing appointments at beauty shops. In Turkey, time spent at the baths rejuvenates both friendships and bodies.

—Paula McDonald, "Travel Diary"

SOPHIA DEMBLING

* * *

The Bus Stops Here

Longing for the open road, the author finds friends
in strangers on the lonely byways of America.

EVERY NOW AND THEN, LIFE BECOMES OPPRESSIVE. DAY-TO-DAY things, ordinarily pleasant, grow tiresome. The same streets with the same sights lead to the same activities, until a day comes when you must flee, if just for a while, from the predictability of your life.

I discovered bus travel in my early twenties, when I was anxious to explore the wheat fields, mountains, and true-life Americana that existed outside my frantically paced, but surprisingly provincial, hometown of New York City. I would buy open-ended bus tickets and travel for a month or two at a time, seeing through the smudged windows an America I had only heard about. I stayed with friends, or friends of friends, or alone in cheap motels. I met unforgettable people—the hodge-podge of American classics that ride the bus—drifters and soldiers, Indians and ex-cons, preachers and heathens, and talkative old ladies.

The bus was the ideal escape. It is a passive activity, requiring only the ability to sit for long periods of time and a tolerance for a fair amount of discomfort. In exchange, it provides a constantly shifting view, endless time for dreaming, thinking and contemplating, and brushes with characters who would never cross my path under any other circumstances.

I loved the constant movement—passing through places and lives, the glimpses of places I had never been, might never be again. I took three or four long trips over several years, each time returning home with a vision that went further, an appreciation for the small vignettes of life, a refreshed attitude toward my place in the world.

But as I grew older and more enmeshed in life's daily worries, those trips began to slip into the past. It had been five or six years since my last one when I began to get that familiar, itchy feeling. I wanted to go, to move, to see.

But it didn't seem as easy as it used to. I had obligations, commitments, and new anxieties about the idea of being out there, all alone. These worries brought their own worries. Were my adventure days over? Was I now just another grinder in a grind? Could that be possible? Could I allow it?

So here I am, with something to prove, sitting on the floor of the busy Dallas depot, waiting to board a bus. My destination is Lewistown, Montana, where I have friends. It is a pretty, small town, worthy of the 36-hour ride.

But what is fun at twenty may be less so at thirty, and I'm fighting doubts. At twenty, the people who rode the bus looked refreshingly "real" to me. Now they look depressingly so. I forgot that some people don't smell very good. I forgot that some people have paper bags for luggage. A very old lady wearing fuzzy blue slippers shuffles by. What if I can no longer sleep in those prickly

> *Women who travel as I travel are dreamers. Our lives seem to be lives of endless possibility. Like readers of romances we think that anything can happen to us at any time. We forget that this is not our real life—our life of domestic details, work pressures, attempts and failures at human relations. We keep moving. From anecdote to anecdote, from hope to hope. Around the next bend something new will befall us. Nostalgia has no place for the woman traveling alone. Our motion is forward, whether by train or daydream. Our sights are on the horizon, across strange terrain, vast desert, unfordable rivers, impenetrable ice peaks.*
>
> —Mary Morris, *Nothing to Declare: Memoirs of a Woman Traveling Alone*

velour seats? An old geezer tries to chat with me, but I'm not in the mood. I'm considering changing my mind.

Still, when my bus is called, I line up to board. I get the last available window seat to myself until the last minute when a woman about my age asks, "Do you mind if I sit here?" What can I say?

The bus is more crowded and noisier than I remember. Nearly every seat is taken. I look out the grimy window and grit my teeth. Things don't look good.

Finally, the familiar slam of the door, the vacuum-packed feeling, the grind and wheeze of the engine, and the bus pulls out.

Miles and miles and miles and miles of West Texas. The girl next to me is pleasant company, although she's a non-stop, seamless talker. We talk about our lives, her new husband, their plans to start anew in Colorado Springs, her artistic ambitions. She is a Christian and tells me a long story about how the Lord cured her chronic yeast infection.

Then she makes a little speech about how she needs to do this, and if I'm not into it that I should stop her and she won't mention it again—and she proceeds to try and save me. She talks fast and steadily, going from her own first experience with the Lord, to the ways he led her to the right things in her life, to Jimmy Swaggart, to *The Last Temptation of Christ*. I look out the window and listen politely, but the landscape is boring, and the barrage of words grates on me.

She's about to launch into abortions when I tell her I've heard enough. She apologizes and is silent for a while. Then she apologizes again. She says she doesn't care if I've had ten abortions. I've had none and tell her so. She says she talks too much. We're quiet for a short time, then resume on friendly terms.

"You won't find no good women in Amarillo."

This wisdom's from the back of the bus, the smoking section, which always gets the rowdies. Our bus has the usual assortment of young toughs, weathered vagabonds and girls who have been around the block. I hear a man telling someone that he lost his wife and kids because of his drinking. One old man has a voice like Wolfman Jack.

We have an hour layover in Amarillo that night. I'm tired and sore. The free restroom stalls are taken; the rest are pay toilets. I don't want to wait. I pull out a handful of change and enter a stall, luggage and all. In the clumsy entry, I drop my change into the toilet bowl. Change is vital in an existence that relies heavily on vending machines, so I fish it out, cursing. A little girl is looking up into my stall from the next. I resist the impulse to kick her.

The only thing even slightly appetizing in the depot snack bar is some gray coffee and a sticky doughnut. My seatmate has arranged to meet her father during the lay over. She hasn't seen him in a year and is ambivalent about the rendezvous—more so when she sees that he has brought his girlfriend. But they're all sitting and eating nachos amiably, if a little stiffly. She takes out her flute—her prized possession that has not left her side since we boarded—and plays what she's learned for her father. It's mostly random notes, but it's a nice sound in the greasy orange-and-white diner.

Back on the bus, she moves to an empty window seat nearby. A plump Hispanic girl sits next to me. Fortunately—as I'm tired and talked out—she's shy and says nothing. I manage to fall asleep with my head on my lap. As I drift in and out, I hear my current and past seatmates marveling at my ability to sleep in that unlikely position. I play possum. I had forgotten that strangers see you sleep.

But that sort of sleep doesn't last long. I'm soon awake again. And cranky. Every muscle hurts. Why did I get into this? What is that noise? It's getting seriously under my skin. Squeeeeak, BANG, Squeeeeak, BANG. The windshield wipers. The night seems interminable. I hallucinate beds.

But eventually I'm lulled by the shifting, rain-smeared scenery. Places appear and then slip into the night. Dark, silent towns, hard to imagine in daylight. Empty roads, seemingly leading nowhere. We stop at lonely bus depots, no more than a sign on a gas station wall. People say goodbye in the light of street lamps. Others step off the dark strangeness of the bus into the arms of loved ones. A small cafe—Edna's Chat 'n' Chew. I want to go in here and have some homemade pie and sit a spell, but we are here only five minutes while the driver picks up a package and exchanges a word with Edna.

Finally I sleep again. I awaken to sunrise in the foothills of the Rockies.

I feel a little sad to see my Christian friend go. I know I'll never see her again and wonder how her life will work out. It's funny how that happens. Strangers...friends...strangers.

The bus from Denver to Cheyenne, Wyoming, is pleasantly empty, and the scenery is interesting. I've had a few hours' sleep, I've got a cup of coffee (however bad), I am definitely somewhere else. Total freedom. Complete independence. I could get off at any small town and just disappear if I wanted to. The country is rolling by, and I have no one to answer to. My only immediate complaint is that the bag of mixed dried fruit I brought to snack on now contains nothing but prunes and figs.

Depot food is inedible. In the past, drivers knew all the best places to make meal stops. Those places provided some of my best memories of past trips, both for atmosphere and food: little cafés with coffee-sippin' cowboys, small-town diners full of farmers talking politics and hunkering down to huge steaming breakfasts, mom-and-pop truckstops with hearty food and oil paintings of trucks.

But the meal stop seems to be a thing of the past. If there's someplace near the depot we can run to for fast food, we're allowed to do that. But for the most part, stops are five minutes and the drivers are not lenient. Often, we're not allowed to get off the bus at all. Some people defy this to hover by the door and smoke cigarettes.

Wyoming is big and sprawling and raw. The sun is bright. Everything looks a lot cleaner than I am.

During my hour-and-a-half lay over in Cheyenne, I have a cup of coffee, wash up in icy cold water (that's all that's available in the restroom), store my luggage in a locker, and wander around the pretty town, buying souvenirs and taking pictures. I feel satisfied that the worst of the trip is behind me—the crowded buses, uninspiring scenery, marathon stretches. Things move slower out here in the West, and I've found the rhythm of the ride.

My next bus is on the Powder River line. The big companies have deserted the sparsely populated West. As a result, I'm tackling the wild West in a van. It seats about fifteen, but there are only four passengers. I have the whole back seat, the width of the van, to stretch out on, and a big picture window to look out of. The midday landscape is eerie, and lonely looking. So much space, so few people. I can't decide if I find it pleasant or unpleasant. I put on my headphones and listen to "Cowboy Country," a radio station out of Laramie. I eat the prunes and figs.

"I don't like to compliment women," an old man says, "they got swelled heads already. But you are one of the quietest little things I've ever seen." I can think of nothing to say that wouldn't just clutter things up.

In Casper, a rosy blond girl with a small boy gets on. She sits across from me. We exchange shy smiles for a while before we begin to talk.

She lives in Sheridan and is going home after visiting her parents and sister in Las Vegas. Married at fifteen—when her family decided to move from Sheridan—she is now nearly twenty. Her little boy is two and a half, and she's pregnant with her second. Her husband is a year older than she. He's part Indian, races motorcycles, likes heavy metal. She speaks of him affectionately.

"I don't know why I got married so young," she says wistfully. She says her sister attends high school in Vegas, is very popular, and works for the CIA. "Everybody thought I would be the one who went to college, that she'd get married and have children," says my seatmate.

Her little boy falls asleep, stretched out between us. In the times we are silent, she gazes solemnly at the sleeping child. The look is full of love, but also sad and resigned.

In Gillette, Wyoming, I meet a woman with a *Seventeen* magazine face who is traveling with her little daughter. She's a full-time missionary with the Jehovah's Witnesses and makes me feel grubby and heathen. So I bum a Marlboro from my seatmate, and we stand together, smoking and shivering in the northern night.

As we wait to leave Gillette, I talk with the old man and a strange-looking little woman of indeterminate age. She has shoulder-length brown hair, wears jeans and an enormous cowboy hat, carries a thermos of coffee at all times, and gets out at every stop to smoke.

"You in your thirties?" the old man asks me.

"I'm thirty." Let's not rush things.

"I'm forty-six," the woman says, in a crow's caw of a voice.

I don't know what to say.

"I'll be forty-seven in a couple of months," she says.

"I got drunk when I turned thirty," I offer.

"I never had a drink," says the woman. "Drinking killed my father. And my two brothers."

I don't know what to say.

The van fills up. It feels like a camp bus for old folks.

Our bus driver, Shorty (he is not particularly short), says we'll be able to run into a Burger King in Sheridan. This is big news for me. After living for two days on crackers and dried fruit, I'm feeling hollow and headachy. Visions of Whalers and fries dance in my head for miles. We get to Sheridan, and there it is. I have to run across a wide, busy avenue to reach it. But though the drive-thru is open, the doors are locked. Walking through the drive-thru would make me look

Thanks to my fellow travelers, every mile of the journey had been a discovery—mostly they were the journey.

"But the discomfort!" Mother's worried neighbor had cried.

"Nothing like it," I told her.

The truth is, I am a hussy of low appetites who always yearns shamelessly for rough travel, and I grab the chance whenever I can to arrive at my destination exhausted, knowing I've earned my goal the hard way. Greyhound and I were made for each other. "It had to be you," I whispered as I watched a great big Americruiser zip past us effortlessly, homing in on the Port Authority after what vast and thrilling distances?

—Irma Kurtz, The Great American Bus Ride: An Intrepid Woman's Cross-Country Adventure

as desperate and downtrodden as I feel, and I can't bring myself to do it.

I'm mad. I'm hungry. I hate everyone—especially Shorty for getting my hopes up. I'm out of coins, and there's nothing in the vending machines I want anyway. I choke down a couple of crackers.

I'm sorry to say goodbye to my seatmate and her little boy and disappointed that her husband isn't there to meet her. So is she. As we pull out, she is talking worriedly on the phone in the tiny depot.

An unbearably cheerful woman with an English accent sits next to me. She gives me encouraging looks, but I'm far too irritable to deal with her. And I'm annoyed that she has moved to the back seat, giving me less room to sleep.

Still, I curl up and manage to doze. The road is in bad shape, and Shorty drives like a maniac. Every time he hits a big bump, we all fly in the air.

Next stop, Billings, Montana, and a brutal lay over—from 1 a.m. to 8:30 a.m. It is to be the real test—the night I've been dreading since I plotted this trip. Bus depots aren't designed for comfort and usually are located on the seedy side of town. I have no doubt the night will be unpleasant. But I have this perverse belief that adventure, like art, requires suffering.

In late-night lay overs, it's best to stick close to the depot. Shorty announces that the Billings depot is locked from 2:00 to 3:30 a.m. for cleaning. He says we can either be locked in or out and that there's an all-night coffee shop across the street. I decide to grab a bite and get back in time to be locked in. I'm glad to have even that much information about the night ahead.

We arrive in Billings at one, as scheduled. I wolf down a big breakfast at the pleasant all-night coffee shop, finishing in time to get back to the depot and be locked in. But the guard has thrown everybody out and is locking the door.

"You can talk to him," he says apologetically, indicating the janitor. "He says he can't clean with people around." I approach the janitor. He snarls. I leave.

The waitress isn't surprised to see me back at the coffee shop. The place is hopping—it's where all the drunks come when the bars close. I'm prime drunk game. An old and particularly pungent one asks me for a cigarette. I tell him I don't have one (true). "You don't smoke?" he wheezes, his breath almost visible. "Why not?"

The waitress, a hearty girl, comes and cheerfully escorts the drunk out. She is proud of what she has done and gets chatty. She tells me she likes to walk around in socks with no shoes.

By 3:30, I have made the acquaintance of a couple of sad, anxious young drunks, and a big boozy one, who has only one story to tell, again and again.

The depot is strictly utilitarian: lockers, plastic orange and green seats, racks of old magazines and books—one of romance novels only. A sign says, "Please buy before you read." There are two walls of video games. One makes noises continually—computer chewing sounds, musical beeps, little tunes.

I talk briefly with the cheerful English woman, who turns out to be Australian. She and her husband, who has the flu and sits wordlessly beside her, have been traveling for seven weeks through Europe and America. They're carrying $800 worth of Venetian glass with them. I marvel silently at her white skirt, still spotlessly clean. She tells me that they have eleven children. "I do twenty loads of laundry a week," she says. She also sells hand-painted clothes and is a social worker. A Remarkable Woman.

Although we never even introduce ourselves, before she boards her bus she hands me a paper with her name, address, and telephone number. "In case you're ever in Australia," she says.

Soon, I'm the only person besides the ticket agent in the depot. It's somewhere in the wee hours of the morning, but I try not to look at the clock. I'm cross-eyed from reading and want a shower and a bed. I stretch out on the floor with my head on my luggage and fall into a fitful sleep.

I'm awakened by a man who looks to be in his thirties, wearing a plaid shirt and jeans that appear to have had several days' wear.

"Hello," he says, taking a seat near me. I surface slowly, feeling thick and achy.

"You're covered with flies," he says. This is true.

I sit up, scattering the flies, and bum a cigarette from him. It's a Camel stud, but I'm grungy enough to handle it. The guy asks me questions, introduces himself. He holds out his hand. I don't really want to shake it. I don't know where it's been.

We don't say very much. A sentence here and there. It seems natural for the two of us to be sitting in commiserative silence— he in an orange chair, me cross-legged on the floor—smoking his cigarettes. Six-thirty a.m. Partners in squalor.

But he smells of old booze. When I mention the fact that he's been drinking, he gets embarrassed. Soon he says goodbye, nice talking to you, and goes away. I'm not sorry to see him go.

It's finally time to board the bus to Lewistown. There are just four other passengers on the full-size bus. The scenery is spectacular here, but I can't stay awake. I fall asleep in my sunny seat almost as soon as we hit the highway. I'm so tired I drool in my sleep and can barely rouse myself to turn my pillow when wet spots accumulate.

I arrive in Lewistown, check into a hotel, take a hot shower, and fall into the deepest four hours of sleep I've ever experienced.

Shell shocked and sore for about a day, I decide the discomfort was intolerable and that I must be too old for the bus. Or maybe they don't cater to passenger comfort the way they used to. I vow, regretfully, that I have bused my last bus. I tell anyone who'll listen how bad it was. I consider flying home from Denver, but after four days in Lewistown, which is as delightful as I had remembered, my feelings about the ride have mellowed and I feel up to the long trip home. Besides, I'm not prepared to give up my youth so easily.

As I settle into my seat and look at dark, quiet Lewistown through the bus window, I am surprised by a feeling of serenity. The seat is a familiar little home.

I have a two-hour lay over in Billings. But I have a new book, I'm clean and rested, and at the end of the line is home. It's not so bad. (A funny thing happens in my stomach, though, when I hear the familiar chomp chomp chomp, ding, tinkle, beep of the video game that serenaded me through that long, grubby night.)

And a wonderful thing happens all the way home.

My buses are all empty. Until Fort Worth, there are never more than ten passengers. I sleep soundly (as possible) both nights. My longest lay over is in Billings. The worst inconvenience I suffer is when my plastic bag of Triscuits springs a leak and covers my seat with cracker shreds.

There is snow on the Rockies. I don't feel much like talking to anyone, so I appreciate the empty buses. I just watch the towns come and go, watch the land crest into mountains and then flatten. I sleep and read and listen to the radio. Toward the end of the ride, I talk a while to a scary-looking guy with tattoos and spiked bracelets who says he's on his way to study marine biology in Daytona, Florida.

We even stop at Burger King and Hardees. I still miss the quaint cafés, but I am grateful to have my stomach filled. One driver impulsively pulls over to a fruit stand. Everyone gets out, but only the driver buys a watermelon.

It is almost the bus as I remember it. All my bad feelings about my ride up are slipping away.

I take back all those vows. I will ride the bus again.

Traveling with me from Denver—or maybe Cheyenne—is a hobo. His greasy gray hair needs cutting, his clothes are grubby and too large, his only luggage is a bedroll as big around and nearly as tall as himself.

He sits near me through most of the trip. When we come into a town, he and I do the same thing. No matter what time of day or night, we rouse ourselves, sit up and look. Look and look.

I suppose, at this point, I appear nearly as roadworn as that hobo. But when my trip is over, I'll take a shower and put on makeup. I'll take my credit cards out of a drawer and put them back in my wallet. I'll return to my job, my boyfriend, my life. I'll be home.

The hobo, staring out the window so hard, may be looking for something. But I'm just looking.

Only when I am nearly downtown do I remember that Dallas—home—is a place I first saw through a bus window.

Sophia Dembling was born and raised in New York City, but at age nineteen discovered life west of the Hudson. She is now a freelance writer living in Dallas, and the former assistant travel editor of the Dallas Morning News.

✳

As a traveler I can achieve a kind of high, a somewhat altered state of consciousness. I think it must be what athletes feel. I am transported out of myself, into another dimension in time and space. While the journey is on buses and across land, I begin another journey inside my head, a journey of memory and sensation, of past merging with present, of time growing insignificant.

—Mary Morris, *Nothing to Declare: Memoirs of a Woman Traveling Alone*

JUDY WADE

✦ ✦ ✦

Romance in the Caribbean

What happens when the vacation fling is over?

IF IT HADN'T BEEN FOR MY INCURABLE WANDERLUST, I NEVER would have met my husband. If it hadn't been for his patience, ingenuity, and inventive communications techniques, we never would have gotten together. If it hadn't been for the gentle charms of the Caribbean, I'd probably still be single.

It began on board a luxury 104-foot trimaran called *Cuan Law*. I had an assignment to do a story on scuba diving and bicycling in the British Virgin Islands.

The enchantment of these romantic isles took over the instant I bounced down the rollaway steps of the little prop plane that brought me to Beef Island from San Juan, Puerto Rico. The night air was pleasantly humid with the fragrance of exotic flowers whose names I knew only from perfume bottles. Beneath the lilting dialogue of the baggage crew, the hums, buzzes, chirps and whirs of night creatures gave exotic mystery to the dark.

Outside the tiny terminal, a lanky islander in a white shirt over neatly pressed khakis pushed himself away from a van and approached me with a smile. "Hey miss, you be goin' to de *Cuan Law*?" At my nod, he swooped up my duffels and gestured toward the van.

Within minutes we were jouncing along in darkness so thick it was almost tangible. Enormous winged insects danced in the headlights' beams. Ahead I could see the glint of lights on water and a rubber inflatable raft tied to a small cement dock. A tan, blond fellow in shorts barely long enough to be decent greeted me with a smile, accepted my luggage from the driver, handed me into the raft, and pointed it toward a string of lights in the bay.

He said his name was Bill.

Within minutes I was being welcomed aboard the largest trimaran I'd ever seen. Scuba tanks were neatly arranged on the aft deck, mountain bikes leaned against safety lines, and Japanese lanterns cast soft shadows on padded benches and varnished tables. Inside, a half-dozen people lounged in the large salon, sipping drinks and chatting. Bill introduced me to the group, then wrestled my duffels to my cabin.

In the days that followed I got to know a couple from Tennessee, a pair of doctors from Texas, a single accountant from Minneapolis, my roommate (a stunning blonde from Philadelphia), and Bill. At first he was just one of six crew members aboard *Cuan Law*, helping me into my dive gear and leading dives that revealed the brilliant fish and coral that have put these islands among the world's premier scuba sites. He'd point out creatures such as a palm-size octopus and needle-like trumpet fish that I would have missed. Mornings often were spent ashore on mountain bikes, exploring tiny back roads sometimes clogged with herds of goats, often passing cheering children who thought the safety flags on our bikes meant we were in a race.

I soon became aware that Bill remembered that my BC was the pink one, and that I preferred white wine as a before-dinner cocktail. During one particular bike ride, when we found ourselves separated from the rest of the group, Bill volunteered that he had "run away from home" and a confining eight-to-five job in the Midwest. He was fulfilling a dream of living in the Caribbean and doing as much diving as possible. He'd been on the boat just over a year, and loved it.

We exchanged tales about my nomadic life as a travel writer and

his duties as a dive instructor/paramedic. After dinners served al-
fresco, we fell into a pattern of meeting on deck when Bill finished
work. With others murmuring in the darkness around us, we'd gaze
skyward, vying to identify amazingly brilliant constellations un-
dimmed by city lights or pollution. The warm Caribbean breeze
was a caress. It was inevitable that we would end up together in his
tiny cabin.

I was sitting on a low sofa in the lobby of the Kathmandu Guesthouse having just returned from the trails of Annapurna. I hadn't washed my hair in ten days; the last thing on my mind was romance. Then, I saw his legs: long, lean, and muscular. I heard he was leaving the next morning for a month's trek to Mt. Everest. Our paths crossed for one moment. Long enough to light a spark.

I continued my travels for another year. And, within days of my return to San Francisco, we met again at a mutual friend's party. Romance, then marriage. It was meant to be.

—MBB

In the days that followed we became better acquainted, sharing moments and experiences without any frantic necessity to
cement a bond. On the Saturday morning that I left, Bill shouldered my duffels and dropped them in the dinghy. We talked of
writing and keeping in touch. But I was certain that after a few
postcards, perhaps a phone call or two, the friendship would fade
into a lovely memory of a week delightfully shared.

Back in Los Angeles, I wrote my thank-you to the yacht's owners, enclosing an envelope for Bill with snapshots we'd taken while
I was there. On a Sunday morning several weeks later I received a
phone call from a rushed-but-cheerful Bill who'd managed to
sneak a moment from the precious few he had ashore to get in
touch with me. I was surprised at how glad I was to hear his voice.

I'd been home about a month when I received a small package
from the British Virgin Islands marked fragile. Inside, swathed in
cotton, was a perfectly formed shell. Wrapped in tissue inside the
shell were a pair of tiny gold earrings in the shape of the shell. For
the first time, I let myself realize that I was dealing with more than
friendship.

To facilitate the long-distance courtship, Bill began recording audio tapes and sending them once a week. He suggested I do the same. Telephone communication, besides being expensive, was difficult because Bill's time ashore usually involved greeting guests and bringing them aboard, leaving little time for personal pursuits. There was no phone on the boat. The tapes filled in the gaps, and helped us learn about each other's families and backgrounds.

Four months after I'd returned home, Bill announced on one of his tapes that he had three weeks off, during which he intended to visit his parents in Florida. He'd also like to spend some time with me in Los Angeles, he said. I was enjoying our fun-from-afar relationship, but I was uneasy about anything closer. As the survivor of a previous long-term relationship, now ended, I was fearful of anything that even hinted of commitment. I used the excuse of travel assignments to gently say no. Bill was disappointed, but accepted my reply optimistically.

During Bill's Florida vacation we talked often. I met his parents by long distance and wondered if I'd made a mistake in telling him not to come. By the time he was back on the boat and our blizzard of letters and tapes had resumed, I knew that the next time he asked he'd be welcome in Los Angeles.

It was ten months between the time I said goodbye to Bill on *Cuan Law*, and when I picked him up at Los Angeles International Airport; and he was as tan and blond and blue-eyed as I had remembered. We'd decided to spend five days of his thirty-day vacation together to see how things went. As it turned out, one month wasn't enough.

Before he returned to the boat, we'd made a commitment. Bill would leave the boat when his contract expired to come to Los Angeles and see exactly where things were going. Within six months of his return, we were engaged, and the following June we were married. We honeymooned aboard *Cuan Law*.

Is there a moral to this story?

A moral most profound.

Sometimes you have to listen to your heart and not your head. The very things that attracted me to Bill for a shipboard romance were what seemed to make him unsuitable as a permanent mate. China blue eyes, sun-blond hair, an all-over tan, and a nomadic lifestyle? Hardly the stuff on which to base anything long-term, I kept telling myself. Thankfully, Bill was smarter about relationships than I.

We return to the Caribbean whenever we can, always remembering to thank the spirits of the wind and sea for bringing us together.

Judy Wade is a travel writer who has written for the Los Angeles Times, Outside, *and* Caribbean Travel and Life. *She is also the co-author of* California *and* Disneyland and Beyond. *A Southern California resident for twenty-seven years, she and her husband now reside in Phoenix, Arizona.*

★

Rome may not have been built in a day, but my decision to go there for the first time certainly was.

I was living in Boston and was dating a man with commitment problems (which may well be redundant, but that's another essay entirely). I had a wonderfully romantic Thanksgiving in mind—just the two of us cooking a magnificent meal, sharing a bottle of wine, toasting our relationship.

But Michael's idea of a wonderful holiday was the two of us breaking bread with an out-of-town woman-friend he'd once slept with. In fact, he informed me one day in mid-November, he'd already invited her.

An unthreatened woman might have been brave and smiled graciously through each course of this turkey *à trois*. A more assertive one might have taken the bird out of the freezer, hit her man over the head with it, and walked out.

Being neither at the time, I decided to make other plans that were so wonderful I'd never give a second thought to what Michael and his old-flame-turned-friend were up to. For me, that could only mean one thing—high-tailing it to Europe.

The next day on my way to work, I stopped at a travel agent's office. She suggested an air-plus-hotel package to Rome for the holiday weekend, and I plunked down my American Express card before you could say "pass the stuffing."

Michael refused to believe I'd actually bought the ticket, right up until

I left for the airport. And while I was having a wonderful time touring the Coliseum, prowling through the catacombs, sipping cappuccino in little out-of-the-way cafés, and buying a pair of butter-soft Gucci boots I still own thirteen years later, Michael was eating Thanksgiving dinner with his lab partner.

It turns out his female friend was just as uncomfortable as I was with Michael's idea of a triangular turkey feast, so she made her own alternate plans. Which just goes to prove that she who laughs last laughs *meglio*.

—Katy Koontz, "Take That!"

✦ ✦ ✦

Obachan & I

*A year living as an exchange student
with a Japanese family leads
to a life-long friendship.*

LITTLE DID I KNOW THAT THE TINY LADY WHO STOOD BEFORE ME on that muggy Tokyo evening more than twenty years ago would have a profound influence on my life. "Have some strawberry juice," she had said as I sat dazed from my first international airplane flight.

Although very tired and not very sure of myself on that first evening in a foreign land, it remains one of my fondest memories. I took the pretty glass of homemade strawberry juice and slowly, tiredly drank in my surroundings—the living room with its tatami straw mat floors and leather couches, the scroll painting hanging in a recessed area of the wall, the television, and the bowl of incense before a picture of a distinguished looking, elderly gentleman. It seemed more like a dream than reality. Everything was so strange and wonderful, especially the woman with the strawberry juice. She was introduced as Kyoko Ono, an already familiar name and the grandmother of Junko, my friend and fellow waitress at an up-state New York resort the summer before.

My plans to study history at Tokyo's Sophia University nearly had fallen through because I had nowhere to live, but Junko had graciously volunteered her aunt and uncle's home as a place to stay for two weeks until something else could be arranged. The two weeks turned into a year, and two decades later the Yokoi family and Kyoko Ono, known to all as Obachan or Grandma, are still like a second family to me. And that year they were my family, and Obachan soon became my best friend.

Although it seems some of her acquaintances thought our relationship a bit strange, to me it made perfect sense. She became my entrée into a world that was at first completely strange and mostly incomprehensible but in the end so comfortable it became difficult to readjust to the U.S. Obachan taught me how to exist in a culture radically different from my own, something I would repeat many times in the future. None of my subsequent experiences can compare, however.

For this was no ordinary Japanese family, and Obachan was far from an ordinary Japanese woman. In fact, I've never met anyone else quite like her. Caught between two worlds—traditional and modern—Kyoko Ono is a maverick. Seventy years ago she majored in English at the university, when higher education for women was nearly unheard of and the study of English almost as rare. Soon after began her life-long involvement in an organization dedicated to improving women's education and status and helping them raise their families better. In her early twenties, she married a man chosen by her parents but refused to wear the huge white headpiece worn by brides during the wedding ceremony that supposedly hides the horns of jealousy. "I didn't have any horns," she said. It was a rather unusual statement for a woman of her day, but she came from a rather unusual family, or so I was to discover.

As the daughter of a military doctor, Obachan grew up in a Japanese settlement in Manchuria. Her interest in things foreign and Christian beliefs set her apart from the average Japanese of her day. And much of the influence came from relatives such as Leonardo Fujita, an uncle and one of Japan's most prominent modern artists, who was known as much for his bohemian lifestyle as his paintings. The first famous Japanese man to marry a foreigner—he married a French woman—Fujita divided his life between France and Japan, and his creations were Western art with a Japanese soul. He had lived in a house on the site where Obachan now lived—the previous one had been burned by the Americans during World War II. Although dead for more than a decade, his presence was felt strongly in the art scattered throughout the house.

And then there was Obachan herself. She only measured 4' 10" or so but always seemed to stand out in a crowd. Whereas most women her age—70 at the time—wore kimonos or conservative dresses, Obachan almost always wore pants, usually grey or brown with her favorite grey sweater. She had a perspective that was rather rare in those days. Kyoko Ono had seen much of the world on trips with her husband, who was vice president of a major Japanese company, and on a fact-finding mission to the U.S. and South America in the '50s, when she represented Tomo no Kai, her women's group, in a coalition of various women's organizations. Her job at Tomo no Kai was, in fact, to be a liaison between its chapters abroad—in the U.S., Europe, and South America—and the Tokyo headquarters.

Getting to know Obachan and her family was an education more valuable than the information contained in my university lectures. Their home near Takadanobaba Station in central Tokyo became my classroom. It was, in many ways, a typical Japanese house with typical daily routines and typical idiosyncrasies. Paper walls dividing the main rooms shook with amazing fury whenever an earthquake would strike Tokyo. Wooden window shutters that slid into the walls during the day had to be pulled out and bolted every evening in a ritual reminiscent of closing castle gates against intruders. A small garden with carefully tended flowers and greenery transformed a small yard into an oasis from the crowded city just beyond the wooden fence surrounding the house. A tiny bathtub contained water that was at first unbearably hot but quickly became a customary way to warm up in a house without central heating. The kitchen, as nearly everywhere, was the social center, where dinner conversation would continue for hours, until one by one we would make our way to the bath.

In that house in Totsuka-machi, Shinjuku, Tokyo, I learned many lessons. Such as how to live harmoniously in a small space, since my room was not much bigger than many American closets. I learned how to understand without always comprehending words. My initial Japanese was minimal at best, and much of Japanese communication is unspoken anyway. I learned to live frugally, not in a financial sense, but in the sense that in such a crowded country, everything is used sparingly and valued greatly. I learned to be forgiving and to forget the past, like many Japanese friends of my parents' generation, whose homes had been burned to the

Like many travelers I know, my first overseas experiences involved studying in a foreign country and living with a family. The Luxembourgish mother of my adopted family was responsible for six children, two acres of garden, cooking three meals a day, and piles of laundry. She was a conservative, traditional woman whose patience, hard work, and humor inspired everyone.

Years after I left Luxembourg and was studying in Paris, trying to survive classes in French and love-life traumas, I would return to Luxembourg for a weekend, just to touch base with a simpler, family-oriented life and for Momma Engels' warm, reassuring hugs.

—MBB

ground by the Americans during the war, but who still accepted me unconditionally. And I developed a feeling of awe for a society in which people treat each other with such respect that department store attendants bow to their customers, and everyone does the best they can at everything they do.

As the year progressed and my Japanese improved, I began to venture bravely forth into what was, at the time, the world's largest city. My classes were at night, and I had plenty of time to explore Tokyo, visit art galleries, and read at the school library. The highlight of the week, however, was lunch with Obachan on the days when she wasn't working at her women's organization headquarters. We'd prepare noodles, fried rice, or leftovers from the previous evening's dinner. It was all delicious, but what we had to say was far more important than what went into our mouths. We would discuss books, tell family stories, and informally tutor each other in the intricacies of grammar and the meaning of words. We spoke in Japanese, English, and a hybrid language that would give us the giggles. Like the time ants invaded the kitchen and contaminated my special lunch of clams in soy sauce. Thereafter, we referred to my feelings for ants as *ari*-phobia (*ari* means ants in Japanese). When I wasn't speaking gibberish, all my young Japanese friends used to tease me that I spoke polite grandmotherly Japanese. And Obachan's very formal English was soon enriched with American slang.

Parks and gardens were Obachan's favorite haunts, and she knew the names of just about every flower imaginable in both Japanese and English. At New Year's, we attended *dezomeshiki*, the firemen's festival, when firefighters perform tricks on ladders and race around carrying heavy hoses before crowds of thousands in the streets of downtown Tokyo. One of my favorite outings was an evening watching the Takarazuka Revue, the all-female dance troupe that performs Las Vegas-style revues as well as more traditional dances, and that was immortalized by James Michener in his book *Sayonara*. But I never saw Obachan as entranced as when she was watching sumo, the traditional Japanese sport, with its gargantuan wrestlers who throw salt over their shoulders as part of a religious ritual before beginning a match. Although not much for TV, Obachan never missed a televised sumo match.

My interests evolved during that year. Although I went to Japan with a desire to learn more about its ancient history, insightful novelists, woodblock-print artists and traditional culture, life with Obachan brought a curiosity for more modern-day concerns.

The women's movement, for example. The spring before I took off for Japan, the first issue of *Ms. Magazine* was published, and I was interested but still not exactly sure what feminism was all about. It didn't take long to learn firsthand, however, from this woman who had spent her whole life bucking tradition and setting an example for others to follow. I followed too, and after returning to the States helped set up a women's study program at Depauw University. Later I became so involved in the feminist movement that Obachan teasingly told me I had become more radical than she.

It was a quiet life I led in Tokyo, with lots of time to think and learn during the first of many adventures in foreign lands. In the years since, I have returned to that house in central Tokyo on several occasions, and my friendship with Obachan and her family is as strong as ever. Hardly a week goes by when I don't think about her, and hope that all is well, and that I will be able to see her again.

Entering that same living room twenty years later on my way to a new adventure in Vietnam, I realized that my life might not have been the same if it weren't for that tiny lady standing once again before me. She gave me the confidence to thrive in a culture unlike any I'd known and showed me the importance of following a path not taken by many others. She also taught me the incredible power of friendship, and how it can last a lifetime, even though there are nearly 5,000 miles of ocean and 50 years between us.

Thank you, Obachan.

Judy Jacobs worked, traveled, and studied in Asia for more than five years and now lives in Oakland, California, with her husband and two sons. Her writing on Asia and the South Pacific has appeared in magazines around the world, and she is the author of Indonesia: A Nation of Islands.

＊

Women in Japan are trained (externally at least) to buttress, build up, and coddle their menfolk, and are simply not expected to have any opinions of their own. My conversations with women of my age (mid-twenties) consisted of their questions and my answers, or my questions and their deflections of them. Of course, there were exceptions: the open-minded and incredibly charming Japanese woman who joined me on a journey through China; the woman I met in a crowded and steamy cafeteria who involved me in a wonderful and unintelligible discussion about nuclear war (I think); and my host mother who is one of the most energetic, self-assured, and lovable people I have met. But generally women I met treated me deferentially, tentatively, and often shied away as though I were a tall and unpredictable extraterrestrial.

—Riki Therival, "Finding a Place in Kyoto," *More Women Travel - Adventures and advice from more than 60 countries - A Rough Guide Special,* edited by Miranda Davies and Natania Jansz

JUDITH MCDANIEL

* * *

Learning to Walk

Standing alone, then stepping out,
begins the path to independence.

AS A KID I HAD BIG FEET. NOW I AM A WOMAN WITH BIG FEET. As
a kid I used to worry about how big my feet were. My mother told
me not to worry, that I had been given a good foundation.

In the eighth grade in 1957 I wanted to wear flats and nylons
to school like the other girls. No way, my father said. I could
choose between oxfords—black and white with laces—or Buster
Brown with laces. But no flats. Not even penny loafers: they didn't
have enough support. I was mortified then.

Today I am grateful, sometimes even smug. Barefoot, my toes
are straight and uncalloused, my arches strong. I can walk or jog for
hours without discomfort, the envy of those friends (I like to
imagine) who bent their toes to get into flats in the eighth grade
or pointed-toe heels not long after.

I tried pointed-toe heels. It was during my mini-skirt days in
Boston. One January morning I was walking back from teaching
class and leaning into a bitter headwind blowing off the ocean
when I realized I had only eight inches of cloth from my waist to
my pointed toes. The rest was nylon pantyhose. It was not surpris-
ing I was cold. After this revelation, it was ski pants and snow boots
all the way.

⋆

The Girl Scouts got me started walking. I was probably only eight or nine when an ambitious leader said we were going to do the Foot Traveller or Day Hiker badge. What I remember is being told we would walk five miles and that seemed like forever to me the night before the hike. It only took two hours. I was amazed. If I could walk five miles, I could go anywhere in my world.

The Girl Scouts also introduced me to the idea of formal walking. I marched in a parade once and carried the American flag. It was a long parade and the flag as heavy. My shoulder and back hurt when it was over, but I had learned something by watching the faces of the people we walked past, learned something about words I had heard but not understood, like patriotism.

In 1960 I was living in Europe and was invited to an international Girl Scout event in Denmark. Five thousand teenage Girl Scouts and Guides from all over Europe and Great Britain walked into a huge stadium. We carried hundreds of flags and marched past the Queen of Denmark and other dignitaries. What I leaned that day was that we were walking for ourselves. I was part of something that was bigger than just me, bigger than the United States. The stream of young women winding in and out of the stadium created a life of its own, an energy of its own, and we all recognized it and were exhilarated by ourselves and what we had created in this coming together.

Years later thousands of us walked to the Pentagon in Washington, D.C., carrying banners instead of flags, but I could still learn from the faces of the people I walked past. I walked right up to the steps of the Pentagon where some folks were being arrested and walked right into the tear gas the special police force lobbed into the crowd to keep us from walking any farther. That day I thought I was walking for someone else, to carry a message for the Vietnamese people who were suffering and couldn't come and walk in protest themselves.

Since that first walk, I've walked to show myself that I could do it. I bushwhacked in the Smoky Mountains and got caught in a snowstorm; I plowed through the mosquito and black fly-filled northwoods of Maine. Sometimes I took these tests alone, sometimes with friends.

I chased the full moon up a hill on a hazy summer night, a night so dark the road was only a memory under my feet. On the hilltop the wind pushed the clouds away for a moment and I could see the mist in the valley; but as soon as I turned back down the hill into the night's dark, I felt like there was no future to walk into and the present was so vague I could only discern it with all of my senses straining toward each sound or smell. Each step was only one step away from an imagined cliff.

That is what a test feels like. I go right to the edge and have to use everything I know to keep from flying off.

My friend says coming down a hill is the hardest thing for her. She has to hold back because her knees can't take the impact. I have strong knees and only watch for safe footing as I let the action carry me forward.

Walking keeps me connected to the earth.

Once I walked into someone's work of art. It was that moment of dusk after sunset and before dark when the intense light makes the colors seem to glow with their own energy. I had climbed the hill to the cornfield and walked over a tractor road I had never been down before. At the bottom of the field were colors so bright I thought I must be hallucinating. Red and pink and purple on a tall stalk. Walking closer I saw it was a flower garden, beautifully arranged, and these were hollyhocks glowing as though they were sun-filled in the half light. I don't know who she was, the artist who planted this garden where only she and the wild things could see it, but I stared and stared until the light was gone.

This year I walked into a theater piece prepared by the universe.

A rainy day. Dog, cat, and me walked to the field down the road to watch the deer grazing at sunset. We thought we were the only actors. The mountains were coming and going behind a curtain of clouds, and puffs of mist blew toward us over the valley. I thought,

if it all ended the next moment, it would have been worth the effort of living just to see that quiet beauty.

Then it got noisy. Something was making a racket the other
side of the hedgerow. I craned my neck to see what it was. And
there was a turkey hen craning her neck to look at me. As soon as
we made eye contact, she ran off up the hill, complaining loudly. I
went back to my contemplation until the noise distracted me
again. I craned my neck to look around the hedgerow once more,
and there she was, craning her neck to look at me. A shouted *gob-
ble* and off she sprinted up the hill. We repeated this ritual dance
several times. The cat was oblivious in the bushes. The dog sat at
my feet, shaking her head in confusion, convinced this was something she couldn't chase or herd.

I found myself walking into an Alcoholics Anonymous meeting
one night when the fog had settled into my chest and head to stay.
I could no longer see where I was going and there seemed to be
nothing to hold onto. I had a knot of fear in my stomach. It was
the most reluctant walking I had ever done and I wasn't convinced
it was the right direction at all. I looked around the room at those
strange people sitting, chatting, drinking coffee. I couldn't possibly
have anything in common with them, I knew; and yet at the end
of an hour I felt I had come home. I met myself in every stranger
in that room.

Sometimes when I expect to walk into a comfortable and familiar place, I am surprised by strangeness. I had been teaching for
years when I looked around one day and realized that nothing in
my academic life felt right to me. The best teaching I could do was
called bad; friends and colleagues, who I thought respected and
supported my work, denied me. For years I believed I had been rejected by academia. Now I know the choices I was making during
the time I taught college were carrying me in different directions,
toward open spaces on the top of hills where the wind pushes the
mist away.

In the autobiography of Harriet Monroe, *Seventy Years A Poet*,
the editor's afterword says that Ms. Monroe died in 1936 at the age

of 76 from a cerebral hemorrhage while climbing the Peruvian Andes to see the Inca ruins. She had been climbing mountains for 40 years.

I have walked myself into a less safe life. I walk on unsafe streets and in unsafe jungles. My heart has walked me into dangerous loving along the way, loving that has made me use everything I know.

Mostly I walk to get to where I want to be.

I hope I can keep walking until I die. I'd like to be climbing a mountain when that happens.

Judith McDaniel has taught at Northeastern University, Middlebury and Skidmore Colleges, and currently is on the faculty at Vermont College. Her poems and stories have appeared in journals and anthologies including: Rivers Running Free, Fight Back *and* Lesbian Poetry. *She is the author of numerous books including:* Metamorphosis: Reflections on Recovery, Just Say Yes, *and* Sanctuary: A Journey, *from which this story was excerpted.*

✳

There are some moments in life that are like pivots around which your existence turns—small intuitive flashes, when you know you have done something correct for a change, when you think you are on the right track. I watched a pale dawn streak the cliffs with Day-Glo and realized this was one of them. It was a moment of pure, uncomplicated confidence—and lasted about ten seconds.

—Robyn Davidson, Tracks

DIANE JOHNSON

★ ✦ ★

Great Barrier Reef

Transformation occurs in the strangest places.

THE MOTEL HAD SMELLED OF CINDER BLOCK AND CEMENT FLOOR, and was full of Australian senior citizens off a motor coach, but when we woke up in the morning a little less jet-lagged, and from the balcony could see the bed of a tidal river, with ibises and herons poking along the shallows, and giant ravens and parrots in the trees—trees strangling with monstera vines, all luridly beautiful—then we felt it would be all right.

But then when we went along to the quay, I felt it wouldn't. The ship, the *Dolphin,* was smaller than one could have imagined. Where could sixteen people possibly sleep? Brown stains from rusted drain spouts spoiled the hull. Gray deck paint splattered the ropes and ladders, orange primer showed through the chips. Wooden crates of lettuce and cabbages were stacked on the deck, and a case of peas in giant tin cans. This cruise had been J.'s idea, so I tried not to seem reproachful or shocked at the tiny, shabby vessel. But I am not fond of travel in the best of circumstances— inconvenient displacements punctuated by painful longings to be home. For J., travel is natural opium.

J. was on his way to a meeting in Singapore of the International Infectious Disease Council, a body of eminent medical specialists from different lands who are charged with making decisions about diseases: should the last remaining smallpox virus be destroyed? What was the significance of a pocket of polio in Sri Lanka? Could leprosy be finished off with a full-bore campaign in the spring? Was tuberculosis on the way back now via AIDS victims? What about measles in the Third World? I had not realized until I took up with J. that these remote afflictions were still around, let alone that they killed people in the millions. A professor of medicine, J. did research on the things that infected their lungs.

He had always longed to visit the Great Barrier Reef. Afterward he would give some lectures in Sydney and Wellington, and we planned en route to indulge another whim: skiing in New Zealand in the middle of summer, just to say we'd skied in August and to bribe me to come along, for I will go anywhere to ski, it is the one thing. For me, too, the voyage was one of escape from California after some difficult times, and was to be—what was unspoken by either of us—a sort of trial honeymoon (though we were not married) on which we would discover whether we were suited to live together by subjecting ourselves to that most serious of tests: traveling together.

A crewman named Murray, a short, hardy man with a narrow Scots face and thick Aussie accent, showed us our stateroom. It had been called a stateroom in the brochure. Unimaginably small, two foam mattresses on pallets suspended from the wall, and a smell. Tall J. couldn't stand all the way up in it. The porthole was seamed with salt and rust. Across the passage, the door of another stateroom was open, but that one was a large, pretty room, with mahogany and nautical brass fittings, and a desk, and the portholes shone. It was the one, certainly, that had been pictured in the brochure.

"This one here, the Royal, was fitted for Prince Charles, Prince of Wales, when he came on this voyage in 1974," Murray said.

"How do you book the Royal?" I asked.

"First come, first serve," Murray told us. Australian, egalitarian, opposed to privilege.

Up on deck, thinking of spending five days on the *Dolphin,* I began to be seized by emotions of panic and pain I couldn't explain. They racketed about in my chest, my heart beat fast, I felt as if a balloon was blowing up inside me, squeezing up tears and pressing them out of my eyes, and thrusting painful words up into my throat, where they lodged. What was the matter with me? Usually I am a calm person (I think); five days is not a lifetime; the aesthetics of a mattress, or its comfort either, is not a matter for serious protests. A smell of rotten water sloshing somewhere inside the hull could be gotten used to. Anyone could eat tinned peas five days and survive, plenty of people in the world were glad to get tinned peas; I knew all that. I knew I wasn't reacting appropriately, and was sorry for this querulous fit of passion. Maybe it was only jet lag.

All the same, I said to J., "I just can't," and stared tragically at the moorings. He knew, of course, that I could and probably would, but he maintained an attitude of calm sympathy.

"You've been through a rough time," he said. "It's the court thing you're really upset about." Maybe so. The court thing, a draining and frightening lawsuit, had only been a week ago, and now here we were a hemisphere away.

The other passengers came on board, one by one or two by two. Cases clattered on the metal gangs. To me only one person looked possible—a tall, handsome, youngish man with scholarly spectacles and a weathered yachting cap. The rest were aged and fat, plain, wore shapeless brown or navy blue coat-sweaters buttoned over paunches, had gray perms and bald spots, and they all spoke in this accent I disliked, as if their vowels had been slammed in doors. They spoke like cats, I thought: *eeeoooow*. Fat Australians, not looking fond of nature, why were they all here?

"Why are these people here?" I complained to J. "What do they care about the Great Barrier Reef?"

"It's a wonder of the world, anyone would want to see it," J. said, assuming the same dreamy expression he always wore when talking about or thinking about the Great Barrier Reef, so long the object of his heart.

I hated all the other passengers. On a second inspection, besides the youngish man, only a youngish couple, Dave and Rita, looked promising, but then I was infuriated to learn that Dave and Rita were Americans—we hadn't come all this way to be cooped up for five days in a prison of an old Coast Guard cutter with other Americans, and, what was worse, Rita and Dave had drawn the Prince Charles cabin, and occupied it as if by natural right, Americans expecting and getting luxury.

I've often said that I never would have married my husband if we didn't travel well together. A compatible travel companion is a rare and wonderful thing. And being a good travel companion is a gentle art involving sensitivity, compromise, generosity, autonomy, teamwork, and sometimes a thick skin.

—Sophia Dembling, "Would You Travel with Yourself?"
Dallas Morning News

Of course I kept these overwrought feelings to myself. No Australian complained. None appeared unhappy with the ship, no satirical remark, no questioning comment marred their apparent delight with the whole ship-shape of things, the cabins, even the appalling lunch, which was under way as soon as the little craft was under way, pointing itself east toward the open sea out of McKay Harbor.

After we lost sight of land, this mood of desperate resentment did not disappear, as J. had predicted, but deepened. It was more than the irritability of a shallow, difficult person demanding comfort, it was a failure of spirit, inexplicable and unwarranted on this bright afternoon. How did these obese Australian women, these stiff old men, clamber so uncomplainingly below deck to their tiny cells, career along the railings laughing crazily as they tripped on ropes? Doubtless one would fall and the voyage would be turned back. When I thought of the ugliness of the things I had just escaped from—the unpleasant divorce, the custody battle, the hounding of lawyers and strangers—only to find myself here, really unmanageable emotions made me turn my face away from the others.

Dinner was tinned peas, and minted lamb overdone to a gray rag, and potatoes. J. bought a bottle of wine from the little bar, which the deck hand Murray nimbly leapt behind, transforming himself into waiter or bartender as required. We sat with the promising young man, Mark, and offered him some wine, but he said he didn't drink wine. He was no use, he was very, very prim, a bachelor civil servant from Canberra, with a slight stammer, only handsome and young by some accident, and would someday be old without changing, would still be taking lonely cruises, eating minted lamb, would still be unmarried and reticent. He had no conversation, had never been anywhere, did not even know what we wanted from him. Imagining his life, I thought about how sad it was to be him, hoping for whatever he hoped for, but not hoping for the right things, content to eat these awful peas, doomed by being Australian, and even while I pitied him I found him hopeless. Even J., who could talk to anyone, gave up trying to talk to him, and, feeling embarrassed to talk only to each other as if he weren't there, we fell silent and stared out the windows at the rising moon along the black horizon of the sea.

There didn't seem a way, in the tiny cabin, for two normal-sized people to exist, let alone to make love; there was no space that could accommodate two bodies in any position. Our suitcases filled half the room. With summer clothing, our proper suits to wear in Wellington and Sydney, and bulky ski clothes of quilted down, we were ridiculously encumbered with baggage. It seemed stupid now. We were obliged to stow our bags and coats precariously on racks overhead, our duffel bags sleeping at the feet of our bunks like lumpy interloper dogs. J. took my hand comfortingly in the dark across the space between the two bunks before he dropped off to sleep; I lay awake, seized with a terrible fit of traveler's panic, suffocating with fearful visions of fire, of people in prison cells or confined in army tanks, their blazing bodies emerging screaming from the holds of ships to writhe doomed on the ground, their stick limbs ringed in flame, people burned in oil splashed on them from the holds of rusted ships, and smells of sewers, smells of underground, the slosh of engine fuel from the hell beneath.

As is so often the traveler's fate, nothing on the cruise was as promised or as we had expected. The seedy crew of six had tourist-baked smiles and warmed-over jokes. There was a little faded captain who climbed out of his tower to greet us now

I have been here eight days. I feel cranky and parochial. What's the point of traveling if one isn't changed—I don't say uplifted—by the experience?

—Barbara Grizzuti Harrison,
Italian Days

and then, and a sort of Irish barmaid, Maureen, who helped Murray serve the drinks. The main business of the passage seemed to be not the life of the sea nor the paradise of tropical birds on Pacific shores nor the balmy water but putting in at innumerable islands to look at souvenir shops. J., his mind on the Great Barrier Reef, which we were expected to reach on the fourth day, sweetly bore it all, the boredom and the endless stops at each little island, but I somehow couldn't conquer my petulant dislike.

It fastened, especially, on our shipmates. Reluctantly I learned their names, in order to detest them with more precision: Don and Donna from New Zealand, Priscilla from Adelaide—portly, harmless old creatures, as J. pointed out. Knowing that the derisive remarks that sprang to my lips only revealed me as petty and querulous to good-natured J., I didn't speak them aloud.

But it seemed to me that these Australians only wanted to travel to rummage in the souvenir shops, though these were all alike from island to island: Dream Island, Hook Island—was this a cultural or a generation gap? I brooded on the subject of souvenirs—why they should exist, why people should want them, by what law they were made to be ugly—shells shaped like toilets, a row of swizzle sticks in the shapes of women's silhouetted bodies, thin, fatter, fat, with bellies and breasts increasingly sagging as they graduated from SWEET SIXTEEN to SIXTY. I was unsettled to notice that the one depicting a woman of my age had a noticeably thickened middle. These trinkets were everywhere. I watched a man buy one, a fat one, and hand it to his wife. "Here, Mother, this one's you," he said. Laughter a form of hate. It was not a man from our ship, luckily, or I would have pushed him overboard. I brooded on my own complicity in the industry of souvenirs, for didn't I buy them myself? The things I bought—the (I liked to think) tasteful baskets and elegant textiles I was always carting home—were these not just a refined form of souvenir for a more citified sort of traveler?

Statuettes of drunken sailors, velvet pictures of island maidens, plastic seashell lamps made in Taiwan. What contempt the people who think up souvenirs have for other people. Yet our fellow passengers plunked down money with no feeling of shame. They never walked on the sand or looked at the colors of the bright patchwork birds rioting in the palm trees. Besides us, only the other Americans, Rita and Dave, did this. It was Dave who found the perfect helmet shell—a regular treasure, the crew assured them, increasingly rare—protected, even, you weren't supposed to carry them away, but who was looking? I wanted it to have been J. who got it.

Each morning, each afternoon, we stopped at another island. This one was Dream Island. "It's lovely, isn't it, dear?" Priscilla said to me. "People like to see a bit of a new place, the shopping, they have different things to make it interesting." But it wasn't different, it was the same each day: the crew hands the heavy, sack-like people grunting down into rowboats, and hauls them out onto a sandy slope of beach. Up they trudge toward a souvenir shop. This one had large shells perched on legs, and small shells pasted in designs on picture frames, and earrings made of shells, and plastic buckets, and plastic straw hats surrounded with fringe, and pictures of hula dancers.

"I don't care, I do hate them," I ranted passionately to J. "I'm right to hate them. They're what's the matter with the world, they're ugly consumers, they can't look at a shell unless it's coated in plastic, they never look at the sea—why are they here? Why don't they stay in Perth and Adelaide—you can buy shells there, and swizzle sticks in the shape of hula girls." Of course J. hadn't any answer for this, of course I was right.

I wandered onto the strand of beach and took off my shoes, planning to wade. Whenever I was left alone I found myself harking back to the court hearing, my recollections just as sharp and painful as a week ago. I couldn't keep from going over and over my ordeal, and thinking of my hated former husband, not really him so much as his lawyer, Waxman, a man in high-heeled boots and aviator glasses. I imagined him here on Dream Island. He has fallen overboard at the back of the ship. I am the only one to notice, and I have the power to cry out for rescue but I don't. Our eyes meet; he is down in the water, still wearing the glasses. I imagine his expression of surprise when he realizes that I'm not going to call for help. What for him had been a mere legal game, a job, would cost him his life. He had misjudged me. The ship speeds along. We are too far away to hear his cries.

*oo often travelling is a Fool's Paradise. I am miserable; I want to get out of myself; I want to leave home. **Travel**! I pack up my trunks, say Farewell, I depart. I go to the very ends of the earth; and behold, my skeleton steps out of its cupboard and confronts me there. I am as pessimistic as ever, for the last thing I can lose is myself; and though I may tramp to the back of beyond, that grim shadow must always pursue me.*

—Isabel Savory,
A Sportswoman in India (1900)

It was the third day and we had set down at Happy Island. Here we had to wade across a sandbar. This island had goats grazing. "This is the first we've gotten wet," I bitterly complained. We stood in ankle-deep water amid queer gelatinous seaweed. I had wanted to swim, to dive, to sluice away the court and the memories but hadn't been permitted to because these waters, so innocently beautiful, so seductively warm, were riddled with poisonous creatures, deadly toxins, and sharks.

"Be careful not to pick up anything that looks like this," the first mate, Murray, warned us, showing us a harmless-looking little shell. "The deadly cone shell. And the coral, be careful a' that, it scratches like hell. One scratch can take over a year to heal. We have some ointment on board, be sure to tell one of the crew if you scratch yourself."

From here, I looked back at the ship, and, seeing the crew watching us, I suddenly saw ourselves, the passengers, with the crew's eyes—we were a collection of thick bodies, mere cargo to be freighted around, slightly volatile, likely to ferment, like damp grain, and give trouble—difficult cargo that sent you scurrying unreasonably on tasks, boozed, got itself cut on coral, made you laugh at its jokes. I could see that the crew must hate us.

Yet, a little later, I came upon Murray tying up a fishhook for old George, whose fingers were arthritic. Murray was chatting to him with a natural smile. I studied them. Perhaps Murray by himself was a man of simple good nature, but the rest, surely, hated us. The captain, staring coolly out from his absurd quarter-deck, made no pretense of liking us, seemed always to be thinking of something else, not of this strange Pacific civilization of Quonset huts and rotting landing barges and odd South Sea denizens strangely toothless, beyond dentistry, beyond fashion, playing old records over and over on PR systems strung through the palms. You felt the forlornness of these tacky little islands that should have been beautiful and serene. I even wondered if we would ever get back to America again. Not that I wanted to. America was smeared with horrible memories, scenes of litigation. Why shouldn't J. and I simply stay here? Why—more important—was I not someone who was able, like the lovely goat that grazed on the slope near here, to gaze at the turquoise sea and enjoy the sight of little rose-colored parrots wheeling in the air? Why was I not, like a nice person, simply content to be, to enjoy beauty and inner peace? Instead I must suffer, review, quiver with fears and rages—the fault, I saw, was in myself, I was a restless, peevish, flawed person. How would I be able to struggle out of this frame of mind? Slipping on the sandy bank, I frightened the little goat.

By the third day I began to notice a sea change in our shipmates, who had begun in sensible gabardines and print dresses, but now wore violently floral shirts and dresses, and were studded with shells—wreaths of shells about their necks and at their ears, hats with crabs and gulls embroidered on. By now I knew a bit more about them. They were all travelers—George and Nettie, Fred and Polly, had been friends for 40 years, and spent a part of each year, now that they were all retired, traveling in Europe in their caravans. Dave and Rita were both schoolteachers, and Rita raised Great Danes. Priscilla was going along on this cruise with her brother Albert because Albert had just lost his wife. Mark was taking his annual vacation. Don and Donna were thinking of selling their Auckland real estate business and buying a sailboat to live on and sail around the world. J. told me that George was a sensitive and sweet man who had lived his whole life in Australia and only now in his retirement had begun to see something of the world. "And he says that the most beautiful place in the world is someplace near Split, in Yugoslavia, and if I take you there, my darling, will you for God's sake cheer up now?" But I couldn't.

Tonight we were dining ashore, in a big shed on Frenchie's Island, in a shabby tin building. Music was already playing on loudspeakers. Groups of people from other ships or hotels strolled around carrying drinks. A smell of roasted sausages, someone singing "Waltzing Matilda" in the kitchen at the back. The *Dolphin* passengers were lined up at the bar and in the souvenir shop. In the big hangar of a room little tables encircled a dance floor, and at one end a microphone stood against a photo mural of the South Seas, as if the real scene outdoors were not evocative. The sun lowered across the pink water, setting in the east, and the water in the gentle lagoon was as warm as our blood. "I wish a hurricane would come and blow it all away," I said to J.

When the diners had tipped their paper plates into a bin, they began to sing old American songs. Sitting outside, I could hear Maureen singing "And Let Her Sleep Under the Bar." Then came canned music from a phonograph, and people began to dance— the ones who were not too decrepit. I tried to hear only the chatter of the monkeys or parrots in the palm trees, innocent creatures disturbed by the raucous humans. J. was strangely cheerful and shot some pool with a New Zealander, causing me all of a sudden to think, with a chill of disapproval, that J., possibly, was an Australian at heart and that I ought not to marry him or I would end up in a caravan in Split. His good looks and professional standing were only a mask that concealed...simplicity.

It didn't surprise me that people liked the handsome and amiable J.; it didn't even surprise me that they seemed to like me. I had concealed my tumult of feelings, and I was used to being treated by other people with protective affection, if only because I am small. This in part explained why the courtroom, and its formal process of accusation, its focus on myself as a stipulated bad person, had been such a shock. It was as if a furious mob had come to smash with sticks my porcelain figure of myself. I had a brief intimation that the Australians with their simple friendliness could put me back together if I would let them, but I would rather lie in pieces for a while.

The moon was full and golden. "What a beautiful, beautiful night," said Nettie from Adelaide, the sister of George, coming out onto the beach. Who could disagree? Not even I. The ship on the moonlit water lapped at anchor, resting, awaiting them, looking luxurious and serene. J. came out and showed us the Southern Cross. At first I couldn't see it, all constellations look alike to me, I have never been able to see the bears or belts or any of it. But now, when J. turned my chin, I did see it, and it did look like a cross.

In the night I had another dream, in which the lawyer had said, "Isn't it true that you have often left your children while you travel?" He had been looking not at me but at a laughing audience. He was speaking over a microphone. The audience wore plastic, fringed hats.

"Not willingly, no," I had said. "Not often."

"How many times did you go on trips last year and leave them at home?"

"Oh, six, I don't know."

"That's not often?"

"Just a day or two each time. A man takes a business trip, you don't call it leaving, or 'often.'" But I was not allowed to speak or explain.

"We're looking at how often you are in fact away from your children."

Here I had awakened, realizing that it was all true, it wasn't just a dream, it was what had happened, not of course the audience in plastic hats. Even though in the end I had been vindicated, I still felt sticky with the encumbrance of their father's hate. All I had wanted was to be free and now I was so soiled with words spoken at me, about me, by strangers, by lawyers I had never seen before, who had

> *Running away doesn't take you away from yourself. Who you are goes with you. If you are lonely or dissatisfied, a trip will only make it worse. Now, to confront difficulty, I stay home. To encounter the world, I travel.*
>
> Mary Morris, "Like Readers of Romance Novels, Some Women Wish to be Taken Away," *The New York Times*

never seen me. It didn't seem fair that you could not prevent being the object of other people's emotions, you were not safe anywhere from their hate or from their love, for that matter. You were never safe from being invaded by their feelings when you wanted only to be rid of them, free, off, away.

In the morning I had wanted to swim, to wash in the sea, to wash all this stuff off, splash; my longing must have been clear, because Cawley, the other deck hand, laughed at me. "Not here you don't, love," he said. "There's sharks here as long as a boat."

The captain, Captain Clarke, made one of his few visits. He had kept aloof in the little pilot cabin above, though he must have slipped down to the galley to eat, or maybe the crew took him his food up there. Now he invited his passengers two by two to his bridge. When people were tapped, they hauled themselves up the metal ladder, helped by Cawley or Murray, then would come down looking gratified. Alfred, who went up alone, suggested that he had helped avoid a navigational accident.

J. and I were invited on the morning of the fourth day, the day we were to arrive at the reef itself in the late afternoon. I went up despite myself. Captain Clarke was a thin, red-haired man sitting amid pipes and charts. He let us take the wheel, and showed us the red line that marked our route through the labyrinth of islands shown on a chart. His manner was grave, polite, resigned. No doubt these visits were dictated by the cruise company.

"But there are thousands of islands between here and the Great Barrier Reef!" said J., studying the charts.

"Souvenir shops on every one," I couldn't help saying. J. fastened me with a steady look in which I read terminal exasperation.

"These islands are not all charted," said the captain. "The ones that are were almost all charted by Captain Cook himself, after he ran aground on one in 1770. He was a remarkable navigator. He even gave names to them all. But new ones are always being found. I've always hoped to find one myself."

"What would you name it?" J. asked.

"I would give it my name, or, actually, since there is already a Clarke Island, I would name it for my wife, Laura, Laura Clarke Island, or else for Alison, my daughter."

"Do you keep your eyes open for one?"

"I mean to get one," he said.

When we went down to the deck again, Maureen was gazing at the waves. "It's getting choppy," she observed, unnecessarily, for the boat had begun to rear up like a prancing horse. "Right, we probably won't make it," Murray agreed.

"What do you mean?" I asked, alarmed by the tinge of satisfaction that underlay their sorry looks.

"To the reef. No point in going if the sea's up, like it's coming up, washed right up, no use going out there. If it's like this, we put in at Hook Island instead."

Astonished, I looked around to see if J., or anyone else, was listening. No, or not worried, would just as soon have Hook Island. They continued to knit and read along the deck, which now began to heave more forcefully, as if responding to the desire of the crew to return to port without seeing the great sight.

"How often does it happen that you don't go to the reef?" I asked, heart thundering. The point of all this, and J.'s dream, was to go to the reef, and now they were casually dismissing the possibility.

"Oh, it happens more often than not. This time of year, you know. Chancy, the nautical business is."

"Come out all this way and not see it?" I insisted, voice rising.

"Well, you can't see it if the waves are covering it up, can you? You can bump your craft into it, but you can't see it. Can you?"

"I don't know," cried I. "I don't even know what it is." But the shape of things was awfully clear; given the slightest excuse, the merest breeze or ripple, the *Dolphin* would not take us to the Great Barrier Reef, and perhaps had never meant to. I thought in panic of not alerting J., but then I rushed to tell him. He put down his book, his expression aghast, and studied the waves.

The midday sky began to take on a blush of deeper blue, and, now that our attention was called to it, the sea seemed to grow dark and rough before our eyes. Where moments before it had been smooth enough to row, we now began to pitch. The report of the prow smacking the waves made me think of cannons, of Trafalgar. In defiance of the rocking motion, the Australian passengers began to move around the cabin and along the deck, gripping the railings, looking trustfully at the sky and smiling. Their dentures were white as teacups.

Here's a guideline for being a good travel companion.

Keep your sense of humor and don't whine. Travel, when you think about it, is a pain in the neck. Any number of things can— and usually do—go wrong. A person who can laugh at adversity is a joy on the road. And by the way, the horror stories are the most fun to tell when you return home.

Then again, if your companion needs to whine a bit, try to be tolerant. Sometimes whining is one of those things that just need to be gotten out of one's system—as long as it's not overdone.

—Sophia Dembling, "Would You Travel with Yourself?"
Dallas Morning News

"Christ," said Murray, "one of these bloody old fools will break a hip. Folks, why don't you sit down?" Obediently, like children, the Australians went inside the main cabin and sat in facing rows of chairs. Despite the abrupt change in the weather, the ship continued its course out to sea. J. and I anchored ourselves in the prow, leaning against the tool chest, resolutely watching the horizon, not the bounding deck beneath our feet, a recommended way to avoid seasickness. In twenty minutes the sea had changed altogether, from calm to a thing that threw the little ship in the air. We felt as if we were slithering along the back of a sea monster who toiled beneath us.

The dread specter of seasickness was promptly among us. The captain, rusty-haired, pale-eyed, as if his eyes had bleached with sea wind, climbed off the bridge and glanced inside the cabin at his passengers.

"Oh, please, they want to go, they'll be all right," I called to him, but the words were swept off by the wind.

The others were so occupied with the likelihood of nausea that they hadn't grasped that the ship might turn back, and they seemed rather to be enjoying the drama of getting seasick. Every few minutes someone would get up, totter out to the rail, retch over it, and return to the laughter and commiseration of the others. The friendly thing was to be sick, so I was contrarily determined not to be, and J. was strong by nature. One of the Australians, Albert, gave us a matey grin as he lurched over our feet toward a bucket. I looked disgustedly away, but J. wondered aloud if he should be helping these old folks.

"Of course they'll use this as an excuse for not going," I was saying bitterly. These barfing Australian senior citizens would keep us from getting to the Great Barrier Reef. My unruly emotions, which had been milder today, now plumped around in my bosom like the smacking of the boat on the waves. J. watched the Australians screaming with laughter, and telling each other, "That's right, barf in the bin."

"This is a rough one," Albert said, and pitched sharply against the cabin, so that J. leapt up to catch him. Murray, tightening ropes, called for him to go back in the cabin.

"Tossed a cookie meself." He grinned at J. and me.

"We don't think it's so rough," I said.

"I've seen plenty rougher," Murray agreed. "Bloody hangover is my problem."

When the captain leaned out to look down at the deck below him, I cried, "Oh, we just have to go to the reef, we have to! Oh, please!"

"What's the likelihood this sea will die down?" J. shouted to the captain. The captain shrugged. I felt angry for the first time at J., as if he were a magnet. It was unfair, I knew, to say it was J.'s fault—the storm, the tossing sea, the *Dolphin,* and of course the rest. J. who had signed us up for this terrible voyage, during which we would be lost at sea, before reaching the Great Barrier Reef, whatever it was, and who had caused the sea to come up like this.

All J.'s fault. If I ever saw the children again, it would be a miracle, or else them saying in after years, Our mother perished on the high seas somewhere off Australia. What would they remember of me? The sight of the boiling waves, now spilling over the bow, now below us, made me think of throwing myself in—just an unbidden impulse trailing into my mind, the way I half-thought, always, of throwing my keys or my sunglasses off bridges. Of course I wouldn't do it.

The ship pitched, thrust, dove through the waters. Yet we had not turned back. "Whoooeee," the Aussies were screaming inside the lounge. Life was like this, getting tossed around, and then, right before the real goal is reached, something, someone, makes you turn back.

"J., don't let them turn back," I said again, for the tenth time, putting all the imperative passion I knew into my voice. Without hearing me, J. was already climbing the ladder to the bridge. I looked at my fingers whitely gripping the rope handle on the end of the tool chest. A locker slid across the deck, back, across, back, and once, upon the impact of a giant wave, a dead fish stowed in it sloshed out onto the deck. Then, in the wind, I heard Murray's thin voice call out, "It's all right, love, we're going to the reef! The captain says we're going to the reef!"

As abruptly as the storm had started, it subsided meekly, the sky once more changed color, now to metallic gray, lighter at the horizon, as if it were dawn. Ahead of us an indistinguishable shape lay in the water like the back of a submerged crocodile, a vast bulk under the surface. The captain had stopped the engines, and we drifted in the water. "The reef, the reef!" cried the Australians, coming out on deck. I shouted too. The crew began to busy themselves with readying the small boats, and the other passengers came boisterously out of the cabin, as if nothing had been wrong. "Ow," they said, "that was a bit of a toss."

"You'll have two hours on the reef, not more," the captain told us before we climbed again into the rowboats. "Because of the tide. If you get left there at high tide, if we can't find you, well, we don't come back. Because you wouldn't be there." The Australians laughed at this merry joke.

J. handed me out of the boat and onto the reef. My first step on it shocked me. For I had had the idea of coral, hard and red, a great lump of coral sticking out of the ocean, a jagged thing that would scratch you if you fell on it, that you could chisel into formations dictated by your own mind. We had heard it was endangered, and I had imagined its destruction by divers with chisels, carrying off lumps at a time.

Instead it was like a sponge. It sank underfoot, it sighed and sucked. Shocked, looking down, I could see that it was entirely alive, made of eyeless formations of cabbagey creatures sucking and opening and closing, yearning toward tiny ponds of water lying on the pitted surface, pink, green, gray, viscous, silent. I moved, I put my foot here, then hurriedly there, stumbled, and gashed my palm against something rough.

"Where should you step? I don't want to step on the things," I gasped.

"You have to. Just step as lightly as you can," J. said.

"It's alive, it's all alive!"

"Of course. It's coral, it's alive, of course," J. said. He had told me there were 350 species of coral here, along with the calcareous remains of tiny polyzoan and hydrozoan creatures that helped to form a home for others.

"Go on, J., leave me," I said, seeing that he wanted to be alone to have his own thoughts about all this marine life, whatever it meant to him. It meant something. His expression was of rapture. He smiled at me and wandered off.

I had my Minox, but I found the things beneath my feet too fascinating to photograph. Through the viewer of my camera they seemed pale and far away. At my feet in astonishing abundance they continued their strange life. I hated to tread on them, so at length stood like a stork, and aimed the camera at the other passengers.

These were proceeding cautiously, according to their fashion, over the strange surface—Mark in his yachting cap, with his camera, alone; the Kiwis in red tropical shirts more brilliant than the most bright-hued creatures; even the crew, with insouciant expressions, protectively there to save their passengers from falls or from strange sea poisons that darted into the inky ponds from the wounded life beneath the feet. For the first time, I felt, seeing each behaving characteristically, that I knew them all, and even that I liked them, or at least that I liked it that I understood what they would wear and do. Travelers like myself.

I watched J. kneeling in the water to peer into the centers of the mysterious forms. Almost as wonderful as this various life was J.'s delight. He was as dazzled as if we had walked on stars, and indeed the sun shining on the tentacles, wet petals, filling the spongy holes, made things sparkle like a strange underfoot galaxy. He appeared as a long, sandy-haired, handsome stranger, separate, unknowable. I, losing myself once more in the patterns and colors, thought of nothing, was myself as formless and uncaring as the coral, all my unruly, bad-natured passions leaching harmlessly into the sea, leaving a warm sensation of blankness and ease. I thought of the Hindu doctrine of *ahimsa*, of not harming living things, and I was not harming them, I saw—neither by stepping on them nor by leaving my anger and fears and the encumbrances of real life with them. Almost as wonderful as J.'s happiness was this sense of being healed of a poisoned spirit.

At sunset we headed landward into the sun, a strange direction to a Californian, for whom all sunsets are out at sea. We would arrive at McKay at midnight—it also seemed strange that a voyage that had taken four days out would take only six hours back, something to do with the curve of the continental shelf. A spirit of triumph imbued our little party—we had lived through storms and reached a destination. People sat in the lounge labeling their rolls of film.

Maureen came along and reminded us that, as this was our last night on board, there would be a fancy dress party. When we had read this in the brochure, I had laughed. It had seemed absurd that such a little ship would give itself great liner airs. J. and I had not brought costumes. In our cabin, I asked him what he meant to wear. Since my attitude had been so resolutely one of noncompliance, he seemed surprised that I was going to participate in the dressing up. Now it seemed too churlish to object. "I know it's stupid, but how can we not?" I said. "It would be so pointed, with only sixteen of us aboard."

J. wore his ski pants, which were blue and tight, with a towel cape, and called himself Batman. I wore his ski parka, a huge, orange, down-filled garment. The others were elaborately got up, must have brought their masks and spangles with them. Rita wore a black leotard and had painted cat whiskers on her face, and Dave had a Neptune beard. Nettie wore a golden crown, and Don a harlequin suit, half purple, half green. I drew to one side and sat on the table with my feet drawn up inside J.'s parka, chin on my knees, watching the capers which now began. "I am a pumpkin," I explained, when they noticed the green ribbon in my hair, my stem. It wasn't much of a costume, but it was all I could think of, and they laughed forgivingly and said that it looked cute.

J. won a prize, a bottle of beer, for the best paper cutout of a cow. I was surprised, watching him with the scissors making meticulous little snips, to see how a cow shape emerged under his hands, with a beautiful delicate udder and teats, and knobs of horn. I had not thought that J. would notice a cow.

"I have an announcement," Mark said, in a strangely loud and shaky voice, one hand held up, his other hand nervously twisting his knotted cravat. The theme of his costume was not obvious.

"Excuse me, an announcement." The others smiled and shushed. "I've had word from my friend—a few months ago I had the honor to assist a friend with his astronomical observations, and I've just had word that he—we—that the comet we discovered has been accepted by the international commission. It will bear his name, and, as I had the honor to assist, I'll be mentioned too. Only a little comet, of course, barely a flash in the sky. There are millions of them, of course. There are millions of them. But…"

A cheer, toasts, Mark bought drinks for everybody. The crew bought drinks for the guests, dishing up from behind the little bar with the slick expertise of landside bartenders. They seemed respectful at Mark's news. I raised my glass with the rest and felt ashamed at the way I had despised Mark's life—indeed a nice life, spent exploring the heavens with a friend—how had I thought him friendless, this nice-looking young man?

"Split, Yugoslavia, is the most beautiful place on earth," George was telling me. "Like a travel poster. I've been almost everywhere by now, except China, but there, at Split, my heart stopped." My attention was reclaimed from my own repentant thoughts; for a second I had been thinking that he was describing a medical calamity, and I had been about to say, "How terrible!"

But no, he was describing a moment, an experience, the experience of beauty. He had the long, bald head of a statesman, but he was a farmer, now retired, from Perth. I was ashamed that it had taken me so long to see that the difference between Americans and Australians was that Americans were tired and bored, while for Australians, stuck off at the edge of the world, all was new, and they had the energy and spirit to go off looking for abstractions like beauty, and comets.

"Let me get you another one of those," George said, taking my wineglass, for a pumpkin cannot move.

"How long have you been married?" asked Nettie, smiling at me. I considered, not knowing whether I wanted to shock them by admitting that we were not married at all. "Two years," I said.

"Really?" Nettie laughed. "We all thought you was newly-weds." Her smile was sly.

I felt myself flush inside the hot parka. The others had thought all my withdrawn unfriendliness was newlywed shyness and the preoccupations of love. They were giving me another chance.

"It seems like it." I laughed. I would never marry J., I thought. He was too good-natured to be saddled with a cross person like me. And yet now I wasn't cross, was at ease and warm with affection for the whole company. Don and Donna were buying champagne all around, and the crew, now that they were about to be rid of this lot of passengers, seemed sentimental and sorry, as if we had been the nicest, most amusing passengers ever.

The prize for the best costume was to be awarded by vote. People wrote on bits of paper and passed them to Maureen, who sat on the bar and sorted them. There was even a little mood of tension, people wanting to win.

"And the prize for the best costume," she paused portentously, "goes to the pumpkin!" My shipmates beamed and applauded. In the hot parka I felt myself grow even warmer with shame and affection. People of goodwill and good sense, and I had allowed a snobbish mood of accidie to blind me to it. Their white untroubled smiles.

In a wrapped paper parcel was a key ring with a plastic-covered picture of the *Dolphin,* and the words GREAT BARRIER REEF around the edge of it. I was seized by a love for it, would always carry it, I decided, if only as a reminder of various moral lessons I thought myself to have learned, and as a reminder of certain bad things about my own character.

"Thank you very much," I said. "I'll always keep it. And I'll always remember the *Dolphin* and all of you"—for at the moment I thought, of course, that I would. J. was looking at me with a considering air, as if to inspect my sincerity. But I was sincere.

"I know I've been a pig," I apologized to him later, as we gathered our things in the stateroom. "These people are really very sweet."

"I wonder if you'd feel like that if you hadn't gotten the prize," he said, peevishly. I was surprised at his tone. Of course it wasn't the prize, only a little key chain, after all, that had cured me, but the process of the voyage, and the mysterious power of distant places to dissolve the problems the traveler has brought along. Looking at J., I could see that, for his part, he was happy but let down, as if the excitement and happiness of seeing the reef at last, and no doubt the nuisance of my complaining, had worn him out for the moment, and serious thoughts of his coming confrontations with malaria and leprosy and pain and sadness were returning, and what he needed was a good night's sleep.

Diane Johnson is an author and screenwriter. The majority of her books are novels, such as the recent works Le Divorce *and* Le Mariage*, but she has also written biographies, and a collection of essays, titled* Natural Opium: Some Traveler's Tales, *from which this story was excerpted. Ms. Johnson divides her time between Paris and San Francisco.*

＊

What is the answer? There is no easy answer, no complete answer. I have only clues, shells from the sea. The bare beauty of the channelled whelk tells me that one answer, and perhaps a first step, is in simplification of life, in cutting out some of the distractions. But how? Total retirement is not possible. I cannot shed my responsibilities. I cannot permanently inhabit a desert island. I cannot be a nun in the midst of family life. I would not want to be. The solution for me, surely, is neither in total renunciation of the world, nor in total acceptance of it. I must find a balance somewhere, or an alternating rhythm between these two extremes; a swinging of the pendulum between solitude and communication, between retreat and return. In my periods of retreat, perhaps I can learn something to carry back into my worldly life.

—Anne Morrow Lindbergh, *Gift From the Sea*

MARY BETH SIMMONS

Women at the Well

*Grace, beauty, and the power of African women
emerge at the traditional gathering place.*

ONE OF THE FIRST STORIES I HEARD IN CAMEROON WAS THE TALE of the industrious Peace Corps volunteer who built a well in the middle of a small village. It seems the closest water source for the community was five miles away, a hefty one way trek for himself, and all the women who went to gather water each day. He contacted federal agencies in the states, and Cameroon, routed out the necessary funds, and during a three month period he and a band of local men constructed the well, a shiny testament to American pragmatism. Legend has it that when the well was completed, the volunteer broke a bottle of beer upon the metal structure, christening it before turning the spigot. As the water flowed freely the people danced and drank from the convenient well, and most, it is said, never returned to it again.

This troubled the volunteer. One day when he saw his neighbor loading up her pushcart with empty water barrels, he approached with a simple question. Why was no one using the well he had constructed for the village? She was shy, but honest, and told him the women continued to make the long journey for water because it was their time to be alone. To gossip. To laugh. To be only with women. When could they find long stretches of time to be away from their husbands when the new well was only a five-minute walk from their compounds?

With this, the volunteer was defeated, but amused. For the new volunteer, such as myself, the story stood as a warning, a lesson, a gentle reminder: before fixing a "problem," find out first if it is, indeed, a problem.

After a few weeks in my village, I became fascinated with simply watching women congregate at the well close to my home. The well legend had captured my interest in the activity of gathering water, but the women, the beautifully different women, held my true attention.

Initially, honestly, the nudity at the well caught my eye. Not because it was unexpected, as I had been told my village was very "traditional." Women would often wear a *pagne* wrapped around their waist, and that was all. What impressed me was the evidence of heavy labor being performed by these half-clothed women. Their exposed upper torsos showed taut bellies, solid upper arm muscles, Atlas-like strength. They could carry twenty-gallon metal barrels on their heads without sloshing a drop over the sides. Their slender hips sashayed ever so gently, enough to create momentum for the walk home, but not enough to rock the balance. I once walked behind a woman and listened for her breathing, wondering if I could detect the strain under which she toiled. Her footsteps slapping the dusty ground were all I heard, coupled with the lazy lapping of water against the insides of the ceramic tub perched on her head.

Though I was fascinated by their competence, I cannot simply dismiss the sheer nakedness of some of the women. I would be lying if I said the nudity did not stir something inside me. If anything, I was finally allowed to test my art appreciation skills, to at last discover if the female body was worth the adoration I had channeled to it. And it was. What pleased me aesthetically was the difference. Before me were no curvaceous white beauties found in the works of the great Masters, yet there was the grace and power of Woman to appreciate. One older woman, well into her seven-

ties, was particularly striking. Her sagging, wrinkled breasts at first
were hideous, resembling well-worn leather billfolds, not a bosom.
But when the sunlight caught dancing beads of water in her gray
stubble hair and a friend came up from behind and touched her
shoulder, her smile, her radiance in that moment was a beauty I
could never have imagined.

The richness of her deep black skin, skin the color of
Midwestern soil, juxtaposed with the stark, parched landscape,
amplified her presence; and as I drew closer my heart ached for
her, for the overwhelming burden she undertook with every gallon of water she fetched for her family. A lifetime of the brutal sun
and suckling children had drained the suppleness from her body,
leaving her ragged, but still gallantly standing.

After she had filled her oversized bowl and lifted it to her head
for the walk home, she stopped, removed it, and went to aid a
friend struggling with her own heavy load. I was taken. If ever
there was a moment when I've wanted to applaud spontaneously,
it was then, but everyone would have detected my voyeurism; no
longer would they have seen me as the nonchalant market shopper I hoped to resemble.

I noticed my own presence in the scene. How disjointing it
was, and sad, when I checked myself, when I mentally gauged my
perversity for imagining what a kiss might be like from her. The
older women of the village followed tribal custom by having a
large button sewn into their mouths, directly above their upper lip.
A sign of beauty, I had been told. And though it was captivating, a
consistent focal point for me with the women, I could only picture them trying to kiss their husbands or lovers passionately. It
seemed they had little control of their mouths. I watched them at
the well drinking water from their cupped hands. They slurped
from the sides of their mouths, rendering the center worthless,
hindered by the obstruction of the bulky button between the nose
and upper lip. How were these lips to form a kiss?

The teenagers, free of the button custom since it is no longer
forced upon little girls, filled their mouths with water and chased
each other around the well, spitting perfect streams into friends'

backs and ears. Their pucker urged me to feel my own mouth, and as my fingers traced my lips I grew thirsty, never had water looked so refreshing. They drank it, played in it, collected it in their barrels—all the while celebrating with an abandon I envied.

As I watched them, I remembered a story a college professor once told me. When she was in her mid-twenties, walking along campus on a warm spring day, she passed a bed of brilliant red poppies and she knew the moment she gazed at them it would be one of the final times she would recognize natural beauty. She called the experience an inner shift; she knew she was losing her grip on the richness and wonders of nature. Her life was transforming into a devoted investigation of the complexities of the world; simple pleasures were losing their appeal.

For me, my fascination with the women at the well acted as the antithesis of my professor's story. Watching the women awakened me, they helped me to fine tune my belief in the power of sisterhood, and urged me to ponder my own connection to basic elements of life: water, sunlight, physical labor, human contact.

One day, while working on an organic carrot display at a natural food store, Mary Beth Simmons realized she wanted more. "More" meant the Peace Corps in West Africa, and more she got. After Cameroon, Mary Beth earned an M.F.A. in Non-Fiction from the University of Iowa and is currently the Writing Center Director at Villanova University.

✳

The woman intently watched my friends and me. She was engrossed in our conversation, as if we were describing precisely where we had placed the bomb on the train.

The conversation must have been hard to follow because it was getting rather rowdy in the bar car of the midnight train going from Cairo to Aswan.

A half-dozen Croatians, geologists, and underwater cameramen from a Zagreb engineering company on their way to repair the Aswan Dam, joined us and passed around a bottle of bourbon. Tongues loosened and topics ranged from the lousy job the Russians did on the dam to the talents of a certain Cairo belly dancer.

It was impossible to tell if the watchful woman was amused because she was covered by a robe and veil. A narrow slit in the folds of fabric, which hid even her eyebrows, revealed those staring eyes. Her hands were still, one resting on top of the other, but her eyes were in constant motion.

Smoke hung in the faint glow of table lights, making the car a surreal cocoon barreling through the night. Egyptian villages, most lit by lone yellow street lights outlining the fringe of date palms, slipped by as we raced south along the banks of the Nile.

The woman was a curiosity. Even a conservative lady from an Upper Egypt village would have taken off at least the veil by now. Was she old, or young? Was she laughing, or was she appalled? But if she was offended, wouldn't she go back to her cabin? All the passengers had luxury sleepers. A woman traveling with her was old, her face uncovered, which seemed to indicate that the veiled woman was young and traveling with a chaperone.

The bartender served them tea, and I asked him about her. He rolled his eyes with obvious distaste, and gave a one-word explanation, "Oman."

So she was from the little sultanate on the tip of Arabia, which meant ultra conservative. She was a long way from home in more ways than one.

Three hours passed and the woman still sat by the window. Her companion fell asleep, her head bobbing on her shoulder.

In the pre-dawn hours, we finally exchanged hotel phone numbers with the Croatians, promising to meet two nights later in Aswan, and we left the bar. The woman remained.

Dawn came, illuminating the lush green of the date groves and the blue water of the Nile. Graceful *feluccas*, propelled by sails full of desert wind, tacked across the river. The cars of Cairo were replaced with briskly-stepping donkeys. Water buffaloes shouldered water wheels. The relentless, undulating gold dunes of the Sahara stretched to the rising sun.

As we left the train in Luxor, I caught sight of the Woman of Oman, her face once again covered with the veil. She was sitting next to the window of her cabin, watching us leave the platform.

She waved.

I looked closely to make sure that was what she was doing. It was tentative, but definitely a wave, which became more exuberant when I waved back.

—Cheryl Blackerby, "The Woman from Oman"

TRACY JOHNSTON

✦ ✦ ✦

Boh Knows Hormones

Menopause stalks the author on a
jungle river trip in Borneo.

WHEN I WOKE UP IN THE MIDDLE OF THE NIGHT WITH A HOT FLASH and heard the rain coming down softly on the tent, I decided to make the best of being awake and go down to the river. I got out in the soft rain and walked quickly and surely in the mist, my face and chest flushed with heat, the breeze cool on my skin, my flashlight poking a tiny hole in the blackness. The canopy was dripping water, but in the slice of sky overhead I could see brilliant, twinkling stars. For a moment I felt the sweet glow of being somewhere extraordinary, the presence of an intangible, undefinable force that breathed down upon me from the wet, lush, almost hypertrophied vegetation of the rainforest.

Then the wet tropical air brought back another infusion of memory, this one less pleasant. I remembered a dream I'd had the night before about the sore in my mouth. It had gotten worse and my gums looked as bad as Gary's [the boatman] feet. Three teeth had actually toppled over and were hanging by tiny threads. I didn't know what was wrong with my teeth, or why they had fallen out, but I remembered knowing for certain that the condition would get worse, and that I would have to keep the whole

119

thing a secret. How would I talk for the rest of my life? I'd wondered. How could I fake it?

It was clear that the dream had been about menopause. I was confronting a transition in life for which my culture had somehow conspired to keep me completely unprepared. I didn't know if all women got hot flashes, or how often, and had no idea if mine were normal or abnormal. I'd heard that emotions were often altered by the change in hormones; could it be that something chemical was making me cautious, even fearful?

I was amazed, then outraged to find myself in such uncharted emotional waters. Why hadn't I read about women going through menopause? I tried to think of female characters in Western literature who were middle-aged, and couldn't come up with a single name. No wise woman; no benignly powerful woman; no free spirit; no one attractive or successful. Where were all the heroines who were over the goddamn hill?

I'd heard, of course, that menopause can be linked to depression, and I knew that some cultures (rural Ireland, for instance) think it causes insanity. But I wasn't prepared for the embarrassment, for the feeling that I'd crossed some invisible line. Yesterday I had been young; today I was middle-aged. A few years ago I would have been on the rocks with the guides, helping them with the boats, and now I couldn't even control my own temperature. Like my teeth, I was beginning to lose things that had seemed part of me, essential to my life.

In the seventies, when I was about to turn thirty, I took off for Mexico and Guatemala with just five hundred dollars and a backpack. I wanted to prove to myself that I was still a free spirit, that nothing had changed. For three months I traveled happily, first with a girlfriend, and then alone. Because I was speaking mostly very simple Spanish, I had no idea if the people I was meeting were smart or educated; simply connecting with them at all seemed magical. I became attuned to the basics: their generosity of spirit, our shared impulse toward laughter.

Then one day, when I was hitchhiking in the Yucatán, an American kid from Florida picked me up. He was traveling in his van, which he'd equipped with a tape deck, ice chest, Coca-Cola holder, and roach clip. We shared a joint, listened to some rock-and-roll, and he told a long, boring story about surfing on Isla Mujeres. Finally he looked at me and said, "And what about you? What's your major?"

I remember saying something about being nine years out of college, but I also remember knowing, then, that I'd reached my limit. Within a week I was heading home. I didn't want to be what I had become: merely young again. I wanted more. I wanted to move on.

On the Boh River, my personal journey was now taking me right up against the same kind of limit, only how was I going to move on when all I could think about were the things I was going to miss? I'd miss looking good and having men pay attention to me; I'd miss being physically confident enough to go at life full tilt. And even worse, some of the things I'd miss I hadn't done well enough yet, or with enough purpose or understanding. It was unfair that just when I was in a position to have great adventures, my time had run out.

Despite the soft tropical night, the facts were coming into focus. Like the river, the world around me sailed on independent of my desires. If I wanted to define myself by facing challenges, I had better stop making them physical. I could take on spiritual challenges, intellectual challenges, emotional challenges—but how, and where, and which ones? The thought loomed up more monstrous, even, than swimming another set of rapids.

It did occur to me that there was something about the moments of happiness and contentment I was feeling on the Boh that might be key. If I was going to reinvent myself, turn menopause into some sort of rite of passage, I would have to look inward.

I heard the rain start to fall softly again and thought of Sylvie and Mike, body surfing in their tiny, moldy tent—sweating, panting, exploring, loving. And although it had a certain fecund appeal, it also seemed like an incredible amount of bother. Suddenly I felt a rush of love for my husband, who, unlike me, had been prone all his life to various fears and terrors. When I have insomnia, he actually likes to hold me in his arms and rub my head and tell me stories until I fall asleep. He may be afraid to go on an exploratory river trip, but he has the courage to offer great love.

Tracy Johnston grew up in Southern California, graduated from UC Berkeley, and has worked as a high school teacher, ceramic sculptor, free-lance writer, and magazine editor. She is working now on a book about marriage in Kano, Nigeria. She is the author of Shooting the Boh, *from which this was excerpted.*

★

Midlife is a time and a state of the psyche. Each of us arrives here sometime during the middle years of adulthood and stays for an indeterminate period of time, as if at a crossroads, before we can go on. It is a time when we passively or actively, consciously or unconsciously, stay on or stray from the course that we earlier embarked upon. What was required of us to get this far, how authentic do we feel, where are we headed? At midlife, we sense that time is passing; we know that this is around the halfway mark and that the rest of life will go by quickly now. We are confronted with the fact that we are aging; we do not have the same body we once had, and much else about us has also changed. A discrepancy may exist between what we have and what we wanted or expected of life, ourselves, or others.

—Jean Shinoda Bolen, M.D., *Crossing to Avalon:*
A Woman's Midlife Pilgrimage

JEAN SHINODA BOLEN, M.D.

✦ ✦ ✦

Quickening: Chartres Cathedral

Spiritual awakening at the sanctuary
of the Mother Goddess in France.

OF ALL THE SACRED SITES THAT MRS. DETIGER HAD PLANNED TO have me visit, Chartres Cathedral was the one that I most looked forward to. Chartres had exerted a pull on me ever since I took art history at Pomona College. In the darkened classroom I had seen the magnificent stained glass windows, flying buttresses, and soaring arches projected on the screen; in the midst of a survey course acquainting us with art from the time of ancient Greece to the present, Chartres seemed to hold something special for me as a place and as an expression of an unprecedented flowering of architecture and spirit in the twelfth century. I remembered that historians were puzzled as to how and why so many Gothic cathedrals were built in a relatively short period; their construction required a concerted outpouring of effort, talent, energy, and financial resources beyond what seemed possible. Of them all, Chartres Cathedral stood out in my imagination. Now, finally, I was a modern pilgrim on my way there.

In marked contrast to the hardships of pilgrims in the days of old, I only had to take a short flight from Amsterdam to Paris and then an automobile ride from Paris to Chartres. When I arrived in France, it was spring and Paris was beautiful. I was to be taken to Chartres by a guide whom I was to meet at the American University. Such was not to be the case however; the guide had had an accident and an American woman who loved the cathedral offered to drive. But once there, I would be on my own.

The next morning she picked me up in front of my elegant hotel. We left Paris and were shortly on a highway that made its way through fields and small villages in a gently rolling landscape. Nothing stood out on the horizon until we made a turn on a rise in the highway and there, unexpectedly close by and silhouetted dramatically above the pastoral countryside, was Chartres Cathedral. I caught my breath, as one instinctively does in the presence of great beauty or mystery.

Next thing I knew we were there. I walked into the gracefully proportioned cathedral and found a group of visitors gathered around an English-speaking guide. I gravitated toward them, listened for a while, and found that this was not what I wanted to be doing. I knew that there was a labyrinth on the floor somewhere and I went in search of it. I found it in the nave, occupying a circular area almost the width of the church. There were rows of

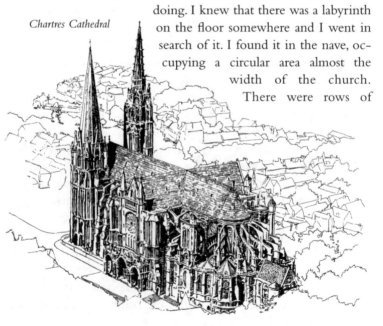

Chartres Cathedral

folding wooden chairs over it, so it was hardly noticeable. I decided to walk the labyrinth, which required that I move each chair, one by one.

This was not the kind of maze one gets lost in. There were no blind endings but instead a path that would take me over every bit of the figure to the center, which, with its circle and six lobes, looked like a stylized flower with petals. The path to the center was its stem. Encyclopedist Barbara G. Walker comments that this design is associated with Aphrodite, Greek Goddess of Love and Beauty.

Later I learned that labyrinths were originally associated with caves and were usually situated at the entrance. In the coolness and dimmed light of the thick-walled cathedral, with the great vault overhead, one can imagine being in an enormous high-ceilinged ritual cave, with its stalagmite and stalactite columns and mysterious labyrinth in the floor. This symbol of the Earth and the Goddess can be found not just here at Chartres but in at least twenty other cathedrals throughout Europe, including Poitiers, Toulouse, Reims, Amiens, Caen, Cologne, and Ravenna. I discovered that Chartres Cathedral, like many other Christian cathedrals devoted to the Virgin Mary, was built on a pilgrimage site that was, prior to Christianity, sacred to the Goddess.

Mary was held in particular

O ften scratched or carved on Stone Age monuments and grave sites, the labyrinthine design apparently represented the soul's journey into the center of the uterine underworld and its return toward rebirth. A labyrinth was not the same as a maze. A labyrinth had only one path, winding but branchless, heading inevitably toward the goal. Designs of this type were common on ancient coins, tiles, floor patterns, and especially tombs and sacred caves.

—Barbara G. Walker,
The Woman's Dictionary of Symbols & Sacred Objects

veneration at Chartres. In the very word *venerate*, the goddess Venus (Aphrodite's Latin name) is hidden. Emile Male, an authority on Chartres, writes that "it was the great centre of worship for the Virgin; the cathedral appeared to be her dwelling place on earth. At Chartres, when the hymn 'O Gloriosa' was sung in her honor, all the verbs were given in the present tense, to demonstrate her presence."

Henry Adams, whose book *Mont-Saint-Michel and Chartres* is a classic, concluded that "Chartres represents not the Trinity, but the identity of the Mother and Son." Mary's cathedral was built where, long before Christianity and even before the Greeks and their deities, the Goddess was once worshipped. Typically, the Great Goddess had a myriad of names. Here at Chartres, she continues to be worshipped in her aspects of virgin and mother, only instead of being called Isis, Tara, Demeter, or Artemis, her name is Mary.

Just as places where the Goddess was worshipped became sites for Christian churches, so too were her symbols taken over. Before becoming Mary's symbol, for instance, the open red rose was associated with Aphrodite and represented mature sexuality. At Chartres, which is dedicated to the Virgin Mary, roses abound. Light streams through three enormous and beautiful stained glass rose windows, and a symbolic rose is at the center of the labyrinth. The path of the labyrinth is exactly 666 feet long. Six hundred sixty-six, according to Barbara Walker, was Aphrodite's sacred number. In Christian theology it became a demonic one.

In the western aisle of the south transept, another mystery was built into the cathedral. Here, according to Charpentier, who writes of the esoteric qualities of Chartres Cathedral, is "a rectangular flagstone, set aslant to the others, whose whiteness is noticeable in the prevailing grey of the paving. It is conspicuous for a shining, lightly gilded metal tenon" (the insertion portion of a joint). Every year on the summer solstice (approximately June 21), a ray of light comes through a clear space in the stained glass window named for Saint Apollinaire and strikes this particular stone exactly at midday. Like the presence of a labyrinth, the timing here hints strongly of an Earth-oriented Goddess tradition embodied in this Christian cathedral.

After I walked the cluttered labyrinth with some difficulty and very little meditative concentration, I wandered through the great church looking at all there was to see. Thus far I was strictly a sightseer, not a pilgrim. Just before leaving on this journey, I had heard that a Druidic well and a black madonna had been found at Chartres. As it turns out, Goddess sites almost invariably have holy wells or springs. I decided to inquire about the possibility of seeing the crypt under the church and found that the shopkeeper at the small gift shop adjoining the cathedral led small groups through the crypt.

When it was time for the tour, a small group gathered, and she locked up her shop and took us to a side door of the cathedral, which she unlocked, and we descended until we were under the church. She spoke in French, which I don't understand, but I read an English description of what she was showing us and heard partial translations of what she was saying from some of the others. Now her friendly and bored shopkeeper expression was gone. Here in the crypt, her passion showed. It was clear that we were with a person who loved this place. Her general demeanor changed. Something about her look made me think she could be a short, solid, medieval friar, with a rope around the waist. And I thought, who knows, perhaps she was.

In the crypt, there is indeed a well, now covered with a locked lid, which is as deep as the taller spire of the cathedral is high. It is an ancient Celtic well about thirty-three meters deep that was once in a grotto. In this low-ceilinged, cool, cave-like, dimly lit chamber under the church, it was easy to imagine a grotto. Long before the Christian era, pilgrims had come to this site and were reputed to have found next to the well a statue of a dark goddess, which was later called a black madonna. She may have been a representation of Isis, the Egyptian mother goddess. Isis was a black goddess whose dismembered son Osiris was resurrected as Horus. Isis was probably the original black madonna, whose worship spread through the GrecoRoman world. Now, in the cathedral above, there is also a black madonna. She is a traditional Roman Catholic figure of Mary wearing a crown, but her features are black.

Once the tour to the crypt was over, there was time for me to return again to the cathedral. Only this time, something in me had changed. I was no longer the tourist; I had become the pilgrim. The descent to the grotto had affected me greatly, and almost as if in response, as I walked into the cathedral this second time, the organist began to play and the magnificent sound seemed to vibrate through the stones and through me.

I found that I was not taking things in primarily with my eyes and mind anymore. I was instead feeling my way, perceiving the energies in the cathedral with my body, responding to the place kinesthetically. For the first time in my life, I felt myself acting like a tuning fork or a dowsing rod. I was aware of something that was neither pressure nor vibration nor warmth, yet seemed to have qualities of all three, centered in the middle of my chest between my breasts and radiating in all directions. As I walked through the cathedral, I found that what I began to think of as "the tuning-fork effect" was greater in one place than others. When I stood at the intersection between the nave and the transepts in front of a cordoned-off altar area, the intensity was the greatest.

Standing there, I felt like holding my arms outstretched, and I had a sudden insight: If I were the same size as the church and were laid out, my arms the length of the transepts, the labyrinth was where my uterus would be. It occupied the "womb" of the church.

When new life stirs within the womb, and a mother has the sensation of her baby moving within her for the first time, it's called "quickening." The same word is associated with pilgrims, who go to sacred places to "quicken" the divinity within themselves, to experience spiritual awakening or receive a blessing or become healed. The seeker embarks on a journey with a receptive soul and hopes to find divinity there. And, as I began to appreciate from my tuning-fork response to Chartres, pilgrimage to a sacred place is an in-the-body spiritual experience—as were my pregnancies.

It is believed that the divine spirit is incarnate at sacred places, both in the sense that the Deity is present there and in that these are places where the divinity penetrates matter, impregnating or quickening the divine in the pilgrim. In Europe, places of Christian pilgrimage are nearly always sites that had been sacred to the Great Goddess before the advent of Christianity.

Charpentier notes that Chartres Cathedral was built on the site that was once the Druids' sanctuary of sanctuaries, on a mound or elevation where there was a sacred wood and a well that was called "The Well of the Strong." Here, carved in the hollowed-out trunk of a pear tree, once existed a statue of a dark woman or a goddess with an infant on her knees, believed to have been made by Druids before the birth of Christ.

The power of the place is in its location. Here ancients came to receive "the Gift of the Earth; something Earth gives like a Mother." Here human spiritual faculties were awakened by what the Gauls called the *Wouivre*, the telluric (magnetic or cosmic) currents that "snake" through the ground and are represented symbolically by serpents. Dolmens or megaliths (large stones) were placed where these currents are particularly strong.

Drawing on esoteric and historical sources, Charpentier says that a particularly strong current comes to a head under the hill on which Chartres Cathedral is built and accounts for its unusual northeast orientation (cathedrals are usually oriented toward the east). He says that a megalithic stone or dolmen may lie buried in the mound, and that it is because of the sacredness of the ground upon which the cathedral stands that among all the cathedrals in France, Chartres is the only one that has no bodies buried in it.

Learning of the *Wouivre* brought other images to my mind: of the famous bas-relief of an unidentified Greek goddess—thought to be Demeter, the Goddess of Grain and mother of the maiden Persephone—arising out of the earth with a snake, wheat, and flowers in each hand; of a Minoan statue of a goddess or priestess, arms outstretched, holding a snake in each hand; of statues of Athena with snakes on her shield or in the hem of her garment, symbolic remnants of her pre-Olympian origins. Might the Great

Goddess, who was in her various manifestations Earth Goddess/Mother Earth, be the provider of sacred energy (the snakes) as well as flowers and wheat? This would explain the images.

In Eastern religions, sacred energy, called *kundalini,* is also symbolized by a snake that lies asleep at the base of the spine (as if in recognition of the significance of this location, in Western anatomy we call the protective shield-shaped bone that covers the end of the spinal cord the sacrum), until it is awakened ("quickened") and rises up through the chakras through spiritual practices. In Eastern physiology, the human body (like the Earth) is seen to have meridians running through it, with acupuncture points at junctions. These points can be stimulated to reduce pain, heal the body, and restore balance and harmony.

On this pilgrimage I first heard of telluric currents and first experienced for myself this energy that is present at places where humans have worshiped for thousands of years, and it occurred to me that sacred places are the "acupuncture points" of the Earth. But I continue to experience the tuning-fork phenomenon, and as a result I tune into the environment wherever I am. I simply quiet my mind and try to feel the response of my body. I tune into an instinctual awareness of the quality of the energy that permeates a place, a sensory intuition that extends to people, animals, trees, and even rocks. In Ireland, for example, I "met" standing stones—each one like an ancient, patient, and wise presence. On a Greek island I came across a grove of old trees in a ravine that had such a malevolent quality, I could not bear staying there.

Mrs. Detiger has the idea that when we visit sacred sites, we are not only affected *by* them, we also are awakening their dormant energies. Maybe so. Maybe the Australian aborigine whose sacred task it is to sing his or her particular piece of the song line that keeps the soul of the earth alive is not superstitious and ignorant, but is doing exactly that. Maybe we can be attuned to Nature; maybe communing with Nature is a sacred dialogue, upon which our spiritual development as a species depends. It was only through my own pilgrimage that I became aware of these possibilities and began to develop a conscious relationship to the Earth as Mother—a living being made up of matter and energy, as are we, with our visible bodies and invisible psyches.

Jean Shinoda Bolen, M.D., is a Jungian analyst and professor of psychiatry at the University of California, San Francisco. She is the author of eight books, including Goddesses in Everywoman, Gods in Everyman, The Tao of Psychology, Ring of Power *and* Crossing to Avalon: A Woman's Midlife Pilgrimage, *from which this piece was excerpted.*

✳

Since history's first epic poem recorded the visit of the Sumerian hero Gilgamesh to a special grove of cedars, certain natural spots scattered round the world—Ayers Rock, Mount Fuji, Canyon de Chelly, the springs at Lourdes, the Ganges River and hundreds of others—have drawn people seeking insight, inspiration, healing or proximity to the divine. Often, the same places have been revered by very different societies. Jews, Muslims, and Christians alike venerate Mount Sinai; the California hot springs that incubated many of the spiritual and cultural changes of the 1960s were once sacred to the Esalen Indians; and many of Europe's cathedrals were deliberately built over pagan springs and ritual sites. Powerfully augmented by the pilgrim's expectations, it seems the special physical properties of what the Bible calls "high places" have the capacity to promote physical and psychological change.

—Winifred Gallagher, *The Power of Place: How Our Surroundings Shape Our Thoughts, Emotions, and Actions*

PART TWO

SOME THINGS TO DO

LYNN FERRIN

✦ ✦ ✦

Across the Steppes on a Horse with No Name

The author follows in the footsteps of Genghis Khan.

SUNRISE. OUR YURT DOOR IS OPEN TO THE GRASSLANDS OF INNER Mongolia.

Six of us are lying under piles of quilts. A two-humped camel ambles by. We have spent the night in one of the world's wackier hotels—30 white yurts and several wooden structures shaped like giant yurts: a bathroom, dining pavilion and performance hall. Chinese tour operators bring groups out here from Hohhot, the capital, to spend one night on the grasslands.

Last evening we dined on Mongolian hot pot and were entertained with regional song and dance. We were expected to respond in kind, so we stood there in our jeans and cowboy boots and belted out "Home on the Range" and "Don't Fence Me In" to the bemused Mongols.

Somewhere out behind the

Yurt

yurts, our horses are stomping and wheezing at the feeding trough.

At this place, Yidui, we will begin our week-long ride.

The romantic appeal of all this was undeniable: to travel over the steppes of Asia on a fast horse, stopping in hamlets and farms for the night, saddling up each morning to ride on. We would be using small, tough Mongolian horses, the ones ridden by the hordes of Genghis Khan, the ones that, in the thirteenth century, took China and most of the Eastern world.

It has taken us a week to get here from San Francisco. On the long train ride from Beijing we passed alongside, then through, the Great Wall. Pressed to the windows, we could see it, running up and down the mountainsides, along the ridgetops, disappearing, then reappearing farther away. The emperors of China built it over the centuries in a futile attempt to keep out the galloping barbarians of Mongolia.

Then we were beyond the wall, in a pale arid country. At night we came to sprawling, smoky Hohhot and slept in a surprisingly glitzy hotel.

Our whole improbable romp was cooked up by one Linda Svendsen, a Montana mountain guide whose tricky knees forced her to trade her climbing boots for a saddle. Somehow she convinced Chinese officials to let her company bring groups of Western riders to remote areas of China, Mongolia, and Tibet.

Most of the fourteen people in our mini-horde are horse owners. There's Fred, an 84-year-old parade rider from southern California; Julie, a 64-year-old endurance champion from Santa Cruz; Whitney, a 25-year-old farmhand from Colorado. Others among us took riding lessons just to come on this trip, including an inventor named Ted, who has developed a huge pop-up internal-frame dome tent modeled after a yurt. His fantasy is to set up his Domad beside its prototype.

I'm here to renew my love-hate relationship with horses. I once rode cross-country over the Canadian Rockies, a week from British Columbia to Alberta, in miserable rain and sleet, terrified of grizzlies, on a very reluctant paint. Later I endured ten days among the Berber villages of Morocco astride a randy stallion that was eager to mount every living creature we encountered, including mules and dogs. Both times I swore I would never get on one of those beasts again, ever. But the years passed, and eventually all I remembered was the thrill, the danger, the hooves pounding the ground beneath me, my hair flying, the horse's guileless eyes. And then along came this ride, too dramatic to resist.

Our route is a 200-mile loop through Ssu-tzu-wang-ch'i Banner. We will pass within 40 miles of what the Chinese call the "Russian border"—Outer Mongolia. Our group will be joined by seventeen Chinese and Mongols—wranglers, guides, cooks, a doctor, various go-fers, and a nerdy government type whose purpose is to "observe." To carry our gear, personnel, and horsefeed, a minibus, a truck, and an outlandish yellow Winnebago camper will accompany us. We will be using some comfortable leather cavalry saddles, and a few wooden Mongolian torture instruments.

Our horses have no names, only numbers. I am assigned to 309, a dark brown steed with a black mane and tail, one white sock, and a brow flecked with stardust. If it were up to me to name him, I'd call him Galaxy. Or maybe Lint.

We ride out through the last gate we'll see for a week. The horses are eager to run.

I had imagined the grasslands to be horse belly deep in emerald grass. But no, there is only a thin frizz of green over the terra cotta earth, flat and drab. We see only a few yurts—most of the nomadic Mongol herders have been resettled into ranching collectives, along with transplanted Han Chinese.

*Not forever
can one enjoy
Stillness and peace.
But misfortune and
Destruction
Are not final.
When the grass
Has been burnt
By the fire of the steppe,
It will grow anew
In summer.*

—Wisdom from the Mongolian Steppe, *Springs of Oriental Wisdom*

The spectacle here is sky—more of it than your eyes can contain, with something different happening in each direction. To the right, unflawed blue; to the left, lightning flashing between gunmetal columns of rain; ahead, a section of rainbow like a stained-glass church window.

We ride 28 miles this first day, and come straggling into Damiao at sunset, our arms aching from pulling on the reins. The streets are lined with people who've come out to gawk at these pale big-noses with the red bandannas. This is Buddhist country, and Damiao was once a great monastic center, with five thriving lamaseries. They were all destroyed during the Cultural Revolution. One temple has been restored by the current somewhat-lenient regime. Inside, a dozen lamas in scarlet robes sit intoning *om* beneath fresh paint and bright new silken banners. They are all old men. We can't begin to know what they have suffered.

In a couple of days we're accustomed to the routine. We rise and breakfast on milk tea with millet, the Mongolian staple. I pull my saddle from the dusty pile and throw it over 309's indifferent back; he always takes the bit easily. We ride for several hours, usually cross-country, until we meet a dirt road and our vehicles parked somewhere near a well.

While the wranglers water and feed the horses, we picnic on the grasslands, then nap, then ride again. Sometimes we all canter along together; sometimes we ride so far apart that the other horses are just specks on the horizon.

Late each afternoon we dismount and walk our horses into a town of mud-walled houses. Usually there is a "guest house," a euphemism for a few grim rooms with lumpy cots and unspeakable latrines. But we always get a pan of hot water for washing off the dust. Then a hearty Chinese dinner appears, often mutton, greens, and rice. We drink beer and the Mongols toast again and again with *maotai*. They sing deep, lusty songs of free-roaming herdsmen. We sing "You Are My Sunshine," and "I Ride an Old Paint." Saddlesore and exhausted, we drop onto our beds in the early dusk.

Our horses trot on through the glaring sun, through rain and under skies full of clouds like a thousand sailboats. Once we are caught in a wildcat storm, the hail hammering the plains in silver sequins, 309 terrified and snorting, our clothes drenched. We pass herds of horses and sheep, even a pack of maybe a hundred Bactrian camels. Sometimes the scenes are surreal: border guards, right out of *Road Warrior,* buzzing along the empty tracks on motorcycles; a town where all the dogs get around on three legs; isolated adobe farmhouses with windmills for electricity, TV antennas and yurts for summer sleeping.

There are no fences in this landscape. The towns have pounded dirt streets, and hitching posts outside the stores. People here ride horses to get places. It strikes me that this may be the only place on earth where the Old West lives. Only this is *China.*

Toward the end of the week, 309 is showing something like affection. When I stand with him in the mornings before we saddle up, he rests his chin on my shoulder, his muzzle soft against my cheek.

One afternoon our horses shuffled through sand dunes; a check of the map shows that this is an arm of the Gobi Desert. That night we stay in a grand oasis called Jianganhe. Its contented people live among tall poplar trees, willows, clear water gushing up out of wells and through fruit orchards and vegetable gardens. We are told that we are the first foreigners to come here.

The next night we are squatting at Dalaiaobao, a remote scatter of rammed-earth houses, with nothing but plains and sky in any direction. Word has spread that we are here, and all afternoon Mongols come galloping in from God knows where to look at us. How they love their horses! How they can ride! They race past our camel-dung campfire, slugging back bottles of beer, laughing like hell, each with one leg in the stirrup and the other slung over the wooden saddle.

Ted carries his Domad over to a yurt where a herder is cleaning a fresh goatskin. In a moment he has unfolded and popped it open, and the yurt is dwarfed by this unlikely shimmering metallic half-sphere. The herder's response is to go into his yurt and shut his little red door.

Our host plays a discordant two-string violin, and tells us glee-fully that during the Cultural Revolution he helped trash the American embassy before returning to the grasslands. The full moon slides above the clouds. Someone produces a ghetto-blaster and we dance to souped-up Chinese versions of Beethoven and Bizet. That night we sleep on dirt floors, six to a room.

Adventure travel. Crazy. You live eleven months of the year blinking into a computer screen, blahing on the phone. And now here you are, streaking across *Mongolia*, please, on a horse. Then, weeks later, all brown skin and taut sinews, you're back at your desk. But you've always come home with some new way of seeing.

For example. Some of these Mongolian settlements—especially those inhabited by transplanted Han Chinese—seem unnecessarily bleak to me. Why doesn't someone plant a tree or a flower—there's water enough. Why don't families build their own clean, private outhouses—there's space enough. Why not a little beauty?

Then, one midnight, something wakes me up. Outside the win-dow, the sky is like nothing I've seen before. I pull on my clothes and slip through the door. A few other people from our group are already there, murmuring, faces turned up to the fantastic dome. We have never been so removed from dirty air and city lights. So many stars! But this sky also has depth to it, so that you can see lay-ers, dimension, stars behind stars. For once I sense my own place: on a planet, hurtling through the cosmos.

And then I realize: if you have this to decorate your nights, you have all anyone needs of beauty.

On the train out of Mongolia to Beijing, our "soft sleeper" car has fresh linens, piles of pillows, an attendant bringing tea, and comfortable bunks.

In the middle of the night the ceiling fans are turned off. I wake up, sweating, and lean over to slide the doors open to the passageway.

In the amber light, old gentlemen in Mao suits are sitting on the jumpseats, smoking.

The train rocks on through the China night. I doze, dream, wake, doze again.

Beneath my pillow run the moonlit rails, and 309's mane is blowing in the steam, his hooves clattering among the rushing wheels. I reach out and catch his mane in my fingers. The wind is in my face. We ride faster, through the grass, through all the Mongolian sky.

Lynn Ferrin was nine years old and knew she was in the wrong place: Texas. One day her father came home and announced the family was moving to Kuwait and her traveling and writing career began. Since then, she has roamed the planet by foot, horseback, kayak, canoe, ship, plane, train, and camel. Currently a freelance travel writer, Lynn was an editor and writer for thirty-seven years for VIA, membership magazine of the American Automobile Association in California, Nevada, and Utah. Her specialty is writing about adventure travel and public lands, and she most recently co-edited Wild Writing Women: Stories of World Travel. *She has lived in a cluttered hillside cottage in San Francisco for almost forty years.*

✳

My love affair with horses has a practical side: riding is a first rate way to travel. It can take you just about anywhere, far beyond the reach of roads, and put you on intimate terms with landscape and weather as you can never be in a vehicle.

—Ann Jones, "Kenya on Horseback," Town & Country

* * *

Surfing is Better than Sex

The power of the sea evokes fear, ecstasy,
and a oneness with nature.

I USED TO SIT OUT ON THE ROCKS ALL DAY LONG ON THE OREGON coast watching my husband surf. After two or three years of that he finally said, "You've got to get out here with me."

The north coast of the Pacific has some pretty cold water, and I didn't want to be cold. But I tried going out with a wetsuit and a boogie board; Tom gave me a few lessons out in the cove. I realized that I could be very warm in a wetsuit, and I felt more protected inside the cove, away from the big breakers. It took a few months to feel confident on the boogie board.

The first wave I caught when I was boogie boarding was one of the best waves of my life. I caught this wave and was rising all the way through it, and I felt like a pro. I was in a pocket in the speed zone of the wave just flying at warp six; I couldn't believe the speed! I kicked out with my board and thought to myself, Yes, this sensation is pretty close to orgasmic. It has to be the closest thing to sex that I've ever known. I've done a lot of things in my life—snowboarding, skiing, waterskiing, hiking, and parachuting from airplanes, trying to find things that are the most exciting to do.

I feel in touch with the ocean. Every day before I enter her, I ask her to give me waves and let me experience her and be safe. I

142

go out feeling that she's going to give me what I am expecting. I paddle out with complete confidence and strength into big wave conditions and think to myself, I'm coming out here to line up and I'm going to find the magic spot. When I find it, I'm going to turn around and ride the wave I'm given, and I'm gonna give that wave the best ride I can. And then I'm going to kick out and come out of the wave safely, paddle back out and catch about ten more like that. That's how I visualize what I'm going to do.

You have to be able to judge your skill level. You can easily drown or get thrown up on the rocks and hurt yourself. You have to look out at the waves and ask yourself, Are these waves too big for me? Are they too gnarly? Are they something I can't cope with? I never surf unless I feel close to a hundred percent confident that I can make it out there, can catch waves, and make it in safely. Gradually, over the years, I've built up my confidence, always knowing when I can ride bigger waves. Now, eight or nine years later, I feel that I can charge just about anything that comes through the cove. Now I can surf waves with twelve-foot faces, even fifteen- to twenty-foot on a perfect day.

Last year, I caught one of the most phenomenal waves of my life. I went down to the cove with two girlfriends, and we were going to catch the "lefts," but once I got suited up at the water's edge, I looked over and saw the most perfect "right" happening just down the beach. It was about six feet high, barreling perfection, and nobody was on it. I told my girlfriends, You go on to where you're going, I'm heading out to that "right."

I happen to be "regular foot" on a surfboard, which puts me frontside on that right-breaking wave. I'm facing the wave when I'm surfing it, which is the most advantageous position to be in. If I'd gone to the other break, I would have been backside, which is less advantageous and not nearly as fun. So I looked down the beach and thought, That wave has my name all over it

It was a hell of a paddle to get out there; there wasn't much of a channel and I was breaking through a lot of waves. I finally got out, waited through about three waves, and then this peak came through, and I thought, This is the perfection peak, this is a perfect right, and I'm frontside on it. This wave was made for me. I turned around and started paddling, and I knew it was going to be the biggest wave I'd ever caught. I started paddling into it on my 8'5" board, which is real hot-dogged out, and caught it.

I dropped in on it, hit the bottom, then came pulling up. The amount of speed I was getting was unbelievable. I came up and hit the top part of the section, hit the turn back down to the bottom, came off the bottom turn, back up again into the lip, and slashed down into the pit. The whole time I was in the green water—not the whitewater—right in the green water, which is the speed section of the wave.

I must have ridden it a hundred and twenty yards, up and down all parts of the wave, until I was just in ankle-deep water. I had the sensation that it had been the wave of my life—it was the euphoria of the century. When I kicked out of the wave, I was so overwhelmed my eyes were tearing up. Then I said, I'm back out there! and immediately started paddling back out for another one, or ten more.

It reminded me of my boogie board wave, but this time I had just surfed a surfboard through the same kind of wave—I had a board under my feet and was pumping it all the way through. It's an amazing feeling—you're harnessing the energy of the wave, and its got so much power. People think I'm half-looney for talking like this, and maybe they can't understand it, but it's like you've got the whole power of the ocean harnessed into the pit of a wave.

I've been involved with feminism for years, and there is nothing that has ever gotten me closer to nature than surfing. You're out there and you have to deal with the ocean, the fear, the survival, the achievements and challenges, and the feeling of ecstasy. All that makes you feel that you've got to stay with it.

My surf buddies are a dozen other women. The men are competitive and cut each other off to get waves, but the women get along well and we all encourage each other. If we're lucky we'll have four women out in the lineup on one day.

I'm the manager of a surf shop, and I tell people who want to get involved with surfing that something will happen out there that you've never had happen before, and you won't understand it until it happens to you.

When you're in the ocean and experiencing its strength, you feel like a magician who just got hold of something that you never thought you would be allowed to have. Something the planet gave you like a gift. It's better than dancing, it's better than sex—you feel that nature just touched you on the nose and said, "That was for you." For a few seconds you are one with that wave. I've never had that sensation before with anything else.

Lexie Hallahan lives on the Northwest coast of Oregon with her husband Tom. They share a love of the ocean and mountains, surfing, and snowboarding. She says: "Carving on a wall of water or on a wall of snow has given us both the exhilaration that life represents."

Thalia Zepatos is a political consultant, traveler, and writer living in Portland, Oregon. She is the author of A Journey of One's Own: Uncommon Advice for the Independent Woman Traveler *and* Adventures in Good Company: The Complete Guide to Women's Tours and Outdoor Trips *from which this story was excerpted.*

*

Full to bursting. The sea accepts, widens *our* reception. We are overflowing and the sea contains us. And then when we are stretched, when we are broadened, opened up to new life, the sea gives us back to ourselves.

—Susan St. John Rheault, *Readings from the
Hurricane Island Outward Bound School*

SHARON DIRLAM

✦ ✦ ✦

Haute Coiffeur Beijing Style

The author is granted an audience
with a Chinese master.

THE WORK UNIT FOR CHINA'S BIGGEST NEWSPAPER, *RENMIN RIBAO* (*People's Daily*), has its own compound, at 2 Jintai Xilu, on the eastern side of Beijing. Within the walls were the newspaper buildings, schools, grocery store, a fried-dough stall, basketball court, workers' apartments, soldiers' barracks, a clinic, and a unisex barbershop. The English-language *China Daily*, where I worked for a year, was also temporarily housed in this compound.

The barbershop was in a small cinderblock building with concrete floor, no heat, and the bare minimum of equipment. I was told the resident barber, Xiao Li, was very good, so instead of going to a Western-style hotel and paying Western prices for a haircut, I came in to his shop. Since I know very few words in Chinese, I brought a drawing with me of what I hoped my hair would like after it was cut.

At eight in the morning, I was the first customer. Xiao Li, the young barber, who wore his slick black hair in a trendy European style, wasn't quite ready to start working. He took my drawing and studied it, nodded, and gave me a thumbs-up sign. But then he pointed to his watch and motioned for me to sit in a folding metal chair by the window. I sat down.

Xiao Li fiddled with a small tinny radio, finally tuning in to a mellow rock number, then heated water for his tea over a portable gas burner. Then he went to the only sink in the shop and brushed his teeth. He spat into the sink, gargled, and spat again, then carefully and slowly washed his hands. He stared at his reflection in the small mirror above the sink, pulled a comb from his pocket and combed his hair slightly, just around the edges. Avoiding my curious gaze as if I were invisible, he proceeded to rub a bit of mousse around in his palms and stroke it gently onto his hair. Then he tore into the process vigorously, backcombing and swirling the hair to his satisfaction before smoothing it all back into place with his comb. Finally he plugged in a portable hair dryer and aimed it at his head, touching the edges of his hairdo with the comb to finish it off.

Xiao Li turned slowly around and stared at himself in the big mirror on the opposite wall, checking himself from all angles, and—still without looking at me—he disappeared behind the curtain that separated the public area from the back of the shop. The entire shop was in a very small room, and I could hear him back there slurping his tea.

By this time I had been in China long enough to know there is no rushing a worker. I had given up the constant undercurrent of impatience and the sense of deadlines that had been my pace in Los Angeles, and had learned to sit quietly, doing nothing. Not really even thinking. Just sitting, with an expectant curiosity. As the Beijingers do. I found this to be a not unpleasant state.

Seeing me sitting there by the window, some Chinese had gathered. The men and women parked their bicycles outside on the dirt and a few came in and took seats alongside me, acknowledging me with a smile and nod. Some were probably customers; others just had come to watch the foreigner (*waiguoren*) get a haircut.

After several minutes behind the curtain, Xiao Li reappeared, ready to begin. He had a small case of accoutrements—combs, scissors, razor, clips, and pins. He motioned for me to sit in the chair in front of the mirror. I moved there, but I gestured to the sink where he had just completed his toilette and moved my hands around on my head in motions that I hoped implied shampoo; and so he waved me in that direction.

I sat down on the small stool he pointed to, with my back to the sink.

The Chinese audience laughed, their hands over their mouths as though not to embarrass me. Xiao Li put his hands on my shoulders and turned me around to face the sink, then gently pushed my head forward. Water and shampoo and more water cascaded over my tightly-closed eyes as he massaged my scalp with his strong fingertips. Finally the worst was over, and he and I filed back to the chair in front of the mirror.

By now my audience inside the shop had grown to ten, and at least ten more were peering in through the window.

Xiao Li studied my drawing again then brandished his scissors, as if he were an artist approaching the canvas with a brush.

He combed my wet hair this way and that. Some of the people who had been sitting in the chairs by the window stood up and moved closer to watch. He snipped and cut and combed and fluffed and snipped some more, with no apparent plan, and it seemed to me that he was taking an unusually long time for a haircut. Finally, he completed his artistry with brush and hair dryer, moving the very short coif this way, then that, down over my forehead and back. At last he signaled that he was finished. He handed me the small mirror.

I turned my head one way and then the other, expressionless, but really pleased with my new hairstyle. I could almost feel his anticipation. I smiled and gave him a thumbs-up. Xiao Li nodded proudly at our audience, a slight smile playing on his lips. All the people in the shop breathed a collective happy sigh. They watched me pay Xiao Li his top price: two *yuan*. Seventy cents, for a perfect haircut.

Sharon Dirlam also contributed "Stranded in Volos" in Part I.

★

It's easy to feel angry at China; every bus is early or late, many clerks are hostile, crowds push and clamor, and boarding trains, planes, and buses demands a physical struggle. People stare openly at foreigners, sometimes gathering in small crowds to observe while rash youths follow you around, trying to practise English and get a foreign address. You can quickly become overwhelmed by a language you do not properly comprehend and by customs, hemispheres removed from your own.

But beyond all this, there's no denying the grandeur of China's natural scenery, its position on the world scale, and the influence it exerts over the rest of Asia. China requires patience, flexibility, and humor. The unpredictability of wandering the Middle Kingdom has its rewards, and for women going it alone, it's bound to feel safer than home.

—Adrienne Su, "An Eastern Westerner in China," *More Women Travel - Adventure and advice from more than 60 countries - A Rough Guide Special,* edited by Natania Jansz and Miranda Davies

CATHERINE WATSON

* * *

Same Place Every Year

Ah…the satisfaction of a couch potato vacation in a Mexican villa.

ONE YEAR AT THE VILLA, THE MOST MEMORABLE EVENT WAS watching a line of black ants transport slices of bright-green leaves and hot-pink bougainvillea petals past the swimming pool.

The ants were coming from somewhere near the mango tree and marching off toward the house, but we never found out exactly where they started or where they went. We could have checked, someone noted much later, but nobody thought of that.

We were in the pool at the time, the ants were trudging along the pool edge right past our noses, and we just hung there in the warm turquoise water and watched them do their thing.

It was like tuning in to the Discovery channel without touching the remote.

That, in a nutshell, is why I've spent ten years of winter vacations renting the same house in Acapulco. Same house, same companions, same cook, same caretaker, same adventures.

Which is to say no adventures.

I go simply because it is beautiful, predictable, peaceful, NOT HOME, warm, sunny, beautiful, predictable.…

We've done this trip so often, people complain when other

people bring the same swimsuit two years in a row. Not enough variety.

We don't like variety in anything else, though. Every year is the same, and that's the great joy of this place: so far, at least, nothing that matters has changed.

Its not-so-great joy is the time-lapse effect of repeat visits: the lady who manages the house—and "lady" is the right word—ages gracefully from year to year, but ages all the same. We age too, between visits.

And the visits connect like film clips, so we seem to age rapidly, as if God is flipping the corners on a stack of our snapshots. Waistlines thicken, wrinkles deepen, hairlines creep upward, jowls creep down. But it doesn't matter here. The villa's the same.

Going to the villa is like renting a summer cabin with palm trees. You know somebody else owns it, and you pay to use it, but once you've paid it's yours. And you can go as brain-dead as you like in that time you've bought.

We go pretty brain-dead.

At the villa, painting your own toenails is an event. Painting somebody else's toenails takes planning. And, wow! Somebody wants to have her hair highlighted? We'd better put that off till tomorrow, when we've got more time. Sometimes, there are real events. One night we saw Queen Elizabeth's ship put out to sea and watched through binoculars until it became an uncertain smudge in the charcoal night.

On other occasions, we've seen whales—or rather the distant white plumes of their breath—and then gone nearly blind staring at the dazzling sea for the next hour, hoping to see them again. Once we saw a mother whale traveling steadily north, while her whale child—a black dot from our distance—frisked around and around her like a two-year-old in a toy store.

We frisk too. Being at a staffed villa is like being five years old. Only better. We have become friends with the people who take care of us each year. They set the schedule; we respond. This is all there is to do: get up in the morning, pull on your play clothes and show up for breakfast. Play by the pool or (if you feel that energetic) go to the beach till lunch time.

Eat lunch. Take an afternoon nap or (if you feel that energetic) write letters on the terrace.

When the sun is pounding full on the pool, go back for a long, lazy afternoon in the water, with squadrons of frigate birds and vultures and pelicans drifting overhead against the blue, blue sky.

(It's not really true that the vultures come closer to check on us as the week wears on. We do move sometimes. Just not much.)

And then comes sunset. It should be capitalized: SUNSET. The biggest production of the day. While the cosmos is working on the clouds, the staff is working on margaritas, and we shower and dress for dinner to the sound of ice in the blender.

"Sunset alert," somebody announces, and we all turn to look. Are there enough clouds to make it gorgeous tonight? Does it rate a ten this time or only the usual 9.6? Is it clear enough at the horizon to see the Green Flash? Ah, the Green Flash.

The Flash is our Holy Grail. We have scanned the horizon for it for a decade, and only a few of us claim to have seen it. The rest don't believe them.

The Flash is supposed to be caused by the last rays of sunlight shining through sea water as if through liquid emerald.... Somebody read that in Somerset Maugham or somewhere, once, I think. Well, somebody read it somewhere.

No, say skeptics, the Green Flash is in your head. When you've stared too long at the last tiny speck of sun, your eyes will see green when the red speck is gone.

The Green Flash argument is only one of our annual certainties.

We know, for instance, that the suitcases of books we've packed won't be quite as appealing as the Agatha Christie or *Vanity Fair* somebody else brought. We know we'll end up trading novels and magazines, and we'll lament the trashy level to which our tastes have fallen.

(Once, before I knew better, I brought textbooks for a graduate course I was taking in anthropology. I spent the week studying yam consumption in Papua, New Guinea, while envying everybody else's *New Yorkers*.)

We know that one night per visit, our whole group will dress up and troop out to a nice restaurant. We know that halfway through the week, one or more of us will get a touch of *turistas*, and we'll all discuss diarrhea at breakfast and blame it on the nice restaurant. We also know that we'll take our nice pills and be fine again pretty soon.

We know that near the end of the week somebody will decide to go "into town," which means shopping for silver or ceramics at the downtown artisans' market, and that will touch off a shopping frenzy in everybody else. One year the shoppers set up their own artisans market in the hall outside our rooms—spread all their treasures out on their beach towels—and the rest of the group got to shop without leaving the house.

We also know that we are not going to stay up until three to go disco dancing at Baby O's. That we will not watch the cliff divers jump off the rocks at La Quebrada. Or go to the bullfights. Or take the sightseeing cruise across the exquisite scallop of blue that is Acapulco's harbor.

Those worthy activities are for our occasional newcomers. We've already done them. Just don't ask us which year; the years kind of blur together.

This kind of vacation falls well below the tourism threshold, and we know it. True, we had to get on a plane to get here, but it doesn't matter much where "here" is.

Which is the point: when you take a villa vacation, you go somewhere to be—and to be taken care of. It is an absolute break, and it could as easily be Hawaii or Key West or Phoenix or the Seychelles, for all we know. We didn't come to interact with the culture. Although we do, in a way. The people who take care of "our" villa have put five kids through college on their share of our rent money, and that makes us feel as if we weren't complete parasites.

One year I went into the villa the moment the taxi dropped us off at the gate and didn't leave the place for a second until the taxi came to take us back to the airport a week later to catch our charter home.

When you have perfection, I figured, who needs to look any further?

(I didn't even go down to the beach that year, just stopped partway down the hillside at the swimming pool. But heck—I could see the beach from the pool deck, and besides, I went to the beach last year.)

Another year, one of us forgot to leave his parka at home, which means he had to wear it all the way to Mexico. He modeled the whole rig—gloves, scarf, hood—for the villa staff, so they'd understand what we were trying to get away from. They were amused.

Why live there then? they wondered.

That's the same question I ask myself about this time every winter—when my eyes get tired of gray and white and start longing for the Green Flash.

Catherine Watson is the award-winning travel editor of the Minneapolis Star Tribune *and the author of* Travel Basics.

★

In my twenties I traveled with a vengeance. Like an addict overdosed on *National Geographics*, I finagled trips to Chile, Hong Kong, East Berlin. I *needed* to see Hong Kong Harbor before the *taipans* with the voluminous red sails disappeared, Borobubur before it was eroded by pollution, Margaret Mead's Bali before the tourists overran it. I was making up for coming from a family that took modest car trips from Seattle, Washington, to Seaside, Oregon, while I craved the Champs Elysée.

I was so amped to know the world that sometimes I charged out on half-price student tickets too fast, too alone, with no ripcord to pull in case of a crash landing. One day when I was stranded in Bogota and a cold terror crept up unexpectedly and sucked my breath away, I got my nails done. Not because I needed a manicure, but for the half-hour of warm contact with a motherly woman that staved off the panic which so often accompanied my youthful adventures.

Now in my forties, I travel slower, to simpler destinations. More at peace with myself, I no longer need the electronic razzmatazz of the Ginza. Now I'm thrilled to uncover small surprises in intimate places, preferably with a good friend nearby. And I no longer travel to escape myself, but perhaps if I'm lucky, a trip will afford an opportunity to get in touch.

—Jo Giese, "Notes From a Fortysomething Traveler," *Moxie Magazine*

MARIA STRESHINSKY

* * *

Mirror of the Holocaust

A museum visit revives family history
and the wounds of the past.

LIKE MANY VISITORS, I WAS NOT EAGER TO GO TO THE NEW UNITED
States Holocaust Memorial Museum in Washington, D.C.—I felt
a responsibility to go. To remember, to pay respects, to learn. To
me, the Holocaust is horrifying history, not horrifying memory.
What I know is that my parents lived through that war, and that
other relatives fought in that war. I thought the museum might
have some answers. And I had some questions.

I know little about my family on my father's side. When asked,
he talks, but in short answers. My father's parents left the Ukraine
in 1922 when Lenin opened the borders for a few years. I know
that my grandparents had many brothers and sisters. I know that
my grandparents went to Harbin, China, where my father was
born, and I know that many of his aunts and uncles relocated west,
to Europe, to Germany. I know my grandmother's maiden name,
Vaisbin, and I know there were other Streshinskys who did not
leave. But I know nothing about them.

For years there has been a nagging question in the back of my
mind, about what happened to those relatives who went to
Europe, or stayed in the Soviet Union, and why I have no family
on my father's side today.

Upon entering the museum, visitors are instructed to take a card, an identity, of a real person who lived during the Holocaust. My card said Rifka Fass, born in Ulanow, Poland, the same year my father was born in Harbin. When the Nazis ordered all of Ulanow's Jews to nearby Zaclikov, Rifka Fass managed to pose as a Polish laborer in Germany. She left soon after, and was heard from only once again. Her fate remains unknown.

With this identity card in hand, I passed through the metal doors of a cold-looking elevator. On the way to the fourth floor, where the exhibits begin, a television mounted in the elevator gave a short introduction to the museum and to the Holocaust. Stepping out onto the dark floor, I was met by a wall-sized photograph of rows of Jews killed in a concentration camp, graphic and disturbing. An uncomfortable silence settled over the museum visitors, and remained throughout the three floors of photo after photo, history lesson after history lesson.

As I circled through the floors, I learned about the Holocaust from the beginning of the rise of Hitler, through the war, Hitler's fall from power, and the liberation of the camps by the Allies. I walked through the halls of the museum reading the plaques of information as carefully as possible, but feeling I wasn't spending enough time, wasn't reading closely enough.

I walked through a train car that carried Jews to the death camps, and stared at a model of Auschwitz with thousands of small naked plaster figures lined up in a giant room, about to be gassed. I heard propaganda speeches made by key figures in the Third Reich. I watched films taken by the soldiers who liberated the camps, and wandered through a room devoted to Anne Frank's story. I learned that while our government refused to bomb the railways leading to Auschwitz, they bombed a rubber factory five miles away, and I learned that 930 Jewish refugees set sail on the *St. Louis* bound for Cuba, only to be turned away and sent back to Europe.

Each visitor to this museum is touched, even scarred, by something they see here. While watching a bank of television screens simultaneously showing the U.S. Army liberating Dachau, the

British Army liberating Bergen Belsen, and the Soviet Army liberating Majdanak and Auschwitz, the woman standing next to me said, "My uncle was there with the American Army. To this day he will not talk about it. I could never ask him to come here."

Three things in the museum haunt me. The first was a room filled with shoes from the concentration camps. I leaned over the railing, looked at these shoes, and it struck me that these could be today's shoe styles. I knew then why this museum is so controversial—why the woman's uncle will not speak about his time in Germany, and why my father doesn't offer information about his family at will. It was only yesterday, and the scars are too fresh.

My second vivid memory is a hall of old photographs of families going about their daily lives before the war. The photos reach to the ceiling; there are thousands of them. I looked and wondered how many of those people are still living. As I wandered through this segment of the museum, it occurred to me that all of these photos could have come from my father's albums, which I loved to look at when I was young. They all had that darkened-around-the-edges look of photos from 50 years ago.

Now I thought: only 50 years.

The last and most startling memory I came away with is this: I walked through a glass hallway with names of villages and cities etched on the glass. A plaque explained that these were lost communities, towns, and cities whose Jewish communities were destroyed as a result of the "Final Solution." The cities were listed by country: Poland, the Soviet Union, Yugoslavia. As my gaze ran down the list of Soviet cities and towns, it froze on STRESHIN. In the name Streshinsky—my name, my father's name, my grandfather's and great-grandfather's name—sky implies "of." I stood staring at the name that must be my family village, knowing then that I didn't need that identity card I had received upon entering the museum.

On the ground floor of the Holocaust Museum, there is a large marble, rotunda-like room with candles lining the walls and an eternal flame in the middle. The sign cautions silence, while visitors light candles, say prayers. As I lit a candle, I looked up to the passage from *Deuteronomy* etched above the eternal flame: "Only guard yourself and guard your soul carefully, lest you forget the things your eyes saw, and lest these things depart your heart all the days of your life, and you shall make them known to your children, and to your children's children."

Maria Streshinsky is on the staff VIA (formerly Motorland), the magazine of the California State Automobile Association. She lives in San Francisco.

✶

I remember.

I remember a solider, a man in uniform, winter woolens, summer khakis. An airman.

I remember a number. 39238853. His serial number, the number on his military identification tag, the one he wore, always even at night, around his neck. I don't know why I remember that number. I seldom think of it. But when I do, or sometimes when I am not thinking about it at all, it is there, in my mind.

I remember letters, letters before we met, letters after he went overseas, loving, longing, despairing, anxious, funny, poetic letters.

I remember hitch-hiking from Pasadena, California to Shreveport, Louisiana. Once a crowd of happy drunks picked us up. I listened and relaxed as Hap told story after story to slow them down so they wouldn't kill us all.

I remember the GI's who called him "the Senator" and came to him for jokes, advice, stories, because he was older than they were and wiser, more experienced and funnier and one of them after all.

I remember cold winter nights in a basement room in Hastings, Nebraska, growling pipes overhead, lying in bed curled, nude, against his long, warm, sleeping body, feeling sated, treasured.

I remember trying to say goodbye, crying so hard I did not see him leave. The fear, the overwhelming fear, that I might never see him again.

I remember wisdom, helpful admonitions. "If anything should happen to me—no of course it won't—but just in case, I want to tell you something. If anything does happen you must marry again. If something happened to you I would: people like us need to be married."

I remember anxiety, apprehension. And waiting, waiting, waiting.

I remember the gray, early morning when the telegram arrived. "The Secretary of War regrets…"

I remember a cross, a grave—Grave Number 70, Row A, in the American Military Cemetery in Epinal, France.

I remember Hap.

I remember Love.

—Betty Ann Webster, "Journey of Remembrance"

BARBARA GRIZZUTI HARRISON

✳ ✳ ✳

Oh Rome!

The author reveals why her heart belongs in Italy.

I AM HAPPY HERE; WHEN I OR OTHERS HAVE BRUISED MY LIFE, I close my eyes against the hurt and think of Rome: as possibility, and hope. And I feel more related to my environment and to my circumstances in Rome than I do anywhere else on earth; I am blessed, intensely delighted, satisfied, and reconciled. The world is lovable when the world is Rome. Everything good in my nature is nourished here. My body feels safe here. When I love the space around my body, I love my body. For the rest of my life I will love Rome and think better of my life for having known Rome. Rome, rooted and ethereal, stretching from earth to heaven, casts aside so little and embraces so much—there's room for me. It is everything; it is elegant, robust, common, spectacular, vulgar, exquisite, and above all, rare. It is Gregorian chant in Sant'Anselmo on the Aventine; it is the gestures of the Trasteverini, their games—*morra*, a game my father played with ferocious patience (he taught me, too, though girls were not supposed to play; when the ancient Romans played it—they called it *micare digitis*—it was always played by two men): two men stand facing each other, and each throws out one or two or three fingers, shouting out the number of fingers he expects, in sum, to see. This game is deceptively simple; I think it is a show of manhood in which guessing—feminine intuition—secures the victory.

Rome is all things high and low. It is like God, it accommodates so much.

My friend Jane tells this story: She was dining with her lover, a Calabrian nobleman, in a little restaurant on the Campo dei Fiori, and, "Oh, wouldn't it be lovely if we could eat outside," she said, it being February, and she in love. "So in five minutes the waiter had a table outside and linen and cutlery and candles [candles being essential, in Rome, to worship and to love], and we were all alone in the Campo, dining just outside the Farnese, Michelangelo's palace; how they love a spectacle," she says; her mouth turns down. "How they love love."

"What a nice story," I say.

"The Calabrian left me," she says.

What Jane means to illustrate is not just that Italians love spectacles but that the love of a spectacle somehow compromises true feeling or masks an absence of feeling, perhaps both—in proof of which Jane gestures toward the fountain we are sitting next to (in the eighteenth century the bathtub of a princess), and to the pergola wound with grapevines overhead. We are having lunch at Otello, a trattoria in a cobblestoned courtyard on the Via della Croce, a block away from the Piazza di Spagna and its fancy shops; it is always cool here, the fountain murmurs green music all the time. Against the wall and in the basin of the fountain are pyramids (red, green, yellow, white, purple) of peppers, pears, tomatoes, grapes, cherries, eggplants, peaches, squash (their green-yellow trumpetlike flowers intact). I cannot comprehend Jane's objection to this cornucopia. It is not typical of her; and if we want a peach, the waiter will pluck one from the pyramid and dip it in the fountain and bring it to us, droplets icy, flesh warm. Nothing is lost, it is not an economy of waste...and yet the Romans are somehow taken to task for this and similar displays, how odd.... Of course, the Calabrian did leave her.

If Romans were "all surface"—as, for example, Milanesi say (but I do not believe them)—why would it matter so much? How graceful the surface is (how lovely the dance). "They prepare a face for the world to see." So do we all. They do it well. That the taxi driver who slammed on his brakes in the Piazza of Santa Maria Sopra Minerva was *acting* his feelings, there is no doubt; he was also *feeling* his feelings.

Things are always happening to Jane. Late one night she calls. On her dark street a man has approached her from behind and seized her breasts. She swings around and hits him with the remains of a watermelon she has brought home from a dinner party. As he sinks to his knees, splattered with watermelon like blood, "Oh, your blond hair," he moans, "your beautiful long blond hair."...The police have come, they are sympathetic and engaging. They will keep a watch on Jane's flat from Monday to Friday.

"What about Saturday and Sunday?"

"Oh, we don't work Saturday and Sunday," they say.

"Who does?"

"*Nessuno* [no one]."

It's just as well Romans are not perfect, one would have to give up family and children for Rome.

"It's just too much to bear," Jane says.

"What is?"

"I could never go back to Chicago again," Jane says.

Well, no.

They have seen so much, perhaps too much, they know so much, nothing shocks them. Cynicism and pragmatism are notoriously easy to confuse. Italians look facts in the face—chosen facts, of course; anyone who looked every fact in the face and gave every fact equal weight would immediately slit his wrists. To the extent to which Italians are not idealistic, it is because they believe in, or have been inculcated with, the idea of Original Sin; they look it in the face. This does not mean they do not want the world to be a better place. It means they have never shared our innocent, cloud-cuckoo-land belief in the inevitability of progress; Italians know that while public morality may be legislated, perfection of intention cannot.

Italians know they are going to die. (Americans have not quite got used to the idea.) You cannot have lived your life in Rome without getting used to the idea—without breathing in the idea—that to dust you will return. This knowledge oxygenates the blood of Romans, and it is this knowledge that animates the living dust we call flesh. The beautiful young men and women at the cafe Rosati in the Piazza del Popolo live so beautifully in the moment because they know they are *of* the moment; they are probably not, are almost certainly not, consciously considering the Four Last Things—Heaven, Hell, Death, and Judgment—but they know they are going to die.

No event in my life, except my death, can ever be greater than that first entrance into St. Peter's, the concentrated spirit of the Christianity of so many years, the great image of our Faith which is the worship of grief. I went in. I could not have gone there for the first time except alone, no, not in the company of St. Peter himself, and walked up to the Dome. There was hardly a creature there but I. There I knelt down. You know I have no art, and it was not an artistic effect it made on me—it was the effect of the presence of God.

—Florence Nightingale,
Florence Nightingale at Rome,
edited by Mary Keele

Romans are invariably more attractive than their detractors; the accused are so much less cynical than their accusers.

Still: "How cynical Italians are!" I heard this time and again in the course of a guided tour to the Catacombs of Santa Domitilla and the Basilica of San Giovanni in Laterano. In the Piazza of San Giovanni in Laterano is the Scala Santa, the staircase which is popularly supposed to be that which Christ climbed for his interview with Pontius Pilate. Our guide was quick to say these stairs are not in fact the stairs climbed by Christ. The prudent Vatican (slow to attribute miraculous properties to venerated objects) has so decreed. (This does not prevent Catholics, including Italian Catholics, from climbing those cruel steps on their knees, from which it is not to be inferred that their penance is in vain. If their pain is an offering to God, then God, it must be supposed, will scarcely reject it, as no gift is unacceptable to Him, even if it is based on a misunderstanding; so we are taught.) The Catacombs, the guide pointed out with forgivable relish, were not in fact a hiding place for early Christians; their Roman persecutors would hardly have failed to notice a mass exodus to the suburbs of Rome. The idea that Christians ritualistically met in the Catacombs derived from Metro-Goldwyn-Mayer. Well, so crestfallen were tourists—including American Catholics, including Protestants and Jews—upon having their beliefs tweaked, you'd think someone had told them that the Trinity was a fabrication of Louis B. Mayer's imagination. (One American Catholic ostentatiously crossed himself.)

Why should Catholics need to have their Catholicism shored up or jazzed up by pastel fictions? To believe in the Holy Trinity is a lot more difficult than to believe that early Christians held powwows in caves. Out of what he must have considered a noisy and bothersome curiosity, I asked the guide if he believed in the Trinity. He looked at me as if I were mad. *"Sono cattolico,"* he said: "I am Catholic." The question answered itself.

Barbara Grizzuti Harrison was born in Brooklyn. She also lived in Libya, India, and Guatemala. She was the author of numerous books, including Foreign Bodies, Unlearning the Lie: Sexism in School, Visions of Glory, *and* Italian Days *from which this story was excerpted. Ms. Harrison died in 2002.*

✳

Forget the Forum, the Colosseum, or St. Peter's. In my opinion the true symbol of Rome is the female breast. Not by chance, Rome's legendary founders, Romulus and Remus, were suckled by a mother with six teats, a she-wolf who found them nestled at the edge of the Tiber. Today, statues of the threesome adorn everything from bridges to fountains to sarcophagi. The six pendulous breasts are always prominently featured. America's founding hero chopped down a cherry tree. Rome's sucked milk.

Thus, even from ancient times, the city has been defined by the mound or the bump. First it was the seven hills so touted by Roman poets and historians. Since the Renaissance, it has been the dome, complete with nipple on top. No city anywhere can rival Rome for the sheer number of domes. From the moment Bramante, in the early 1500s worked out his scheme for the little chapel called the Tempietto, domes began to pop up around town like mushrooms in a damp field.

Now, Rome's skyline is a pattern of breast-shaped domes in any number of colors and sizes. Indeed, breasts, the prototype of the dome, are so closely linked with the Roman concept of a church that when the seventeenth-century builders of Sant'Ignazio ran short of funds, they painted on the ceiling an awe-inspiring *trompe l'oeil* dome seemingly equal to, if not surpassing, that of St. Peter's. This was the Baroque's most outrageous, but certainly not only, instance of dome envy.

Rome's horizon notwithstanding, it is difficult to walk even a block without confronting at least several pairs of bona fide breasts. Newsstands are a sure bet. The otherwise respectable *Express*, an Italian equivalent of *Time* or *Newsweek*, always, regardless of current world crises, features a bare-breasted woman, or several, on its cover. Similarly, billboards, even those adjacent to the Vatican, frequently feature this favorite cross section of the female anatomy. Last summer, the city was wallpapered with a pair of well-formed, well-bronzed breasts. THESE WON'T FADE BY CHRISTMAS, the sign said. It was, of course, an ad for photographic film.

—Libby Lubin, "European Journal," *European Travel & Life*

RUTH BOND

Granny Shoots the Rapids

A senior overcomes fear to fulfill a dream.

EVERY TIME WE VISIT FRIENDS IN ARIZONA, WE ARE DRAWN AS IF by a magnet to visit the Grand Canyon rim. To gaze down into that indescribable gash in the earth is always an overwhelming experience. It reduces one to an insignificant place in the natural world. Here we admire God's glory below us. And here also, on each visit, I have longed to take a trip down the river glimpsed so many times from above.

Rafting the Grand Canyon was a longstanding dream, but one that, at age 68, with arthritis, I was sure I would never actually live. My husband Bill's twice-operated on back ruled him out as a companion, so I resigned myself never to get to the bottom.

Then I received a call that reawakened the dream. Our youngest daughter said, "Mom, let's you and me raft the Colorado through the Grand Canyon." I answered "Let's go!"

I didn't, of course, just pack up and take off. I needed to consult Bill. I was worried that *he* would worry too much about the rigors of the trip—the nine-mile hike I'd have to make from the rim of the canyon to the river, the 100-degree-plus August heat, the camping out, the risks of being thrown from the raft, in short, the physical toll that might be exacted from the woman he had married 45 years ago. I didn't want him to be afraid.

But Bill surprised me. "Go for it," he said. "I know you can do it."

And that became the rallying cry for my adventure of a lifetime, an eight-day rafting trip on the Colorado River.

What kind of people go on a raft trip? We were a diverse group of every age and description, but all shared a passion for the beauty of what we were seeing, and an abandonment of our everyday lives that led us to connect with each other simply as fellow adventurers. We fifteen rafters from several states were a mix of singles, husband-and-wife teams, and parents-and-kids groups. We were a lawyer, a librarian, a free-lance writer, a factory owner, a technician, a young mother who needed some "away time," four college students, my daughter—

Guided adventure trips—such as white-water rafting—are particularly good for solo travelers because of the camaraderie that develops when a bunch of crazy fools flirt with death together.

—Sophia Dembling, "Going Solo is a Pleasure All by Itself," *Dallas Morning News*

and me, a retired school teacher. We were an about equal mix of men and women. And we had fun together. The worries I had before the trip about being accepted into an adventuresome crowd disappeared on Day One.

The rafting itself was the real high. We spent five to seven hours every day floating downstream from our departure point at Phantom Ranch, ending 138 miles away at Diamond Beach near Lake Mead at the end of the canyon.

But the word "floating" certainly doesn't describe our transit through the swirling, rolling rapids we encountered two, three, sometimes even four times a day. Some rapids were gentle, but others were high-riding, drenching experiences. The big rapids offered opportunity for passengers to push their limits by "riding snout"—sitting atop the front of the raft, on the end that bucks and kicks like a wild stallion. And I did it! I rode snout, holding on in elation as the snout rose above, then plunged into, the waves of the rapids.

Another highlight was camping out each night on soft sand. This was my first experience sleeping under the stars. Seldom did we sleep inside our tents because we were too anxious to watch for falling stars, to feel the cool breezes and hear the gentle sounds of the river, and to listen to the rustle or whispers of campmates nearby. My daughter and I would hold hands in the dark, watching silently until we saw four shooting stars, then with a tired, "I love you" we would close our eyes and slip off to sleep.

And the food! Breakfast and lunch included all one could wish for—fresh fruit, eggs, pancakes. Dinner was the day's *piece de resistance*, with filet mignon or stroganoff, sweet-and-sour pork, or delicious Mexican dishes. You name it, we had it complete with fresh green salad, vegetable, and dessert each night. The boatmen were gourmet cooks in an outdoor kitchen.

One day we all wore Indian war paint and acted accordingly. One evening by the campfire we sang and accompanied ourselves on kitchen instruments. Other nights we played games and told stories. By the end of the trip we had become a close-knit family. One's age and accomplishments in the outside world faded into insignificance in this atmosphere of sharing.

Although I was the oldest person in the group, I was never singled out as someone who needed help. However, on hikes up side canyons where the boulders were big, I usually found a boatman nearby to assist me with a pull or a push. I plunged into pools below waterfalls with all the others, and learned much about the canyon's evolution from a fellow who worked for the U.S. Geological Survey, other rafters, and the boatmen.

I will never forget my ride though the sometimes unnavigable Crystal Rapid. Everyone else was asked to hike over a high, rocky cliff to avid shooting this dangerous stretch of water and rock. Only three rafts, piloted by boatmen, heavy with our food and packs, would shoot Crystal. But because my arthritis made this particular climb impossible for me, I was designated as one of the seven persons to go through the lower part of the rapids in the smaller boat, which was guided not by oars like the others, but by the communal effort of paddling passengers.

I remembered Bill's "you can do it," and paddled for dear life. Emerging from the chaos of Crystal into the last eddy with a twist, rush and plunge, I heard a roar of applause and whistles and cheers from the cliff above me. To me, it was the accolade of a lifetime.

But finally, and most specially, the best part of my trip was the renewal and satisfaction of my relationship with my daughter. We shared memories, old and new ideas, experiences.

At the end of eight days in the canyon, and after a tearful parting with my daughter in Phoenix, I came home to Bill in Ohio. He tells me my midnight arrival at the Cleveland Airport was one of the funniest sights of his life. I emerged from the airplane, hair wildly askew after ten days without a "do," backpack bouncing, jeans wrinkled, tennis shoes worn, holding a victory fist above my head and shouting, "I made it! I made it!"

The other passengers probably wondered what was the big deal in surviving a Phoenix-to-Cleveland flight, but Bill knew better.

Ruth Bond taught history, government, and comparative religions for 25 years before retiring. She has been married for 53 years, has four children and four grandchildren. In her spare time she gardens and does volunteer work for her church, woman's book club, and the Stan Hywet Historical Society. She enjoys telling stories and loves to travel. She cannot type and has never used a computer.

★

Ten or fifteen years ago, normal people in their fifties, sixties, and seventies didn't go hiking in the Rocky Mountains or learn to paddle a sea kayak off the coast of New Zealand. They didn't sell their houses to buy a van and camp around Europe or stay with a family in Japan. That was for the kids. Most Americans believed that once you hit fifty, it was downhill into retirement and old age. Maybe there'd be a bus tour or two along the way, with fellow travelers shouting for the guide to turn up the microphone. But if you were a widow or had a non-traveling spouse, the only acceptable vacation was a week with Aunt Thelma or your grown children.

—Marcia Schnedler, *The Seasoned Traveler*

PAULA MCDONALD

⋆ ⋆ ⋆

Buried Treasure in Baja

There's something out there in the desert....

SECRET CAVES ON A BROODING BAJA MOUNTAINTOP. CAVES WITH a curse and buried gold. An army deserter holed up and hiding out for years with only a lonely bugle call drifting down the mountain to carry his coded signals to someone far below. A renegade on the run who died with his treasure unspent.

For almost 100 years the stories have circulated virtually unchanged. Stories about lost treasure on a haunted mountain just a few miles south of the California-Mexico border. Stories about an American army colonel who once lived and died up there with his secrets and his sins.

You may already know The Colonel. Maybe you've just never known his name.

Anyone who has ever crossed the border south of San Diego and headed down the toll road toward Rosarito will remember the two strange mountains that suddenly dominate the eastern horizon as you approach the little coastal town. In the middle of miles of flatlands, an odd pair of landmarks seem to loom up out of nowhere—mountains as different as good and evil twins. One is a friendly-looking mesa so flat it seems sheered by a machete, and perhaps the perfect, peaceful place to have a picnic if you could ever reach it. Next to it huddles a rugged, raggedy jumble of peaks, sullen-looking and hunkering down into the desert with a shape that defies some easy handle like "Camelback." A dark, unfriendly mountain that doesn't invite picnickers. *El Coronel* it is called. "The Colonel." He chose his hiding place well.

There has always been a consistency to the stories about *El Coronel*. From simple legends about the mountain being haunted and some old man who lived up there and died, to the detailed adventures of children, now grown, who explored the caves 35 years ago—and found gold! The consistency is that the locals believe the stories. And they believe The Colonel never got off his mountain with the gold.

These ongoing talks are not just typical small town gossip to be taken lightly. Solid, sensible businessmen such as 57-year-old Hugo Torres, owner of the prestigious Rosarito Beach Hotel remembers hunting owls on *El Coronel* when he was young, and remembers friends who found paper money and currency up there. Juvenal Arias, head of the Rosarito Historical Society, remembers well a cave from his childhood explorations and clearly recalls witnessing young friends as they brought out gold coins. Gonzalo Rivera, an employee at Calafia Resort, found a legend scratched on wood in one of the caves and carried it around in his pickup truck for years. And last summer, Alex Lopez, a twenty-year-old student who had been drawn to the mountain all his life, camped there overnight to meditate. When he awoke, he found a rock next to his campsite with the startling image of a skull seemingly etched on its surface. No one was surprised.

Something happened up there a long time ago. And something remains on that mountain today. Gold or a ghost. Or both.

Of course, I had to see for myself. I wanted to meet *El Coronel*—the mountain and the myth—face to face, and only one man could help me do both. The man whose ancestors had scratched the area's first ranch out of the desert dust 220 years ago and built Rosarito's first building—a stable—where a luxury resort and historic monument now stand. The man whose family was given the brooding mountain in 1863 by Porfirio Diaz, along with all the land from Ensenada to the mesa. Only this man could still tell all of the story because his great-grandfather had actually known The Colonel; his grandfather had watched him move surreptitiously from cave to cave and had listened to the sound of his lonely bugle as the notes drifted down empty canyons. One descendent was now the recipient of the legend—a man who still lives somewhere out there today and who has spent most of his life on a horse roaming that mountain.

I met Guadalupe Uvaldo Machado in Hugo Torres' hotel office. Hugo had somehow managed to arrange the meeting for me because Machado has no phone. But he showed up on time, a quiet, solid man in jeans and boots who looked like he'd be far more comfortable standing up in his stirrups, squinting for a lost steer, than sitting in a high-backed leather chair in a tycoon's modern office. It took him awhile to size me up, but finally he decided, based on some intangible, that if I had sensible shoes and could ride a horse without whining, he'd take me to the caves and tell me the story of The Colonel. I jumped at the chance.

We met at dawn in Rosarito three days later, Machado with his beat-up truck hauling horses, and me hauling along a buddy to translate and two backpacks stuffed with sandwiches and lots of water. Together we headed out of town and east up a dirt track into a land of folded hills and hawks, quickly leaving the rusted cars, the last of the power lines, and the whole 20th century behind.

Machado started the story as we unloaded the horses in the late dawn mist, part-way up the mountain—as far as the truck could go. Seven hours later, still in the saddle on the toughest ride of my life, I was convinced: The Colonel had been real and I was a believer in buried gold.

Machado's grandfather had been a child in the late 1800s when The Colonel first appeared. He was an American army ordnance officer who had deserted with the army's money. Somehow he found his way to that mountain, a three-day horseback ride from San Diego along the old Spanish trail, *El Camino Real*—the Royal Road of trade that once ran all the way from the tip of Baja to San

Francisco to avoid the Pacific's coastal pirates. In those days the trail swung inland at a big rock south of Rosarito, ran along the base of *El Coronel*, then past the mesa, and on up to San Diego.

Perhaps The Colonel chose the mountain because he could see the caves from *El Camino Real* just as you can see them from the toll road today if you know where to look and when. He was on the run, heading south into the safety of Mexico, and he would have had to ride that way. Near KM 39, where the cave-pocked, west face of *El Coronel* looms closest to today's road, he must have been able to see the dark splotches on the side of the mountain. And a tough renegade, looking for a spot to hide out, would have realized the caves offered the perfect place.

The area was isolated. Only the few scattered ranches, clustered around where Rosarito would someday be, broke the empty coast-line between San Diego and Ensenada, the territory's primitive capital. And the mountain was ideal. Virtually inaccessible and in-finitely defensible. Like Cochise's stronghold, the highest caves are built into sheer cliffsides. Standing in the mouth of one, I could see all the way to the coast when the fog lifted that day, and everything in between. There would be no sneaking up on *El Coronel*.

With his eyes fixed steadily on those caves that first time, he must have found the rugged ride getting there reassuring. It terri-fied me—and my translator, a tough cookie himself.

There is no trail to The Colonel's caves. No easy just-head-east path. Without Machado's sure-footed horses, raised there, we would never have made it. And, at times, the way seemed almost impossible, even for them. Hours of tacking back and forth across skittering rock slides too steep to climb—or descend—directly. Miles of shoulder-high chaparral and mesquite tearing at the horses and at us. Breathless transverses across crater rims that had fallen away on both sides, leaving only a foot-wide path of shale unstable enough to make a Grand Canyon mule shudder.

The horses had a hard time of it. Only a riderless colt, follow-ing fearlessly after its reluctant mother, seemed to scramble up and down the endlessly unfolding canyons without hesitating. The other three horses had to be forced, continually. Possibly The

Colonel had to force his horse, too. And he probably smiled. No one was going to follow easily.

It took hours to reach the first cave. Hours of constantly changing terrain and aching thighs that had long since turned to agony from alternately using them to urge on the balking horses or to hang on for dear life whenever they finally decided to head straight up or straight down the next challenge. Only Machado seemed implacable. He'd been this way before, and I blessed him for stopping to rest the horses often so that I could unclench my legs. "They'll drop like stones if you push them too hard on this mountain," he said, and, indeed, my horse did on the return ride when I stopped too long to stare at a single lonely grave out there in the middle of nowhere. He just flopped down on the grave with me still in the saddle.

Unburdened, all three horses had collapsed earlier on the final small plateau below the peak while Machado and I scrambled up to the last cave on foot. This one was almost invisible from below. But pulling our way up, the opening suddenly appeared, hidden behind thick brush. A rough, century-old mesquite fence still guarded the entrance, and the charred remains of countless fires were still sheltered farther back. But nothing else. How had he found this place originally? And why had The Colonel used so many?

Machado's grandfather had said The Colonel moved from cave to cave, guarding them all. And each of the caves he occupied was well-hidden. The biggest, which we never reached that day, had only been discovered years later when a storm broke off a tree shielding its entrance. How many more were till undiscovered? No one ever approached too close when The Colonel was alive, but they all knew he had gold. Buried and moved and moved again. It trickled down the mountain bit by bit.

The bugle was used to call its carrier, Machado's great-grandfather. Whenever The Colonel trumpeted his message across the canyons to the mesa, Juan Machado appeared a day later. And ingots went to Ensenada, a few at a time. Was he cashing in slowly, quietly, so as not to attract attention? But what went wrong? He was there for years and then, suddenly, he was gone?

Some say he died. Some say he was killed. No one says he left. Time simply ran out on him and it's not hard to imagine how. That bleak, inhospitable mountain must have been a raging torrent of water in the winter rains, a baking, waterless hell in the dry season. If our horses went for a day without water, how far did The Colonel have to go? And what did he eat? Machado says there are deer, wildcats, and rabbits up there, but my eyes saw only lizards and bones that day. It couldn't have been easy.

Maybe the mountain just finally won. A foothold finally faltered. A rock or rim gave way and he was gone. Or broken. Or sick somewhere. And alone.

I sat on the rim of his cave late that afternoon, looking out over one of the most beautiful views in Baja. From the top of *El Colonel* you can see forever. But, God, it's lonely! Did he curse his treasure as he died?

Somehow, it simply ended. He never came down and neither did the gold. A mystery. As big a mystery as Guadalupe Machado is, perhaps. Out on the ledge, while he emptied the sand and stones out of his boots that day, I asked why he hadn't gotten himself a metal detector and just dug up the damn mountain. He smiled and shook his head very slowly, as though he were speaking to a child.

This is what he said, exactly: "I am a poor Mexican. I have a good horse, my cattle, good boots, a good hat, warm clothes, a good woman, and my children have food. What more do I need? Digging gold is the kind of thing *gringos* do."

He was serious. And he's right. We are different. It's hard for *gringos* to just let things lie. We didn't find any gold that day—we were looking for legends instead—but someone will.

As I sat there, letting the ashes from The Colonel's fires sift through my fingers, I looked at Machado, and wondered who it would be. He was still smiling. The last few grains of soot and sand slipped out of my hands and we stood up to head back. Empty-handed.

This time.

Paula McDonald is an award-winning travel writer and bestselling author

who lives in Mexico. She writes a regular column on Mexico for California
magazines and newspapers. She plans to go back to the mountain.

✷

I came to Mexico and fell in love.

I didn't fall in love with the museum curator who pursues me like a treasured artifact. Nor with the handsome policeman with bristling black mustache who wants to drive me to the beach on his official motorcycle.

No, the one who has captured my heart is Tito Baeza de Ramero, the 49-year-old mother of a large family who took me into her home two months ago as a paying guest. She is a beautiful *prieta*—dark skinned with thick black hair and silver streaks twinkling at her temples. She has laughing eyes and a smile made crooked by the loss of a few teeth on one side.

Doña Tito announces to her friends and relatives that she wants to adopt me, which pleases me greatly. She fixes coffee for both of us in the mornings, when the family has gone off to work and school. We talk about life and the day ahead. She includes in every declaration of future plans the conditional phrase, "if God is willing." "If God is willing, I'll make fish stew for lunch." Or, "We'll go to the beach at Puerto Escondido on Sunday, if God wants it."

Each time I leave the house, she solemnly blesses me, saying, *"que le vaya bien."* When I return home, she quizzes me immediately, "Where have you been?"

"Out for a walk, to visit Yuyi."

"What did you eat?"

"Only a cup of coffee."

"Ah good, I'm saving something special for you."

—Thalia Zepatos, A Journey of One's Own: Uncommon Advice
for the Independent Woman Traveler

JANET FULLWOOD

⋆ * ⋆

Baby on Board

Traveling cross-country by car with a new baby,
the author learns by trial and error.

FIRST, THE DIAPER. THEN THE LONG UNDERWEAR, THE LIGHT-weight sleeper, the blanket sleeper, the bunting, the hat, the mittens. Come on, Willie, don't cry. See the stars? See the tent? This is camping. It's fun!

And it was—despite the fact that our infant son won't remember a thing about Monument Valley, the Grand Canyon, Las Vegas, New Orleans, and other places that unfurled on our 4,077-mile cross-country trip last October. But his father and I will. We'd do it again in a minute. And we cringe to think that the nay-sayers almost talked us into staying home.

"You're awfully brave," friends with children said, shaking their heads in gestures that implied some awful, secret wisdom, when we mentioned the proposed trip with our three-month-old. "What if he gets sick? What if the car breaks down in the middle of nowhere? What if it's too cold for him at night? What if his eardrums pop in the mountains? What if he gets dehydrated in the desert? What if something happens *to you*?"

There was no end to the "what ifs" that clouded my mind as I, with mere weeks of motherhood under my belt, contemplated driving coast-to-coast with a baby on board. But there was a big carrot on the end of the stick: we were in the market for a car, and my mother-in-law had made us a deal on her good-as-new old one that we couldn't refuse. The catch: we'd have to come from Sacramento, California to Tampa, Florida to get it.

The good news was that we had the entire month of October at our disposal. We could take our time, smell the roses, pull over and minister to our little one's needs whenever he fussed or got hungry. Little Will, we figured, would be happy wherever he was, just so his parents were near.

And so, shipping camping gear ahead (to keep expenses down, we planned to tent it every other night), we flew to Florida, baby and car seat in tow. A week later, with an ice chest wedged behind the driver's seat and a trunk so full it had to be sat on before it would close, we headed north on U.S. 19, up the flat west coast of the Sunshine State.

In preparing for this trip, I thought that I had thought of everything. We had diapers aplenty, a pallet for the baby to sleep on in motel rooms or the tent, a quilt to spread on the ground during rest stops, a selection of toys, a bucket for washing soiled clothes, a collapsible stroller, the pediatrician's phone number, the insurance card. (Since the baby was being breast-fed, we didn't have to bother with formula or baby food.) Yet, we hadn't been underway half an hour before Will, who immediately had fallen asleep in his rear-facing car seat, woke up and began to fret. From my position in the front seat, he could not be consoled.

Now reality set in. How had I failed to anticipate that a three-month-old child might not be happy staring backward hour after hour, day after day, while his parents sat contentedly up front, watching the world go by? Boredom, up until now, had not entered into our little one's life.

Moving Mom to the back seat, next to the baby, made him happy, but not me. Was I condemned to ride across the country in cramped quarters, shaking a rattle and cooing incessantly to keep our little one entertained? California suddenly seemed a long, long way away.

Reprieve came later, when we discovered that the infant car

seat in which Will was confined would fit between my husband and me in the front seat of our midsize car. To give the driver enough elbow room, though, the person riding shotgun had to sit lopsided, squinched over on one haunch, right thigh hard against the door. The upside to this uncomfortable positioning was that we could interact constantly with the baby, who clearly enjoyed looking up into our faces as much as we enjoyed looking down into his.

So travel with children is possible, but why bother? Well if travelling is one of your major pleasures in life, why stop? Children can increase the hassles in travel, but they also make it even more fun. Tony and I have taken Tashi and Kieran to places we had visited before, and have found that it is a new experience with them in tow. We meet more local people: parenthood is universal so we immediately have something in common with most people we meet. The experience is fascinating for us and the children enjoy it and benefit immensely from meeting other people and playing with their children.

—Maureen Wheeler, *Travels with Children - a travel survival kit*

Our route across America, determined by whim on a day-by-day basis, took us through territory that, for the most part, neither my husband, Daryl, nor I had explored. Forgoing the interstates for more interesting secondary highways, we hugged the Gulf Coast from Florida to Texas, angled up across Texas to northern New Mexico, moseyed from Santa Fe to the Grand Canyon, tooled up to Zion National Park and down to Las Vegas, then through Death Valley and up the backside of the Sierra to Yosemite National Park and home. Some nights were spent in motels, and some with friends or family. The most memorable ones, however, came when we pitched our tent.

The first night out, we paid $19 for a waterfront campsite at St. Andrews State Recreation Area, on the Florida panhandle coast. The steep price (never have I paid more to camp) proved worth it, if only for the opportunity to set up our campstove and sauté some fresh jumbo shrimp which we had picked up along the way. And the beach was superb, the sand sugar-fine, with water clear as glass and a fishing pier where anglers were seeing lots of action.

Little Will, who spent the evening perched on the picnic table in his carseat or playing on a quilt on the ground, took to the camping life like an old pro. Well, almost like an old pro. When he awoke in the night and had difficulty getting back to sleep in strange surroundings, I took him into my sleeping bag, where each of us awakened the other every time either of us moved. None of us got much sleep that night. But for a first time out, we did fine.

My husband and I had to admit to a feeling of pride as, at each place we camped, people came out of the woodwork to talk with us about traveling and camping with a baby. In Florida, a young man fishing with his father was visibly relieved to hear all was going well. "My wife and I are expecting a baby next month," he said, "and I was thinking that camping was out, at least for a couple of years." At our campsite in Palo Duro State Park, Texas, where a cold front dropped nighttime temperatures below freezing, a retired couple from Mississippi chucked Will's bundled-up chin and lavished us with praises—only to lament in the next breath about their daughter, whom they said would hardly take her six-month-old son out of the house. At Monument Valley, Arizona, and again at Yosemite, we heard similar refrains. And while we did meet and see other families camping with kids young enough to be carted around in backpacks or strollers, we never encountered another infant.

Not that all was hunky-dory as America unfurled, state by state, east to west, beneath our wheels. Some days Will slept a lot and was the picture of cooing baby happiness when awake. But other days he fussed incessantly, and I thought I would go mad if I had to sing another song or shake another ring of plastic keys to keep the tears and the wails at bay. We pulled over and took time out when it got too bad, but there were occasions, I guiltily admit, when I took the baby out of his safety seat and held or nursed him in the moving car.

And then there was the matter of fatigue. Daryl and I had planned to take turns driving. But it was I, not he, who had to get up several times each night to put the little one to my breast. As a result of continual sleep deprivation, my energy was sapped by early afternoon and it was all I could do to stay awake behind the wheel. In total, I conducted the chariot over only about 200 of the 4,077 miles logged.

From my passive position in the passenger seat, where I alternated looking out the window, at the baby, and at a lapful of maps, America flipped by in colorful little snippets. There were the tired towns of the Deep South, graceful antebellum homes juxtaposed against faceless strip shopping centers which seemed to be dripping with ennui. There was historic Fort Morgan, Alabama where our stroller bogged down in the sand, forever gumming up the wheels, as we waited for the ferry across Mobile Bay. There were the road signs advertising gumbo and *boudin* in southeastern Louisiana and 24-hour self-service earthworms in Texas. There were the two nights we spent sleeping on the floor of a friend's French Quarter apartment in New Orleans, with the sultry notes of a saxophone serenading us from the nightclub below. And then the musty motel room in Lake Charles, Louisiana, and a four-day break at my par-

With liftoff, Stephanie, our three-year-old, had gum to equalize the pressure in her ears. Nicolas, our one-year-old, of course, had my poor breast again. Steve, my husband, was reading. Once the seat belt light went out, squirmy boy and I were off. He decided that he needed to explore the jet. Up and down the aisles we went.

On the first few passes, our fellow passengers smiled and made sweet comments to him. The looks became less agreeable when he began wailing when I wouldn't let him handle someone's under-the-seat baggage, their shoes, or drinks. As the hours passed and we traversed the aisles, dodging passengers, flight attendants, and their carts, I realized this was true life travel with kids. How many of us have had the opportunity to walk across America in a 747?

—Nancy Saarman, "Walking Across America by Plane"

ents' house in Fort Worth, Texas, where Will fell happily into loving arms.

As anyone who has driven across Texas knows, the Lone Star State seems to drone on, monotonously, for what seems like forever. But take the back roads and you get a different, and much more interesting, perspective. The cotton harvest was in progress on the high plains when we drove through, and fluffy white bolls littered the roadsides. I picked one up for Will's baby book—an unlikely souvenir, but one that, for his parents, will vividly recall the day we drove through Turkey, Quitaque, and Claytonville.

Somewhere near the Texas-New Mexico border, it's impossible to say where, the landscape undergoes a subtle change and you know you have entered The West. Suddenly, the land seems bigger, the people smaller, the settlements scruffier around the edges. In northern New Mexico we were charmed by adobe architecture and sagebrush-mottled landscape, and astonished by the red wasteland that composes most of the enormous Navajo Indian Reservation which takes the better part of a day, at highway speeds, to drive across.

We camped one night on the reservation, at Monument Valley, where huge sandstone monoliths familiar from a lifetime of Western movies rear up from the red desert floor. Our campsite, on a promontory overlooking the formations known as the Mittens, afforded an unforgettable sunrise view. Will, who by now had grown accustomed to the camping life, snuggled with his parents as we watched the dramatic landscape outside the tent flaps turn from gray to purple to red.

The desert, I mused as we drove endless hours across it, was all about colors and life and death. Las Vegas, with its billboard promises of cheap lobster dinners, lured us as much for hot showers as anything else, but one night in its surreal stew of bright lights and milling people was enough. Death Valley was awesome—and blisteringly hot—and the climb out of the depression was almost too much for our laboring car. We drove north on U.S. 395 through Marlboro Country, turned west, entered Yosemite

National Park, and dropped down into Yosemite Valley just hours before the first snowfall of the season closed Tioga Pass, over which we had just driven.

Little Will slept most of the day, missing some of the best scenery of the trip, but enabling us to make good time. Halloween day at Yosemite—our last stop before home—was bright, crisp, magical, frozen in time. I hugged my son, smelled his sweet smell mingled with the smells of the wild, and committed the moment to memory.

Being with our son 24 hours a day was, I thought, like watching him through a time-lapse camera. In the month we were gone, he seemed to change from infant to child. Back in Florida, at fourteen weeks of age, Will was still dropping every rattle or object we inserted into his clenched fist. By Arizona, at age seventeen weeks, he was shaking the rattle vigorously—even if he did miss now and then and hit himself in the head.

Since Will was not yet able to creep or crawl, taking him into restaurants and other public places was no problem. If we timed it right, he would fall asleep in his carseat, which doubled as a tabletop infant chair, as we ate. Nor, with a baby this young, did we have to curtail outdoor activities. At the Grand Canyon, our little one hiked contentedly with us all day, snugly ensconced in a fabric "front pack," where he could doze even as we walked. At Zion National Park, he rode on my husband's shoulders for a good two miles. In Death Valley and again at Yosemite, he looked out wide-eyed at scenery that also enthralled his parents, and never made a peep.

After having my child, I realized that women are superior to men. But I don't see how women could go through this—carrying a baby, nurturing it and being responsible for its formation—and not understand that we are the most powerful people in the universe.

—Sister Souljah,
Arizona Republic

One day, his father and I know, little Will will grow up and want to go back to the places we visited on our cross-country trip. I can just hear him now, telling me that seeing the Grand Canyon at three months of age doesn't count. Probably he'll ask us over and over again to tell about the time he got kicked out of the Stardust casino in Las Vegas for being under age, or about how he came to be in fourteen states before he was four months old.

What I'll remember most about the trip is how I didn't want it to end, how I wished we could just keep on going, driving from sunset to sunset with our little one between us, savoring this special time as a family.

Janet Fullwood, a mother of two boys who never slow down, looks back on this time and can't believe life ever was so simple. Besides being Mom, Janet is the travel editor at the Sacramento Bee *and was published in the anthology,* I Should Have Stayed Home: The Worst Trips of Great Writers.

★

I know flying to Europe
sitting in the airport, waiting to line up
hearing loud speakers screaming
"paging Jeffrey Hanson"
in the bathroom, coming out of your booth
stewardesses powdering noses.

I know flying to Europe
shoving through the isle
heading for third class
oh, the smell of that airplane
smells like bad butter
people stomping, hurts my ears,
sounds like herds of elephants,
engines roaring, rattling cold windows,
shaking brains.

I know flying to Europe
walking to the bathroom, vacant
feeling like a sardine,
suddenly, an air pocket,
gripping handle
green whirlpool flushing.

I know flying to Europe
watching Ren and Stimpy
repeat itself, tiny TV
drinking purple soda,
reaching for the barf bag,
purple.

I know flying to Europe.

—Anna O'Reilly, Age 10, "I Know Flying to Europe"

* * *

Rainforest Symphony

*An all-women's hike through the Amazon rainforest
with two barefoot professors.*

*"Para bailar la bamba
Para bailar la bamba
Se necessita una poca de gracia…"*

HOW PERFECT IT WAS: DANCING TO AN OLD FAVORITE SONG PLAYED by new friends: Moises on guitar, Segundo on spoons, Juan on metal flashlight, and Jorge on bar, concocting superb pisco sours deep in the Amazon rainforest. The homegrown band, our jungle guides by day, had come together this night to provide the entertainment for a serendipitous celebration—the birthdays of two of fifteen women brought together for a two-week experience of the Peruvian Amazon.

The party, halfway into our trip, was a surprise for us all. The cake was a beauty, even if the cake pan was the tin from which the capybara, the largest (and cutest) member of the rodent family and temporary camp pet, was served. The birthday gifts were presented by Juan Antolin, our multilingual Indian guide/storyteller/teacher/artist, who had split open a calabasa gourd, cleaned and polished each half until smooth, then painstakingly carved an appropriate design for each birthday celebrant: for Laura, 32, a bird we had seen that morning, the *hoatzin*, which

Capybara

187

is linked to the prehistoric archaeopteryx; for Jayne, 33, a pink freshwater dolphin, with which she had swum the day before. Their names, the date, and Juan's signature also were engraved, making it a souvenir of a birthday they'd never forget.

A diverse group we were—women aged 27 to 67, from both East and West Coasts. We were a college professor, auto mechanic, social worker, chef, librarian, secretary, rancher, writer, and several artists. Six were grandmothers, active and enthusiastic, who set an inspiring example of "aging" for the rest of us. Several were avid birders, others had never hiked nor camped before!

Yet hike we all did, through the rainforest behind Carlos, Juan, or Moises, our "barefoot professors." From them we began to learn not only to recognize countless medicinal and food plants, bird and animal sounds, but to move quietly, carefully, and efficiently with our senses open and our hands touching nothing. On our first morning hike, Juan showed us a tree hosting millions of tangarana ants, whose bites are so painful they have been used by the natives to torture unfaithful spouses. We also saw trees with sharp, black, sea urchin-like spines. Even after those two lessons deeply imprinted on our consciousness, it was difficult to break the habit of using hands for balance as we walked trails which were sometimes narrow and muddy.

Yet, the hiking was neither ominous nor difficult. We'd break into small groups according to how far we wanted to go: an hour or two, perhaps half a day. The pace was slow, the better to delight in a fleeting encounter with a neon blue Morpho butterfly alighting on a trailside leaf, or a bright red flowering bromeliad emerging from the forest of multitudinous greens. As we honed our microscopic vision, we tuned into the tiny world of the industrious leaf-cutting ants. Marching in columns with their flags of cut leaves, they cleared a path to the nest they were building—a mile away and as large as a garage!

This was the rainforest we'd all read so much about, fast disappearing in Brazil, more slowly, if inexorably, here in Peru. To experience its wondrous fecundity with all our senses was the reason most of us had flown from Miami to Iquitos, stayed overnight at a city hotel in that once-booming rubber capital, then made the dreamlike ten-hour journey upriver to a rustic lodge we'd call home for the next twelve days.

Our arrival at camp was illuminated by a full moon. It shone on the log pathways that had led us up from the river, beneath African tulip, mango and guava trees, past the round screened-in dining and neighboring hammock rooms, to our *tambos*. Each of these native-style thatch-roofed cabins, built on stilts to accommodate the rise and fall of the river, would house four of us in two semi-enclosed rooms. Beds were single mattresses on top of wooden platforms enclosed in mosquito netting.

Dinner awaited us as it would every night with slight variation: moist tender white fish straight from our Yarapa tributary or stewed chicken with rice or boiled potatoes, fried yucca—a staple of the region from the manioc plant, fried bananas, and the freshest salads of sliced cucumbers, beets, and carrots dressed in lime juice. Twice, after successful fishing trips, we ate the piranha we caught—small, fried and defenseless; tastier was the dorado, and most succulent of all, the arapaima, known in the region as *paiche*, the Amazon's largest fish, weighing up to 400 pounds.

Lit at night by gas lanterns, the dining room served as our social center: from morning Nescafé to evenings over tall bottles of Cristal beer, talking, playing cards, poring over the small but vital library of books on the natural history and wildlife of the region. On many nights a softly strummed guitar accompanied passionate, haunting Latin American folk music played by Alberto Flores, from Leticia, on the Colombian border, or Marie Yvonne, born into a tribe of Paraguayan Indians 58 years ago and adopted as a baby by a French professor. Some of us would stay up late, singing along with the songs we knew; then we'd fill our canteens from the large bottle of purified water and head to bed.

We began to know the lowland jungle that surrounded us in a variety of ways. When we explored its interior on foot, walking beneath the tree canopy which deeply shaded and pleasantly cooled our steamy path, I felt like a tiny Alice in a Wonderland of towering trees, muscular roots, and nests the size of soccer balls.

The liana vines that link the forest into a virtual maze were strong and sturdy enough for us all to swing out our Tarzan fantasies. And when we were quiet and lucky enough, from time to time we watched the real jungle gymnastics of spider or howler monkeys. We also learned survival skills: how to drink from the water vine that traps fresh rainwater in its spongy cells; how to build a *tambo* or a backpack with palm leaves; and how to recognize some of the jungle fruits, such as the aquaje palm which the natives use as a "female hormone." The taste of white liquid oozing out of a small machete-cut Carlos etched in a tree was immediately identifiable as milk of magnesia.

More often the forest was a passing green wall lining the banks of our river highway, the Yarapa. This tributary branches from the mighty Amazon close to where it is formed from the merging headwaters of the Ucayali and Marañon Rivers. Daily we would pile into two simple outboard-powered wooden boats—about twelve of us per boat—for outings I grew to love all the more as my bottom got accustomed to the hard wooden thwarts. Each excursion—to a neighboring village or to a lake to swim with the pink dolphins or to the trailhead of a hike to an early morning convocation of hundreds of brilliant blue-and-gold macaws—was another step in piercing the mystery of the green wall. For we began to recognize the bare limbs of the kapok tree silhouetted against the sky; and to search the upper branches of the cercropia trees for the three-toed sloth with its mystical Mona Lisa smile; and to watch for a hanging orapendula nest or a tiger heron perched quietly in the early dawn light. Once, our boatman, Segundo, spotted a glistening yellow-and-grey fifteen-foot anaconda coiled asleep on the riverbank and brought our boat a few feet away so we could watch it in safety.

Wherever we went, animal and bird watching became the focus; yet, while the animals were ever elusive, we were always rewarded with the spectacle of brilliantly plumaged birds. Most common were the long slender yellow-billed herons that fluttered noisily from their riverside perch at the approach of our boat; the ring-and-belted kingfishers diving for fish; and the groups of parrots and parakeets that squawked back and forth across the river.

Carlos was masterful at identifying them all by their calls, habits, and habitats, and at guiding our naked or binoculared eyes to the right branch of the right tree. During one optional 5 a.m. birding trip, he began by directing his flashlight at the early birds in the pre-dawn darkness. As the rainforest began to blush with the mauves of dawn and fill with the sounds of a world awakening, he softly called to them. By the time the light blazed golden, we had disembarked and followed him along a trail to intrude upon a sand bittern bathing in a marsh and three silver-beaked tanagers shaking themselves dry. That morning we identified 45 different species before returning ravenous to camp for breakfast. After eating, we excitedly located each of these in an oversized copy of *Birds of Venezuela* in the camp library.

But we still find the world astounding, we can't get enough of it; even as it shrivels, even as its many lights flicker and are extinguished (the tigers, the leopard frogs, the plunging dolphin flukes), by us, we gaze and gaze. Where do you draw the line, between love and greed? We never did know, we always wanted more. We want to take it all in, for one last time, we want to eat the world with our eyes.

Better than the mouth, my darling. Better than the mouth.

—Margaret Atwood,
Good Bones and Simple Murders

Since it was late July, well into the dry season, the rivers were getting lower each day, so plotting a route was never certain. There were times we were slowed down on small channels choked with lovely purple water hyacinths, amongst which jumped small striped yellow-and-black angelfish. At such times, Segundo would quickly cut off the engine, pick up his machete, and help Juan or Moises hack a pathway as skillfully as they did inside the rainforest. Early one morning, en route to see the macaws, we hit a "traffic jam" on the tributary. Vegetation-choked and obscured by low-lying branches, the narrow waterway could only handle one boat at a time, which caused a lineup of five small dugout canoes, their fisherman silent and patient.

Carlos' 70-year-old mother accompanied us on many outings, buying their catch from passing fishermen and selling or trading her herbal medicines to the river dwellers (*riberenos*) scattered in small villages along the way. Lithe and strong, the Señora would disembark and scamper up the steep, often muddy river bank, to return with a basketful of food and bottles of mysterious potions. According to Carlos, she is one of the most sought-after healers in Iquitos, drawing wealthy clients from as far away as Lima. One night she let us apply a thick yellow liquid from one of her bottles to soothe our mosquito bites. She treated a number of us for ailments ranging from fever to indigestion and showed us a plant resin used to purify the blood, the leaves of which are used for childbirth and nursing.

We may never use the healing or jungle survival skills learned in the Amazon, but life for most of us has changed. To inhabit, even for a moment, a world in which macaws and monkeys and Morphos live wild and free is to affirm the majesty of life, even as we must be haunted by the specter of its destruction.

An artist in our group captured the Amazon's vitality in a painting she gave me. The painting will always link me back to those July days when life was stripped to the basics, and clarity of thought and sensory awareness were at a peak. Her painting depicts the magic of the nights we motored upriver, when we would turn off the engine and drift for an hour, perhaps an eternity. Under a sky ablaze with more stars than we'd ever seen before, illuminating the river with their reflection, we would listen to the jungle symphony of tree frogs, howler monkeys, and the plaintive cry of the *ayaymama* bird, and contemplate our own place in the universe.

Still contemplating her place in the universe, Carol Canter finds clarity harder to obtain in Oakland, California, where she lives, than in the Peruvian Amazon, to which she longs to return.

★

Four nights before this I was sleeping on the ground when I was awakened by something that seemed to be pulled over me.... I woke, glanced down, and was horrified to see a snake. I had handled snakes at the Cairo zoo, but that was one thing and this was another. A snake crawling over one at nighttime is a clear and not a pleasant proposition. I grabbed it just below the head, crawled out of my (mosquito) net, and walked about fifty yards to a rock where I smashed its head. I was afraid I should cause too great a commotion if I fired. I had always in mind the Indians might desert me and take the canoes, especially after Vlhesek's death. They were very superstitious.

Two of the men woke up and I asked for my medicine chest. The wretched thing had bitten me below the knee the moment I had stretched out my hand for it. I didn't know whether it was poisonous or not, but the beast had a flat head and, as I know some of that kind are poisonous, I took no chances. With my scalpel I cut across the bite and pushed in two halves of a tablet of permanganate of potash. I wasn't happy for a little time, and though trying hard not to find myself panicking, having searched through my baggage, I eventually found a mirror; I hadn't used one for months. I examined my face carefully to see if I was going black or grey or had a queer colour on my lips. Except I seemed a great deal thinner, with big dark rings under my eyes, nothing seemed to be amiss—foam at the mouth was lacking and all my other imaginative ideas. I decided on coffee, a walk and sleep, and if I was going to die, it was a fine spot for it, and I was at peace with the world—so anyway there was nothing to worry about.

—Violet Cressy-Marcks, *Up the Amazon* (1932)

* * *

A Spree in Tennessee

The Ladies' Discoursive and Digestive Society
hits the outlet mall.

WORLD PEACE WAS IMPORTANT, AND THE ECONOMY CERTAINLY A concern. But the issue of the moment was clear: would my lingerie hold out until I could hit Pigeon Forge?

It's a question that comes up late every summer, as friends and I plan our annual purchasing pilgrimage to eastern Tennessee. It's not that I couldn't buy undergarments beyond the borders of the Volunteer State, but somehow the tradition has become so deeply ingrained that it just feels wrong to belly up to a Bali counter anywhere other than this most overt mecca of outlet malls.

And this fall, the excitement would be multiplied again and again, as twelve good friends, and strong-hearted shoppers, booked a cliffside chalet in the mountains of Gatlinburg and revved up their credit cards.

Traveling in October, we billed our weekend excursion as a Christmas shopping trip dedicated selflessly to our families, friends, and loved ones. Any group that calls itself the Ladies' Discoursive and Digestive Society knows more than a bit about euphemisms.

Yes, the loosely knit, genteel group dedicated to talking and eating—no dues, no rules, no worries—would head south for a spiritual retreat of mark-downs, close-outs, and rack-rattling clearances. Our little LDDS caravan of bachelorette two-seaters, mom's soccer van, and an executive Volvo would roll from the Ohio River to the Smoky Mountains, fueled by a bottomless fount of diet soda, dainty snacks on the quarter hour, and a *hajji's* enthralled vision of discounts to come.

The Ladies' operational headquarters? A rental chalet burrowed into a Smoky Mountain hillside, its two-story glass face afire with autumn sun. Perched just above the frost line, we looked out to bare limbs dipped in Waterford.

But, alas, no Lady can eat scenery, and dainty nibbling is indeed part of the group's pledged mission. Nothing coarse, nothing vulgar, to be sure, just delicate morsels of cake, cookie, chip, and chocolate—for protein—available around the clock. Yes, the chalet's oak table, boarding-house broad, seemed up to our array, and its refrigerator cold enough for the LDDS waters of life, diet soda and chablis.

Soon settled with a tidbit and a toast, it was time for mission-eve strategy. No shopper who wanted to see her little chalet again dared roll down the mountain to Pigeon Forge's legendary strip without a vetted plan.

Some of the Ladies were old bargain pros, knowing that one side of Pigeon Forge's central Parkway held all the nuts and bolts of life—Corning/Revere, Black & Decker, Oneida under one red roof—while a dueling green roof on the opposite side of the street sheltered all the luxurious fun—Liz Claiborne, Harve Benard, and Anne Klein in a glitzy designer row.

The veterans planned to sprint to the red-roofed, practical Factory Merchants Outlets mall in the morning, get their chores over with, and leave the entire afternoon free for wallowing up to their elbows in Claiborne, Klein, Barbizon, J.G. Hook, and Stone Mountain bags, lined up like confectioneries in the green-topped Tanger Factory Outlet Center.

The novices, on the other hand, needed to set their own targets and pace amidst the daunting bounty—180 outlet stores in a tourist town of 3,200. Eager to learn, they rifled through brochures and quizzed the old masters on the eve of the initial attack.

This Gitano shop—was it anywhere near the Nike outlet? Did we think the Bugle Boy outlet would have XL sweaters for her husband, large shirts for her brother, and boys' pants for her son? Would the Palm Beach store be better in the morning, or should they scout out J. Crew first?

Could we advise, oh wise ones, on the current status of merchandise? Was it all last season's, the skirts too short when they should have been long, the sheets too chintz when they should have been striped? Or were the bargains so terrific that it wouldn't matter if they were selling love beads and bell bottoms?

Well, we paused sagely. You needed to be a savvy shopper. Some of the clearance racks were sagging hopelessly with pitiful pups, too homely to find closet space with even the most charitable shopper. Many others were tagged about what you'd pay at home, and Tennessee's extra 2.5 percent sales tax left you with a burden instead of a bargain.

But others were true treasures, worth every inch on the closet rod, and every cent on the monthly bill. Veteran shopper Janet spoke glowingly of her white glazed flowerpots, a steal at Dansk. To this day, they still hold the lush geraniums she stair-steps from her walk to her porch.

I reminisced about a discouraging weekend expedition, searching in vain for business suits and silk blouses. Then, just as Janet and I were ready to head out of town, laden with nothing more hedonistic than sheets, towels and a Black & Decker mini-mincer, we popped into the green-topped Tanger Mall for one last troll. There, beneath the faithful Evan-Picone sign, was my mother lode.

That year's coordinated silk suits and blouses on their third mark-down. How had I ever doubted?

Why not a sweater to go with that, Janet suggested, and a pair of pants to stretch the outfit? Sure, why not, it was all on sale.

Then, there was just time for a quick look into a little shirt and sweater shop just down the mall. There, lining the wall, in shades from plum to bronze, was the ultimate quarry. Silk blouses, usually stitched and labeled for big-time department stores, were still wearing their no-status maker's labels, and price tags to match.

In a bold, Trumpesque gesture I've never made before or since, I looked brazenly at the "No refunds, no exchanges" sign, waved to the rack, and nodded to the sales person.

"I'll take one in every color," I told my gaping audience. I didn't try one of them on and I've been wearing them ever since.

Encouraged, inspired, nay, transported, the neophyte outletters slept lightly, woke early, and met the merchants as they unlocked their doors.

Some tackled housewares, while others joined the formidable lines at Oshkosh, braving all for their little ones back home. Still others took them as they came—the socks store next to the ribbon outlet next to the bakeware shop. The hunters paused only for a stand-up slice of pizza between storefronts, their bagged spoils at their feet.

Somehow, in this artificial atmosphere of ultra-bright fluorescent lighting, miles of linoleum, and simulated music sifting down from the speakers, it somehow seemed right that Royal Doulton was British cheek-by-jowl with polyester pants suits.

My God, were we beginning to understand Las Vegas? As with Vegas' monomania, we were cocooned in an artificial glow that seduces you into counting neither time nor money.

But how much more practical we were than those poor souls at the gaming tables! Would they come home with new speckleware turkey roasters, or bathroom ensembles in just the right shade of peach? Would they count among their winnings a glamorous new power suit that would leave 'em speechless in the boardroom?

All this and more we unveiled each evening during the Ritual Display of Purchased Goods—presented with pomp and pageantry over wine and cheese.

No purchase was too small or too mundane to miss its moment

of glory. Was that not the cutest toddler jean skirt you'd ever seen? Or the best-looking mixing bowl this side of Julia Child's? The Ladies even demanded a glimpse of the annual stash of unmentionables.

And, we assured each other over crinkling shopping bags and tinkling wine glasses, each and every one a bargain.

Betsa Marsh is a Cincinnati-based travel journalist whose lingerie purchases follow natural progression.

★

What's a bargain? My American Heritage dictionary says, "Something offered or acquired at a price advantageous to the buyer," from the old French *bargaignier*, meaning "haggle in the market."

—MBB

KATHLEEN CLARK

✦ ✦ ✦

Blood from Stone

Egypt's antiquities speak.

I WAS ABOUT TO TURN 50 WHEN I DECIDED TO GO TO EGYPT. I wanted to take a trip to let myself know that life was going to continue to be good, or even to be better, after that fateful age.

I'd received a brochure in the mail describing the trip and had promptly thrown it away. I considered it to be in the category I labeled "spiritual bullshit." Maybe "hubris" would have been a more accurate term. Supposedly there was to be some special energy available to the earth on January 11, 1992. People were convening at different spots over the earth in order to "anchor the energy." For some reason the earth couldn't figure out how to do this without us human beings meditating or dancing or doing intricate rituals.

I tend to disbelieve this sort of thing although I continually find myself on the fringes of it and having a terrific time, energetically speaking, whether I believe the prevailing dogma or not. As this included a few pilgrimages where this "Doubting Thomasina" managed to survive and flourish amongst the "true believers," and as I actually prefer that type of adventure in spite of myself, I located another copy of the flier and signed on.

Now anyone else, I figured, would be getting out books on Egypt in order to prepare for such a trip: archeology, mythology, Egyptology. It's all fascinating stuff to anyone with an ounce of curiosity. I knew that. I told that to myself. But somehow I just couldn't arouse any interest. Instead, I was deeply into the books of Anne Rice. *The Vampire Chronicles* were consuming me. I was living the immortal life with Lestat and friends, coping with what it means to be living eternally, to be out of time, drinking the blood of the innocent (or not so innocent), and dealing with the dark side. I couldn't pull myself away.

Well, you can imagine how tickled I was as I realized that the last book was turning into a book about Egypt. It helped me to understand why I'd been sticking with *Queen of the Damned,* which was slow going and not as vitally interesting as *The Vampire Lestat* and *Interview With a Vampire.* I'd been doing my homework. *Queen of the Damned* contained all the information about Egypt I needed.

According to the brochure, the climax of the trip should have been on January 11 when I was in the king's chamber of the great pyramid, lying in the sarcophagus, or in the queen's chamber, asking my divine self to help me create right action and right livelihood in the year to come. But it wasn't. I enjoyed that experience, but it was a little rose on the icing. The cake, the main event was in the Cairo museum the day before.

We were there with our guide. She was dark with beautiful almond eyes. She called us *Habibi,* beloved, and knew what we would most want to see. We had been her charges for almost two weeks, following her out into the desert and up the Nile from temple to temple. Our little group of 25 women had dressed ourselves in bangled scarves and learned to belly dance. We had haggled in the markets for magic statues, half-animal, half-human. We had fended off the advances of men who thought we were beautiful and wanted to marry us. We had met the pantheon of gods and goddesses and had become believers again asking for their help. We had experienced the sweetness and power of Setmet the lion-faced goddess, had invoked the spirit of Isis, mother of all, and Ra, the sun god had warmed us. Our very cells had been steeped in the deep memories of the past. Maybe our own past. We had lain on the ground at Sacara, the temple of healing through sound, and become one with the earth, howling our pain at separation. We had felt the fierce and unforgiving timelessness of this desert land. We were tired, and I was saturated. I couldn't bear to go with the group. Not only that, but I discovered I wasn't interested in anything in that dusty old, crowded museum. It took me a while to make my peace with that. After all, this was a once in a lifetime occasion for me, how could I waste it in boredom. I figured somewhere there must be something that would speak to me. I quickly walked through the room with King Tut's treasures. Nothing there. Nothing of wood or papyrus or lapis lazuli called to me. Eventually I found myself on the second floor balcony overlooking two massive stone statues two stories high.

It was King Amenophis II and Tgi. They had been sitting together, meditating side by side for centuries. They stared forward motionless, her hand resting on his knee, his hand covering hers. They were so calm and peaceful in their Divine Marriage. "I want to be them," I wrote. "I want to be eternal beauty, timeless and immortal. I want to be this land, stark and massive. I do not want to be a human pulled hither and yon. I want this eternal balance, power, and sweetness, focused and unyielding." Separate, and yet joined, they embodied for me the perfect relationship. As I cried my anger and anguish at my own failed relationships, they seemed to speak to me in some incomprehensible way from deep within the stone. They began revealing to me the nature of the body, of what it means to be a hand or a foot or a mouth. I felt the essence of hand pouring into my body, the ecstasy of foot, the sweetness of mouth, the love of heart flowing through hand. The more I stood there and looked, the more they showed to me. They revealed to me everything I am and everything I aspire to be. They were lifeless, unmoving, impassive, carved out of stone, the images of two people long dead, but they were not speaking to me of death, they were showing me about life, eternal life. I felt their timelessness, agelessness, immortality, and I knew I wanted it too. I felt as I had felt when I'd been in India and the love began to pour out of my guru's feet into my body, suffusing me with love. The devotees had said, "He is God. He is goodness. He is sweetness. He is love." But he had said, "I am only a mirror. I am only a mirror of you."

Now these silent stone statues were the mirrors reflecting back to me the truth of my own timelessness and eternal being, indefinably sweet, loving, immovable, and yet constantly flowing.

Suddenly, I knew that Anne Rice had stood exactly where I was standing on the balcony in the museum at Cairo. She'd stood before the feet of the stone gurus and cried the energy of their eternal love, timelessness, and beauty everlasting. She'd felt the fierceness of this land and had been able to capture it in her books and convey this sense to me. I had received it from the books but only in this moment could I see her genius. I felt I was at the birthplace of an idea. I felt she'd taken the energetic experience and had transformed it into a highly readable story. She'd done something that I now understood as a possibility for me. Her ability to use words to communicate the energy of Beingness was what I wanted for myself. My body was thrilled with delight and awe as I was touched with the synchronistic perfection of this moment. Who was reading *The Vampire Chronicles* in Egypt? Who was standing and experiencing those frozen statues as living beings? Who needed to be inspired by an author taking the energy of a particular experience and transforming it into a story which communicates that precise energy so well? As far as I knew, no one. No one but me. I received the revelation with wonder and thanks. Then I went downstairs, fought my way through the crowd, and bought a postcard so I wouldn't forget.

Born and bred for the suburbs, Kathleen Clark has spent the latter part of her life trying to escape. She now lives in Santa Fe, New Mexico, and is carrying on an intense and passionate affair with a cello.

★

Moreover, in this country it could be said that a heart beats in all things, even in the sun which was named, blessed, and implored like a god and tenderly loved like a human father, and even in the dark stone of the tombs...you will contemplate the indefinable reality and will finally understand the words of André Malraux: "The Egypt which first invented eternity is also the most powerful actress in life." So do not set out with the intention of discovering this country. It is Egypt which, by your good fortune, will take possession of you.

—Henri Gougaud and Colette Gouvion, *Egypt Observed*

PAMELA MICHAEL

* * *

The Khan Men of Agra

Taking a chance in an Indian train station.

ONE GOOD THING ABOUT MONSOONS: THEY SURE KEEP THE DUST
down, I thought to myself, peering out the milky window of the
Taj Express. I surveyed the approaching station from my uncertain
perch between two lurching cars, ready to grab my bag and disembark purposefully. Despite the early hour, the platform slowly
scrolling past me was packed with people.

Of the dozen or so bony hands struggling to wrench my suitcase from my hand as I stepped off the train at Agra, perhaps two
were porters, four or five were rickshaw drivers, three or four were
taxi drivers, and maybe a couple were thieves. The sudden rush of
mostly barefoot men in states of undress ranging from rags to
britches, brought me face to face with the difficulty of "reading"
a person's demeanor or intentions in an unfamiliar culture. What
to do?

I already knew from my few days in New Delhi that I would
have to choose one of these men—not because I didn't want to
carry my own bag, but because I would be hounded mercilessly
until I paid someone to do it for me. It's a defensive necessity, and
an effective hedge for women traveling alone who must rely on
their own wits and the unreliable kindness of strangers—the taxi-

wallah as protector and guide. In Delhi, though, the competitive tourist market is based more on ingenuity and charm than intimidation. Many of the drivers had developed very engaging come-ons, my favorite being the rickshaw driver who purred, "And which part of the world is suffering in your absence, Madam?"

My reluctance to hire anyone apparently was being interpreted as a bargaining ploy. Several men had begun to yell at each other and gesture toward me, ired by the low rates to which their competitors were sinking for the privilege of snagging a greenhorn tourist fresh off the train. Not wanting to see the end result of such a bidding war, I handed over my bag to the oldest, most decrepit-looking of the bunch, deciding I might be able to outrun (or overtake) him if I had to and also because he had an engaging (if toothless) smile.

Triumphant, he hoisted my bag on top of his turban and beckoned me to follow as he set out across the tracks. For the first few minutes the old man had to fend off a persistent few rival drivers who thought they could convince me to change my mind by casting aspersions on the character, safety record, and vehicle of the man I had chosen, whose name he told me, was Khan, Kallu Khan.

Half way through the station, in a particularly crowded spot, Kallu handed my bag to another (much younger and, I theorized, more fleet-footed) man. "Hey, wait a minute!" I protested. "My cousin Iki," Kallu assured me. "So, what's he doing with my bag?" I asked. "Helper," I was told. I went into red-alert and quickened my pace to keep up with Iki and my luggage. As we reached the street it began to rain again, part of the deluge/blue sky monsoon cycle to which I had become accustomed. Over my objections, Iki put my bag in the trunk of their car, a battered Hindustan Ambassador that was unmarked except by mud, no reassuring "Agra Taxi Company" emblazoned on the door. "Thief might steal suitcase in back seat, Madam," Kallu explained. I acquiesced—the dry shelter of the "taxi" looked inviting and I was worn down by the ceaseless demands on my ability to communicate, decipher, make decisions, find, respond, protect, etc., that travel entails, even in a four-star situation, which the Agra train station was decidedly not.

Once underway, my relief at having escaped the crowd and rain was somewhat dampened by my realization that I was on a rather deserted road with two men who were probably making the same kind of un- and misinformed assumptions about me that I was making about them. I peered out the rain-streaked window to my right to get my bearings and to take in some of the sites I had come to India to see. I was also tentatively toying with escape options. All I could see was a blur of red, towering overhead and as far into the distance as I could make out. The Red Fort, of course. I had done my homework, so I knew the walls were 70 feet high, surrounded by a moat. On my left was a long stretch of sparse forest, separated from the roadway by a crumbling, low iron fence.

Suddenly, Iki pulled the car over on the left and stopped alongside a broken place in the fence. Kallu got out of the passenger side and opened my door saying, "Now I show you something no tourist ever see, Madam."

"That's all right," I said, "let's just get to the hotel. Tomorrow is better," I demurred.

"Please Madam," he insisted and, sensing my concern about my suitcase, he added, "Don't worry, Iki stay here with your bag."

I was already chastising myself for being so naive and trying to decide how much real danger I was in when I looked—really looked—into Kallu's eyes for the first time. They were kind; kind and bloodshot, but kind. In an instant I made the sort of decision that every traveler has to make from time to time: you decide to take a risk, trust a stranger, enter a cave, explore a trail, act on intuition, and experience something new. It is this giving oneself over to a strange culture or environment that often reaps the most reward, that makes travel so worthwhile and exhilarating.

As if to affirm my decision, the rain stopped. "OK, Mr. Khan, you show me," I said. We walked down a muddy path through a stand of

Ambassador sedan

stilted trees, leaving Iki behind, smoking a *bidi*. My courage faltered a couple of times when I caught a glimpse of a spectral, loin-clothed man through the leaves, but I said nothing and slogged on, hoping for the best.

It came quickly and totally unexpectedly: an enormous mauve river, its banks aflutter with river-washed tattered clothes hanging from poles and vines—work in progress of dhobi-*wallahs*, the laundry men. Directly across the river, luminescent in a moisture-laden haze, was the Taj Mahal, seen from an angle that, to be sure, few tourists ever see and shared with affection by a man who clearly derived great pride from its grandeur. The monument's splendor was all the more striking, its manifest extravagance even more flamboyant in contrast to the faded homespun garments flapping rhythmically in the humid monsoon breeze. We could only stand there and beam at each other on the shores of the mighty Yamuna, the Khan man and I. I like to think it was a sweet kind of victory for us both.

Pamela Michael is a freelance writer, radio producer, and education consultant. She is the editor of The Gift of Rivers, *co-editor of* A Mother's World, A Woman's Passion for Travel, *and* Wild Writing Women: Stories of World Travel, *as well as the author of* The Whole World is Watching. *Currently, she is the director of The River of Words Project, which she co-founded with U.S. Poet Laureate Robert Hass. She lives in Clayton, California.*

*

I grew to love stations as much as I dreaded them in the early stages. They seem bewildering ant-heaps until you find your way around, but you can always get help from coolies (wearing red waistcoats for identification) who know platforms and departure times rather better than the station staff. Fellow travelers, too, are infinitely helpful. Indians are well aware of the impenetrability of their booking system for foreigners and love to help out.

—Una Flett, "Lonely You Come?" *Women Travel: A Rough Guide Special*
edited by Natania Jansz and Miranda Davies, et. al.

GRETEL EHRLICH

✦ ✦ ✦

The Source of a River

A search for beginnings traverses wilderness,
wildness, and the soul.

IT'S MORNING IN THE ABSAROKA MOUNTAINS. THE WORD *absaroka* means "raven" in the Crow language, though I've seen no ravens in three days. Last night I slept with my head butted against an Engelmann's spruce, and when I woke, it was a many-armed goddess swinging around and around. The trunk is bigger than an elephant's leg. I stick my nose against it. Tiny opals of sap stick to my cheeks where the bark breaks up, textured: red and gray, coarse and smooth, wet and flaked.

I'm looking for the source of the Yellowstone River, and as we make the day-long ascent from a valley, I think about walking and wilderness. We use the word "wilderness," but perhaps we mean wildness. Isn't that why I've come here, to seek the wildness in myself and, in so doing, come on the wildness everywhere, because after all, I'm part of nature too.

Following the coastline of the lake, I watch how wind picks up water in dark blasts and drops it again. Ducks glide in V's away from me, out onto the fractured, darkening mirror. I stop. A hatch of mayflies powders the air, and the archaic, straight-winged drag-onflies hang blunt-nosed above me. A friend talks about aquatic bugs: water beetles, spinners, assassin bugs, and one that hatches, mates, and dies in a total life span of two hours. At the end of the meadow, the lake drains into a fast-moving creek. I quicken my pace and trudge upward. Walking is almost an ambulation of mind. The human armor of bones rattles, fat rolls, and inside this durable, fleshy prison of mine, I make a beeline toward otherness, lightness, or like a moth, toward flame.

Somewhere along the trail I laugh out loud. How shell-like the body seems suddenly—not fleshy at all, but inhuman and hard. And farther up, I step out of my skin though I'm still held fast by something, but what? I don't know.

How foolish the preparations for wilderness trips seem now. We pore over maps, chart our expeditions. We "gear up" at trailheads with pitons and crampons, horsepacks and backpacks, fly rods and cameras, forgetting the meaning of simply going, the mechanics of disburdenment. I look up from these thoughts: a blue heron rises from a gravel bar and glides behind a gray screen of dead trees, appears in an opening where an avalanche downed pines, and lands again on water.

I stop to eat lunch. Emerson wrote: "The Gautama said that the first men ate the earth and found it sweet." I eat bologna and cheese and think about eating dirt. At this moment the mouth frames wonder, its width stands for the generous palate of consciousness. I cleanse my taste buds with miner's lettuce and stream water and try to imagine what kinds of sweetness the earth provides: the taste of glacial flour or the mineral taste of basalt, the fresh and foul bouquets of rivers, the desiccated, stinging flavor of a snowflake.

As I begin to walk again, it occurs to me that this notion of eating the earth is not about gluttony but about unconditional love, an acceptance of whatever taste comes across my tongue: flesh, wine, the unremarkable flavor of dirt. To find wildness, I must first offer myself up, accept all that comes before me: a bullfrog breathing hard on a rock; moose tracks under elk scats; a cloud that looks like a clothespin; a seep of water from a high cirque, black on brown rock, draining down from the brain of the world.

At treeline, bird song stops. I'm lifted into a movement of music with no particular notes, only windsounds becoming watersounds, becoming windsounds. Above, a cornice crowns a ridge and melts into a teal and turquoise lake, which, like a bladder, leaks its alchemical potions.

On top of Marston Pass I'm in a ruck of steep valleys and gray, treeless peaks. The alpine carpet, studded with red paintbrush and alpine buttercups, gives way to rock. Now, all the way across a valley, I see where water oozes from moss and mud, how, at its source, it quickly becomes a river.

Emerson also said: "Every natural fact is an emanation, and that from which it emanates is an emanation also, and from every emanation is a new emanation." The ooze, the source of a great river, is now a white chute tumbling over brown bellies of conglomerate rock. Wind throws sheets of water to another part of the mountainside; soft earth gives way under my feet, clouds spill upward and spit rain. Isn't everything redolent with loss, with momentary radiance, a coming to different ground? Stone basins catch the waterfall, spill it again; thoughts and desires strung together are laddered down.

I see where meltwater is split by rock—half going west to the Pacific, the other going east to the Atlantic—for this is the Continental Divide. Down the other side, the air I gulp feels softer. Ice bridges the creek, then, when night comes but before the full moon, falling stars have the same look as water falling against the rock of night.

To rise above treeline is to go above thought, and after, the descent back into bird song, bog orchids, willows, and firs is to sink into the preliterate parts of ourselves. It is to forget discontent, undisciplined needs. Here, the world is only space, raw loneliness, green valleys hung vertically. Losing myself to it—if I can—I do not fall.... Or if I do, I'm only another cataract of water.

Wildness has no conditions, no sure routes, no peaks or goals, no source that is not instantly becoming something more than itself, then letting go of that, always becoming. It cannot be stripped to its complexity by CAT scan or telescope. Rather, it is a many-pointed truth, almost a bluntness, a sudden essence like the wild strawberries strung on scarlet runners under my feet. For half a mile, on hands and knees, I eat and eat. Wildness is source and fruition at once, as if this river circled round, mouth eating tail and tail eating source.

Now I am camped among trees again. Four yearling moose, their chestnut coats shiny from a summer's diet of willow shoots, tramp past my bedroll and drink from a spring that issues sulfurous water. The ooze, the white chute, the narrow stream—now almost a river—joins this small spring and slows into skinny oxbows and deep pools before breaking again on rock, down a stepladder of sequined riffles.

To trace the history of a river or a raindrop, as John Muir would have done, is also to trace the history of the soul, the history of the mind descending and arising in the body. In both, we constantly seek and stumble on divinity, which, like the cornice feeding the lake, and the spring becoming a waterfall, feeds, spills, falls, and feeds itself over and over again.

Gretel Ehrlich's essays have appeared in The New York Times, Harper's *and* The Atlantic Monthly. *She is the author of* The Solace of Open Spaces, Heart Mountain, A Match to the Heart, This Cold Heaven, *and* Islands, Universe, Home, *from which this piece was excerpted. She divides her time between California and Wyoming.*

*

The garden was our universe. It stretched downhill in a solitude peopled with birds, frogs and tadpoles, and hedgehogs in the twilight, which we carried home in a ball and waited to feed with milk when they unrolled. The place had once been an orchard and was filled with fruit trees of every sort; and its gentle life busy with tiny incidents in the sun and dew—its loneliness—with only an old gardener, usually out of sight, and my father among the daffodils—and the careless abundance—circles of fruit on the ground beneath their boughs—gave it an atmosphere which I have never met again except in the descriptions of Eden in *Paradise Lost.*

—Freya Stark, *The Journey's Echo: Selections from Freya Stark*

✦ ✦ ✦

Pedals and Pubs

The adventure changed when her tire,
and spirits, began to deflate.

AFTER THREE HOURS OF SLOGGING OVER THE HILLS THROUGH the ever-present Irish mist, I heard a hiss from my front tire and knew I had a problem. It had been hours since I'd seen the sun, my leg muscles screamed, and my rear end burned. My only companions, some black-and-white cows plodding across the road, were indifferent.

For ten hypnotic days I had cycled, without a glitch, along the Ring of Kerry and through the Dingle Peninsula in southwestern Ireland. I had wheeled down narrow roads aflame with red fuchsia and yellow gorse, through frog-green hills crossed with stone walls, dotted by medieval ruins, and grazed by baaing sheep. Gliding through myriad shades of green, I felt the earth roll under my pedals, smelled the peat bricks burning, and tasted the salty air of the coast, where the ocean foamed onto the rocky shore.

This was my first trip to Ireland, and I was traveling alone. Had I booked a tour with a bicycle company, a support vehicle and a guide would have come to my rescue to repair my tire. But an organized bike trip didn't fit my loose schedule or my slim budget: I was traveling around the world on a shoestring.

My vehicle was a heavy black rented bike with a basket in front, like the wicked neighbor lady rode in *The Wizard of Oz*. I stashed my bags in the basket, spent my nights in small B&Bs, and ate in local pubs.

For me the advantage of exploring rural Ireland by bicycle was the slow pace. I could stop often, breathe the fragrant air, absorb the verdant landscape…and remember every heart-pounding hill that passed under my wheels.

But now, with a leaking tire and a soggy spirit, it was time to break for coffee and a scone—or better yet, a Guinness. From the crest of the next hill, I saw cottages with gray slate roofs in the distance. One chimney rose above the others, pouring out the signature plume of peat smoke. I figured it was the village pub.

After a few more minutes of low-tire pedaling, I was there. As I tramped into the pub's inviting warmth, I felt conspicuous—but the man behind the worn wooden bar put me at ease. When he served my Guinness, he grinned and asked, "Can you sing?"

Now where else would a bartender ask this question of a young woman who stood dripping water on the floor?

"Of course I can sing," I answered. Lord Guinness loosened my tongue, and out flowed "When Irish Eyes Are Smiling," which my mother used to sing to me at bedtime. An old man in tattered tweed coat and cap stepped up to the bar, squared his shoulders, sucked in a deep breath, then belted out, "Mine eyes have seen the glory of the coming of the Lord."

Men left their darts and conversation to gather round.

"Sing another one, Yankee," they urged and then joined in. A dozen tunes later, when I was ready to leave, the impromptu choir members insisted on paying for my brews and then escorted me to the door. As I pushed it open—miracle of miracles—the sun was shining once again.

When the men saw me start to wrestle with my little bicycle pump, ineptly trying to fix my flat tire, they organized a work party. The baritone fetched a repair kit from his barn, and as they worked I passed around my entire stash of Cadbury bars. It didn't take them long to patch the leak, and as I pedaled off, I turned and waved.

There are all kinds of adventure. Biking through a land of hills and mist pushed me physically, but my real discovery was cultural: The sun in the Irish soul is expressed through song, and the smile in Irish eyes is contagious.

Marybeth Bond is a writer and a consultant in the adventure travel industry. In addition to this volume, she is the co-editor of A Woman's Passion for Travel *and* A Mother's World, *and the author of* Gutsy Women: Travel Tips and Wisdom for the Road *and* Gutsy Mamas: Travel Tips and Wisdom for Mothers on the Road. *She lives in the San Francisco Bay Area.*

★

I have many opportunities to take my husband along on my travels and often do. But when I travel alone, it's an entirely different trip. Instead of being focused on the person with you, you are more observant, more attuned to every sound and detail. And you are much more likely to meet people.

—Kimberly Brown, "The Joys of Solo Travel"

JOY SCHALEBEN LEWIS

✦ ✦ ✦

Legacy of Love

Travels with Momma in the old country.

"*CIAO,* CECILIA," SHOUTED MY MOTHER AS WE LOOKED DOWN across the steep vineyard. "*Dove stai?* (Where are you?)" she cried.

A door from a lone hut nearly lost in the great green vines opened. A humped figure dressed in black waved. Her dress was muddy, her shoes torn. At 90, this frail woman still worked among the grapes of Massa Marittima, the Tuscan hill town where my mother was born. She hobbled towards us, leaning deftly into her cane.

"*Bella, cara, tesora,*" said this strange bundle of crumpled black reaching up to caress my face. She was calling me "beautiful, dear, treasure." I bent down to kiss my great aunt. Once, more than half a century ago, she had held my mother's little-girl hand in the piazza. Now, her hand clasped mine.

In the days that would follow, many more hands would clutch mine and lovingly stroke my face. My mother had finally lured me to Italy to meet the relatives. At the time, I was 23 and not particularly keen about vacationing with my mother in the old country. But, when she insisted on paying my way, I couldn't resist. And I was, at least, faintly curious about her place of birth.

My mother, the fifth of seven children, was christened Ida Pia Eleka Arnella Elena Androvandi. Honestly, she does have all those names. As a child, I used to impress my friends by rattling off her name-litany as a tongue twister. But that was all I'd concede was different about my mom. I preferred her to be 100-percent American, not Italo-American, as she would identify herself.

I never could understand why she was, well—so darned Italian. You know, kissing everyone and making such a big fuss about the family. As for all those people back in Italy with odd names—they were her relatives, not mine.

And then, her childhood had been so poor: not enough to eat, living in two small rooms, no running water, no electricity, owning only two dresses and no other outfits when my grandmother took her brood to a new life in America.

They had settled in southern Illinois in 1923, where my grandfather had been working in a coal mine for several years. In the New World, my mother, at age nine, had enough to eat but not much more. Throughout her girlhood, she never even had one doll, ever!—a fact she told me every time she reminisced about her childhood.

I, in contrast, had a new doll every Christmas. My growing up was a carefree and secure existence with two younger sisters and a brother in a well-off Milwaukee suburb.

"Joy-a, get into the car." After only one day in Italy, Mother had taken to pronouncing my name Italian style. "We're going to drive Cecilia back to Massa Marittima and then meet your Aunt Anita." She was in her element. At last she was opening the doors of her childhood to me. Clearly, Mother was in command.

For one thing, she knew the language. I didn't. What's more, people in Massa Marittima treated her like visiting royalty, hugging and kissing her, calling her name as she walked the cobbled streets, bringing her gifts of welcome. She'd been back several times and had become a kind of town heroine. And just because I was her daughter, I, too, was instantly beloved.

I was impressed.

I was also astonished by the beauty of Massa Marittima, a walled, medieval stone city teeming with arches, alleyways, stepped passages, red-tiled roofs, green shutters, and wrought iron balconies rimmed with flower pots. Below, olive groves, vineyards, and wheat fields reached ten miles to the sea. On an exceptionally clear day, I could see all the way to the resort town of Follonica and even beyond to the island of Elba where Napoleon had been exiled.

Massa, as locals call their hometown of 10,000, was immaculate, just like my mother's house in America. And its people—many had her same handsome features: fine bones, narrow hips, straight noses, blue eyes, smooth light-olive skin. And the women, petite like her, were "dressed to kill," as mother says, and does. That meant looking "*molto bella,*" especially when promenading arm-in-arm in the piazza at dusk.

Massa Marittima, acclaimed for centuries for its artisans and nearby silver and copper mines, is sectioned like a three-layered cake. At the bottom is the "Borgo" (little village). At the top is the "Cittanova" (new city), where my mother was born. In between is "Cittavecchio" (old city). "All eyes notice you here," Mother warned, frowning at my Bermudas and tennis shoes as we strolled into the main square.

How proudly she showed me the nooks and crannies of her memories—the big stone basins at the foot of the hill where she washed clothes as a small girl, the huge clock tower with its sweeping view of the valley, the frescoes in the mighty Romanesque Cathedral, and her favorite place to play—the so-called "500 Steps," a steep, wide passageway leading to the Cittanova.

And then, of course, there were all the *parenti*—relatives. Each morning over cappuccino in the piazza we'd review who was who.

"Let's see," I mused, "the old woman in the hospital, with the broken hip is Maria—another great aunt. Narisco is the man with the little farm who gave rabbits to GI's during World War II; he's your cousin and therefore my second cousin."

"No, no," she interrupted. "In Italy, you don't have second or third cousins—just cousins."

Before long, the names of my mother's relatives no longer sounded so foreign: Mazzini, Liana, Sergio, Caesare, Bruno, Fulvia, Nuncia, and a whole string of others were now my family too. I liked having an Italo-American mamma. In Massa Marittima, she was bequeathing me my inheritance.

One day, my mother announced she had something special to show me—the tiny two-room apartment where she had lived with her four cousins and two brothers. It was on the fourth floor of a run-down building at the end of Via Bogetto, an area where the poor miners lived when my grandfather was a young man.

"We're lucky," she said. "The rooms aren't occupied. They're going to be renovated." Excitedly, she opened the door and said, "This is where I took my very first breath."

I entered cautiously, not anxious to confront what I thought were bleak memories. There they were: the walls and floors of my mother's childhood—as dark and dreary as I had imagined. And here was the hearth where she'd severely burned her elbow, the tiny back window where my grandmother sat wet-nursing other women's babies to earn a few lire.

I couldn't wait to get out, to leave this molding old building that testified to my mother's dismal start.

Yet, my mother lingered cheerfully, recalling instead games she had played with her "toys"—pebbles from the street—and the good minestrone her mother cooked and how all her sisters and brothers giggled together on one mattress. Finally, outside again in the bright, fresh air that was Massa, she sighed happily. "It's fine to return to the past, but I live for today," she said simply.

"*Andiamo!*" Let's go.

My mother is now seventy-something and still, like me, making almost annual pilgrimages back to Massa. She remains a happy woman, full of life and Italian embraces. In fact I've only seen her cry once.

It happened precisely a year ago, on Mother's Day, when I gave her a present I'd bought in Italy. When she saw what was in the box, she was flabbergasted. Tenderly, she lifted the gift and clutched it to her breast. "*Bella, bella,*" she murmured over and over.

At last my mother had a doll.

Joy Schaleben Lewis may reside in Milwaukee, but her temperament and spirit belong to Massa Marittima, the splendiferous town where everyone calls her "Gioia, figlia della Ida" (daughter of Ida).

★

Mama's passport photo says it all. The impish grin is brighter than the white curls, the wrinkle of smile deeper than the wrinkles of age.

She's happy. She's going somewhere. With me.

The mugshot proves I shouldn't have waited so long to invite her.

We'd talked about a big trip we'd take "sometime," but I married and got even busier at home and work, and summers and years passed with no adventure together.

Then Daddy died.... Out of those sad days of winter came a sense of urgency. Time and life were galloping past, and I needed to catch up.

—Mary Ellen Botter, "A Promise Kept," *The Denver Post*

PART THREE

GOING YOUR OWN WAY

* * *

Into the Kingdom

A trek into remote Bhutan opens
the door to another world.

"DID YOU HEAR THE SINGING LAST NIGHT?"

We were riding downhill along a rocky causeway fringed thickly with pine trees and knotted banks of rhododendrons. Since we left the Lama's retreat, Karma [our guide] had hardly spoken. We had taken our cue from him, travelling silently, each wrapped in our own thoughts of the things we had seen.

"That *dread...*" Tom had privately described it to me as "that dreadful caterwauling," but one look at Karma's face made him think better of it. "I mean, er, those songs. You bet."

"Were they not beautiful?"

"Hmm." Falsetto.

"They made me feel somewhat sad."

"I expect they would," Tom agreed with funereal solemnity.

Karma sighed. "One day...one day I too will go and live in a cave for some years. Meditating. Praying. I spoke to the Lama about these things you know: he has told me never to give up hope. Someday, the time will be right. Who knows, it may be sooner than I think."

He gave us a knowing, sideways look.

The last thing we needed at this stage was to lose Karma. It was a worrying thought.

"What about girls?" Tom said hopefully. "You have to give them up you know."

In his less zealous moments Karma was rather partial to them, as we had often seen.

"And food," I added. "No more chillis; no more cheeses."

Karma's pack bulged with cheeses, now the most remarkable— and odiferous—shapes and colours, which he had stocked up on in Tashigang.

"You'd have to live on just one bowl of rice a day. A very small one, I should think. Just enough to keep you alive."

Karma looked gloomy. "I know. It is indeed a sticky problem. I will have to be strong."

We rode on in silence. There was a stubborn streak in Karma, and I could tell that it would take more than these arguments to change his mind.

At midday we came to a small pass with a prayer wall at the top. The stones from which it was built seemed immeasurably ancient, weathered and smoothed by the elements. In a band around the centre were some cracked slabs of slate on which we could just trace the outlines of a *mantra*. I loved these characters; their faded imprints gliding like dancers over the lichen-mottled rock.

Beneath us fell a landscape quite different from any that we had seen over the past few days. The rocky pathways, cataracts, and deep forests were behind us; instead, here were smooth pastures falling evenly to a wide,

> *Wherever one wanders in the mountain wilderness, to the farthest inhabited places and the highest mountain passes, the signs of holy places are the religious monuments and symbols, the mani-stones, chorten-reliquaries and prayer-flags. The mystic OM MANI PADME HUM are cut into stone and rocks and into the slabs of prayer-walls. This holy formula cannot be translated literally; its deeper meaning is felt by all, that the divine power—born in every human being, but covered with the dust of ignorance—might become manifest within us.*
>
> —Blanche C. Olschak, *Bhutan: Land of Hidden Treasures*

green, flat-bottomed valley, along the middle of which a river flowed, its waters as brown and stippled as little trout.

I had a sudden, instinctive feeling that we had crossed some kind of boundary. For all its wild beauty, the mountainous land we had been travelling through had a desolate feel to it. This, on the other hand, was a pastoral place. The grass was marbled with tiny yellow and white flowers, and the familiar wooden jangle of yak bells floated up to us from below. I thought how pleasant it would be to sit down there in the sun or fish for a while by the banks of the river. Someone, somewhere, was playing a pipe.

At the sound of the horses approaching, impatiently tossing their bridles, the tune stopped. From behind a rock a man emerged. He stared at us, motionless, with a look of surprise. Although he was obviously only a herdsman watching over his grazing yaks, his bearing was proud, like a warrior.

I stared back at him, transfixed. He was extremely tall for a Bhutanese, with a powerful, muscular body and smooth, bronzed skin. His eyes were very dark, fringed with black hair which fell thickly to his shoulders like an engraving of a medieval knight. In one hand he was carrying a curious five-pointed black felt cap. As we drew closer I saw that from one ear he wore a piece of scarlet thread tied with a lump of turquoise; from the other hung two tiny gold nuggets and a cluster of emerald-coloured bird's feathers. The top half of his body was swathed barbarically with animal skins.

The next instant the man had turned on his heel, striding with arrogant grace down the hillside, and was gone. I felt a strange constriction in my throat. We had reached Bragpa country at last.

According to Sangay [another of our guides] we had several more hours of riding to go before we reached Mera. The horses, perhaps sensing our excitement, did nothing to ease this last stretch. They jostled and barged one another, and behaved in a thoroughly disobliging way. Karma's horse, oblivious to its rider's saintly thoughts, threw him clean off into a puddle and refused to be caught, while the ponies, taking advantage of the confusion, rushed off into the boggy ground near the river where they proceeded to plunge about gleefully, up to their bellies in thick, evil-smelling slime. Mine, for once, was the only one to do what it was told. It plodded meekly along, doubtless only the temporary effect, Tom said, of a raging hangover.

We journeyed on, fording rivers, criss-crossing streams, climbing hills, and passing through steep gorges, their skylines topped with a thick, green icing of unbroken forest. To pass the time, Karma told us a story, an origin myth of how the Bragpas first came to these remote valleys, sometime long ago before the dawn of time.

"These people came originally from Tibet, from a strange place where there was a big mountain, the largest in all the world. This mountain was so tall, and so wide, that the people who lived behind it could never see the sun, and for most of the time they lived in complete darkness. One day the King of Tibet ordered these people to flatten the mountain, so that he could see the sun again. This made them very much afraid, because the mountain was so great that they knew it was impossible. So instead they killed this king, and then fled from the country.

"Soon they came to a huge cliff. There was no way forward for them now, so in despair they threw all their animals off the top of this cliff, one by one, and then they jumped off themselves, expecting to die. But they did not die, and nor did their animals, for the protective deity of the cliff saved them. And this way they came to Bhutan.

"And this is why the Bragpas are still so rich, for each of them owns many yaks; and why even today," he concluded rather dubiously, "there are no yaks left in Tibet."

As he was speaking, the gorge we were following narrowed, and without warning the path swung up the cliffside. We pulled ourselves, panting, up some rough steps in the rockface, slipping clumsily in the loose scree. When we reached the top at last, the sun was sliding behind the hills. Spread out beneath us,

Yak

glowing in the last tiger-striped fingers of dusk, lay the village of Mera.

I had always imagined our caravan making a triumphal entry into Mera. Of course, I was wrong.

We rode in slowly, bunching the horses as closely together as possible. That same constricted feeling gripped at my throat, but this time it was not due to excitement but to a distinct tremor of alarm.

"Do you think this is a good idea?" I whispered nervously to Tom, but he was too busy looking around him to reply. It sure as hell was too late to do anything about it now.

At first only a few people saw us arriving, but as our procession drew in, more and more came out of their houses, lining the path as we passed by. Others appeared from the nearby pastures about the village, or strode up from the river below it. When they drew near enough to see us clearly, they stopped still, watching us like the others with expressionless, hooded eyes. No one approached us, no one spoke. We advanced into Mera in utter silence, followed by a hundred or more hostile eyes.

The first Bragpa we had seen on the way to Mera was a mysterious but magnificent being. The sight of 50 of them, when we were none too sure of our reception, was terrifying. Like the first, the men wore tunics made from animal skins, and their legs were clad about with enormous sinister-looking leather leggings. As they watched us pass, their wild hair whipped across their faces in the wind. It was not until now that I realized that all of them, down to the smallest boy, wore sharp knives, also sheathed in skins, at their belts.

Sangay led us into the centre of the village to a house enclosed within stone walls. Unlike the other houses, which were mainly single-storeyed and made from stone and clay, this one was bigger than the rest and had carved wooden window casements and a tree-trunk ladder leading up one side, like the usual Bhutanese homesteads.

We tethered the horses in the courtyard, and went inside. Upstairs we found three interconnecting rooms. All were empty except for the second which had an enormous chest in one corner, which looked as though it may once have been used as a shrine of some kind, and a wooden bed. Outside we heard the sound of voices, both men's and women's, coming from somewhere below us.

At first the sound was barely perceptible, a soft murmuring like the wind over the mountains, but gradually it began to increase in volume. From the windows, Tom and I looked down into the courtyard: it was full of Bragpas. Behind them, others were still streaming in through the gateway into the courtyard; from the fields, and woods, and the furthest houses they came racing towards the house as though it were a magnet, until the whole space was packed tightly with a sea of milling, barbarous-looking bodies. At the sight of our two pale faces looking out nervously from above, a shout went up. Hastily we withdrew.

"Oh dear," I said, and sat down on the bed.

Then came the invasion. First one black-hatted face popped round the door, then above it another, and another, until the whole room was seething with people.

With relief I saw that most of them were women, although they were easily as impressive as their fearsome-looking menfolk. Instead of knives, many of them were carrying bottles in their hands filled with a colourless, cloudy-looking liquid. We stared at one another in silence. Then, jabbering at the tops of their voices, they started to unscrew the bottles, making signs for us to drink.

"What's in them?" I asked Karma suspiciously.

"*Arra*, I expect."

"Oh."

"You must drink, or they will be insulted."

This, obviously, was to be avoided.

It is the custom in Bhutan that everyone carries his or her own cup from which to drink. In Tashigang I had bought myself a little bowl made from varnished rhododendron wood which I now brought out from my bag. It was filled, and I took a sip.

"Groo!"

The *arra* flowed through me like firewater.

The women beamed with satisfaction, and started to refill the bowl.

"*Khadinche-la*. Thank you. That's enough."

In vain I tried to take the bowl away from them, but they were too quick.

"Shi-shi-shi!" They made more drinking motions.

"*No!*"

"Shi-shi-shi!"

"Oh, all right," I took another gulp. "Wah!"

You must have your cup filled three times, Karma explained, before you can refuse. By the end my head was swimming, but the ice had been broken. I also saw that the varnish had been stripped completely from the bottom of my bowl.

The women gathered in around us. Like the men they wore the same five-pointed felt hats, but instead of skin and leather they were dressed in tunics made of striped homespun, with woolen jerkins dyed a bright earthen red over the top, and small, square shawls over their shoulders. They wore their hair long, tied up in plaits like Tibetan women.

It was their jewels which intrigued me the most. Each wore several heavy necklaces made from rough lumps of amber, coral, turquoise, and intricately engraved beads of solid silver. The same stones fell in clusters from their ears, often circling their waists, too, on chains which jangled like jailers' keys with amulets, scrolls, old coins, and charms to bring good luck. Silver rings adorned their fingers and their arms were cuffed with heavy silver bracelets. When they moved they clanked, as though sheathed from head to foot in armour plating.

There was one woman whom I noticed particularly. She was rather older than the others, most of whom were young girls, and less elaborately adorned. Her face was plain, but deeply creased with laughter lines. It was she who had been the first in through the door, and she, too, who had been the most insistent that we drink our fair share of the *arra*. Her good-humoured persistence was such that she had defeated even Tom, who referred to her affectionately afterwards as "Bagwash." I found out later that her name was Dechen.

Tom went outside to see to the luggage, while Dechen conducted an intensive examination of what was left: namely, me. The others stood around attentively while she fired questions, patiently translated by Karma.

"She wants to know if you have had any children?"

"No."

"She is not believing you."

There did not seem to be much to say to this. Dechen was undeterred. Gently she started running her hands over my chest, feeling my breasts like a detective after some vital clue.

"Wah!" Karma's eyes popped with horror, and quickly he hid his head in his hands.

After some squeezing and prodding, she smiled knowingly and started to undo the opening of her own dress. Triumphantly, a long, rather wrinkled brown breast was produced from the folds of homespun. I was not too sure what to make of this. Out of politeness, I gingerly prodded it, composing my face into what I hoped was an admiring look. Evidently I struck the right note; there was a murmur of approval all around.

"She says that she has had lots of children," came a despairing, muddled voice behind me.

"Really?" This was getting interesting. *"Ming gha chi su?* What are their names?"

But too late.

"Wooo…no!" Squinting out from between his fingers, Karma had caught sight of the proffered breast. This was too much. Crimson in the face, he bolted from the room. Peals of laughter floated mockingly after him down the ladder. We thought it was a great joke.

Even to the Sharchops, as the majority of the Eastern Bhutanese are known, the Bragpas are an enigma. The beauty of their women is legendary, as is the excellence of the yak cheese and butter they produce, but these were the only things that we had been able to discover about them with any certainty. We were lucky to find them in Mera at all, for these high pastures are only habitable for four months of the year. In the winter, when their lands become snowbound again, they move with their livestock down into the lowlands, roaming as nomads until the spring thaws return.

Our first impressions were quite unfounded. The deathly silence on our arrival had not been the result of hostility, but of astonishment—and who could blame them—for any visitors, let alone strange foreign ones, are virtually unheard of in these remote parts.

The village consisted of about 70 houses built closely together on a gentle expanse of open hillside, as smooth and plucked as a cricket pitch. Unlike the houses in most other Bhutanese villages, these were relatively simple buildings. Most were single-storyed with small windows, which made their interiors even darker and smokier than usual. We were able to wander freely wherever we chose, although on our walks it was never long before we would be ushered ceremoniously into someone's house to drink butter-tea with them, or a cup of *arra*. *Arra* featured highly in the Bragpa ideal of hospitality.

Inside, the houses were arranged in much the same way. There was no furniture, only a stone hearth in the centre of the room. In the absence of any chimneys, smoke from the fire would circle up through the room into the blackened rafters, eventually seeping out through cracks in the roof. Usually we emerged from these visits looking like chimney sweeps, our faces and clothes covered in sooty smuts. A few spare clothes hung from pegs on the walls, and bunches of dried chillis and maize swung from the beams overhead. Sometimes there would be sacks made from animal skins, or pots of sickly-smelling, fermenting maize covered with leaves ranged around the walls. At night the household would wrap themselves in blankets and lie down by the hearth to sleep.

I found these details intensely absorbing. While we sat, often half-blinded by the smoke, blinking at each other over our cups of *arra*, I would make elaborate mental inventories: one wooden spoon, three metal pots, an uncured sheepskin (smelly), one pair of quilted boots with curly toes (traded across the border with Tibet?), and so on. I was struck, too, by their self-sufficiency, and by the careful ways they had to ensure that nothing was ever wasted. Once I saw a family cutting up the carcass of a yak that had just been slaughtered. One man was sitting on the roof carefully cutting up the meat into thin slivers which he then arranged over the roof to dry. Another was scraping the hide clean of the re-maining blood and sinews, which he then placed in a basin; the women picked off the loose wool from the pelt, which later they would spin into yarn for weaving. The fat, the intestines, the bones, horns, skull, and even the hooves were meticulously sec-tioned off and kept for some later use.

There were few minutes in the day when the people of Mera were not working, and yet, once again, I was impressed by the tran-quillity and gentleness of their way of life. Outside each house was a raised wooden porch on which the whole family would sit out when the weather was fine. The women's looms were usually po-sitioned there, and woven baskets of maize and buckwheat were laid out to dry in the sun.

The men spent much of their day up in the high pastures with their yaks. All but the youngest children would keep watch over the livestock in the nearer fields, and we would often see groups of two or three of them playing games with piles of pebbles to pass the time. When they were not weaving, the women spent much of their time spinning wool on wooden spindles. They were ex-tremely skilled at this, and could do it walking, sitting, standing, or even, I began to think, in their sleep, for they never seemed to go anywhere without their spindles bobbing up and down at their sides. By the end I began to think of them not as tools at all, but as a kind of natural extension of their own bodies.

Once I persuaded Dechen to show me how it was done. The spindle is spun round with one hand, and while it is turning I was shown how to let out the wool, which is held in the other hand, pulling and stretching it through the fingers until it reaches the required tautness and width. What appeared to be so effortless in her hands turned out to be horribly difficult. I could not get the spindle to spin, and the wool tied itself around me in knots, and finally snapped. Hastily, I handed it back, afraid of becoming a social disaster. It was plain that no one was very impressed by my efforts.

I found it soothing to sit out on the porch with Dechen and her family, which sometimes I would do for hours on end while Tom was out photographing. I used to watch the women sorting wool, or listen to the rhythmic swish and click as they worked on their looms. It was peaceful, for we could not speak much, except with gestures and the odd phrase. Although I did not like to admit it, I was not up to doing much else.

The weeks of almost continual travelling had been exhausting for all of us. For me this was not helped by the fact that my cold had been maturing steadily ever since the night we spent at the Lama's temple. I could no longer breathe through my nose at all, and my ears were blocked; at times it felt as if my whole head was weighted down with lead. When I blew my nose, torrents of

It would not do to over-romanticize this way of life. It is extremely tough, even for an unusually tough people. Since nearly everything that they use and consume is made themselves, from their ploughshares to their kitchen pots, their lives are filled with constant work, from before dawn until nightfall. One bad harvest, one spell of unseasonal weather can spell disaster for an entire community. Despite this it seemed to me that they had a certain quality of life that we have lost. There was a serenity about everything they did. Their labour, although constant, was unhurried; their family life, despite the absence of any form of privacy, was gentle. Their children and their old were cared for; women and men treated each other naturally and with affection. I never heard a raised or angry voice. They were at peace with themselves and with their world.

—Katie Hickman,
Dreams of the Peaceful Dragon:
A Journey into Bhutan

unearthly-coloured green mucus filled my handkerchief like lumps of disgusting *blancmange.*

My debility had its own advantages. This enforced stillness meant that I spent much of my time in Mera watching and absorbing these quite ordinary things. The experience of travelling is usually an active one: we probe, we enquire, we deliberately seek things out, go to them, rather than letting them come to us. Here, I was seeing things in a passive but entirely natural way, as and when they happened. Despite my weariness I found it deeply satisfying. For me, this is what travelling is ultimately about: getting under the skin of things—to the heartbeat beneath. For a time, just for a short time, I was no longer on the outside looking in, but on the inside myself.

I had come to Bhutan seeking mystery, and I had found it in plenty. I had also discovered something else, something I can only describe as innocence, or a kind of purity. The satisfaction I felt answered some deep nostalgia within me, a strange atavistic longing to grasp at the roots of man's existence: at his most fundamental bonding with the land and with the natural world around him.

Katie Hickman has lived in Europe, the Far East, and South America and was educated at Oxford. She is the author of A Trip to the Light Fantastic: Travels with a Mexican Circus *and* Dreams of the Peaceful Dragon, *from which this story was excerpted. She lives in London with her husband, photographer Tom Owen Edmunds.*

★

It seems that there are two distinct Bhutans for me. One is the remote Himalayan Kingdom, last remaining Shangri-la, mystical, almost magical place described in guidebooks and glossy travelogs, with scenery beyond words, peace beyond imagining, and people of such friendliness, generosity of spirit, and contentment that they are special indeed. Remarkable as it seems, this is a true picture.

But it exists alongside the other Bhutan. The Bhutan of sheer slog and drudgery for its people, where ill health, illiteracy, ignorance, and a terrifying low life expectancy prevail; where people lead short lives made painful, both physically and emotionally, by hardship. I sat in my friend's house in the village the other evening, and her mother looked at me carefully and said, "We go to the fields every day and we become old women very quickly. You teach in school all day and you will become old very slowly." She is right. Yet slowly things are changing.

—Lesley Reader, "A White Ghost in the Himalayas," *More Women Travel: Adventures and advice from more than 60 countries - A Rough Guide Special* edited by Natania Jansz and Miranda Davies

TANIA AEBI WITH BERNADETTE BRENNAN

* * *

Alone at Sea

*Alone on a 26-foot sailboat, the eighteen-year-old author pushes
her limits as she sets the record for the youngest person
to circumnavigate the globe.*

OCTOBER 23, 1987, ANOTHER DAWN—MY 37TH ALONE ON
the North Atlantic. Around me, the sea is a liquid mountain
range of heaving swells, and I'm really scared. The winds and
waves have been steadily increasing since yesterday, when they
veered from southeast to northeast. *Varuna* has been knocked
mast-down to the water countless times during the night, and
I haven't been able to relax, sleep, eat, or think about anything
other than staying alive. Following now are the biggest waves
I've ever seen—probably 25 feet. It's almost winter and I've
pushed my luck. The weather can only get worse.

Four feet above, avalanches of white water crash across
Varuna's back, swamping the cockpit. In the cabin, everything
that hasn't been battened down has been thrown off the
shelves. Pots, pans, cans, and tools clatter together in the lockers. I'm wedged into my bunk, my foot stretched across to the
sink to stop me from being thrown around the cabin. There
are still 880 miles to go until home. I want to see the Statue
of Liberty. I want to take a hot bath and eat something good. I
want to see my family....

I stuffed my logbook onto the shelf behind my head, struggled out of limp long johns, and stripped down before beginning the contortions of getting into foul-weather gear—first the overalls, then the jacket. It was useless wearing anything beneath the gear because it would have been stupid to jeopardize the precious dry clothes by wearing them outside, where they'd be soaked in seconds. I fastened the hood around my salty head, which was matted into itchy, sticky clumps of hair and crying out to be washed. Practically the only kind of shower I had been able to provide myself during the last month at sea was the occasional unexpected wave that crashed over me, increasing the sodium level on my skin. There was not a drop of fresh water on board to spare for the luxury of a wash. Even though I sprinkled myself liberally with talcum powder, my skin pinched up from the salt and my bottom was covered with sores from sitting on damp cushions for so many weeks. The cold, salt-encrusted lining of the foul-weather gear rubbed against my naked skin like broken glass, and I had to step into it at least ten times a day.

Crouched on all fours and peering out through the dark blue Plexiglas slats that sealed the companionway, I choreographed my next move and waited for the null moment between waves to lurch into action. OK…almost ready…ready…NOW! Quickly removing the slats, I clambered out to the cockpit and added one more bruise to the scars covering my legs.

"Come on, Tarzoon," I coaxed my feline buddy, "if you want to come out, now's your chance." He blinked up at me from the safety of his corner in the bunk, looking for assurance. *Varuna* leveled for a moment and Tarzoon leapt through the companionway, sniffing the air and sticking close. "It's kind of ugly out here," I confided, snapping the umbilical cord of my safety harness onto the lifelines of the boat and looking up the mast to the sky. No change from yesterday. If anything, it was worse. The wind velocity was gale force and holding between 40 and 50 knots. Rain pocked the water around *Varuna*, and low-hanging dark masses canopied us. The last piece of land that these black clouds had shadowed was America, "maybe even New York," I said aloud, and the thought made the gloom seem almost friendly.

"We are so close, Tarzoon, and I have these feelings, New York feelings." If we continued on at this speed, we would have about eight more days left; if we dropped back to our average speed until now, it could take another fourteen.

Already I could feel the pulse of New York and could almost smell civilization in the air. I sensed the vibration of the subway, and as the ocean mimicked the noise of rattling tracks, imagined being on the Lexington line #6 heading uptown. Soon, God willing, I'd be home. Home, after two and a half years of seeing the four corners of the world from the deck of this little 26-foot sailboat. The gray horizon to the west was full of promise.

Landfalls were not alien to me. I had emerged from the ocean void to stand in awe of jagged cliffs of the Galápagos, the verdant dream world of South Pacific islands, the cities carved from the rock of Malta. *Varuna* had shown me a world of physical challenge and jaw-dropping beauty; of ancient cultures; of generosity in the face of unspeakable poverty; a world where a smile is the greatest gift you can give or receive. Out of the past two and a half years, I had spent 360 days alone at sea, pressing ever westward, ever homeward. This final landfall would close the circle, end the dream, and begin the most daunting unknown yet.

I squinted into the howling winds, hypnotized, watching every wall of water catch up, lift *Varuna's* stern, and take us surfing down its crest. With just enough

> *Single-handed sailing presents challenges that are especially appealing to the adventurous woman.... Crewing on a boat has little to recommend it as long as the women members are confined to the galley and take their orders from the male skipper—it's not much different, in fact, from being on dry land. Single-handed sailing, however, gives a woman a unique opportunity to be in sole command of her own destiny, to test her independence and courage, to extend her sailing skills, to pit her physical strength against that of the sea, to push self-reliance to its limits, and to survive.*
>
> —Mary Russell, *The Blessings of a Good Thick Skirt: Women Travellers and Their World*

time for me to crouch and hang on, the crest of another thousand-gallon mountain broke and engulfed us. Water rushed up my pants legs and leaked into my hood and down my neck, and slowly the cockpit began to drain as *Varuna* lurched drunkenly onward. Making the adjustments to the windvane, I took a 360-degree scan of the barren seascape. As far as the eye could see, there was nothing—nothing but angry graybeards marching toward an eternal horizon.

Tarzoon meowed by the companionway, wet and matted, desperate to get inside to safety before the next drenching. Following him below, I peeled off the wet rain gear and turned on the radio. The BBC announced that things were going better in New York since Black Monday, four days before. We had been at 50 degrees longitude then, in the midst of a flat calm, almost two-thirds of the way across the Atlantic. As the announcer described the Wall Street crash, I had been studying my chart, staring at the place where we were now, wondering how it would feel to be here. Now I knew.

Tuning in to Radio France and clutching onto handholds, I stumbled the two steps toward the toilet, which was out of commission. It was always closed up at sea, where I was surrounded by the biggest toilet on earth. I didn't need the little white pot and transformed its closet into a hanging locker with lines holding everything in. I wrapped the gear over one line as it dripped down on the floor, threw a dirty mop-up rag over the new puddles in the cabin and rearranged the kerosene heater and bottled water. The heater fell over again with the bucking motion, dribbling some fuel, stinking up the small confines and making me dizzy. "More than enough kerosene," I thought. "Wish it were water. I have only five bottles left. I hope it'll last."

Putting my thermal underwear back on I saw Tarzoon chewing away at the coral fan Olivier had given me to bring home. "Stop it, you little monster!" I reprimanded, taking it away from him for the 50th time. It refused to stay in its lashings on the wall and kept tumbling down to my bunk and Tarzoon's teeth. Picking it up, once again I admired the intricacy of its lacy white fronds, thinking about Olivier and remembering how much he loved to dive in search of shells and underwater life. The fan had come from the San Blas Islands between Columbia and Panama, and I remembered that it was one of the first things that I had remarked on in *Akka*, Olivier's boat. Here on *Varuna* with Tarzoon, after nearly circumnavigating the planet, it was disintegrating.

"I wonder what he is doing now," I said aloud. "If he was able to come to the United States, perhaps he's at the American consulate, applying for a visa. If he wasn't able to come…" My emotions and energy were already stretched to their limits and I knew better than to risk the torture of negative thoughts. But it was no use. Although I tucked the fan away in the toilet closet, safe from harm, everywhere I looked were reminders of Olivier, the quiet man who had become a part of my life in Vanuatu in the South Pacific. Without him, I knew, I would not be here today.

We were both crying when we kissed each other goodbye, and I finally broke away from the little island of Malta, not knowing when or if we'd ever see each other again. Ahead of *Varuna* was the Mediterranean and then the North Atlantic. Olivier was headed back to his home in Switzerland. Our lives, which had been so closely aligned for so many months as we voyaged together around half the world—he aboard the *Akka* and I aboard *Varuna*—now seemed filled with uncertainty. Only time would tell.

At sea, the crashing, banging, and moaning sounds of a sailboat battling through a storm, however discordant, come together in a symphony of chaos. Any unusual sound or movement that disrupts it immediately stands out—like now. There was a slight knocking noise against *Varuna's* hull at the bow, and I turned toward the sound. The big jib, saved for lighter winds, was lashed down up forward and was working itself loose, with the metal eye at the foot of the sail beginning to bang against the hull with each wave. It had to be retied before it was dragged overboard.

Pulling my gear back on, I crawled outside and clipped the harness onto a jack line as *Varuna* buried her bow in every wave. "I might as well get this over with right *now!*" I yelled and barreled forward, splashing through the water on deck, grabbing the rails and the lifelines along the way and viciously stubbing my foot against a chain plate.

"Oh, for Christ's sake!" I screamed, as another wall of water threw *Varuna* over on her side and drenched me. My hood blew off and my hair whipped about my face as I reached the pitching foredeck. I held on and began to work free the waterlogged knots in the line, gathered the sail, rolled it up into a wad, and relashed it, quickly navigating my way back to the cockpit. At the spray hood, I took a quick check of the horizon, the deck, the rigging, and the frothing ocean one last time before dashing inside. When I replaced the slats, the howling din diminished as the radio welcomed me back with Bob Marley's "Coming In from the Cold." I sat in a heap on my bunk and glanced at my watch. It was only nine a.m.

The wind continued to cry through the rigging, the same sound as when it keened through the pine trees behind my family's house when we lived in Vernon. My thoughts drifted back to the days of my childhood, to my parents, and to our lives of such confusion that the fury of today's ocean almost paled by comparison.

inds. To blow us down and then to bring us home. To blow us back unto ourselves. Fill our sails and brim our hearts.

—Susan St. John Rheault, *Readings from the Hurricane Island Outward Bound School*

Looking at my hands, I smiled to see that they were now more callused than my father's had ever been during his years of eking out a living doing construction work. The day-to-day dampness at sea had soaked so deeply into the skin that the calluses now peeled off in shriveled white hunks. I thought of how proud my father was going to be; I had finally finished something other than a meal. My father, the collector of experiences, the gifted Swiss artist of boundless energies, had almost sent me to my doom. Although I might have set off on the voyage of his dreams, somewhere along the way, I had created my own.

For better or worse, my life was now woven from a different thread than that of the loved ones to whom I was returning. Very soon, I'd see the differences I had only read about in letters. I'd see my best friend from high school, Rebecca, whose first baby, my goddaughter Kendra, was one and a half years old already and whom I'd never seen. Many of my friends had gone away to college. Three had become heroes in the music world whom I had read and heard about in *Newsweek* and on the BBC.

Tony, my brother, wasn't in tenth grade anymore, but in college at Stonybrook. My sister Nina was in her third year at Cornell; and Jade, the youngest, was in her senior year of high school. We had all done our best to correspond and keep in touch by means of tapes and phone calls over the past two and a half years, but as the months passed and as the landfalls became more distant from home, I sensed in the letters and in the rare static-free telephone calls that our lives had diverged more radically than I ever dreamed possible. Did they feel it, too? I wondered if I would ever fit in again.

My life had been a mixed package of wild circumstances until the day *Varuna* carried me out of New York Harbor at age eighteen. I thought back to that day and recalled the frightened girl I had been, filled with such unbridled visions of the future. Today, I found myself envying her innocence. Now that she had learned the perils of the game, I wondered if she would ever again be brave enough to pay the price for a dream of such dimensions.

My bony knees were outlined through the thin long-john fabric. Although I was not as skinny as I had been in the Red Sea, I still hadn't accumulated any insulation. The Red Sea, which separates like a forked serpent's tongue the continent of Africa from the countries of Asia, had almost finished me with its searing heat and relentless headwinds. Unable to sleep for more than thirty minutes at a time for twenty days as a result of the weather, the sea conditions and a continuously breaking engine, I was overcome with dizziness and fever spells, and my normally 120-pound frame had shrunken to a skeletal 105 by the time *Varuna* arrived in Egypt. I hadn't regained enough strength before setting out through the Mediterranean, and had paid the price by almost losing my boat and my life 200 miles off the coast of Spain, with only a brief respite in Gibraltar before heading across the Atlantic. I had no choice. The deadline was bearing down like a grizzly after a field mouse and I had to carry on.

The New York I was coming home to could never be the same as the one I had left at eighteen, but the names still felt as alive as nerve endings, and the sounds of them on my lips as we got closer were like a soothing mantra. Greenwich Village. Tri-BeCa. SoHo. Memories of home became clearer as the final miles ticked into *Varuna's* trailing taffrail log.

Tarzoon rubbed his nose against my face and I was brought quickly back to the present *Varuna* canted downwind. "How's my little buddy?" I asked, taking him in my arms and scratching his belly. His purrs warmed my heart. I reached up to the swinging net over my head and pulled out the bags of pumpkin seeds and cat treats. The little hammock, a present given to me in Bermuda, my very first landfall, contained vegetables, snacks, odds and ends. When I first hung it across the cabin, it had been a brilliant white, but now it was gray, hanging by its last threads as if waiting for me to get home before retiring.

My mind was spinning, more from the pressure of homecoming and new beginnings than from fear of the surrounding storm. For thirty months and 27,000 miles, there had been no uncertainty about the future. Every day, my objective had been clear—to head westward, to return home. For every storm, every calm, every emotional how and high, the one thing I could always count on was that eventually it would become a memory. Today, my mind was riveted on the future. The most daunting landfall of all lay ahead, on that horizon to the west. I was returning to a home that could never be the same as the one to which I said goodbye a lifetime ago.

At the age of eighteen, Tania Aebi left New York on a three-year solo circumnavigation of the globe. The story was chronicled in her book, Maiden Voyage, *from which this story was excerpted. She has since earned her captain's license and has chartered boats to lead flotillas and teach groups of women how to sail all over the world. She now lives in Vermont with her two boys.*

★

For those of us for whom a comfortable bed, running water, and the probability of living at least until tomorrow is of prime importance, the phenomenon of the traveller appears as incomprehensible as it is intriguing. Here are people who have succumbed to the treacherous seduction of the unknown, who actually choose to put their lives at risk by climbing the sheer and icy face of an avalanche-ridden mountain; who sail alone in frail craft through towering seas; who will eat maggots and river insects if nothing more palatable is on offer, and who can live, day and night for months on end, in the shadows, and the promise, of the unknown.

It is easy to dismiss such people as oddities—as indeed they are—to be relegated to the bedlam of flat-earthers, freefall divers, or indeed writers. That they exist cannot be denied, but the strange, uncomfortable world they occupy lies well outside our everyday experience and can be dismissed, we tell ourselves, as an irrelevancy. We can shrug our shoulders and return thankfully to the twentieth-century world of microwave food and answerphones, glad that the only risks to our health are the predictable ones of smoking, eating hydrolyzed animal protein, or making a kamikaze dash across a city street.

—Mary Russell, *The Blessings of a Good Thick Skirt:*
Women Travellers and Their World

⋆ ⋆ ⋆

Polar Encounter

*At age 50, the author became the first woman to ski
to the magnetic North Pole, accompanied by her
Inuit husky named Charlie.*

IT WAS ONLY SIX O'CLOCK, SO I DECIDED TO HAVE A HAVE A leisurely breakfast of a bowl of granola, milk powder, coconut flakes, raisins, and butter mixed with warm water. I sat on my sled to enjoy the full effect of my first breakfast of the expedition only to find that after the third spoonful it was frozen. So much for leisurely breakfasts! I added more warm water and ate the rest as fast as possible. Then I melted enough ice to fill two vacuum bottles with water and a carbohydrate powder.

The dry Arctic air holds little moisture, causing quick dehydration of the body, which, in turn, causes early fatigue and reduces the body's ability to keep warm, so fluid would be just as important as food to keep my energy reserves up. I put my day's supply of crackers, cashews, walnuts, and peanut butter cups in my day food bag along with the two vacuum bottles and slipped everything down into the front of the sled bag. Then, remembering Charlie's appetite for crackers, I added a few more.

Last to be packed was the tent. I was completely engrossed in finding a way to twist the tent ice screws out of the ice so that my hands wouldn't scream in protest when suddenly I heard a deep, long growl coming from the depths of Charlie's throat. In a flash I looked at him and then in the direction in which he was staring. I knew what I would see even before I looked. A polar bear!

It was a female followed by two cubs coming from Bathurst Island, slowly, purposefully, plodding through the rough shore ice toward me. They were two hundred yards away. With a pounding heart, I grabbed my loaded rifle and flare gun and carefully walked sideways a few steps to Charlie, who was snarling with a savagery that caught my breath. Without taking my eyes off the bear, I unclipped Charlie from his ice anchor and, again walking sideways, I led him to the sled where I clipped his chain to a tie-down rope. The bear, now only 150 yards away, wasn't stopping. Her cubs had dropped back, but she came on with a steady measured stride while I frantically tried to remember all the Inuit had told me. Keep eye contact, move sideways or slightly forward, never backward, stay calm, don't show fear, stand beside a tent, sled, or other large object to make my five feet three inches appear as large as possible. Don't shoot unless forced to. Don't wound a bear, you'll make it even more dangerous, and never run. Repeating to myself, "Stay calm, stay calm," I fired a warning shot to the bear's left. The loud explosion of the .338 had no effect. On she came. I fired a flare, landing it a little to her right. Her head moved slightly in its direction but she didn't stop. I fired another flare, this time dropping it right in front of her. She stopped, looked at the flare burning a bright red on the white ice, then looked at me. She was only one hundred feet away now.

By this time my nerves were as tight as violin strings and my heart could have been heard at base camp. The bear began to step around the flare, and I dropped another flare two feet in front of her. Again she stopped, looked at the flare and at me. Then she fixed her tiny black eyes on Charlie, who was straining at the end of his chain, snapping and snarling, trying to reach her. She looked back at her cubs. I could sense her concern about Charlie's snarling, rabid act and her cubs. She waited for her cubs to catch up, then moved to my left in a half circle. In spite of my sore fingers, I fired two more flares in quick succession, trying to draw a line between her and me. She stopped, then moved back toward my right. I fired two more flares and again she stopped. She seemed to want to cross the line of flares but was unsure of the result and of Charlie, so she elected to stay back. She kept moving right in a half-circle, still one hundred feet away. Finally, with a last long look, she plodded north with her two new cubs trotting behind her, their snow-white coats contrasting with their mother's creamy, pale yellow color.

The whole episode lasted fifteen minutes but seemed years long. I was a nervous wreck. My hands were shaking as I stood still holding my rifle and flare gun, watching the trio slowly move north. But in spite of the mind-numbing fear that still gripped me, I could feel deep down inside a real satisfaction. I now knew that I could stand up to a bear in the wild, stay calm enough to function and still remember the words of wisdom from the Inuit. With Charlie's help, I had passed my first test. The bear had been completely silent as it had approached and moved around me on paws thickly padded with fur on the undersides. I was thankful for Charlie's warning. Now he had stopped growling and snarling but still stood rigid, watching the bears as they zigzagged in and out of the rough ice, hunting for the seals that lived in the cold waters beneath the ice. He seemed to hardly notice the giant hug I gave him. He was still on guard.

Helen Thayer is a professional mountain guide, former discus thrower, and U.S. National Luge Champion (1975). At the age of 50, she skied solo to the magnetic North Pole. Six years later, she and her 65-year-old husband, Bill, became the first and the oldest married couple to walk to the North Pole. Helen, Bill, and their husky live in Snohomish, Washington. This story was excerpted from her book, Polar Dream: The Heroic Saga of the First Solo Journey by a Woman and Her Dog to the Pole.

*

While I am often accused of being a bit short-sighted, I maintain that no one could mentally prepare for the yawning vastness of the Arctic. It happens so fast—going from the comforting close quarters of the cockpit to the wide open space. There was no sign—none—of others. Absolutely nothing to connect to the civilization just left behind: no power lines, forgotten twist ties or signs. The only footprints were cloven, clawed, or padded. Worse, there was no one to look at and say "Oh boy, *now* what have we gotten ourselves into?" Nervous giggling simply requires more than one person.

—Liz Cornish, "Humor Loves Company: An Arctic Circle Solo,"
Canoe & Kayak Magazine

ANNE DAL VERA

✦ ✦ ✦

Endurance on Ice

*A day in the life of an Antarctic expedition
for four American women who skied
to the South Pole.*

THE COLD WIND STUNG MY FACE AS I PULLED A 185-POUND SLED over the ice at eighty-five degrees south latitude in Antarctica. The temperature was zero degrees. I cursed the wind as I bent to pull against it, then turning, I saw the perihelion, a rainbow around the sun. It filled the sky with the brilliance of thousands of particles of ice reflecting the light. Sun dogs, or false suns, shone on either side of the sun, and a band of white light stretched horizontally around the sky.

It was November 20, day twelve of the American Women's Antarctic Expedition (AWE). I was enjoying this spectacular scene with three other women— Ann Bancroft, Sue Giller and Sunniva Sorby—as we skied and pulled sleds with our food and equipment from the edge of Antarctica to the South Pole— 678 miles, the distance from

The four women involved in the expedition included expedition leader Ann Bancroft, mountaineer Sue Giller, ultra-marathoner Sunniva Sorby, and the author, Anne Dal Vera.

Their goal was to traverse the Antarctic pulling all of their supplies on sleds, without the help of dogs or motorized equipment. The expedition left on November 9, 1992, and reached the South Pole on January 14, 1993.

—MBB

Denver to the Mexico border. Our sixty-seven day undertaking was a challenge in every respect: physical, emotional, spiritual, mental, and financial.

We camped in two tents, two women in each tent, changing tent partners every eight days. This gave us the opportunity to get to know each other better and to keep good communication in the group.

A typical day unfolded something like this. We woke up at six a.m. and one woman in each tent lit the stove and boiled water for hot chocolate or mocha java. She then got her mittens, socks and hat down from the drying rack and cared for her feet, taping on moleskin to prevent blisters, or foam pads to relieve tendonitis. As she cooked breakfast, her tent partner got up and prepared for the day. We ate as much hash browns and cheese and sausage (or oatmeal with cherries) as we could. Then we put on sunscreen, sunglasses, layers of pile clothes, wind pants, wind jacket, socks, boots, gloves, mittens, and a down jacket. Dressing was a difficult task in a small tent with an overstuffed stomach!

Emerging from the tent at eight, we packed our stuff sacks of food, clothes, and equipment into the sled, laying the sleeping bag and its waterproof cover on top. We greeted the two women from the other tent and asked how they were as we rolled up the tents and slid them into the sleds. Sue gave us the magnetic bearing for the day, to keep us heading south. Finally, we buckled ourselves into the harnesses of our sleds, adjusted our compasses, and skied off in single file.

The first two and a half hours of travel were measured by the steady progress of the sun from our left shoulders toward our backs. I usually needed to warm up a bit before pulling hard. The first break was very welcome, as Sue and I were almost always starved. We sat on our sleds and drank hot water and ate gorp, cookies, cheese sticks, and crackers. After a few minutes of talk and rest, the cold seeped into our bodies and we knew we had to move on. We reluctantly took off our down coats and swung our hands to warm them. Then we skied for two more hours. One of us led by sighting on a distant spot of bright light or a shadow and following the compass bearing. We took turns leading, enjoying the feeling of discovery and freedom and the exertion of pulling hard and making the first tracks. Those who were following could occasionally let their minds wander or take photos. When the terrain wasn't too challenging, I tried to remember the words to songs of struggle of people in other places and times.

We skied hard like this for up to ten hours a day, with a break every two hours. At the end of the day, around 8:30 in the evening, we set up the two tents. One woman in each tent started dinner while the other finished securing the tent and sleds for the night. She also piled up a stack of snow blocks by each door of the tent, which we later melted for our water.

Dinner was a creative endeavor: beans and rice, or mac and cheese, or pasta with sausage and tomato sauce. We often had soup and grilled-cheese sandwiches for an appetizer. I made apple crisp a couple of times. Sometimes we baked oat scones, biscuits, cornbread, or gingerbread. We had quite a bit of variety in our food, which prevented most cravings. Usually one of us cooked while the other relaxed or wrote in her journal. Our tents functioned as bedroom, living room, dining room, and kitchen—all in the space of a double bed plus four feet. In the constant wind, the tent fly flapped in a staccato rhythm, making communication with the other team members difficult, if not impossible.

Melting snow for the next day's breakfast and thermos bottles was the last task of the day. On cold nights we took a hot water bottle to bed. But often the solar radiation in the tent at night was enough to keep us quite warm, as we had twenty-four hours of sunlight. November at the South Pole is actually summer, so sometimes we even had to unzip our sleeping bags to cool off! If we were efficient, we managed to get seven hours of sleep before the alarm went off signaling the start of another day.

As expedition leader, Ann Bancroft kept track of the "big picture" of the project. Sue Giller was expedition navigator, while Sunniva Sorby made sure we kept the correct procedures for the research that was done and kept record of our use of medications in the first aid kit. My role was expedition food planner. I worked with a dietitian to plan the food and obtain donations of everything from bacon and butter to beans, dried cherries, and pasta. I continued to make sure we ate well on the expedition.

For Ann, the past four and a half years had been a constant push of letter writing, phone calls, and meetings to work out the myriad details necessary for a nearly million-dollar expedition. She had a wonderful sense of humor, a big dream, and the desire and determination to achieve her goal. It was on the 1986 dogsled journey to the North Pole with the Steger expedition (where she was the only woman), that she was smitten with love for polar regions. She brought together more than two hundred volunteers to work together and form the American Women's Antarctic Expedition Foundation. Ann also selected the other members of the team from women recommended through the mountaineering and dog-sledding communities.

Sunniva Sorby coordinated the research on the expedition. At thirty-one, she was the youngest member. Although Sunniva joined the team only three weeks before we left the U.S., she put her life in order quickly and embarked on this grand adventure with her whole mind, body, and spirit. Her cheerfulness in spite of illness and injury was remarkable. Sunniva had muscle spasms in her neck for the first week, then she came down with bronchitis. When that cleared up, she got tendonitis in her feet and sprained an ankle. She remained determined to continue on and became aware of new lessons in dealing with pain.

Holidays brought an opportunity to celebrate and renew our spirits. Sue turned forty-six on November 15th. We sang "Happy Birthday" and had a little party with balloons and magic candles on gingerbread cake—all of us in one small tent! On Christmas, Santa visited us from the North Pole, pulling a sled loaded with goodies. Stockings hung by our air vents were filled with small treats and we cooked scrambled eggs with cheese and peppers for a special breakfast.

As I spend time in wilderness, I develop a strong attachment to the land. Antarctica is an incredibly beautiful place. Although we didn't go where the penguins live, we saw snow sculptures of dolphins leaping into the frozen air. And, we were blessed with an ever-changing landscape as the wind sculpted the snow into unique wave-like shapes called sastrugi. Quite often we would pull our sleds, creaking and groaning, over six to eight inch ridges of snow.

Sue, Ann, and I all got minor frostbite on our thighs from opening the side zippers of our wind pants for ventilation and from having to "drop trousers" to pee so often. We learned to go very quickly!

As I toiled to pull my sled over cold hard sastrugi, I often asked, "Why am I doing this?" I came to realize that there were many reasons. Although I had taught cross-country skiing for fourteen years and led year-round outdoor trips for the past ten years, I was now ready for a personal challenge. I am an experiential educator. I ask people to take risks as they learn about themselves in the outdoors. I think I had begun to question the meaning of my work in experiential education because I hadn't done the risk-taking and introspection that I was asking my students to do. Training with the AWE team and skiing to the South Pole provided me with the challenges I needed to learn about myself in relation to the land, and in relation to a small group of women.

It seems a contradiction and denial of their sex that women should risk the very thing which only they can nurture and sustain, namely life itself. Yet despite being hemmed in by society's barriers, their vision obscured by fixed horizons, their growth stunted, and their potential to develop forced into the narrow channels leading to marriage and motherhood, women throughout the centuries have managed to transcend their condition and reach out for the world. The reason is clear. If they are to do more than simply give life—if they are to enrich it as well—then the journey must be made which takes them beyond the physical and mental confines set by society. That women are capable of grasping this aspect of their destiny has been ably demonstrated by those pioneers who, valuing freedom more than conformity, have walked out into the world and taken possession of it.

—Mary Russell,
The Blessings of a Good Thick Skirt: Women Travellers and Their World

I love wilderness and cold climates. Skiing in the wilderness is my passion. I knew I had the skills and the ability to enjoy the rigors of travel in extremely cold conditions with a small group of women. I believe that life is to be lived fully. When an opportunity arises to live in a way that you are ready to live, it makes sense to go for it.

Only now am I beginning to realize the real intensity of working so hard and relying on a group of four women. We each had our hard times and received the caring support of the other three. And we were each called upon to give everything we had in patience, strength, and humor. We did have disagreements, but no major fights. I find that I have a deep respect and appreciation for the qualities of each of these courageous women. We are all so different, and we used our different qualities to work together as a team, drawing on each woman's strengths. Sue put her energy into efficient camping and travel, taking care to keep the equipment in good shape, and getting enough sleep. Sunniva was indomitably positive and cheerful in spite of her painful illness and injury. Ann's unflagging determination and desire inspired us to continue when we were weary. I gave hugs, sang songs, and tried to encourage the others. We found that although we got annoyed by some idiosyncrasies, we still valued and needed each individual and the qualities she had to offer the group. Ironically, it was often the trait I admired most in a woman that would annoy me. I became irritated by Sue's efficiency, which, while necessary, seemed to be like a roommate's compulsive need for a spotless kitchen. My interest in her personal life no doubt irked her as well.

I am sure that each one of us felt held back at some time and felt that she held the others back at other times. But as Ann once said, "That's part of traveling in a group. I didn't come here to do a solo trip."

When we were tired and didn't want to go on, how did we get motivated to continue? We encouraged each other. Usually, when one of us was feeling particularly tired or was hurting, the others had the strength to cheer her on. We also remembered the support from friends and family and even strangers back home. Often, I thought of the effort put into getting us to this incredible place.

The pressure of making miles each day was always on our minds. We had to make some difficult decisions about whether to travel or rest on some days. It required an exchange of information from all of us, keen examination of our physical conditions, and an estimate of the toll the daily exertion was taking on our bodies. As a result, I think I have a better understanding of what it means to set a goal and work toward it. It requires pacing, endurance, focus, and concentration.

I was curious to see where my limits really were. Just when I felt I was about to break from physical, mental, and emotional exhaustion, I would find another ounce of energy and go on. It must have been a deep spiritual resource fueled by the power of the land, ice, snow, and wind. On December 17th, day 39, I felt extremely weary of the struggle. I had skied up to sixty-nine miles with tendonitis, which produced a painful throb with each step. The ibuprofen I took masked the pain for a while, but I was not healing. I felt more and more depressed. Finally, at a break, I lay down on my sled and cried. Ann asked, "What's wrong, Anne?" Sunniva walked over to me and rubbed my back and listened to my tales of pain. Sue told me that when she had been feeling bad in the first weeks of the trip she noticed all the sparkles in the snow and it reminded her of all the people who loved and cared for her. I began to feel much better and was able to continue to ski. Later I switched medications, to Arnica Montana, a homeopathic remedy. Within four days my tendonitis had healed and I was happy once again.

Through the trip, I began to see that the way to go on in the face of adversity was to believe in myself; to trust that I would be able to continue even in pain, even in loneliness. By pushing my limits, I learned the line between discomfort and danger. For example, after each break, my hands cooled off. I had to take off my down coat and put on the sled harness and skis. My hands would often become almost numb as I began to ski. I would take off one pole and swing my arm vigorously to get the blood flowing back into the fingertips, then switch my poles to that hand and swing the other one to get it warm. I would do this as I skied. I knew the

edge between very cold hands and numb hands meant the difference between pain and frostbite. I constantly checked my face as I
skied to feel if the skin exposed to the wind had become numb. A
mental checklist of each part of my body kept me very aware of
life-sustaining blood flowing to each cell.

One discomfort we faced was the absence of a shower. It is
amazing how well one can wash with a bandanna and a cup of
warm water. Still I longed for a refreshing plunge in a bath. So one
day I worked up a sweat, then stripped off my clothes and rolled
in the snow! It was as wonderful as a sauna and a swim.

On January 13th, after sixty-six days of pulling the sleds uphill,
Sunniva spotted the buildings of the scientific station at the South
Pole—about fourteen miles away. We skied steadily toward it all
day on January 14th. At 6:30 we were greeted by three construction workers who told us that they had been anxiously awaiting
our arrival. As we covered the last two miles to the Scott-
Amundsen base, waves of scientists and support workers came out
to greet us. The warm welcome was completely unexpected. I felt
very energized by the excitement these people had for our
achievement. Along with a feeling of great satisfaction at reaching
the Pole, we came to the realization that we had made history. We
were the first all-women's expedition to ski from the edge of the
continent to the South Pole. Ann Bancroft is the first woman to
cross over ice to both the North and South Poles.

This expedition never received corporate funding, although we
approached more than 250 corporations. Only Marlboro, the cigarette manufacturer, expressed interest, and the expedition members decided not to sell our souls to the makers of tobacco or al-
cohol products. One corporate executive reportedly told Ann
Bancroft, "Maybe…if you take a man along…." Other companies
were fearful that if the women got hurt it would be bad for their
image. Some didn't want to sponsor a women's expedition because
they assumed that all the team members were lesbians. A lot of
suggestive remarks were made both directly and indirectly: Two
women to a tent? Gonna keep each other warm? Such homopho-
bic assumptions weren't made about Will Steger's 1990 all-male

Antarctic Expedition or the Reinhold Messner/Arved Fuchs ski traverse of Antarctica.

Now that I am home, people often ask me if I would do this again. I pause, reflecting that the challenges of this journey are still with me. Financing a $900,000 expedition is a major undertaking. Over half of the expedition's $900,000 budget was paid by $12 to $25 donations or by sympathetic supporters who bought the $12 AWE t-shirts. The smallest gift was $5, the largest $10,000. The AWE team members are still working hard to pay off the rest of the debt. We wonder what it will take to convince corporations that it is in their best interest to support women who are experienced in their field and who choose to take on new challenges and continue in the face of adversity. Through my slide show and talks I have become a public figure, which is very new to me, and not something I willingly sought out. Leaving loved ones for a long period of time to work harder than I have ever worked before, day after day, demanded that I learn to pace myself physically and sustain myself mentally, spiritually and emotionally. Still, I long to return to the ice, the cold wilderness of quiet, the pure air that carves sastrugi. I long to travel light and fast....

Anne Dal Vera guided outdoor trips for women and taught co-ed wilderness courses in Alaska and Minnesota. She currently works as a Wilderness Ranger in Colorado. She wrote about the AWE expedition in Another Wilderness: New Outdoor Writing by Women, *edited by Susan Fox Rogers and published by Seal Press. She writes poetry and is working on a book about the AWE expedition, integrating her experience with insights about how women work together.*

✳

I began to wonder again why I, and so many others like me, should find ourselves in these recondite places. We like our life intensified perhaps. Travel does what good novelists also do to the life of every day, placing it like a picture in a frame or a gem in its setting, so that the intrinsic qualities are made more clear.

—Freya Stark, *The Journey's Echo: Selections from Freya Stark*

⋆ ⋆ ⋆

Alone in the Outback

On an epic journey across Australia with four camels and a dog,
the author wrestles with joy and despair.

THAT EVENING THE CAMELS PLAYED IN THE WHITE DUST, RAISING
balloons of cloud that the fat, red setting sun caught, burst and
turned to gold. I lay on a foot-thick mattress of fallen leaves which
scattered golden jangles of firelight in a thousand directions. Night
calls and leaf sighs floated down to me on the breeze and around
me was a cathedral of black and silver giant ghost-gums, the thin
sliver of platinum moon cradled in their branches. The heart of the
world had been found. I drifted into sleep in that place and allowed the mountains to fade along the rim of my mind. The heart
of the world, paradise.

I decided to stay in that place as long as the water held out. I
planned to enter the sandhills and ride out to those distant mountains. But first the camels must rest. There was feed here to burn.
Salt-bush, camel thorn, mulga, everything their little hearts could
desire. Diggity [her dog] and I explored. We found a cave in Pine
Ridge which had Aboriginal paintings plastered all over it. Then
we climbed a narrow, treacherous rocky gap, the wind howling and
whistling down at us. We pulled ourselves up to the flat top, where
freakish rock strata ran in great buttresses and giant steps. The trees
up there were gnarled into crippled shapes by the roar of the wind.

Along the distant horizon I could see a sandstorm being whipped up into a cloud of red, straight out of *Beau Geste*. Further west, we discovered ancient desert palms, called black-boys. Rough black stumps shooting out fountains of green needles at the top, all huddled together by themselves, like an alien race left behind on a forgotten planet. There was a haunting hallucinatory quality about this place. I felt swelled by it, high as a kite. I was filled with an emotion I had not felt before—joy.

Those days were like a crystallization of all that had been good in the trip. It was as close to perfection as I could ever hope to come. I reviewed what I had learnt. I had discovered capabilities and strengths that I would not have imagined possible in those distant dream-like days before the trip. I had rediscovered people in my past and come to terms with my feelings towards them. I had learnt what love was. That love wanted the best possible for those you cared for even if it excluded yourself. That before, I had wanted to possess people without loving them, and now I could love them and wish them the best without needing them. I had understood freedom and security. The need to rattle the foundations of habit. That to be free one needs constant and unrelenting vigilance over one's weaknesses. A vigilance which requires a moral energy most of us are incapable of manufacturing. We relax back into the moulds of habit. They are secure, they bind us and keep us contained at the expense of freedom. To break the moulds, to be heedless of the seductions of security is an impossible struggle, but one of the few that count. To be free is to learn, to test yourself constantly, to gamble. It is not safe. I had learnt to use my fears as stepping stones rather than stumbling blocks, and best of all, I had learnt to laugh. I felt invincible, untouchable, I had extended myself, and I believed I could now sit back, there was nothing else the desert could teach me. And I wanted to remember all this. Wanted to remember this place and what it meant to me, and how I had arrived here. Wanted to fix so firmly in my head that I could never forget.

In the past, my bouts of gloom and despair had led, like widdershins (water-worn gulleys), to the same place. It seemed that at that place was a signpost saying "Here it is," here is the thing you must push through, leap free of, before you can learn any more. It was as if the self brought me constantly to this place—took every opportunity to show it to me. It was as if there was a button there which I could push if I only had the courage. If I could only remember. Ah, but we always forget. Or are too lazy. Or too frightened. Or too certain we have all the time in the world. And so back up the ravines to the comfortable places where we don't have to think too much. Where life is, after all, just "getting by" and where we survive, half asleep.

And I thought I had done it. I believed I had generated a magic for myself that had nothing to do with coincidence, believed I was part of a strange and powerful sequence of events called fate and I was beyond the need for anything or anyone. And that night I received the most profound and cruel lesson of all. That death is sudden and final and comes from nowhere. It had waited for my moment of supreme complacency and then it struck. Late that night, Diggity took a poison bait.

We were running low on dog food, and I was too lazy, too high to want to go and shoot some game for her. So I rationed her. She woke me up sneaking sheepishly back into the swag. "What's up, Dig, where've you been, little woofing?" She licked my face profusely, snuffled her way under the covers, and snuggled as usual into my belly. I cuddled her. Suddenly she slunk out again and began to vomit. My body went cold. "Oh no, no it can't be, please, Jesus, not this." She came back to me and licked my face again. "It's OK, Dig, you're just a little bit sick. Don't worry, little one, you come and snuggle in here and get warm and you'll be OK in the morning." Within minutes she was out again. This couldn't be happening. She was my little dog and she couldn't be poisoned. That was impossible, couldn't happen to her. I got up to check what she had brought up. I remember trembling uncontrollably and droning to her, "It's all right, Dig, everything's all right, don't worry," over and over. She had eaten some dead animal but it didn't smell rotten, so I repeated to myself that she couldn't be poisoned. I forced myself to believe it yet I knew it wasn't true. My head raced through what you do for strychnine poisoning. You have to swing them around your head to make them get rid of it all, but even if you do it immediately there's virtually no chance of survival. "Well, I won't do that anyway, because you're not poisoned, you're not poisoned. You're my Dig and it can't happen to you." Diggity started wandering around retching violently and coming back to me for reassurance. She knew. Suddenly she ran away to some acacia bushes and turned to face me. She barked and howled at me and I knew she must be hallucinating, knew she was dying. Her two mirror eyes burnt an image into my brain that will not fade. She came over to me and put her head between my legs. I picked her up and swung her round my head. Round and round and round. She kicked and struggled. I tried to pretend it was a game. I let her down and she went crashing through the undergrowth barking like a mad dog. I raced for the gun, I loaded it and went back. She was on her side convulsing. I blew her brains out. I knelt frozen like that for a long time then I staggered back to the swag and got in. My body shook with uncontrollable spasms. I vomited. Sweat soaked into the pillow and blankets. I thought I was dying too. I thought that when she licked me, I had swallowed some strychnine. "Is this what it feels like to die? Am I dying? No, no, it's just shock, stop it, you must go to sleep." I've never been able before or since to do what I did then. I shut my brain off and willed it into unconsciousness.

I woke well before dawn. The sick, steely, pre-dawn light was enough to find the things I needed. I caught the camels and gave them some water. I packed my belongings and loaded up. I felt nothing. Then suddenly it was time to leave that place and I didn't know what to do. I had a profound desire to bury the dog. I told myself it was ridiculous. It was natural and correct for the body to decay on the surface of the ground. But there was an overwhelming need in me to ritualize, to make real and tangible what had happened. I walked back to Diggity's body, stared at it, and tried to make all of myself face what was there. I didn't bury her. But I said goodbyes and thank-yous and I wept for the first time and covered the body with a handful of fallen leaves. I walked out into the morning and felt nothing. I was numb, empty. All I knew was I mustn't stop walking.

I must have walked thirty or more miles that day. I was afraid to stop. Afraid that the feeling of loss, guilt, and loneliness would swamp me. I pulled into a wash-away and built a bonfire. I had hoped to be so exhausted that I would fall asleep without having to think. I was in a strange state. I had been expecting a lack of control over my emotions, but instead I was cool, rational, hard-edged, accepting. I decided to finish the trip in Wiluna, not because I was wanting to run away from it, but because I felt that the trip had ended itself; had reached some psychological conclusion, had simply become complete, like the last page of a novel. I dreamt that night, and most following nights for months, that Diggity was all right. In my dreams I would relive the sequence of events, only it always turned out that she survived, and that she forgave me. She was often human in these dreams, and talked to me. They were disturbingly vivid. I woke to the reality of loneliness, and was surprised at the strength which enabled me to accept it.

It may seem strange that the mere death of a dog could have such a profound effect on someone, but, because of my isolation, Diggity had become a cherished friend rather than simply a pet. I'm sure, had the incident occurred back in the city, surrounded by my own kind, the effect would not have been anywhere near as great. But out there, and in that changed and stretched state of mind, it was as traumatic as the death of a human, because to a large extent she had become just that, she had taken the place of people.

I was woken that night by the most chilling, hair-lifting sound I had ever heard. A soft, high-pitched keening that got louder and louder. I had never been afraid in the dark, and if I heard a sound I couldn't place, it didn't disturb me too much. Besides, Dig had always been there to protect and comfort me. But this? Ripples ran up and down my back. I got up and wandered around camp. Everything was perfectly still, but the noise was now a continuous unmodulated wail. I began to recognize the first tell-tale signs of panic—this noise had to have a rational explanation. Either that, or I was going mad, or some spirit was out to drive me that way. Then I felt the first stirrings of breeze. Of course, the noise I was hearing was the wind whistling through the top tips of the trees. There had not been a breath of turbulence on the ground, but now the pre-dawn wind, that solid unflagging front of cool air, was chilling me to the bone and making the coals of the fire glow red. I crawled back into my swag shivering, and tried to get back to sleep. I would have given anything just then, to be able to hold that familiar warm dog flesh—the need was like a physical ache. Without her, I was suddenly susceptible to all those swamping, irrational feelings of vulnerability and dread.

Most of the rest of that week or ten days was a timeless blur. The ground travelled under my feet unnoticed until some piece of country shocked me out of my mental machinations. I kept getting the odd sensation that I was in fact perfectly stationary, and that I was pushing the world around under my feet.

Robyn Davidson is an Australian adventurer and writer best known for her remarkable overland journey from Australia's Red Center at Alice Springs to the Indian Ocean at the age of 27. Her book about the experience, Tracks, *has been translated into more than ten languages, was transformed into a* CD-ROM *product and photo book called* From Alice to Ocean: Alone Across the Outback. *She is also the author of* Traveling Light *and numerous magazine articles. This story was excerpted from her book* Tracks.

✳

Where there is a heart, there is heartache. Open up your heartache.
　　　　　　　　　　　　—Inez Baranay, *The Saddest Pleasure*

✦ ✦ ✦

The Broken Heart
of Don Manuel

The author interrupts her travels, and lingers to love.

CONFESSION: I WAS A KEPT WOMAN. A MISTRESS PRIVILEGED TO sleep late, drink champagne with breakfast, and not give a thought to mortgage payments, stopped-up toilets, or office politics. I didn't work at the time, at least not from nine to five. My "job" was making one man feel good, and that man was Don Manuel Estevez de la Fuente Fria.

Don Manuel, a Spanish aristocrat with waxed handlebar *mustachios* and a 24-karat family seal ring on his pinky, was generous, flamboyant, and accustomed to getting what he wanted. Fortune had been good to him: he had wealth, friends, an indestructible liver. His capacity to enjoy life was as boundless as his line of credit.

There was a once-in-a-lifetime quality to our meeting. One does not meet a Don Manuel on any street corner, after all. No, men like Don Manuel move in charmed circles against a backdrop of starry nights, hugging the equator. They inhabit splendid old mansions in towns with names like Sans Souci or Isla Verde. They make grand entrances.

Don Manuel did not walk into my life, he *sauntered*, with a bottle of Moet in each hand and a fetching, if foul-mouthed, parrot perched on his left shoulder. He found me pacing outside a café, where a friend—already late—was to meet me for early evening *tapas*. His commanding gaze danced flamenco across my anatomy with undisguised admiration.

"Don Manuel Estevez de la Fuente Fria, *a sus ordenes* (at your service)," he introduced himself, bowing from the waist.

"*Torpe* (clumsy)!" squawked the parrot, dislodged by the gesture and struggling to right itself.

"*Callate, maldito* (be quiet, damn you)," ordered Don Manuel in a whisper at once mellifluous and menacing. Turning to me, he smiled, drew himself up to his full height, and gallantly extended his arm. "Will you accompany me?"

I took his arm, and remained glued to it for more than three years.

Not that being the mistress of a man with a dozen-syllable name was my idea of self-actualization. Though I might have once mused about such a life, I had mountains of my own to climb, a profession to pursue, and a ticket home tucked away in the pocket of my bulky winter coat.

Still, I dallied. Don Manuel's ebullient magnanimity proved too great a temptation. Each time I'd book a flight, he enticed me back with a serenade, a party, or a new car. When he bought me a beachfront condo, my resolve went limp as week-old ceviche. I moved in.

He visited me there several times a week, always bringing a gift of flowers or bubbly, sometimes parking his parrot on my bedpost. There was no presumption in the man. He treated me with the indulgence of a doting father (which he was old enough to be), the ardor of a schoolboy courting a first love.

Still, I was restless, and twenty, and never for a moment doubted that the future was one endless blank check awaiting my endorsement. Surely Don Manuel, a free spirit himself, knew better than to expect a butterfly to roost. But passion has a logic all its own. People tilt.

The trouble started the day Don Manuel went for a physical exam, his first in years, and came home with a wired-up contraption strapped to his torso. A heart monitor. The poor man, suddenly peaked and ancient, collapsed onto my sofa. When he spoke his voice had a tremor.

"*Mi amor* (my love)," he said, "I'm kaput. The doctor says my left ventricle could give out at any time."

"No, heavens, no!" I exclaimed, throwing myself into his arms—and nearly shattering my ribs against the monitor's rock-hard shell.

"If I must die, let me die making love to you," he intoned breathily, thrusting his chest out even as his shoulders sagged under the weight of the diabolical little machine.

"Do you really think that's a good idea?"

The words were not a question but rather an expression of the most dire mortification. The specter of Don Manuel expiring of cardiac arrest sprawled atop me stark naked at the height of orgasm flashed before my eyes.

We made love in a tangle of wires and surgical tape, hanging on each heartbeat. The monitor's needle took off like a rollercoaster.

"Are you all right?" I asked him.

"*Estupendo* (stupendous)!" he assured me.

His hardware clanked, then revved briefly, and finally went still.

"I may not have long to live," he told me afterward, dropping to his knees beside the bed with as much elegance as his wiring permitted, "but however much time I have—a day, a year—I want to spend every second of it with you. Marry me and I'll make you a rich widow."

Far be it for me to pooh-pooh the heartfelt entreaty of a dying

> *I once had a six minute love affair with—who else but an Italian—on a platform in the Verona train station. I had got off one train and was completely puzzled how to catch the next which was momentarily due to leave for Munich. A young man—and I also was younger in those days—came to me, offered to carry my bag, hurried to the right platform, declared his undying love for me, agreed, if I would like it, to come with me to Munich for a holiday, agreed not to when I, regretfully, said I was meeting a friend, kissed my hand, again declaring his eternal love and helped me on to the already moving train. Twenty years later it is one of my most charming memories.*
>
> —Jan Haag, "Last Minute Terror"

lover, but at the tender and self-absorbed age of twenty, I was in no hurry to be a widow, neither was I eager to spend the next twenty years of my life with a moribund man. Not wanting to inflict the death blow, I hedged. Don Manuel's *mustachios* drooped.

"*Pobre diablo* (poor devil)!" the parrot piped in from the bedpost.

"*Callate, por Dios* (be quiet, for God's sake)," sighed Don Manuel.

The following day the dying man returned to the doctor and was told there had been a mistake. His heart was fine. He'd live to be a hundred.

Don Manuel revived but our romance expired. We parted a few months later, gingerly, without rancor. I shipped the car, furnishings, and miscellaneous trinkets he had bought me to the States, sold the condo, and used the cash to finish college. We corresponded for a time, then lost touch.

For me there has never been another Don Manuel Estevez de la Fuente Fria. His effervescence was epic, his pluck immortal. Wherever he may be, among the living or the dead, I raise my glass in fond salute.

Itinerant writer Germaine W. Shames has written from six continents on topics ranging from Latin lovers to sex-crazed swamis. Her essays have appeared in such anthologies as Cupid's Wild Arrows *and* Travelers' Tales Mexico *and is the author of* Transcultural Odysseys. *She was last spotted trailing a gypsy caravan through Transylvania, having celebrated her 40th birthday in questionable company at Dracula's Castle.*

✳

> Whoring? I guess I thought it was part
> of the adventure, that I was smart to get
> sex, interpreter, companion in one
> package, but by increments of mornings,
> this brown face has grown dear upon my pillow.
> Across the jittering spoons on the dining
> car table, I watch her laugh at jokes in her
> comic book as we ride north to trek the hills.

She won't like that, thinks walking's for the poor,
for farmers and now she's a city lady

who taxis, paints her fingernails. Her father's
a farmer. He sold, first her sister, then her,
to a man from Bangkok when the droughts came.
The two support ten who, in good years, gather
in the rice sheaves, but never enough to buy

back even one. I paid the bar a month's fee.
We went to Koh Samui. Scared, she walked
the beach but wouldn't go into the sea
above her knees unless I held her. We took
the shells she'd chosen in the sand and presents

from Bangkok to the farm. The family was
polite but formal like a nineteenth century crew
lined up to meet the captain's wife who brought
aboard bad luck. She's taught me Thailand, given
me a purchase on the culture, until

she and the country have become a chord
in memory, not separate notes. That body,
each breast sweet as brown domes of raw sugar
sold in the market, has the softness of
soil clouding round the plow in paddy water.

Two weeks, then I go back to work, to college.
I bought her a diaphragm, urged the pill –
her sister's on her third abortion. Maybe
I can send a small check from time to time.

—Karen Swenson, "Getting a Purchase," *The Landlady in Bangkok*

STACY ALLISON

⋆ ⋆ ⋆

Triumph on Mount Everest

Despite an abusive husband and shattered self-esteem, the author
summoned the spirit and courage to climb peak after peak
and become the first American woman to reach
the summit of Mount Everest.

I COULD SEE IT NOW, OFF IN THE DISTANCE. THAT LAST GLINT OF white against a powder blue morning sky. Two hundred yards away. A slow uphill walk in the thin air, perhaps fifteen minutes. Each step a physical strain against the altitude, the desolate air, the sudden bursts of high-velocity wind. But there it was, almost close enough to touch. A few more steps, and I would.

But first, the ridge. It slopes up from the left at about 35 degrees, then peaks to the right as a series of cornices—ridges of overhanging ice and snow, poised above a sheer 8,000-foot drop. A stress fracture in the snow, crawling up the ridge a few feet to the left of the dropoff, marked the fault line. I kept to the left of the crack in the snow, trying to avoid riding a broken cornice down into Tibet, but still keeping a buffer between my path and where the slope turned steep and fell away on the left.

The worst was behind me, but I was so high now, so exposed. A sudden gust of wind, I thought, could lift me right out of my boots and sail me all the way back to base camp. Or one of these icy overhangs could snap. Or I could catch a crampon on my pants and tumble down the other side of the ridge. Death was everywhere. I forced it down and drilled myself onward. I went as fast as I could, one foot down, then the other. Walking with my ice ax, chunking the tip into the snow. Keeping an eye on the stress fracture, on the bottomless slope to my left. Glancing up, seeing the end of the ridge in the distance. The end of the ridge, and the end of the world. I could make it. As long as I kept moving, I was going to make it.

Pasang was on the ridge now, following my steps about seventy yards behind me. In the distance I could see the Koreans, small specks of color sitting in the snow. They were on the summit. I was so close. But I couldn't think about it yet, not with these cornices, the drop-off, the stress fracture swerving between. I had to follow that line, and keep moving. I was still digging for breath, feeling the thunder in my chest, still keeping tabs on my numb toes. And still climbing.

The air looked like crystal. The sky was so blue, the sun gleaming yellow and powerful. Even in the cold the rays felt palpable, as if they carried a physical weight. I could see everything. Up above, a few wispy clouds skimmed by the sun, riding the highest winds in the firmament. Behind me, I could look down into Nepal. All but a few of the tallest peaks were covered by thick, billowing clouds. The sky was clearer above the brown plains of Tibet, spread out ahead of me. I could see the plains, rolling away, and closer in I could see the Rongbuk Glacier, where I'd been standing exactly a year earlier.

Now I was 75 feet away. Walking carefully, minding the crack in the ridge and the tip of my ice ax, my crampons squeaking in and out of the snow. *One foot in front of the other.* Fifty feet. Closer to the Koreans now, close enough to see them snapping pictures of each other. So close, but I wouldn't let myself feel it yet. Not until I was there. Something was swelling inside me, but I pushed it down. I had to keep moving, stay focused on the crack, the steps, reaching out with my ice ax, pulling in another two feet. Taking another step, then another, and reaching out again. Walking faster, feeling the adrenaline starting to flow, surging through my veins and running hot into my fingers and even my dulled toes.

Twenty-five feet. It was unbelievable. Now I knew I was going to make it. I could see the Koreans talking on their walkie-talkie. Just beyond where they stood, I could see blue sky.

Ten feet. This was it. I checked my watch—just past ten-thirty. September 29, 1988. The Koreans were watching me now, the leader reaching out to shake my hand. "Good, very good!" he called, and beneath my oxygen mask I smiled. But I barely heard him, and kept going, those last few feet to where it ended. It was so strange. After everything, I was walking onto the summit of Mount Everest. It was right there, I could see it clearly just ahead of me. The last few steps, just a little higher, and then there was nothing. The end of the ridge, and then nothing but that clear, empty air.

I stopped climbing.

There was nowhere else to climb.

I was standing on the top of the world.

I felt it now, everything I'd kept bottled up as I came up the ridge. It billowed up from my core, a blinding wave of emotion. I could finally let it all go, the months of controlling my thoughts, of channeling all my energy toward this one purpose. Behind my glasses my eyes blurred. I was wide open now, and I was aware of everything. The wind in my hair, the sweat on my back, the blood washing through my wrists and ankles. I made it. For myself, for Steve and Jim, for everyone. I was standing on the top, looking down on the world. It was real—that fragile dream I'd first had so many years ago. The vision I'd nurtured so carefully over the years, the one I almost lost touch with last year. I had taken it back and it had all come true. I was strong enough. I was good enough and lucky enough...and I had come out the other end. After everything, I finally had.

Pasang was still ten minutes away. So it was just me. A small patch of snow, a lot of sky, and me. The cloud of emotion thinned, then vanished. My eyes were dry again. I took little steps and turned around on the snowy crest of the summit, this way to look over Nepal, then that way to see into Tibet. Behind me the

Koreans hung together in a tight circle, laughing and chattering to their base camp on the walkie-talkie. Now I felt strange. *I was on top of the world, but I was alone.* This wasn't how I wanted it to happen. During all those years of wishing, dreaming about it, working for it, I never once imagined I'd be alone when I got to the summit. I wanted to hug someone, to make this dream explode into life by seeing it reflected in someone else's eyes. But I was on top of Mount Everest by myself.

Then Pasang came up. He pumped his ice ax in the air, hooting and yipping with everything he had left in his lungs. The Koreans looked up from their radio and greeted him, slapping his back, pumping his hand. The sight popped the lid off my emotions again, and I walked over to him, reaching out to Pasang and wrapping him in a bear hug. "We did it," I said, my eyes going hot and cloudy again. "We really did it."

The Koreans were putting their packs on now, taking their first steps down the ridge. Then they were gone. Pasang and I had a minute or two to stand alone on the summit, then it was time to get to work.

Back home, we'd engaged donors by promising to entwine their own names with the summit. Now that we were really on top of Everest, we had to provide the payoff. Opening my backpack, I dug in for the Honor Roll, the small roll of microfilm listing the names of all the people who had donated money to our expedition. I scraped a shallow pit in the snow, laid the roll of film inside, and covered it over. But our corporate sponsors expected a more tangible kind of testament. I gave Pasang the camera, then reached into my pack for the corporate banners.

There were 25 of them wrapped in a stuff sack, some as small as a handkerchief, a few as large as a tablecloth. I planted my pink flamingo in the snow, then sat down and unrolled the first banner. Pasang snapped a few photos, and then we moved on to the next one, then the next. The task soon grew tedious. My smile started to hurt, and I began to get cold. To make things even more difficult, the wind was blowing up again. The gusts kept blowing my parka hood off my head. That made me worry about holding up the larger banners—what if one blew out of my fingers?

After a while, I pulled off my oxygen mask and took a stab at breathing the thin, cold air of the jet stream. My body felt it immediately but my head stayed clear. It seemed livable, and it made me think of Jim and Steve. I wished they had come up with me.

During the half-hour it took to shoot the corporate photos, Pasang and I were all business. Once we were done, however, we had a few minutes to ourselves. We snapped a few pictures of each other, and I shot a series of panoramas. Then I reached into my pocket for my own artifacts. Climbing the mountain gave me something to take away. It felt only appropriate to leave a small part of me behind. I had a little piece of turquoise a Tibetan yak herder had given me in 1987. He'd lived in the shadow of the mountain for his entire life, but never dreamed of climbing it, so I promised to take something of his to the top. I had a baggie of blessed rice I took from our altar at base camp the day we set out for the summit. I had a prayer scarf, a snapshot of me with David, and, finally, a Susan B. Anthony silver dollar.

I looked at my watch. It was getting late now, after eleven. We didn't have that much time, but I still felt I had to ground myself. I thought about the mountain's spirit. The Mother Goddess of the Earth. I thanked her for

*C*homolungma, *the Tibetan name for Everest, means "Goddess Mother Earth."*
—MBB

being kind enough to let me climb her. I prayed she'd let me get down in one piece, too. I looked at my watch again, and saw I'd already been on top for close to 45 minutes. I caught Pasang's eye and gestured down. He looked surprised.

"Now?"

"Soon. In a minute," I said.

We stood together, looking out over the world beneath us. I wanted to remember everything. The cold, dry air between my lips, the wind pushing against my back, the way the silvery wisps of cloud jetted across the sky. I needed to remember it, to keep the image deep inside the vaults in my memory bank. This was the top of Everest. The dream of a lifetime. I looked around. There had to be something for me to latch onto. A perfect image I could remember that would objectify why I'd come, for now and forever. But nothing came into focus. It was hard to believe, after so many years, but the summit of Everest was just snow and ice. A mountain summit, pretty much like any other mountain summit. I was contemplating this when Pasang looked over at me and said: "We spend two months getting to the mountain, carrying things up the mountain, climbing the mountain. We work like dogs, then spend so little time on top, and now we go back down. What's the meaning?"

I shook my head. How do you define ambition? People do strange things—stand on their heads, play computer games, write 100,000 prayers to Buddha. You find your talent, and see how far it will take you. You do what makes you feel the most alive.

Stacy Allison, in addition to mountain climbing, runs a construction business and travels the country giving lectures. She and her family live in Portland, Oregon. She is the author, with Peter Carlin, of Beyond the Limits: A Woman's Triumph on Everest, *from which this piece was excerpted.*

★

Most people climb mountains for the sheer challenge and exhilaration of it. But for 46-year-old Laura Evans, a five-year breast cancer survivor from Ketchum, Idaho, climbing represented her hard-won victory over cancer, and a way to help other cancer victims fight back.

Laura Evans, along with a team of seventeen breast-cancer survivors climbed Aconcagua, a 22,834-foot mountain in the Andes of western Argentina. The team members represented a cross-section of breast cancer survivors: several had lost both breasts; others, including women in their early thirties, were battling the hot flashes and moody-blues of surgically-induced early menopause; a number of women were still nearly bald from chemotherapy.

Their shared goal was to raise $100 a foot climbed per team member to fund breast cancer research, for a total of $2.3 million, so they knew every step counted.

"Only three of us got to the summit, but we were everyone on the mountain, everyone on the expedition. We all reached important summits for ourselves," said Nancy Knoble.

People don't have to climb mountains to prove there's a life beyond cancer. I think what the expedition did was to celebrate that life is for living. For each of us who had life-threatening diseases, it's important to go on, to find important and joyful things, focus on them and enjoy the fulfillment of your dreams, whatever they may be.

—Carole Jacobs, "The Breast Cancer Climb: Mind over Mountain,"
Shape Magazine

LYNNE COX

✦ ✦ ✦

Even a Babushka

An endurance swimmer shocks Inuits and Soviets
in a swim for peace across the Bering Strait.

WE MOTORED SOUTH IN THE *UMIAKS* [WALRUS-SKIN BOATS] ALONG the craggy shores of Little Diomede toward the southern tip of the island where we would begin the crossing. Ethereal clouds and mist swirled around the island, and the air was filled with the smell of sea birds and salt and was charged with expectation.

I had to try to calm myself, to focus on what I was about to do, not to be distracted or overwhelmed by it all. I told myself to take it slowly at first. Take off your sweats. Let your skin cool down to the air temperature. Be prepared. The water will be colder. Wait until everyone's ready before you get in. I looked at our tiny flotilla: the villagers in their *umiaks* waiting excitedly and the crew turning the boats into position. Bill told me he thought everyone was ready. How cold is the water? I wondered, but I didn't want to know for sure, I was afraid it would psyche me out.

I peeled my sweat suits off quickly, put them in a bag so they would stay dry, put on my swim cap and wrapped my goggles around my hand. Then I climbed up onto the zodiac's pontoon, focused, told myself once you start, don't stop for anything. I took a deep breath then slid feet first into the Bering Sea.

276

It felt like cracking through ice as I plunged down into the dark gray water, then popped up and swam as fast as I could toward Little Diomede. I touched shore, waited for a moment for everyone to check their watches, and then pushed off the rocks and began a three-mile sprint for Big Diomede.

> *Lynne wears neither a wet suit nor insulating grease over her thin swimsuit.*
>
> —MBB

I couldn't see where we were headed, the entire Strait was covered in fog, and the walrus-skin boats which were supposed to be beside me, guiding me, were behind. Be patient, I told myself. But I knew that I couldn't be. For the average person, survival time in 42-degree water is twenty minutes. I knew I had trained for this, to increase my survival time, but every moment I strayed from course reduced my chances of making it across. I looked back at Bill and Jan: they were fiddling with the equipment. They should have been keeping track of what was happening. I lifted my head and yelled, "Bill are we going straight or what?"

Bill looked up from the equipment, realizing I was disappearing in the fog in front of them. "Straight," he pointed and asked Pat and the guide in the journalists' boat to move in on either side of me.

I was swimming as fast as I could move. It was like being on the very edge of life. The water was so intensely cold, I had to be so aware of my body. My fingers were together. I wasn't losing fine motor control, but my hands were numb. I had to wait to feel the push of water against my thighs to know if my hands were pulling any water. I was sprinting to stay warm, to stay alive. I glanced at my shoulders. They were turning white, but at least they weren't blue.

In the zodiac, Jan and Bill were shouting at me. Jan was wearing a complete dry suit in case he had to jump into the water to drag me out. Bill was hunched over, trying to retain body heat. Bill hated the cold as much as cats hate water.

"We need to take your core temperature." Jan grabbed the receiver, which looked like a portable mine sweeping device, and

positioned himself on the zodiac's pontoon. Bill moved to the opposite side to counterbalance Jan while I swam to within two feet
of the zodiac. I rolled over onto
my back and began backstroking
as quickly as I could go. I wasn't
producing as much heat as I did
swimming freestyle. Heat was
being drained from my body,
heat that I would never get back.
Jan was trying to hold the receiver near my stomach. He was
trying to catch a moving target
and waves were bouncing him
up and down. A surge heaved the
zodiac; Jan nearly flew into the
water but caught himself and
tried again. This was slowing me
down. I didn't want to wait. I was
getting colder. Bill stared at a dig-
ital read-out in his black box and said they got my temperature. It
was 97-degrees.

The first question anyone wants to know about Lynne Cox is how she tolerates cold, COLD water. Lynne's body fat percentage is 33 percent (20-26 percent is typical for women and female runners can go as low as 13 percent) and is evenly distributed. Her body density is about the same as salt water, which means she doesn't have to expend effort to stay afloat...and high VO_2 max help her resist hypothermia in water as cold as 38 degrees.

—Michele Kort, "The Big Chill,"
Women's Sports Fitness

"Right, she's cooling down a bit. Lynne are you all right?" Bill
asked.

"Yes, this is great," I said, laughing, trying to cover up that the
outside of my body was freezing. I didn't want them to panic and
pull me out of the water. I had to appear warm. But I was worried. I hadn't expected to lose so much heat so soon. Without
knowing exactly how cold the water would be and how it would
affect me, Bill, Jan, and I decided that I had a three hour time limit.
By then, the water would have cooled my peripheral area down
and after the swim was completed, we expected my core temperature to drop. We didn't want it to drop too far, so we were racing
against the cold and against time.

Jan knew I was using a lot of energy. He asked me if I wanted
something to eat but I couldn't stop, not for anything. I was hoping we were moving forward. I couldn't tell; there were no refer-

ence points. Our visibility was less than 50 meters. I kept hoping
the Soviets knew we were there. We had had no communications
with them. With the fog they couldn't see us.

We have to be past the half-way point by now, I told myself. But
there was no sign of the Soviet ships. My body felt the water for
vibrations. I listened for the deep sound of a ship's engine. There
was nothing new.

Clouds were swirling tightly around us, closing out the light.
Our visibility was less than ten feet. It was as if we had become de-
tached from the world. A blip of warmth on a cold gray sea like
tiny stars in the blackness of space. We were in a void between two
lands. Do they know we're out here, I wondered? Have we drifted
too far north? Was the current stronger than we had expected? Did
we miss Big Diomede? We only had a four-mile-long target to hit.

I moved closer to the *umiak,* feeling my breath shorten. I didn't
want to be lost in the fog again. The fear was still there. It had
never left. Maybe it was an instinctual fear for survival—something
my mind would never override.

David checked the compass. He noticed he was 30 degrees off
course. David said something to Pat in the Inuit language. Both
boats made sharp corrections to the left.

 Suddenly, the current was broaching the left side of my head.
What are they doing, I wondered? Could we be off course that far?
Don't they realize that every moment we stray off course we di-
minish our chances of making it across? But then I thought, how
can you expect them to know how important it is to maintain a
direct line? You've never worked with them before and they never
believed you'd get in the water. How could they? No one on Little
Diomede swims. When they fall into the water they don't believe
they'll survive and so they drown. Why would they think you're
any different?

A heavy sleet began falling. My body ached from the cold. Bill
and Jan waved me over for another reading. I rolled over onto my
back. I was getting impatient. These readings were taking too long.
Every time I slowed down I felt myself get colder. Cold tremors
were running up my back. Jan couldn't get the reading. He waved

me away, then waved me back for another attempt, but I ignored him. I had to get warm. I had to swim faster than before to get warm. It was more important to be warm than to get a reading. The goal was to get across.

skimos call themselves "Inuit." They were the only people living in the Arctic for thousands of years. "Eskimo" is an Indian word meaning "eaters of raw meat." The Inuit are masters at tracking polar bear and seals across the Arctic ice, but the idea of swimming in the Arctic waters, which freeze over in the winter, is foreign to them.

—MBB

A few minutes later Jan called me again and I rolled over onto my back. The receiver wasn't working. They were fiddling with it. The cold was biting into me. I decided at that moment, I couldn't slow down again.

Suddenly, we made another sharp correction to the left. Why can't they stay on course? Have we missed Big Diomede? Have we drifted into the Chukchi Sea? Is that why the Soviets haven't found us? Where are you? Are you out there? Can you hear us? Please find us. God, don't they know how much we want to see them? To go this far and then miss them. Oh, that would be so horrible. I can't think that. I can't. Maybe my mind can travel beyond my body. Maybe they will hear my thoughts. Picture the Soviet boat. Tell them where you are with your mind. This could work. If invisible wavelengths can be transformed into sound and light, maybe the Soviets can hear my mind. Try it. Try anything. We're over here. We're here, my mind shouted.

I didn't know it then but Pat wasn't sure where we were. He told Bill that he and David had only hunted as far as the border area. He said he didn't know what the currents were like beyond that point. Pat asked Bill what direction he thought we should take. Neither Bill nor Pat knew how far we had already drifted. Bill suggested that we continue heading south to compensate for the northward current. Pat agreed.

Suddenly I felt the water tremble beneath my body. It was a boat. I could hear it through the water. The crew heard it too. They were staring into the fog. The boat was circling. It was them! Who else could it be? They were searching for us! They were so close we could hear their engine. But the sound was changing. Their boat was moving away. Oh God, no.

The crew was shouting and waving but in the fog their voices were muffled, their hands were unseen.

Jim began making catcalls. Jan fired a flare gun. We heard the motor. It was louder. When I looked up on a breath, I saw Claire bouncing up and down in the *umiak*. Jack was pointing and shouting, "Look Lynne, there they are! It's them. It's the Soviets!"

A gray 30-foot boat emerged slowly from the fog.

"Yea! Yea!" I shouted. In my mind I had imagined this moment—our boats meeting in the middle. But I could never have imagined the way I would feel at that moment, the complete joy. There the Soviets were, in real life. But it didn't seem real. It was as if we were living in a dream.

The swirling fog was melting in the warm sunlight. We had crossed the U.S.-Soviet border. We had crossed the international dateline. We had moved from the present into the future.

"What day is it?" Claire cupped her mittened hands around her red face.

"It's tomorrow!" I shouted gleefully. At that moment I knew my life and the world would never be the same.

The crew's excitement and energy rippled across the water to me. But there seemed to be something wrong. The Soviet boat was keeping a distance of twenty yards.

Why? I wondered. Were they unsure of us? My arm strokes reach out into the gray sea. Each hand reaching farther into the future.

Slowly the Soviet boat moved within fifteen yards of us. Every time I looked up to breathe I tried to see the reactions of the Soviet crew. They were immobile and stone-faced. Had we made a mistake? Had something changed? Were they upset I hadn't phoned them? Were they angry that we hadn't given them our exact starting time? I smiled. They didn't smile back.

A cold chill rushed deep into my body. I was tired, giving the cold the chance to penetrate deeper. Bill noticed this immediately. I told him I was okay. But my arms had no feeling.

"Your stroke rate's dropped to sixty-six. Pick it up," Jan coached me.

Stop looking up. You're wasting time. That's why you're getting cold. Turn your arms over. When I looked up, the fog had parted and the rocky cliffs of Big Diomede were towering above us. Before us were rocks. Bill said that I was 50 meters from shore. My heart leaped.

Suddenly, the water temperature dropped from 42 to 38 degrees and the cold popped the breath out of me. All I wanted to do was finish. We were almost there. But the Soviet crew was talking to Rich and Jack and pointing to something about half a mile down the beach. I could see a small black cluster on the white slope.

"The Soviet people are waiting for you over there," a man with curly brown hair shouted excitedly from the Soviet boat.

Bill told me I could stop now. If I stopped now, I would have succeeded.

"How far is it to the snow bank?" I asked.

The curly haired man turned and asked the captain of his boat then translated for me. They said it was half a mile.

"Bill, can I stop now?" I asked, trying to decide what to do.

"Yes. Yes. You can finish right there." His tone was urgent.

I just wanted to finish, to succeed, to get warm.

"She's going into shore," Bill said with relief in his voice.

But when I looked down the beach and saw those people standing there, I asked myself, will you be satisfied if you stop now? Everything that you have done has been to extend yourself, to go beyond borders. You have had to go beyond your physical and psychological borders. You've gone beyond the political and cultural borders. And you've had to go beyond the borders people placed around you. Everything everyone has done to get you and themselves to this point has been about extending themselves beyond their own borders. Believing when there was little to believe in, hoping when there was little to hope for, and now you can stop. You're ten yards from shore. If you stop now, you will make it. This water is freezing. I've got to consider how cold it will be when I climb out onto Big Diomede. No you don't. You're wimping out.

"You can finish on that rock." Bill was leaning so close to the water.

I took a few more strokes forward. You've got to decide now. The crew is preparing to land. I have to try. I turned left and began sprinting. I glanced at Bill. He looked surprised and worried. He must have thought I had become disoriented.

"Bill, it's all the way or no way," I said, reaching deep within myself beyond anything I knew I had.

The crews on all the boats were leaning forward in anticipation and were cheering. I looked into their faces. Draw from their energy, I told myself.

The current was flowing directly into us at one knot, reducing my speed by half. I angled toward them, remembering that Dennis had told me that the current would be less there. He was right.

"Look, you can see the people!" Jack urged.

There were 30 or so black figures on a snow bank. I watched my hands pulling through the water. They were ghostly white. The water was six degrees above freezing. I imagined the people onshore extending an invisible rope, pulling me towards them. I could see the colors of the Soviet people's clothes, red, blue, green. They were slipping on the snow bank, running to the water's edge.

Bill was telling me I had to sprint to make it to shore.

Where could I find the speed now? Remember all those sprints you had to do at the end of every single workout? Sprint with everything you have left. Come on. Go.

The journalists' boat zoomed ahead. Men in military uniforms were setting out small wooden ramps. The journalists jumped out of their boat. The sea floor rose up to meet me. There were real life-sized people above me on the snow bank.

We were less than ten meters from shore. I looked up. A man in a green uniform was reaching out to me. I pulled off my goggles and stuck them in my mouth. I needed my arms for balance. I tried to crawl up the incline, but I slid backward. The three men were

You are as powerful and strong as you allow yourself to be.

—Robyn Davidson, *Tracks*

extending their arms as far as they could. They were speaking Russian. It was really Russian! I leaned back and threw myself forward and reached up as far as I could. The man in uniform caught my hand and pulled me up. Our eyes met and we smiled.

All those years, all the hope, all the effort dissolved into that very moment. We had made it! All of us. We had reached beyond our borders and they had reached beyond theirs. We had made it! I was too happy, too sad, too overwhelmed to speak. It was too much.

Someone was talking to me. A man. He was taking off his coat and putting it over my shoulders. Another woman with reddish brown hair was piling blankets on me. They were so heavy I could hardly stand. Too many thoughts were racing through my mind. Too much emotion in my heart. The curly haired man was kissing my cheeks as if I were a long-lost relative. He was so happy, so excited. Someone wrapped a green towel around my shoulders. My feet were wobbly. Bill and Jan were standing behind me ready to catch me. Bill was saying, "We've got to get her to that tent, we've got to get her warm."

The curly haired man was talking rapidly in my ear in English. He told me his name was Vladimir McMillian. He was a reporter for Tass. His mother was Russian and his father was American. He met her during World War II, married her and stayed in the Soviet Union. That was why he spoke English so well. Vladimir had been selected to serve as a translator for us to the Soviet press. Vladimir began introducing them to me: "That man is from Radio Moscow. The woman is from *Pravda*. He is with Bremia, it's Russian television, it's called 'Time,' like your 'Sixty Minutes.'" There are many others who would like to interview you now."

Bill was insisting that we go to the tent but Vladimir asked me if I wanted to meet the welcoming party. The Soviets had helicoptered people from all over the country out to meet us. There was Vitaly Medjannikov, the Soviet national swim coach. A world champion boxer, the governor of Siberia, the commander of a military garrison, and a Siberian Inuit woman.

The Inuit woman was a small pretty woman with dark hair and eyes. She kissed me on both cheeks and handed me a bouquet of wildflowers. She had gathered them from her village near Magadan on the Siberian mainland. The flowers were the same as I had seen on the Alaskan mainland: fireweed, forget-me-nots, aster, and goldenrod. She said that Alaska and Siberia had once been joined. This was something the Inuit people knew. They had family on both sides of the Bering Strait. They were separate, but after today they might see each other once again. I told her I hoped they would. Maybe this was a beginning. She smiled with tears in her eyes. And Vladimir pulled me away. He said the Soviet press wanted to conduct a news conference. I didn't realize what I was getting into.

Their questions were direct and difficult. One reporter from Russian television asked me, "Do you think your swim will contribute to a reduction of nuclear missiles in the United States and Soviet Union and further the INF treaty? Do the American people view the Soviet Union as the evil empire? Why did you make this swim? What do you feel now?"

The television cameras were rolling, and the lights and the microphones were in my face. It was all I could do to concentrate on the questions. I didn't want to look stupid, but I was so tired, and so cold, and my body was struggling to warm itself. Who did they think I was? No one had told me what to say. No one had briefed me. And how could I even speak for the American people? I tried to sort out my thoughts and feelings. And when I responded my speech was slurred.

Vladimir translated what I said to the Russians, "The reason I swam across the Bering Strait was to reach into the future, to cross the international dateline, and to symbolically bridge the distance between the United States and the Soviet Union. It was to generate goodwill and peace between our two countries, our two peoples. I would not have swum here if I believed that this was the evil empire. I can't say if this swim will contribute to the reduction of nuclear weapons, but I hope it does. We need to become friends." I said.

The media fell silent for a moment and nodded in agreement. I think they thought I would have a prepared speech for them. But these were spontaneous answers, ones that required considerable thought, but there was no time for deep thought.

In the background, Bill was saying, "We've got to move her. She's cooling down."

The reporter with Radio Moscow asked in English, "Who were corporate sponsors?"

Suddenly I was so embarrassed. I saw all that the Soviets had done: they had moved ships, helicopters, people, everything, to this island. Later I would find out they had spent more than a half-million dollars. What could I tell them? That no U.S. corporation had supported us? That none of them believed in us? I didn't want to embarrass the U.S. Should I tell them the truth, that I had to take out a loan to cover the expenses of the researchers and myself? I didn't want them to think that the Americans wouldn't value the Soviet effort. I didn't want them to think that no one in the U.S. cared. I didn't want them to think I was a wealthy American and did this on my own. I thought for a moment and said, "Our sponsors were the American people. They were individuals from all over the

Lynne has files of rejection letters from corporate giants, such as Coca Cola, IBM, and AT&T, whom she contacted more than 75 times during a 12-year period. But for her swim across the Bering Strait, Lynne had many supporters on a grass-roots level. A six-year-old California girl who had been taught swimming by Lynne gave the entire contents of her piggy bank—$24.85 in change. Private individuals she had never met sent checks in the mail. One Pennsylvania woman donated in the memory of her deceased mother who had believed strongly in world peace. The Los Alamitos Swim Team held a Swim-A-Thon and raised $250. Rocky Boots (not worn during the swim), and Monotherm, a company that makes rectal probes, were sponsors. In the end, Lynne took out a personal loan to cover her flight to Alaska.

—MBB

United States. There were old people and children and just ordinary people. They were the ones who supported us. We had some support from companies like Rocky Boots and Monotherm." My teeth were beginning to chatter harder.

They didn't understand. Didn't corporate America, the free enterprise system support you? Didn't you get paid millions of dollars for doing this?

Rich and Vladimir tried to explain grass-roots support. The Russian media continued asking questions.

"Bill, my legs are going, I can't do this any more," I said.

"Look Vladimir," Bill said, "her temperature is dropping. It could affect her heart. We've got to move her immediately. Can you walk, Lynne?"

I couldn't flex my feet or grip with them. I didn't know how I was going to walk barefoot across the ice. But two Siberian Inuit women suddenly emerged from the crowd. They presented me a pair of sealskin slippers. Vladimir explained that the slippers were made by the Inuit who lived on the Siberian mainland in the Chuckotka's Lawrentia region. With the help of the two women I put them on. They were beautiful beaded slippers and they fit perfectly. How did they ever know my size? I wondered.

The walk to the tent was 200 meters. Later I would tell Bill, I thought it was a mile. We slipped and slid on the ice and when we finally arrived at the tent, there was a cot with a heavy sleeping bag, extra blankets, and hot coffee. Standing near the entrance of the tent was a woman with reddish brown hair.

Everything we had requested was there except for the babushka, the colorful shawl. I was disappointed. The babushka symbolized the Soviet Union and warmth.

My body started shaking violently. My hands felt like clubs. I pulled the coiled wire out of the bottom of my swimsuit. One end had been attached to me before the swim, the other end I handed to Jan and he plugged it into the monitor. Vladimir came into the tent and told me the woman with the reddish hair was a Russian doctor.

"Go ahead and get into the sleeping bag. Make sure to place the reheaters, those hot water bottles, behind the back of your head, under each arm and in the groin area," Jan said, stepping out of the tent.

The woman doctor was using hand gestures to tell me to take my wet swimsuit off before I climbed into the sleeping bag. It was one thing to be naked in front of her, but another in front of the men on my team. I pretended that I didn't understand, but she wouldn't let me get away with it. Quickly she placed the hot packs around my body at the key sites. She didn't speak English and I didn't speak Russian. But it didn't matter. She kept feeling my cheeks with her hot hands and leaning on top of the sleeping bag to give me the warmth from her body. My breathing was fast and rapid like I was running a sprint. My body was working hard to generate heat.

"Her temperature's still 97. It's amazing it has stayed that high," Jan said walking into the tent with Bill and checking the monitor.

"Her skin is very cold though, probably about 40 degrees," Bill said, feeling my arm.

They set the defibrillator down on a table. The Soviet doctor saw it, stood up, and shook her head vigorously. She thought they were going to use it on me. And she stood between them and me.

Bill saw her and said, "It's just a precaution. I'd better find Vladimir. Jan, would you check her heart?"

Jan opened the bag and put the cold stethoscope on my chest. It was like a chunk of ice.

"Sounds strong and even," Jan said. "You okay?"

I nodded and covered my head with the sleeping bag so I could breathe into it and trap more heat. The Russian doctor wanted to see my face. She pulled the bag back down. Cold air hit my face. I slid deeper into the bag. Too cold to talk.

Jan put the cold stethoscope on my chest again. Shivers raced up my spine. I told him that I was doing fine. Bill noted that my temperature had risen to 97.5. It amazed me how hard my body had to shiver and breathe to rewarm. I was so tired.

The Soviet doctor leaned on me again to give me her body heat. She looked at me with such concern.

In the background, I could hear voices and people singing in Russian and in a different language; it sounded like they were having a party.

I wanted to see what was happening. Rich came inside and told me that the Soviets had set up two buffet tables and that there were waiters in white smocks serving hot tea in china cups, dried fish and bread, and chocolate-covered coconut candy. On the cliffs above the tables were two army officers watching everyone with binoculars and taking pictures.

It was a Siberian beach party. I wanted to join them but I was still too cold.

About an hour later, when I finally felt warm, I looked up at the doctor, who was leaning over me, and said, "Hi, my name is Lynne, what's yours?" We laughed.

"My name is Rita. Rita Zacharova." Quickly she took pictures of her family from her wallet.

"Your children?" I asked.

"No," she said, and then she said something I didn't understand.

"Not children. I babushka."

"You're a babushka?" I asked.

"Yes." She nodded quickly. "Gran children." She pointed to the pictures.

Then I realized that babushka doesn't only mean shawl. It also means grandmother. Rita Zacharova was my babushka.

A moment later, Rita reached into her bag and excitedly handed me a gift—a beautiful hand-painted lacquer bowl decorated with bright orange, red, and gold flowers. I thought, What can I give to her? I picked up my cap and goggles and handed them to her. Rita motioned that she couldn't take them. When I insisted, she accepted them as if they were precious gifts.

Claire Richardson asked me if I had heard what had happened with the Inuit from Little Diomede crew and the two Siberian Inuit women we met when we touched shore. Claire said that this was the first time in 40 years that the Inuit on Little Diomede had met with relatives from Siberia. Before 1948 the border had been open. The Inuit on both sides were allowed to go back and forth freely. But in 1948, Hoover closed the border. Claire said Pat had tried today to communicate with Zoya and Margaret, the two Siberian Inuit women who had given me the sealskin slippers. Pat wasn't able to speak with them because they spoke a different Inuit dialect called Siberian Yupik. But many of the elders on Little Diomede were walrus hunters and they used to hunt and trade with the Siberian Inuit. Pat knew the elders on Little Diomede could understand Siberian Yupik so he called Little Diomede on his two way radio. The elders on Little Diomede translated as all the villagers on Little Diomede crowded around the receiver in the community center to listen to the conversation.

Margaret Guchich asked about the walrus hunting and whaling around Little Diomede. She said it wasn't good for the Inuit in the village of Magadan, on the Sea of Okhotsk. She said that most of the whales were gone. Margaret also asked about John Kiminock, who had sailed from Siberia to Nome in the 1930s and never returned. The elders knew John. He was 86 years old and lived in Nome. They asked Margaret about his family, whom he hadn't heard from for over 50 years. Margaret said two of John's sisters had died, but three were still alive....

Claire and I were walking down to the *umiaks*. On Pat's short wave radio we suddenly heard singing. The villagers on Little Diomede were singing Siberian Yupik songs they had memorized from old records. They performed them for Zoya and Margaret. Zoya and Margaret listened and then they sang along. Over the short wave, the people on Little Diomede listened to Zoya and Margaret singing the old Inuit songs. And when they finished, the audience on Little Diomede applauded. Zoya and Margaret's eyes filled with tears. Mine did too. I wondered if the border could remain open for them and for all of us.

Our trip back to Little Diomede that afternoon was calm; the sky was clear blue and the silvery water shimmered as we motored back across the Bering Strait. All the villagers came out to greet us. They were dancing and singing the same Yupik songs we had heard on Big Diomede.

At age 15, Lynne Cox shattered the men's and women's world records for swimming the English Channel. After her historic swim across the Bering Strait, President Reagan and President Gorbachev toasted her at the signing of the first INF treaty. Most recently, her story, "Swimming to Antarctica," appeared in The New Yorker. *"Even a Babushka" was excerpted from her unpublished manuscript,* Beyond Borders.

✦

The reason why men and women set themselves the challenge of going beyond the limits of everyday endurance are numerous, complex and mysterious. Few can articulate their motives and fewer still feel it necessary so to do. Their actions speak for themselves. It is usually only after the journey has been completed that travellers will allow themselves the luxury of attempting an analysis, constructing a package of reasons which seem rational and can be presented to the questioner as a sort of peace-offering.

Most, however, are in thrall to a driving force within them which pushes them onward—a force which they seem powerless to resist. The force has no name but its function is to explore the potential of the human species to adapt to conditions that are both challenging and dangerous. By so doing, it increases our potential for survival.

—Mary Russell, *The Blessings of a Good Thick Skirt:
Women Travellers and Their World*

ANN ZWINGER

★ ★ ★

A Cave with a View

Fascinated since childhood with the tale of Robinson Crusoe,
the author follows in his footsteps.

ENSCONCED IN ALEXANDER SELKIRK'S SEASIDE CAVE, I LOOK through its entry arch, which frames a warp-dyed silk landscape, woven of lavender and dove gray, above a celadon ocean. The moment I first stood in front of it, a sense of familiarity washed over me. It was so exactly what I had imagined—the cobble wall in front, the framework of poles in the doorway, the yellow flowers dotting the grass—that I felt as if I had walked into an illustration from *Robinson Crusoe.*

Selkirk was the real-life model for Daniel Defoe's fictional Crusoe. The stiff-necked navigator of the British privateer *Cinque Ports*, Selkirk had come to mistrust both the vessel and her captain and demanded to be put ashore. Accordingly, in October 1704 he was deposited here on Isla Más a Tierra, largest of the Islas Juan Fernández, 400 miles off the coast of Chile.

Although Selkirk changed his mind and begged to be taken back on board, the *Cinque Ports* sailed off into the Pacific Ocean without him. And his first instinct had been correct: the ship foundered near the mainland, and those who didn't drown were imprisoned by the Spanish. Selkirk, on the other hand, remained here alone until 1709, when he was picked up by two other British privateers.

Now I'm here to be a modern-day Robinson Crusoe and to enjoy for myself the isolation of Selkirk's cave, near a small embayment called Puerto Inglés.

In Selkirk's time the island was empty, but today there is a village of some 500 people at Bahía Cumberland, on the northeastern tip of this roadless island, whose translation name means "closer to land" (as it is, compared to its sister, Más Afuerta, "farther from land" by about 100 miles). About 30 years ago the Chilean government changed the name of Más a Tierra to Isla Róbinson Crusoe.

I came into the airport on the island's southwestern tip a couple of days ago, flying the two hours from Santiago in a twin-engine plane. To me Más a Tierra looked very small in that immensity of sea, at the mercy of an unfriendly surrounding medium that had been working on getting rid of the island for the last three million years.

A line of white surf scribed its edge, white feathery cartouches on the sea's map. Tufts of clouds stuck to its promontories, and anvil-shaped El Yunque, at 3,000 feet the island's highest point, wore its clouds like a cardinal's hat. It dominated the eastern end of the island, a deeply dark green terrain, sharply ridged and crimped.

From the airport I hitched a ride on a small boat to the village of San Juan Bautista, a rock-and-roll ride along the volcanic cliffs of the island's north coast. As we rounded the headland into Bahía Cumberland, a charming Monet painting hung before me: blue waves peaking into sprightly whitecaps; opulent, thickly green mountains, colorful roofs; and fishing boats, white with dark green trim, bobbing cheerfully at anchor.

In the village I got supplies (including home-baked bread, there being no bakery on the island) to take with me to Selkirk's cave, and arranged for a boat to drop me at Puerto Ingles and leave me to my solitude.

It was not an easy landing. We threw an anchor out about 30

feet offshore, cut our motor, and rowed to a rock outcrop. I jumped off the boat as it heaved up against the jagged, slippery rock, taking advantage of the upward motion to be thrown to shore. I left fingernail marks in the basalt.

Selkirk's cave is larger than I anticipated, the ceiling high, the floor as clean as if swept—in short, cozy. I've set up housekeeping, pitched my tent, hung my backpack and rain suit on spikes in the wall, by my own inclination doing what Defoe scripted Robinson Crusoe to do. It must be a human reaction to a new place where you find yourself alone; recreate the familiar.

I join other households already established in the porous, abrasive walls. In the hundreds of holes, spiders have spun silk, closing the apertures to form pencil-width tunnels, interspersed with small fresh ferns in other cavities. Numbers of infinitesimal ants nest at the base of one of the upright poles that form the screen of the cave, surrounding the pole with little granules of excavated soil. They are so tiny that when one trails across my bare toes I never feel it, only know it's there if I happen to glance down.

After setting up housekeeping, the second thing I do when out alone is walk the bounds, define this new world that is mine to prospect.

To the west of the cave a broad meadow opens, the end of a small valley, including more flattish ground than anywhere else on the island except around Bahia Cumberland. As I walk, hundreds of half-inch grasshoppers spring up out of the grass like gray ghosts, crackling spirits, invisible until they fly.

A fresh bubbling stream a foot wide runs through the meadow's edge. Beside it, dew-beaded spiderwebs drape a shrub. In the stream, masses of extra-peppery watercress surround lavender mint and blue speedwell and small dock plants with rosy seed heads. I follow the water to where it gurgles into the cobble beach. Never more than ankle deep, it has cut no channel but twinkles out through the grass.

From the puddles pop little frogs, each of which would fit on a quarter. One mystery of islands is how plants and animals get there.

The eggs of these frogs perhaps came on the feet of migrating birds, which also carry seeds. Essentially dark olive green, the frogs' only distinctive markings are three black stripes that converge in the eye, and adorable pale pink feet. (I hear them singing at night, tiny bursts of amorous longing, a gentle trilling that befits a creature small enough to sit under a watercress leaf.)...

When one is out alone, life takes on a much different rhythm, governed mainly by dawn and dark, the weather, and one's stomach. The rest of the time is up for grabs. I eat at odd hours, explore a lot, see the same place from different directions, note how early the thistles open, how late before the grasshoppers are active, when the land snails are out.

This morning, in a tuft of grass, I find two snails in *flagrante delicto*. Their silvery paths have tinseled the dirt by the cave, but until today I've seen only empty shells, usually with the spine broken through, as if they'd been eaten. These snails wear fresh lustrous shells—chocolate bands on cinnamon, interlined with cream. Their bodies are palest dove grey with a tinge of peach, lightly speckled, tentacles and horns turning slowly like radar antennae.

With the woodland around Puerto Inglés gone, the terrain has dried out and is less hospitable to indigenous species. Chonta, the lovely palm endemic to Más a Tierra, and which "abounded in the island" in Selkirk's time, has all but disappeared because its satiny white wood with glistening black bands made it a natural for carved objects. The sweet heart of this palm, also called "cabbage tree," provided Selkirk's favorite food, but the harvesting killed the tree. The few left are in difficult-to-reach places in the high country, their slender, glossy green boles neatly ringed by leaf scar lines.

I eat most of my meals on the beach, not wanting to drop any tidbits in the cave and encourage the hordes of ants that long ago dug their nests here.

Among the lumps of white shells worn to nubbins, and a few red and ocher pebbles, the volcanic beach cobbles stand out—

doorstop size, beautifully rounded. Many charcoal gray ones, full of gas when they hit the atmosphere, are evenly pitted with tiny holes. Others have larger holes as if they'd been worked by boring clams. Marveling at permutations of color and shape, I wonder from what depth within the earth they came, what minerals they carried, how quickly they cooled, how long did the ocean tumble them to create this size and this perfection.

Within moments 35 dark red crabs appear close by. Number 36 skulks in a crevice right beneath my feet. Some are busily feeding, scarcely missing a beat in transferring food to mouth, scraping minute scraps off the rocks, first right, then left. Their little white claws make them look white-gloved, dainty dowagers enjoying high tea. Others hold their claws poised, like wind-up toys just run down, needing to be rewound.

I begin on the chicken leg I've brought with me from the village. As I nibble, a scrap of skin drops off and I leave it, intending to pick it up later, forgetting what quick scavengers crabs are.

One crab picks up the whole piece in one claw and drags it like a security blanket across the rocks. Most rocks here are porous, and the crab's progress is purposeful and secure. Then it starts up the face of a gray cobble so smooth it has difficulty getting anchored. At the crab's most vulnerable moment, precariously hanging by only three feet, a second crab scuttles up from beneath and grabs the skin. A tug of war ensues, and the skin parts, leaving each with a snippet.

As time goes on, I become more and more entranced with the crabs and come to share meals with them just for the pleasure of watching them operate. For breakfast one morning I have bread and cheese. What I toss into crevices reappears quickly. A phalanx of crabs advances up the rocks, each with a corn-kernel-size piece of cheese held out in front, as carefully as a child taking a present to his teacher....

One misty afternoon, while tea water heats, I begin rereading *Robinson Crusoe*. It is *nothing* like the magical book I remember from childhood. Reading it today is watching a writer's mind develop an idea: choosing to set the action on an island in the

Orinoco River of Venezuela, stretching a stay of four years into twenty-eight, giving Crusoe a native to convert (the inspiration may have been a Mosquito Indian named Will, inadvertently left on Mas a Tierra in 1881), expounding a theme of man's struggle against temptation and his dominion over the natural world.

Instead it is Selkirk's own account I enjoy—published as the story he told Edward Cooke and Woodes Rogers, the two privateers who picked him up in 1709, and Richard Steele, who interviewed him in 1713 soon after he returned to England.

Selkirk came home well-to-do from his share of the proceeds from a Spanish galleon that Rogers captured. But after being lionized a short while, he returned to his father's house in Scotland, where he increasingly spent his days alone. He hollowed out a cave in a hillside and bemoaned the remembered tranquility of his island. Discontented, he returned to sea in 1717 and died there in 1721.

For my final day at the cave, I've saved walking up the ridge between the two drainages that make the stream, saved its high view for the last. Mists still flow and recede from the mountains, but today the wind comes in from the ocean and pushes them back whenever they creep downward. Big waves hurtle shoreward, with spray blowing off the crests like ostrich feathers....

Wistfully, I want to stay longer. The world unfolds slowly here, holding its secrets, parting with them one at a time. Just when I smugly think everything is familiar, I go out for a ten-minute walk, come back three hours later with an arm-long list of questions, having found still another alluring cranny that should be explored tomorrow.

I am loath to part with this day. I look down on all the places I've so contentedly wandered, the peacefulness of it all, the torn-paper profiles and the textures, the high cols through which the mists decant, a quiet in which I fancy I could hear a crab sneeze.

I continue to plod the ridgeline, soak up the splendor of opulent woods and jagged ridgelines, soil dark as a coffee bean, trees green as life. Selkirk's words filter back to me: "Never have I been so happy as when I lived on my little island."

*Ann Zwinger is addicted to solitary journeys to faraway places with strange
sounding names; writing about her travels is simply her way to legitimize an
unconventional lifestyle. She is the author of numerous books, including* The
Mysterious Lands, Beyond the Aspen Grove, Land Above the Trees
(coauthored with alpine ecologist Beatrice Willard), Run River Run, *and*
Shaped by the Wind and Water. *She lives in Colorado and is currently
editing a book, with her daughter, on the psychological aspects of how women
relate to wilderness.*

★

The shell in my hand is deserted. It once housed a whelk, a snail-like creature, and then temporarily, after the death of the first occupant, a little
hermit crab, who has run away, leaving his tracks behind him like a delicate vine on the sand. He ran away, and left me his shell. It was once a
protection to him. I turn the shell in my hand, gazing into the wide open
door from which he made his exit. Had it become an encumbrance? Why
did he run sway? Did he hope to find a better home, a better mode of
living? I too have run away, I realize, I have shed the shell of my life, for
these few weeks of vacation.

—Anne Morrow Lindbergh, *Gift from the Sea*

✦ ✦ ✦

Guardians of the Dark

A mother and her daughters learn more
than Spanish on a trip to Mexico.

"ARE YOU SCARED, MOMMY?" MY SEVEN-YEAR-OLD DAUGHTER whispered in the backseat of the battered Mexican taxi. The driver accelerated, swerving into the left lane to pass a farm truck full of cows. The pale, hazy sun slipped behind the mountains. It would be dark before we arrived. Night descended quickly as we roared through the desert toward San Miguel de Allende.

My queasy stomach, more than the forced smile on my face, spoke the truth. I was very nervous about our maniac driver, the lack of seatbelts, and how long it was taking us to get to our destination. Annalyse, the seven-year-old, squeezed my hand, snuggling her head into my shoulder. She thinks I am invincible, I thought with a sense of irony. Her mom, the author of a book called *Gutsy Women*, felt like an un-gutsy wimp. I could be so brave when I was alone, but add the responsibility of traveling with my daughters and I was going into an attack of insecurity.

I avoided an honest answer and calmly, if not confidently, responded, "Sweetie, whenever I travel somewhere I've never been before, I'm both excited and uncomfortable." I explained, "I am just wondering what our host family will be like. During meals together will we be able to communicate? We don't know very much Spanish do we? I bet they don't know much English either. I hope our teachers at the Language Institute will be as nice as your first-grade teacher this past year."

In the silence that filled the dark cab, I realized for the first time this trip wouldn't be easy. I wished there was another grown-up along to help me keep an eye on my exuberant, wandering blonde daughters. Why was I so insecure about going to Mexico alone with my kids? Before marriage and motherhood, I had traveled alone around the world for two years. I used to be a confident traveler. Motherhood seemed to have taken the "piss and vinegar" out of my wanderlust. It had made me wary and cautious.

I could blame it on traveler's fatigue. We were exhausted, having survived three flights to Mexico City. Of course, the flight was "direct" but that didn't mean it was nonstop. News programs in the U.S. had warned us about the violent crime in and outside the Mexico City Airport. We held hands to stay together in the crowded terminals. Julieclaire and I wore our backpacks over our chests, instead of on our backs, to thwart pickpockets and thieves. Outside the terminal there were no benches for weary travelers at the curbside bus stop, so we stood waiting for over an hour for the bus to Quaretaro. I was exhausted from watching our luggage, protecting my children, and keeping them entertained.

Aboard the Primera Plus deluxe bus while Julieclaire and Annalyse napped, I nervously thumbed guidebooks during the four-hour trip. At the bus stop we hailed a cab for the hour journey to our final destination, a Mexican home in San Miguel de Allende.

The scrubby countryside of the highlands of central Mexico ended abruptly as we drove into town. We passed shops and bars with men spilling onto the unpaved streets. Where were the traffic lights, the neon signs, and fast-food establishments I saw in other Mexican towns? Where were the narrow cobblestone streets and the charming colonial villas described in the guidebooks? Our cabbie stopped twice to ask for directions. When we careened around a corner into a dirt alley, I was sure we were lost or being taken for a ride. Our decrepit cab lurched to a stop as the grizzled driver pointed with pleasure at a messy handwritten sign on a white-washed wall, "Jaimi Nuno." That was the street address I had given him. I slumped back in stunned silence. This neighborhood had no reassuring streetlights, no pedestrians, no trees, and not even a stray barking dog. It was deserted and dirty. When he found the house address, my stomach churned. I didn't want to get out of the taxi. The darkness, silence, and poverty of the scene were intimidating.

The cabbie wanted no part of my hesitation or insecurities. He dumped our luggage on the street, grabbed his pesos, and sped off. We pounded on the wooden door and hoped for the best. Annalyse's tiny warm hand found its way into my clammy cold fist. Julieclaire impatiently scuffed her foot in the dirt.

A short woman with charcoal-colored hair threw open the door, grabbed my free hand, and pumped it in an energetic greeting. She was wearing a starched white apron over a somber black dress. Her unlined face made me guess she was in her thirties. She introduced herself as "Lourdes," and wasted no time welcoming Annalyse and Julieclaire with hugs.

Julieclaire, at ten years old, was almost as tall as Lourdes, who took charge, leading us through an empty garage and into the main house chattering nonstop in staccato Spanish. Her monologue, of which we didn't understand one word, cheered us up as we stacked our heavy luggage in a corner of what was to be our new home for the next fifteen days.

My children were hungry and I wanted to be taken care of. Lourdes knew intuitively what we needed. She led us into a large, empty dining room and seated us at the only piece of furniture, a lace-covered table. She brought in bowls of cornflakes and cold milk. Ah—reassuring cornflakes! I remembered another time, when I had been on the road for over nine months, alone. I discovered cornflakes on a restaurant menu in southern India and relished every bite as I was transported back to Ohio and my childhood breakfasts. Cornflakes had been my emotional link with home. And now, lifetimes later, my daughters also found a bowl of familiar cereal reassuring. Removing her apron, Lourdes smoothed down her glossy hair, smiled and sat down at the table with us. Little Patrick, her cheerful five-year-old son, climbed onto her lap and furtively glanced at the girls. He made funny faces to get their attention. Julieclaire made goofy faces in return, and our laughter echoed through the bare rooms.

After our snack, Annalyse and Julieclaire argued over who would get the bigger drawer in the dresser for their clothes and who had to sleep with mom on which bed. As we unpacked our suitcases in our tiny dark bedroom, Patrick peeked through the half-open door. He was fascinated by these two foreign girls who were squabbling as they pulled hair bows and games out of their bags.

Meanwhile, Lourdes gave me a tour of her three-bedroom, one-dining room, cement-block home, showing me what I would need to know—how to use the key to lock the front door, where to find purified water to refill our water bottles for drinking and brushing teeth. We climbed up a narrow set of chipped cement stairs to the flat roof that served as the laundry. Lourdes showed me the clotheslines where we should hang our damp towels. A big enamel wash-tub, with a wooden washboard and bars of soap stood in the corner. This is where I would hand wash our clothes and hang them up to dry.

Wooden clothespins held sheets and underwear on the clotheslines. They crisply flapped in the balmy summer breeze. A crescent moon was pasted against the black-velvet sky. A myriad of stars competed with each other for space in the heavens. I was awed by this nocturnal beauty but pleasure lay shrouded beneath fatigue and sobering maternal responsibility.

Lourdes held back the corner of a drying sheet and motioned for me to follow her through the laundry to the other side of the open roof. I was unprepared for the sight that awaited me. Dominating the city's panorama was a pink Gothic cathedral with ornate steeples aglow with tiny lights. We could hear the children below, giggling together in the bedroom. They were playing peek-a-boo. I let out a sigh of relief.

Lourdes spoke to me in slow sentences. My knowledge of French helped me to piece together her Spanish words. Lourdes was divorced, living alone with her children. She supported them by taking in language students as boarders. In addition to Patrick, she had a twenty-year-old son who worked the night shift in a dry cleaning factory and an eighteen-year-old daughter who was still in school and spent most of her time with her *novio*, boyfriend. With a shrug and resigned, laugh she explained that her teens were rarely at home.

Lourdes attended elementary school for four years and could read and write "a little." She considered herself fortunate, because after her divorce, she kept the house (but little else). Now I understood why the rooms were sparsely furnished. Julieclaire noticed there were no pictures on the walls and not a book to be seen in the home.

When Lourdes finished speaking I wanted to tell her about my family, my life. Many times in my travels I have confided in other women, often relative strangers. I have told them secrets about my loves, my losses, my insecurities. Under the regal moon, Lourdes and I stood for a while in silent female communion. Then I tried to explain my fear.

I pointed to the dark empty streets below and asked her in my schoolbook Spanish: "I am with my daughters. My husband, their Papa, is not with us. No other adult is with us. Is it possible to walk in the streets at night?" We wanted to go after dinner to the main square, to sit on the wrought-iron park benches near the bandstand to watch people or hear the mariachis play, to see the peddlers offering candy and the old men get their shoes shined. But there are no lights here. I motioned to the dark and deserted street below and asked, "No one is in the streets. I am afraid. Is it a problem? Is my purse safe? Are my girls safe?"

Lourdes reached out and looped her arm through mine. She was small but solid and smelled as fresh as the hand-scrubbed washing that hung around us. As we stood arm in arm, amid the fluttering laundry, I knew she understood my distress. She pointed to a nearby rooftop. I saw two women rocking in chairs, quietly conversing as they watched the streets below. They were partially hidden by their own drying laundry. I was surprised, for I hadn't noticed any other life in the neighborhood. She motioned to other rooftops and open windows where women sat, witnesses to the dark and silent night.

"No problem, Señora. Many women watch out for you. No problem to walk in the streets at night with no man," she assured me.

I had traveled to San Miguel to experience the customs and the language but the lasting legacy of our journey was this female kinship, we confide in and support each other. My daughters and I learned some Spanish, shared in another family's life, walked confidently in the dark, laughed at ourselves, and ate too much ice cream. Most importantly, we returned home, forever changed, surer of ourselves, strengthened, stretched, and having touched other women with our spirits.

Marybeth Bond also contributed "Pedals to Pubs" in Part II.

✳

Everywhere I went—Karnataka, Kashmir, Rajasthan—people stared the long bold stares of undisguised interest that Indians are known for. They couldn't fathom why I would want to travel alone. They asked, "Where is your husband?" "Why has your son let you come here by yourself?" The seclusion of 1,000 years of purdah lingers. An Indian woman moves about under the close protection of her family. The inevitable male guardian—father, brother, husband—stands ready to scramble for train tickets, squabble over prices, shield her from the outside world.

Some days I would have welcomed a guardian. At times I felt tired and bruised from making mistakes and backing up to try again. But I knew I had been right to come. I had never felt so alive! I had never seen or heard or smelled or felt or remembered so completely. India woke me up, compelled me to pay attention, stretched me beyond limits I thought were firm. I loved India and myself in it. I wanted to stay forever.

—Jo Broyles Yohay, "An Old Promise Kept"

★ ★ ★

A Close Call

Traveling with Grandma leads to a strange proposal.

OMA HAD NEARLY STARVED TO DEATH IN INDIA BECAUSE SHE couldn't eat spicy food and the Indians douse everything, even fruits, in chili. Fortunately, the Pakistani cuisine is mostly *beena masala* (without chili), so Oma had been eating her way back up to 110 pounds ever since we arrived in Karachi a week earlier.

In the Thatta market we bought dried fruit, nuts, and yogurt from open-air stalls along the roadside and called it dinner. By then it was nearly dark, the unspoken curfew for women in Muslim countries, so we hurried back to eat in the safety of our hotel room.

We stumbled up two flights of unlit stairs. Oma clutched my wrist with one gnarled hand and groped the grimy stairwell with the other. Reaching the third floor, we followed a row of dusty 40-watt bulbs to cubicle 309. Inside, we both plopped down on our saggy mattress and placed the food between us. We spooned down the fresh homemade yogurt and chased it with dried fruit and nuts.

We had just finished eating when someone knocked on our door. "Who is it?" I called from the bed.

"I am night clerk. The son of owner of hotel sends you tea. Do you accept?"

Oma and I looked at each other. She nodded her graying head. Well, why not? We were getting used to Pakistani hospitality, and I hadn't drunk my quota of tea for the day. I unbolted the door.

The clerk, a dark and wiry old man with tousled mustache, stood outside with a wooden chair in one hand and a silver tea tray in the other. He set the chair down inside our room, then offered us each a steaming shot glass. After he'd excused himself we noticed a third glass on the chair.

A few moments later, a short, rotund man with an olive complexion appeared in the doorway and asked if he could join us. He shook hands enthusiastically, his plump fingers crushing mine, then picked up the extra glass of tea. I checked out his receding hairline, bulging midriff, aviator-style sunglasses and guessed him to be about fifteen or twenty years older than I, perhaps in his mid-forties.

He repositioned the chair directly in front of Oma and sat down, carefully arranging his flowing *shalwar-kameez* (traditional baggy pants and knee-length tunic). Addressing her in faltering English, he began, "Madame, my name is Ali Hassan Khan and my father, Zahid Khan, built this hotel."

At the mere mention of his name, I felt my stomach turn. A member of the infamous Khan family right here in our room! That afternoon, while Oma had napped, I'd witnessed a riot in the town square. In the midst of shouting and gunfire, a young man had told me about the evil Khan family who had exploited the Thattanis for centuries. No wonder this guy had gems dripping off his pudgy fingers and gold chains lining his hairy chest. I stifled the urge to ask him where he'd been this afternoon. Probably holed up inside guarded walls.

"Our family owns much of Thatta City." He paused for dramatic effect as if to let the depth of his words sink in. Then he continued loudly, "Of course you noticed my family palace beside the famous Blue Mosque?"

"Well, no," admitted Oma, in her soft, sweet voice. "We just arrived this afternoon."

"Ask anyone which house is grandest in all of Thatta." He swept the air with one hand as if pointing the way. "That, of course, will be my family palace." Then he gulped his tea in one slurp and set the empty glass on the dusty floor. Meanwhile, I took my first cautious sip.

"Maybe we'll see your palace tomorrow," said Oma politely.

"Of course, of course!" he continued. "I will send my driver over first thing in the morning. Then my servants will prepare a splendid feast in your honor."

"Oh, I'm sure that won't be necessary," said Oma, giving me one of her oh-wouldn't-that-be-delightful looks.

"Madame, I insist. It will be my pleasure." He grinned at Oma like a fat Cheshire cat, but never once glanced in my direction though I sat next to her on the bed. That puzzled me. Why

akistan men not OK" (teek ne he), *she explained. Her husband and brother had sent her over to save me from the stares. Her son was sent to get me a cup of tea for my headache and I was taken around the old fort with the family. Her husband and sons paid me the customary compliment of not acknowledging or addressing me except to make sure that I wasn't getting lost in the crowd. The family was the first in a long line of people who were to help me out. My vulnerability was double edged. As a woman, I was open to harassment but also equally open to great hospitality and kindness from people amazed to find me traveling alone and unprotected in their country.*

—Susan Wetherall,
"A Cautious Enjoyment,"
*Women Travel, A Rough Guide
Special,* edited by Miranda Davies
and Natania Jansz, et al.

was this guy so hot for my grandmother? Probably some kind of pervert. Obviously he was too comfortable here in Thatta to care about immigrating with her to the U.S.

"You may wonder why I wanted to meet you this evening," he continued, leaning his cloyingly perfumed body toward Oma. "But not often have we the honor of entertaining foreigners in Thatta City. Some visit the tombs or the Blue Mosque, but only for a few hours, then return to Karachi. So when a young American woman and her honorable *dadimah* (grandmother) checked into our illustrious hotel, my clerk rushed to inform me. How many nights will we have the pleasure?"

I nudged Oma's knee with mine. She handed me her half-empty tea glass, then patted me lightly on the thigh. "Well, I'm not really sure," she replied, an expert at neutrality.

"I hope it will be for quite some time. Thatta offers much to see. I can escort you wherever you like."

"How wonderful," Oma said, clapping her hands in delight. "I'm sure we'd love to see the sights, don't you agree, dear?" she gushed.

Without waiting for my answer, Ali insisted, "Of course you shall tour my family's entire estate. We own more than 1,000 acres of date palms. Also I can show you our buffalo cows, goats, and Arab horses, more than possible to count." He inspected his manicured nails, then added, "And obviously you will want to see my mother's collection of jewels. She has more than any woman in Thatta." He cracked his knuckles one by one, as if taking inventory of his own ring collection.

"I hope your granddaughter will also be impressed."

Aha! So he finally recognized my presence. I was beginning to wonder if I would ever be included in this conversation. But still he kept his beady black eyes focused on Oma.

"Dearest *Dadimah*, I must confess something to you." He leaned forward and lowered his voice. "I lost my beautiful wife two years ago. We were married only ten months and Allah had not yet granted us children. She was a good, pious girl and I miss her very much, but I cannot spend the rest of life grieving. I am just 26 years old...."

I nearly choked on my tea. This balding Pillsbury Dough Boy was actually two years *younger* than I!

"And, *inshallah*, I want to remarry. Unfortunately, most of my remaining female cousins are already married and the others do not please me." (Oma and I later learned that marriage between first cousins is quite common in Pakistan, unlike India where marriages are often arranged between complete strangers.)

"There are many other beautiful girls in Thatta," our host continued, "but they are not from my class."

"I see." Oma raised her eyebrows slightly. I could tell from her expression that, like me, she was amazed he would reveal such intimate details about his personal life. I hated to imagine what might have killed his poor wife.

Ali settled back in the spindly chair and crossed his thick arms. The haughty arrogance returned to his bloated face. "When I beheld your granddaughter today, she pleased me very much. That is why I had to meet with you tonight. I am asking permission to marry her."

Dead silence.

I, along with my eager suitor, anxiously awaited Oma's answer. I'd had countless marriage proposals in numerous countries, but none quite like this.

Oma glanced nervously at me, then turned to our host, "Why are you asking me? My granddaughter doesn't need my permission to get married."

Oh no, she's tossing the ball into my court. Now I'd have to deal with him. How could I tactfully tell a privileged pillar of the community that he was the last man on earth I'd want to marry.

"Excuse me, Madam," he said, "but here in Pakistan we must seek permission of eldest member of family and I am assuming that would be you." He raked chubby fingers through what was left of his hair. "I can offer you ten buffalo cows."

I couldn't believe my ears. This poor excuse of a man had actually offered to buy my hand in marriage for *ten* buffalo cows! Should I be flattered or insulted? Was that a fortune or was I going for peanuts? Oma leaned forward and appeared interested, as though considering his offer. But she didn't even like milk! Maybe she wanted to up the ante. Surely her only grandchild should be worth at least *fifteen* buffalo cows.

"Obviously your granddaughter is living with me in my palace, but for you, *Dadimah*, we build fine house. You will have servants of your own."

Waited on hand and foot! Now who could resist that offer? I could smell the orange blossoms of my bridal bouquet already.

While I sat in stunned silence, Oma ushered the nice young man to the door and thanked him for his hospitality and tea. She promised to think over his generous offer and assured him that we were quite comfortable in his lovely hotel, then bolted the door with a resounding bang the instant he left.

The next morning before daybreak, Oma and I crept down the darkened hall and stairway, then slipped across the deserted highway. Frantically, I flagged down the next bus heading north.

After that, any time Oma got the least bit irritated with me, she would look me squarely in the eye and say, "I could have traded you for *ten buffalo cows*, you know."

Carole Chelsea George will do almost anything to avoid working nine-to-five: professional racquetball, magazine writing and photography, tramping by freight train, remodeling Victorian houses, self-publishing books, teaching Adult Education, owning a juicebar, flea marketing, renting out rooms in her house…and traveling around the world for several years with her grandmother, Dr. Gertrude Snider Tempe. Currently Chelsea lives in Santa Cruz, California, and is working on a book entitled, Travels with Oma.

★

Anywhere vaguely official, such as fancier hotels, newspaper offices, or tourist offices, could somehow provide a reliable male escort. The tourist office in Bhawalpur provided me with a guide whom they proudly asserted was the only man they would trust in the whole town. We motorbiked through the desert and I even managed to get some painting done. Resorting to male escorts—in reality, bodyguards—may seem to be copping out, but the alternative, staying in self imposed *purdah* within four walls of a hotel room, seemed a worse defeat. My escort from the tourist office had helped out women travelers before. Two other girls had once come to the office, depressed, upset, and terrified of Pakistan. I sympathized with their story. The continual harassment by Pakistani men: low wolf whistles in my ear, oppressive attention, verbal abuse ("fuck me, baby"), made my hotel room seem distinctly inviting.

The combination of sexually liberated women in the bygone age of the hippie trail and widely circulated Western pornography make up a formidable myth of the Western woman as a whore, a myth that cannot be exploded by a single woman traveler wearing a *dupati* for protection. Women, on the other hand, did not seem to hold this view of Westerners and were kind, warm, and anxious to gently correct mistakes that I made in public so that I wouldn't put myself in embarrassing or dangerous situations, saying "sit here with us," "stand here for your tickets," etc. I met women everywhere, in the telephone exchange, on buses, in post offices where friendliness and concern bridged all language and cultural barriers.

—Susan Wetherall, "A Cautious Enjoyment," *Women Travel, A Rough Guide Special*, edited by Miranda Davies and Natania Jansz, et al.

LUCY MCCAULEY

⋆ ⋆ ⋆

What I Came For

*The search for answers to a family mystery leads
to stronger bonds.*

THE ORANGE CLAY PATH TO THE CEMETERY IS NARROW AND LIES
at a right angle up the mountain. Carlos drives up anyway, oblivious to the danger and the cliffs on either side falling into the cav-
erns between us and the volcanoes Santiaguito and Agua. As the
jeep climbs, the gears grind on the pitted dirt road, and my head
slaps the metal ceiling.

I imagine us rolling backward on these roads, muddy from the
rains that are relentless during this season. I imagine the jeep
rolling over the cliff and that we are left to die, having come all this
way from the States to Guatemala and now up this mountain to
see my grandfather's grave. Mother sits up front with her childhood friend, Ana Pérez, who was with her the night her father was
killed. I sit in back with Ana and Carlos's son, José, a green-eyed
boy who wears the sweet, simple face of Down's Syndrome. I've
overheard Mayan women say, when we've passed them on the
street, that José's expression "holds the knowledge of God."

My mother is showing me where she grew up. Planning the
trip, we never even had to say it aloud: we would leave the men—
our husbands—behind. It was important that it be just she and I, a
mother showing a daughter exactly what had happened.

Now the road becomes smooth. We drive past two men with machetes and bare feet and a woman balancing a basket of corn on her head. Past men and a small boy walking bent at the waist with wood tied in bundles on their backs, secured with a leather strap across their foreheads. Up the last lick of the road, where a tiny girl, black eyes on us, drinks from a spigot connected to a spring.

The jeep stops. We're on level ground at last, on a hillside overlooking green canyons. Nearby, coffee plants reflect sunlight off their waxy leaves. Volcanoes tower in the distance on either side.

My grandfather's grave is the first in the cemetery and one of the few with a cement tombstone. The rest are mostly Indian graves with wooden crosses. We find one large tomb buried in bushes away from the footpath. It marks the grave of seventeen unknowns who died in the eruption of the volcano Santa María in 1902.

I look at my grandfather's grave and I wonder what makes a man choose to live near a volcano. On his tombstone is his name, Frank McKoy, and the name of his ranch, the *finca El Rosario*, the Rosary. Born November 12, 1895, died April 1, 1942. April Fool's Day. It was also Easter week. The tomb is engraved with a cross surrounded by Easter lilies.

Cement covers the rectangle into which they lowered Frank McKoy almost fifty years ago. Carlos takes out his machete and hunches down, forehead moist, and hacks the stringy grass that has grown long over the cement edges.

My mother and I stand on either side of the grave, and I think about her standing here with my grandmother fifteen years ago, the last time they came back for a visit. It was Nana's last trip here before she died. She came up that same washed-out mountain road to this grave, but she wouldn't go back to the ranch where it had happened.

Now here I stand with my mother, my grandfather beneath our feet. Three generations together. We pose for pictures. Mother rests her hand on one side of the tomb and I lean against the other. We smile for the photograph that we will show when we get home; it will grow yellow around the edges and I will one day show it to my grandchildren. I feel odd smiling for a camera while leaning against a tombstone, especially when the person buried there died young and violently. I have that urge to laugh that always comes at inappropriate moments, like during a church sermon or at a funeral of someone I never knew. I try to think of something else. I think: I wonder if I'll ever make it back up this mountain or if my children will. I might be the last in my family to see it. Maybe it will be covered over by lava from a volcano. Maybe my children won't need to come here as I have.

We climb back into the jeep and drive down the path. An Indian family walks up toward the cemetery carrying baskets of bread and fruit. They will picnic with their dead ones. One man carries a plucked chicken by the neck. In his other hand he holds a wreath of white and black tissue paper wrapped in plastic.

Halfway down the mountain, we get a flat, and we all climb out. My sandaled feet sink into red clay, soft from the rains. A fly hovers with an urgent buzz near my ear. I watch Carlos use his machete to pry loose the spare from its rusted stand on the back of the jeep.

From nowhere, a man approaches us. He wears fatigues, heavy boots, and a machine gun strapped across his chest. I don't know if he is military or guerrilla. I have heard the stories; sometimes each side dresses as the other. No matter; I fear both. Two more men with machine guns appear from around the bend in the road. Carlos is jacking up the car. Now there are ten or fifteen of them coming around the bend, up the narrow mountainside. Soldiers, unquestionably. The first man stops at the jeep and asks what the problem is.

Little José draws close to the soldier, who is now leaning on the jeep. The soldier's hand rests on his machine gun, and I imagine him moving a finger slightly and then watching as José's sweet expression collapses and he falls to the ground. And then I imagine all of them, the twenty or more who now surround us, moving their fingers slightly, making each one of us fall into the mud on this narrow mountain road, spattering blood and red clay onto the jacked-up jeep, a minute's walk from my grandfather's grave.

But no, I am merely feeling dramatic. I am titillated from the visit to the cemetery, from watching as men in fatigues surround us. The soldier says something to José. José snaps to attention and slaps his hand to his forehead in salute. The soldier smiles, pats him on the head, and gives the signal for the group to continue up the road.

Today we almost flew over the mountains to Tikal, to see the Mayan ruins that archaeologists have found beneath centuries of overgrowth. But the rains began again, and I had visions of our faces through the small, square window of a tiny plane pelted by wind, flickering through lightning. When the time came to leave for the airstrip, neither Mother nor I said a word; we let the hour pass.

Now the rain has stopped, leaving the bricks on the streets of Retalhuleu a shiny red. I pass a school where the doors are open wide to let in cool air. The sound of a classroom of typewriters drowns my footsteps. I look at things my grandfather looked at half a century ago: white walls, tiled roofs, pathways lined with smooth, flat stones.

Though Guatemalans call this the "land of eternal spring," I knew this country's beauty was deceptive. Guatemala has often topped international watch groups' lists for numbers of human rights violations in the Western Hemisphere. Underlying the still serenity of its landscape, behind the gentle round faces of its indigenous people, Guatemala is a place of fear. During the last 30-plus years of the country's underground civil war (between army "death squads" and guerrilla groups), some 100,000 people have been found dead; 40,000 more comprise the desaparecidos *—people who have simply vanished. Changes to more "democratic" presidential regimes in recent years have done little to…ensure the safety of the indigenous people.*

—Lucy McCauley,
"Up the Volcano"

Years ago, when I asked my grandmother, why Guatemala? she didn't answer. I don't think she ever understood it herself. We'd sit there in her kitchen, in the same North Carolina town that she and Frank McKoy had left so many years before. And she'd tell me how first he went to Guatemala alone, a man of thirty, his hairline already revealing the forehead above each temple. Then he returned to the States to marry her, bringing a platinum ring with five diamonds, one for each Central American country existing at that time. He took her away from her girlhood home, an antebellum house with wide white columns, to live in a box of a house in the jungle, with no electricity or plumbing. She left her mother and four sisters behind with her wedding china and silver still packed in tissue paper, just as they'd come from the department store.

Nana told me stories of riding sidesaddle wearing a full khaki skirt, of wading through flooded rivers on horseback, and killing scorpions and snakes in the house. Later I'd ask her, what happened that Easter week, fifteen years after they'd arrived in Guatemala? And she'd tell me the legend I'd heard since childhood, from her, my mother, and my aunts, a story so carefully crafted with details that it seems almost a brilliant fiction.

She said no one knew. She guessed it was a cattle thief; someone had stolen four of the neighbor's cows the week before. She awoke one night to the sound of a gunshot. She looked over and saw that my grandfather had left their bed. She thought maybe he was out shooting an opossum trying to get the chickens. It wasn't until morning, when he hadn't returned to bed, that she saw that his rifle still leaned silently against the bedpost where he always kept it. He was found dead in the yard.

She would never say that it was she who found him, though I knew from Mother that it was.

Now here in Guatemala, I am obsessed with my grandfather's murder. I think how perhaps I am looking for nothing less than pieces of myself, of what the last two generations have left me here to find. I take three buses to get to the center of Guatemala City, to the National Library, where the librarian carries out from a back room the oversized, bound volumes of newspapers from 1942.

In *El Imparcial*, I read about war, headlines my grandfather missed, from Wednesday, April 1, the day of his death. *"Las Fuerzas Polacas en Libia son Temidas por el Eje,"* and *"Vitebsk a Punto de*

Caer." Headlines about a war that my grandfather was anxious to join, but past forty and having already fought in one war, he had been rejected at the enlistment office.

I search through the papers—days, weeks, months after my grandfather's murder. No story, not even an obituary. The *Vida Social* section of the paper is disproportionately large, filled with gossip about socialites and advertisements featuring drawings of glamorous women with hairsprayed coifs. I find few obituaries: a car accident or two, one man killed when a tree fell on top of him in a lightning storm. The librarian tells me to give up looking for murders in the papers of that era. It was during President Ubico's time, he smirks, referring to one of a string of Guatemalan dictators. "There was no bad news," he says.

Fluorescent light streams through a crack in the bathroom door at the hotel La Huella in Retalhuleu. Mother is throwing up again. Her stomach has never been what it ought to be, she says. As children, whenever we vomited, she would too. Tonight it is from memories and too much time gone by. I lie on the bed listening to her and to mariachi music coming through the open window from the streets. I have something important to tell her, but I decide it can wait.

Earlier today we saw the mayor of Retalhuleu, Antonio Rios. When we were introduced, Antonio said, "Your mother is a legend around here." Then he and Mother sat down and talked about the jitterbug contest they'd won at the country club. And about how Antonio used to swim up the Samala river to my grandfather's ranch to see my mother.

Frank McKoy's *finca* was impressive, he said. Cattle, coffee, bananas, chickens. The chicken

A finca is any kind of land or property that yields a regular income. The finca El Rosario was both a cattle ranch and a farm.

—MBB

coop was very clever; my grandfather had built it to look like a little house.

The mayor said my grandfather was *"muy buena gente."* Good people. No one who'd known him would have wanted him dead.

He looked at my mother with his full brown face edged with white hair. He asked her how old she was now, and she said 60. He said he was 64. They both began to laugh.

Mother was animated, speaking rapid Spanish. Now and then she forgot how to say a phrase, and she would alternately laugh or become impatient with herself. I thought how she still feels part of this, how in her mind she's often still here with the boyfriends she'd dated before she and Nana moved back to the States when she went to college.

When I was small, I used to come home to the sound of Trini Lopez or Edie Gormé singing romantic Spanish *boleros* from the stereo, and my mother's voice from the living room singing along. She would be cleaning house, fiercely polishing furniture or washing windows while pronouncing each word in her high vibrato. A teenager again in Guatemala being courted by dark young men.

We stepped into a tiny car with the mayor. A chauffeur, round stomach bulging beneath a white t-shirt, shut our doors.

At Antonio's house, his wife, Lourdes, a trim woman with startled black eyes, walked out to greet us, forcing a smile for her husband's childhood *gringa* girlfriend and her daughter. Inside, they showed us pictures of their five children and nine grandchildren. They showed us the scrapbooks filled with news clippings about Lourdes, the Coffee Flower Queen of 1948 and later the first woman pilot to solo in Guatemala. I felt jealous for my mother.

Mother asked for a Coke, and I saw beads of sweat on her forehead and upper lip, despite the springlike weather of the rainy season. She was white. Probably something she ate or drank. And this was all just too, too much.

Later, I met the mayor's cousin, Fernando, while my mother rested. He is nicknamed "the Buzzard" for his dark, bony throat. Silver hair flew from his wide forehead. His body was restless, and every time he shifted in his seat, he hopped to a different topic. He told me he could stay for only a drink or two because he was due at his Rotary Club. He founded the club 30 years before, he said, with 50 members, but now only a few of them remained and they might have to disband.

Finally, with a hand holding a lit cigarette, Fernando ran his fingers through his hair and began to talk about my grandfather. He had been a teenager when Frank McKoy had his ranch on the outskirts of town. Your grandfather received the Flying Cross in the first World War, did you know that? he asked. The Buzzard knew about the medal because he had seen it, he said, pointing to his eye as if the image were still there. My grandfather was buried in his military uniform, the medal pinned to his chest. His open coffin was paraded through the streets of Retalhuleu on the way to his grave on the mountain.

The Buzzard lit one cigarette with another; it was long after he was supposed to leave for his Rotary Club. Whoever killed your grandfather, he said, had probably been found long ago, had confessed, and had been shot on the spot without a trial.

When I asked why anyone would confess to murder, the Buzzard looked at me gravely. Back then, he said, they had ways of getting information from people.

Now the fluorescent light goes out and Mother returns to bed. We lie in the dark and are silent awhile. But soon Mother begins to talk about how, when her father died, Nana took all of his white linen suits and had them made into skirts and jackets for herself. He'd always worn white, even on horseback. Nana horrified her Catholic friends by walking through town wearing white linen as mourning clothes and only a single band of black encircling her upper arm.

And now Mother recounts to me again, as I knew she would, the story of the night her father died. She was at Ana Pérez's vacation house on the coast, and the victrola played "Lady of Spain" over and over. She remembers a flock of birds flying past her window, making a horrible noise. And in the morning, as she braided Ana's hair, her hands shook. Then she put on black socks instead of the red ones that the maid had set out for her.

And when, just before lunch, a messenger from the city—a

German expatriate—rode up to the house, she thought something must have happened to Ana's daddy, because he was already so late in picking them up to go to town. But the German was coming for her.

We have no schedule today, just a late lunch in town with Carlos and Ana. We lay in silence for a long while this morning. But now, as we dress, she tells me how she and my father fought before she left. This is my mother's first trip back here without him. He is afraid of what she'll find in old boyfriends' eyes. She is too.

I don't want to tell her that I am about to leave my husband. When we first arrived, I took off my ring. It lies in a zipped pocket in my suitcase, wrapped in a handkerchief like contraband. I told Mother, before she had a chance to ask, that I wouldn't be wearing my ring because it might attract a thief. She looked up at me from her unpacking but said nothing.

She knows; just as she knew to put on black socks.

I want to tell her that I am about to leave my husband. I want to talk of how excruciating human relationships can be, of those unspeakable mornings when you awaken next to him, panicked, thinking: this is my life.

I suspect there is something in Mother's nature that mirrors mine, that has always raised the question of leaving. But also something that has answered again and again, No.

I am afraid she will try to talk me out of it.

The tires of the Rover hobble over rocks and pits and snapping twigs. Carlos slams on the brakes to point to a woodpecker. *¡Mira como vuela el!* he says, black eyes wide. Look how he flies! We stop again where two men with pliers are mending a barbed wire fence. Is this the way to the *finca El Rosario?* asks Carlos. Yes, answers one, keep going down and turn just before the bridge. His fly is open. A gold tooth shines from his mouth.

The bridge is the one my grandfather built. I recognize it from Nana's photographs. My grandfather sits on horseback on the bridge, dressed in white. He's waving his hand, calling to my small mother and the ranch dog, Guardia, who stand nearby. The river rushes beneath them in great white peaks. Now it is only a shallow stream.

We climb out of the Rover in front of a green iron gate. Rosario, says Mother, reading the inscription aloud. Beads that one clutches and counts, that send up prayers for forgiveness and protection.

There's a padlock. We squeeze through an opening on the side and begin to walk where my grandfather rode his horse after posing for the photograph. Up this narrow road, dusty and lined on either side with fences that are alive, grown from pito thorns that form a wall. Up the road with pastures on either side, we walk and walk until finally we see it.

The *finca* house is a slanted red roof sheltering white-washed walls. It looks unchanged from photos I've seen, taken 50 years ago. We stop, blocked by the fence. It is utterly silent here.

Up ahead is a hut with tractors and trucks scattered in front. Carlos shouts, Are there any people here? A cowboy hat bobs from behind a tractor and moves toward us. The man is short and graying, with large brown eyes that are wet and kind. He clutches a machete. He says he is Andrés Renój; his father once worked for my grandfather. The ranch owners live in town and keep the house locked up, he says, but he could show us around.

Still holding his machete, Andrés takes us to see *"una obra,"* a work, of my grandfather's. We walk past tractors and through a small field, stopping where water gushes into an opening in a red brick hut. Inside, he says, there are ancient pumps that still work as they did when Frank McKoy put them in, still pushing water into rusted wheels that turn, making electricity for El Rosario.

Andrés walks us past the main house and behind a shack where children in sun-faded clothes are playing. We stop in front of something that looks like a tombstone. A goat sits leaning against it. The stone, Andrés says, marks where a tragedy occurred. Frank McKoy was found dead here, by the place where a chicken coop once stood. I think of the "little house" the mayor described.

Someone has carefully painted over letters that were once engraved but are now almost worn away. Falleció, McKoy, 1 Abril.

*In Latin America, the
place where a person ac-
tually died, where the soul left the
body, often is marked by a cross or
stone. Loved ones will visit the site
and lay wreaths or flowers, just as
they will at the actual grave and
tombstone.*

—MBB

Here he fell. The year, 1942, is
worn too much for even the
anonymous painter to read. I ask
Andrés if he has ever heard who
might have shot him.

"Pancho Maldonado," he says
simply.

Of course, no one knew for
sure, he adds. But the villagers
had named Maldonado. Everyone knew that Frank McKoy was
found dead in front of the coop, he says. He'd heard a noise in the
night and had left his rifle behind, thinking it was just a monkey
he needed to scare off. But instead he found a thief, who shot him
in the back. Maldonado was the biggest chicken thief around.

I stare at the ground where my grandfather was shot, at the
stone. The goat leans against it, a severed rope around his neck, legs
bent and curled beneath his body and his head tucked away so that
I can't see his face. I watch him sleeping on this ground where half
a century before my grandfather lay, probably alive for a while,
hoping someone had heard the shot. Your beloved Frank was killed
for a couple of chickens, Nana. It wasn't a cattle thief at all.
Nothing so dignified.

I have a rush of morbid curiosity. Did he fall on his face or his
back? Where did the bullet enter his body?

We follow Andrés into the fields. In the distance is the volcano
Santa María. Clouds or smoke cover the top. I think of the tomb
in my grandfather's cemetery, of the seventeen people there who
had been covered by Santa Maria's eruption in 1902. Fields stretch
out before us. Two pastures, Mother says, are named San Francisco
and Santa Elisa, for Frank McKoy and Nana. The owners who
bought the 1,100 acres before Nana and Mother left Guatemala
gave them those names.

We walk farther into the fields. Mother points to a stump where there once stood a large red Castaña tree with branches that stretched out like arms. She tells me how once she was playing in the yard and saw a monkey sitting in the tree and a cowboy named Mateo approaching it. Mateo had gnarled, deformed fingers that clutched a shotgun. My mother tried to stop him, swatting him with a stick she picked up, trying to protect the monkey. But Mateo shot him anyway, putting a hole in his stomach. She watched as the monkey used his long fingers to pluck leaves from a branch of that glowing red Castaña tree, trying to plug them into the hole in his belly before Mateo finally shot him dead. There was no reason, she says. The cowboys never ate monkey.

Now we leave Andrés and walk back down the dirt road, past the fields and the live pito-thorn fences. Past the Santa Maria towering in the distance, the pastures San Francisco and Santa Elisa and the stump of the red Castaña tree. We open the iron gate and return to the bridge, where I walk across once and then climb below. I look up at the stones and the wooden planks Frank McKoy laid.

I think about these last three generations of my family. About how my family passes down photographs and stories, but mostly memory. Mostly memory of loss. Surely, my grandfather came to Guatemala looking for some lost part of himself. I wonder, did he find it? And my grandmother carried around the memory of a lost husband. She held it somewhere in the cavity of her mouth and in her throat, and sometimes she seemed to choke on it when she told her stories. My mother too holds the memory, of a father, a country, of youth. It has settled deep into her belly. It makes her sick and it makes her sing.

What is left to me is a memory of a memory of a memory, of loss, that has now become a sort of poignant longing. In its third generation it seems to have migrated down to the soles of the feet. It keeps me moving, propelling me toward people and away from them again.

I am beginning to understand this: those mornings, awaking startled at the sight of my husband, at my own unhappiness; it was memory rising from a dream to shake me. As if to say, Remember? There was more that you wanted.

I awaken from a nap at Carlos and Ana's *finca, El Cuenco,* where we are visiting our last night before returning to the States. The afternoon showers that lulled me to sleep have stopped, and Carlos is going to take us to the *"puente,"* the swinging bridge. We must leave at once, he says, slipping leather driving gloves over wide brown fingers. It will be dark soon and then he would never maneuver the muddy road.

We pile into the rusted jeep—Carlos, Mother, and I. My seat in back comes loose and plunges me to the floor when we begin to move, so I cross to the other side. Ana Pérez stands at her door, with one arm around little José's shoulder. He waves goodbye, and I watch his face, trying to detect a glimmer of the divine.

Carlos says something funny that I can't hear over the grinding gears, and Mother laughs as we round the first corner. It is sharp and steep but there is plenty of room for the turn. Mother talks to Carlos about his coffee crop, his workers, his house. The jeep passes through wet greens on each side and over thick mud. The sky is black with impending rain or darkness, I'm not sure which.

The gears grind loudly. Carlos is using his whole body to push the clutch and thrust the stick with his gloved hand. Mother has stopped talking. The shoulders of the road grow suddenly narrow. On one side is a bank of dirt that rises into the mountain and could flip us over if we hit it. On the other side is a cliff hidden by coffee shrubs that beat against the door of the jeep as we pass. Beyond the shrubs is a drop of 100 feet or more, though it is hard to know; the shimmering greens below could be the tops of tall trees or just small coffee shrubs.

Carlos grinds the gears again and rounds a hairpin curve. My muscles contract, but in my head I hear music. Lady of Spain, I adore you. I think of my mother's hands shaking as she braided young Ana Pérez's hair, of the black socks she put on.

I grasp the back of Mother's seat, and she turns to look at me, eyes wide. Carlos has changed suddenly from the nice man who took us to my grandfather's *finca*; now he is a big, dark, sweating man hunched over a gearbox and making hairpin turns on muddy cliffs. I think, we could roll down the side of this cliff, I could die here in Guatemala with my mother, just because we wanted to see a swinging bridge.

Up ahead is another sharp curve, turning onto a bridge of two small planks. We hit the turn, cross the bridge, and Carlos shifts down again to climb the next grade. I hear tires slipping in place.

He drives a little farther and finally stops. In my rush to get out I pinch my finger in the door. I'm nauseated and already dreading the trip back.

I stand at the opening of the swinging bridge. The sides are ropes, frayed and barely waist-high. The bridge floor is wooden planks, some rotting, spaced widely apart. Below lies a river full from the rains. The river is level with the house on *El Cuenco*, a quarter-mile down, a distance it took us a full 30 minutes to drive.

Carlos is already part way across. I hear someone approach from behind me. It's a man with a child on his shoulders, small legs wrapped tightly around a short, thick neck. I am terrified for the child crossing an unstable bridge, at such a height, where she could sway and topple from those shoulders like a sack of flour.

Mother stands by the jeep, examining coffee beans, ripe and red, in bushes on the roadside. She chatters about how coffee is roasted, how on the ranch she used to shuck the two red berries from every pod. When she finally approaches, Carlos chides her out onto the bridge. She passes me, whispering how she's been on this bridge a hundred times and she's still afraid.

I have a picture of her here, taken on one of her visits probably twenty years ago. It is a color snapshot, square with a white border, and she is standing in the very center of the bridge. She wears white shorts and holds a straw hat. Her pink-lipsticked smile betrays no fear.

And now there she goes again, smiling again, with her blonde hair freshly rolled and styled at the hairdresser in Retalhuleu, walking across that bridge of rotten planks and frayed rope. She looks like an ordinary tourist, protected by her naïveté, visiting an attraction from a guidebook. My mother, who grew up in this country and once watched a monkey stuff leaves into his bleeding belly, and whose father died in some ludicrous struggle with a bumbling chicken thief. Here, now, she walks in white pants, like a tourist who will leave this bridge uninjured and go on to the next point on a travel itinerary. Who could fly unharmed in a tiny plane in the rain over the mountains to Tikal. I think of my grandfather and of long-silent volcanoes that suddenly erupt and bury people. I think how the jeep that brought us here almost slid into the ravine, leaving nothing of me but perhaps a carved stone or cross to mark a spot on the roadside.

Now the wind picks up and the bridge swings violently. I stare at the bridge and remind myself: I am a tourist. My finger throbs, and I am still sick to my stomach. I walk onto the bridge, horrified at my quivering legs, trying not to look down, but needing to so that my feet won't slip into the gaps. I look up to see the man with the child on his shoulders reach the other side. Still trembling, I walk toward Mother and Carlos, only a few yards out, the bridge bouncing, its rope sides drooping and going taut again with each step I take.

I reach Mother and Carlos and stop, unsteady. My tongue is dry. I clutch the frayed sinews of rope with sweaty hands. Mother, I hear myself whisper. She looks at me and nods, then drops her eyes to the river. I think how on gray mornings, she too has been startled awake by memory.

For a moment, I think I might continue my walk across the bridge. Instead I lean ever so slightly into my mother's shoulder. It is a comfortable shoulder; it accepts my weight naturally and completely, and I think that I will stay there a while.

This is what I came for.

We have left them behind, her husband, my husband. We have journeyed beyond their reach, and we stand here shivering in our fear. Yet, nesting our shoulders together, on this bridge of ropes and rotting planks, I feel oddly safe. We have conjured my grandfather's ghost, and put it back to rest again. The bridge holds steady, and I follow my mother's gaze a quarter mile down, into the pounding river, full from the rains and red clay spilling from the bank.

Lucy McCauley is the editor of Travelers' Tales Spain, Women in the Wild, *and co-editor of* A Woman's Path. *Her work has appeared in such publications as the* Atlantic Monthly, *the* Los Angeles Times, Harvard Review, Salon.com, *and* Fast Company *magazine. A freelance writer and editor, she divides her time between Dallas, Texas and Cambridge, Massachusetts.*

*

So I had made a decision which carried with it things that I could not articulate at the time. I had made the choice instinctively, and only later had given it meaning. The trip had never been billed in my mind as an adventure in the sense of something to be proved. And it struck me then that the most difficult thing had been the decision to act, the rest had been merely tenacity—and the fears were paper tigers. One really could do anything one had decided to do whether it were changing a job, moving to a new place, divorcing a husband, or whatever, one really could act to change and control one's life; and the procedure, the process, was its own reward.

—Robyn Davidson, *Tracks*

MARIANA GOSNELL

* * *

Sky Queen

The time for gypsying by air is not over.

I WOULD BE GOING IN MY OWN AIRPLANE. I OWNED A LUSCOMBE
Silvaire, model 8F, built in 1950 in Garland, Texas. It sounds luxurious to own your own airplane, but when I bought mine it cost
less than most cars, $3,100.... I called my plane *Zero Three Bravo*,
its registration number, or rather the part of the number I gave out
as a radio identifier after the first call-in.

I bought it as a kind of getaway from New York City, where I
lived and worked, a weekend cabin that moved. On days when the
city seemed particularly punishing to body and spirit and the point
of the job particularly well concealed, I'd sit in my mini-office
halfway up the side of a 40-story building in midtown Manhattan
and gaze out the window at a sliver of sky, a ribbon, a rivulet of
blue, and think: there's lots more of that out there. And it's all waiting, waiting for me. From my roller chair I'd mentally zoom off
into the blue and keep on going, out into a country that has the
most little airports of any country in the world, over 12,000 of
them, in almost every geographical niche and on almost every kind
of terrain, with almost every kind of person on them (although
aviation has more than its share of the tinkerers, dreamers, escapists,
and leathery-faced loners).

On one such day not so very long ago, when even the leaves on the trees in Central Park had an oily film on them, and there wasn't anything on the streets that didn't seem sad or hurt or tired or ugly, the gaze out my window turned into a stare. I couldn't take my eyes off that ribbon of blue. It held me as the blue of an air hole must a person trapped under the ice, whose continued breathing depends on reaching it. I asked for three months' leave from my job and got it, arranged for the daughter of a friend to stay in my apartment and hold mail, and assembled eight bags and boxes of a size that could be squeezed into the plane's baggage compartment in back of the seat (almost everything in the Luscombe involves a squeeze). In them I put, for emergencies, a portable still (for making drinking water), folding saw, signaling mirror, waterproof matches, morphine pills (against pain after a crash), water-purification tablets, a device for trapping fish (brought without conviction that I could use it), plus wheel chocks, tiedown pegs, harmonica (I liked to picture myself in some barren place, out West preferably, sitting on a ramp, leaning against one of my tires and playing a haunting tune, never mind that I didn't know how), space blankets, clothing, cologne (Vol de Nuit, of course), cameras, food, books. I filled a whole box with books, as if I were going into semiliterate country, or to place that didn't speak my language. I planned to put the box on my right seat in place of a passenger, so that the plane's center of gravity would be well forward of the baggage compartment, and to use the top as a table for holding snacks, notepads, and charts....

I'd be going solo. Flying is an activity that allows you to indulge your passion for solitude, or society, or both. For me, society on the ground at chummy little airports, and solitude in the air (mostly). I enjoyed taking people up flying with me, but I enjoyed even more being alone in a cockpit beyond their reach. To be sitting in some nameless cube of air, or standing, an anonymous human being, on the grounds of some unidentified little airport was freedom of a different sort from just leaving the ground.

There was sure to be adventure in such a trip. Despite claims to the contrary by people who flew in more pioneering days, the time for gypsying by air is not over. The sky is bound now with electronic airways and bulging with control zones, planes are being made faster and with more instruments than ever, the land is increasingly paved, hedged, and peopled, but the *impulse* to go up and tool around the sky is the same as it was when planes were all wood, nails, and glue, and aviators wore riding breeches and boots. As a pilot you still want to separate yourself from the firm ground you were born on and float among treetops and clouds, zipping over countryside that has cars only inching across it, marveling at the new view you get of your neighbors' yard, dazzled by the sight of light lying on a field, lake, or hillside in a way you've never seen it, testing yourself constantly for skill and courage, just you up there with your craft and the elements, either of which could kill you. In the last quarter of the century that began with the first powered heavier-than-air flight, there is still adventure in flying a small plane cross-country, still risk, still surprise, still sport, still fun.

Unencumbrance being the goal, I made only a few rules for the trip. Go into only small airports if possible, fly low where sensible and don't fly at night. I once met an airline pilot who regularly flew thousands of miles for his airline, to Europe and Asia, many of them at night, but he absolutely would not go up in his 182 after dark. "It's one chance I won't take," he had decided. I decided too that over unknown terrain at night I wouldn't take the chance and made it a rule so I wouldn't be tempted, since flying in the light-spangled darkness can be enchanting.

I would, however, take the chance, everyday if possible, of flying low, under 2,000 feet, even though it isn't as safe as flying high, or as fast, usually, or as comfortable, and I'd have to do most of my navigating by chart rather than by radio. When you're high there's the grandeur of abstraction (clouds, sun, and earth-plane), but the far-off earth is a picture. Down low it's more sensual, given the texture and narrative; you see the nap on the grain field, the white dog chasing the green car, the yellow blooms deep in the swamp nobody else can see. You may even be in the picture yourself (look, there's a shadow, a bar with light shot through it, running over the hill).

So, on a day when flowering linden filled New York City with such a heart-rending sweetness that it almost weakened my resolve to be off, I climbed into a rented car with eight bags and boxes, rode the 30 miles to Spring Valley airport, phoned Flight Service, told Al and Bill and Helen goodbye, went down and stood by my plane, and began to drag my (cold) feet. I asked the friend who drove me to the airport to take a photo of me standing next to the cowling of the plane, which had painted on it the outline of a goshawk (someone suggested that play on my name; to my regret it was often mistaken for a parrot or pigeon). He took six, and I did a long, careful preflight inspection, stuffed the bags and boxes into the baggage compartment, polished the windows, drank a last cup of hot tea; then there was nothing for it but to go. The friend, who never liked the idea of this trip anyway and made it clear he preferred kites, waved me off. I pulled on the starter, taxied out to my tiedown, did an engine runup by the end of Two-Six, turned into the runway, eased in the throttle, went rolling down, lifted off, climbed away, and rocked my wings, for him.

For many years Mariana Gosnell reported on medicine and science for Newsweek *magazine. She took a leave from her job for a three-month adventure, flying solo across America in her single-engine tailwheel airplane. She is the author of* Zero 3 Bravo: Solo Across America in a Small Plane *(the journal of her trip), from which this piece was excerpted. She was born and grew up in Columbus, Ohio, graduated from Ohio Wesleyan University, and now lives in New York City.*

✳

Courage is the price that life exacts for granting peace. The soul that knows it not knows no release from little things; knows not the livid loneliness of fear nor mountain heights where bitter joys can hear the sound of wings.

—Amelia Earhart, *Readings from the Hurricane Island
Outward Bound School*

✦ ✦ ✦

Travels with Clarence

There is no better journey than the one that takes you home.

THE FIRST DAY I SAW CLARENCE MCQUIGGLE WAS THE SAME DAY I came out of my tree. I mean that literally. You see, I'd been in the Redwood Forest in northern California during an unkindly wet spring, and my cheap little Canadian Tire tent proved itself useless in those rains. That's when I found my tree. Redwood trees are massive; they dwarf people. The rain was soaking me and my backpack right through to our insides. The enchanted forest was losing its charm as I looked around that empty campground for a place to set up my tent. Then I spotted her. She was a hollowed-out redwood with an opening like a cave, big enough for me to crawl inside and stay dry. Once inside I realized this tree was big enough to lie right down in. So I'd found a home for the night, a dry home, and it wasn't going to be another night in that lousy tent. As I settled in with my sleeping bag, I wondered if anybody had

In the interest of privacy, the names in this story have been changed.
—MBB

ever lived in this tree before, perhaps a gold miner, an Indian princess or a deranged hermit.

I was twenty years old and on my very first solo journey of discovery. That spring was the first time I'd ever tried hitchhiking. After the initial free ride down the Banff-Jasper Highway in the Alberta Rocky Mountains, I believed I was hooked on the freedom of hitchhiking forever. I felt like a female Jack Kerouac on the road, full of exhilaration and fever for adventure. And it's so easy. Best of all are the characters who pick up hitchhikers. People of this planet have so much to find out about each other and what better way than through the noble and neglected art of hitchhiking to discover how different people experience their part of the world. And if I ever felt they might experience it in an unpleasant sort of way, I always carried a few cloves of raw garlic in my pocket that I could start chomping down on at any time to deter any would-be aggressors. Fortunately it never came to that—raw garlic itself tasting unpleasant. So whether in naïveté or wisdom, I hitched out to British Columbia then south down the rugged west coast, stopping many times along the way for further adventures and various waitressing jobs, then on to that northern Californian land of the green-leafed giants where we realize how small we really are.

It was three days before I got out of my tree. It took that long for the rain to stop. But I didn't mind one bit. I was starting to identify with the Buddha—insights, revelations, cramped legs. I don't think I actually slept that much, not that it wasn't comfortable; it was the ideal hovel, but I was too elated to sleep. How many chances does a person get to live in a tree? Everything around me became electrified and alive: the steady beat of the falling rain as it splashed down through the leaves onto the forest's dark floor, the rumble of a nearby brook; the very air I breathed seemed charged with an energizing mist. Towering redwoods took on subtle details. It was as if I were seeing everything for the first time or as I had seen the world as a child. A vibrant green was taking over the forest, a green that could never be found in a paint store. This green was passionately awake and wildly alive and for those three days, so was I.

I remember looking out of my tree's entrance, feeling like a spy, awe-struck at the stately and all-knowing presence of those ancient kings and queens of trees all around me. They'd seen rain like this for many hundreds of years. The history of the world was ever-unfolding while they stood strong and solid: as empires came and went, as wars to end all wars never ended, and as people searched for answers they never seemed to find. I felt humbled sitting in and among those pillars of wisdom because I was learning from them that a constant search for answers is futile. These trees didn't question their existence and their life; they were life, perfect in every moment of their existence.

> *hile the stream badgers the solemn hemlocks, I stop to touch the fallen tree. It is remarkably alive in its decomposing. I fancy I sense a pulse under my fingertips, as the tree gives its life over to new forms—moss and grub worms. The blond, damp splinters witness to surrender, to the yielding of life to life, and death to life. Receiving the gift of the tree, I bow and walk on.*
>
> —Karen Monk, "Spirit Walk,"
> *Another Wilderness: New Outdoor*
> *Writing by Women,* edited by
> Susan Fox Rogers

I'm not quite sure now what it was exactly, nor was I even sure a week after leaving the tree, but something happened to me in there that changed me forever. I only know when the rain finally did stop and the sun broke through out of the bluest sky I'd ever seen, everything seemed different to me. When I walked back out onto the road, I got a ride from an ordinary friendly sort of guy, or so I'd think today if I were to meet him, or I would have thought before my stay in the tree. But then, after my monumental awakening in solitude, this particular human had me baffled. He talked on and on about his job as a lumberjack, the economy, the weather.... I watched in horror as the words emptied out of his mouth, all strung together yet meaning so little. The drone of his voice faded as it struck me: this is it? There's so much MORE, I wanted to shout. But I couldn't. I was barely able to utter a word to him. What could I say? Tell him to go and live in a tree for a while and then we'd talk? I worried myself that I'd lost the ability to communicate with my fellow humans forever. Fortunately that never happened. Like a powerful summer storm that bolts down on us suddenly then leaves the world freshly stimulated and clean for a brief while, the intensity of the experience gradually diminished as time passed. Vibrant green became just ordinary green again. Practicality and Canadian Tire tents weren't always a bad thing. It's hard to hold on to that which we try to grasp. Maybe those insightful moments of brief encounters with revelation aren't meant to last forever. Life would look pretty different if they did. But somewhere deep inside of me, those three days living in a tree left an imprint on my soul which can never be washed away by anyone or anything, even the heaviest of rains.

Now to get back to Clarence McQuiggle which is the story I wanted to tell before getting sidetracked with the tree thing.

When the alien-like lumberjack dropped me off at a gas station on the coast I was dying of thirst so I bought a drink at the roadside store and sat outside on the porch. I shut my eyes and aimed my face right into the sun. That's when the noise came—blaring country and western music, the worst of its kind. I opened my eyes to observe the specimen in front of me.

He wasn't what one would call a big man although he must have weighed a good 250 pounds. But most of this seemed to be concentrated into some sort of eerie tabloid, "Man gives birth to a giant watermelon" shape, set above his low-riding polyester brown pants. His sweep of dirty-silver hair blocking out one eye tried hard to give the effect of distilled youth but fooled nobody. He was probably 65 years old. Oddly, his legs were short, skinny even, which struck me as funny since he and his stomach took up so much space perched on top of his equally large, luxury-style motorcycle. It was the legs that made him appear ridiculous.

Even more impressive was the collection of sprawling odds and ends strapped onto the back of the motorcycle: a Disneyland pillow, a frying pan, a clear plastic bag of socks, a bag of squished hot dog buns, a carefully folded Texas flag, a box of assorted chocolates, a sombrero.

The country music was exploding from this beast of a machine's stereo speakers. It had to be an expensive bike, probably brand new too. The man wore a brown leather jacket which was far too small

for him and those '70s-style zippered ankle boots. He sauntered up
to the porch and bought a double ice-cream sundae at the counter,
extra chocolate sauce, no nuts. He left the music on for everyone's
enjoyment. "Howdy there. Where ya from?" Oh no. My backpack
was giving it away that I wasn't a local. I felt like saying I wasn't
from this planet but decided it would be safest to say I was from
L.A. instead of Canada. It might deter any further conversation. It
didn't work. He proceeded to tell me how he'd just been "verbally
harassed by California delinquent brats"—even worse than the
kids who had laughed at him when he was going through Texas,
he explained. I could have laughed myself as I imagined the reaction he must have been causing throughout the country on his
motorcycle crusade promoting sappy country music and a fully
bloated ego and belly. Stereotypical loud American, thought I.

"Clarence McQuiggle's my name. From Tarmfoot, Nova Scotia."

"Nova Scotia? You're Canadian?" So much for stereotypes. "Me
too. I haven't met another Canadian in ages. I'm from Ontario."
We shook hands.

"Well, they had a big tornado in Ontario," he told me proudly.
"Most of them up there in Ontario are dead. Yep, big tornado."

"What! There must be ten million people living in Ontario.
They can't all be dead," I pleaded as I thought about my family and
friends lying devastated or dead while I'd been contemplating the
wonders of rain and eternity in a tree.

"Well, not all dead I guess. It did hit one town though. Yep,
pretty bad. So where ya headed?"

It struck me at this point that I wasn't exactly sure where I was
headed. There'd been a debate going on in my head between the
"Live for the moment" version of life versus the "plan ahead, set
goals, work towards the future" perspective. Just then I wasn't too
clear which side was winning. Certainly the tree experience scored
some points for the "live for the moment" ideal. It was one of
those summers of the kind they like to call coming of age or the
turning point in novels, when we try to figure it all out, think we
have, find out later we never really knew anything but at least we
had a good time, which is something after all. I had just finished

my second year of university and was on one of those disaffected youth quests for deeper meaning, more immediate experience with life itself rather than just reading about it. I loved my free-spirited wanderings facing life head on even if the occasional rain storm, dark night, or encounter with the west coast's superiority complex did put me off sometimes. Clarence's inquiry into where I was headed forced me to think about all this. After all, it was a logical question. Living for each moment, the accumulation of what actually makes our life, the journey itself rather than the destination—all this seemed reasonable to me. But it was a lot harder work than I had thought it would be.

"I guess I'm headed for adventure."

"Adventure? Nope, don't know that town. All kinds of crazy names for these California places, eh? How'd ya like to go for a ride on the bike with me. Great day for a ride."

"Geez, that'd be great but are you kidding? Look how packed down it is already with all your stuff. My backpack's pretty heavy."

"Nah, there's always room for more," he told me as he picked up my backpack and shackled it down on top of his cargo. Completely amazed at the ease with which he could accommodate my backpack on top of everything else, I thought of protesting some more then thought, why not?

"Well okay," I said. "I'd love to go and it is a gorgeous day."

M y first big trip was hitchhiking around New Zealand with a friend for six weeks. We were both in wheelchairs. No one believed we were hitchhiking; they'd drive by and just wave. We carried bungee cords so our chairs could pack easily into cars or trucks.

We spent six weeks traveling the North and South Islands. Our longest wait for a ride was three hours. Every night (except two or three) we were invited to stay in people's homes who we met hitching. People fed us and gave us grand tours of their communities.

—Susan Sygall with Thalia Zepatos, *A Journey of One's Own: Uncommon Advice for the Independent Woman Traveler* by Thalia Zepatos

He handed me an extra helmet and off we sped up a winding steep road that ran along a cliff overlooking the ocean. When I looked down I could see giant waves pounding against the cliff bottom. Beyond that the violence and expanse of the sea thundered out into forever. It was spectacular. I was surprised at how undeveloped this part of the coastline was. I'd always imagined California to be packed with people everywhere, the last stop for people who come from somewhere else, 20th-century pioneers in search of the golden life who left their lives and the cold back East. But here in the northern part of the state, the land appeared empty of those people.

"This is fantastic!" I shouted over the roar of the engine. Adrenalin-laden ecstasy tangoed all through me like it never would consider doing when driving enclosed inside a car. Mundane concept—windows. The wind wrapped itself in a rage around my body and whirled itself through my hair. The ocean mist cooled and dampened my skin while the sun warmed me to my core. I was a *part* of it all.

"Yep, fantastic is right," Clarence shouted back. "She's a beauty."

I didn't mean the bike but I guess it was okay too. I meant the whole thing, roaring through the countryside up high over the sea with the sun and wind slapping me in the face. I was free and alive. My mind didn't travel to the future or the past for a second. I was living for the moment. I realized that this is it. This must be the way to live.

If I'd only known that the path to enlightenment could also be found by bumming a ride with a possibly pregnant Hell's Angel wanna-be bound for the open road, I might never have bothered with living in the tree. Then again, who can say? We're only twenty years old once, and must make use of every hovel and eccentric we come across. Otherwise, how are we to know what to make of this life?

Maybe an hour passed by of meandering our way along that coastal road. But it could have been much more than an hour. I had lost all concept of time since I was living for the moment and all. Clarence slowed down and pulled into a scenic lookout on the cliff's edge far above the spray of the sea. He took off his helmet and walked John Wayne-style to take a look below.

"Some view this is. They call *this* a scenic lookout? They've never been to Nova Scotia." I think he was trying to impress me, somehow.

"But this is beautiful. Look at the way those waves are thrashing against those jagged rocks down there and there's no development here at all." I tried to say this politely. After all, he had just given me an hour, more or less, of the most blissful ride I'd ever had.

"Nope, sure ain't like Nova Scotia."

Forget it, I thought to myself. Let him miss the beauty.

"I'm headed back there now, can't wait," he said. "I'm going north to B.C. and straight east all across Canada to Nova Scotia. Should be back home in ten days or so. Wanna come with me? It'd be free for you and I've got this extra helmet anyway."

I fixated on his face for ten seconds without saying anything. Was he serious?

"Oh no I couldn't. That's crazy." A thousand thoughts railroaded through my head on the pros and cons of this most unusual offer. He was a total stranger. Yet, he did have an endearing kind of helplessness or naïve quality about him; I knew he was perfectly harmless. But travel thousands of miles across the continent with the guy? My head reeled. It would solve my current financial problem, that being I had absolutely no money on me except for a Canadian paycheck from the Alberta lodge I'd worked at and couldn't cash in the United States. And I always wanted to travel by motorcycle. It could be the perfect way to get back to Canada.

The idea, absurd at first, began to grow on me like an out of control weed. Suddenly, euphoria swept through me at the thought of the wind ripping through my hair along this powerful coast, then forging our way through the crude passes of the heathen Rockies, flying straight and reckless across the endless prairies, to migrate back to my forested home province of Ontario—which I was missing—then maybe farther east through Quebec, out to the salty dampness of the Maritime coast with its pastel-coloured, warm-hearted fishing villages. All that air to breathe in with the sun warming my face, feeling the raw power of speed with so much to see, always, all around me, revelling in the single and pure moments of the journey itself.... If I could only get him to lose the corny country music station....

"Okay Clarence. I'd love to go with you." For the second time that day, Clarence McQuiggle and I shook hands.

Clarence McQuiggle was a terrible driver. So bad in fact, that I considered changing my mind about the entire whacked idea even before we reached the Oregon border later that afternoon. But of course it was too late by then. I was hooked. I'd become a full-fledged motorcycle mama in the intervening Zen-induced moments of a two-hour ride of rapture. Except for the drone of the engine, we were experiencing a place of grandeur and eloquent silence. Or at least I was. Clarence seemed to enjoy the experience of speed.

When we veered for a time away from the coast and blasted along a near-traffic-free road obscured from the sunlight by a forest of 200-foot redwoods, I felt a pang of remorse and guilt for zooming past these intimate giants, now my friends, at such a pace. These tree gods deserved reverence and quiet contemplation, but I could hardly shout that out to Clarence. He was like a madman possessed, intent on taking off through the forest into flight perhaps, trying to defy gravity and beer gut all at once.

He did eventually come to a squealing halt, thank god. A sign saying, "WELCOME TO OREGON" by the roadside caught his attention as would every other "welcome to" sign for the next 5,000 miles. Clarence began his camera search through every luggage container and duffel bag strapped onto that machine. I stood by, completely in awe, at how much junk he, or rather we, were lugging. Clarence McQuiggle was a packrat, a souvenir storer, a heavy hoarder.

"Here's the damn thing. Now take a couple pictures of me in front of the sign. Make sure I'm not blocking out 'Oregon.' Gotta show my friends back home."

Clarence has friends? I tried to imagine this "Clarence-friends" concept as I stood, camera in hand, while he posed with his weight on one leg, hand on hip, head cocked, half-zipped leather jacket trying gallantly to conceal its portly contents. Snap: the state of Oregon welcomes Mr. McCool-quiggle. Look out all of you west coast-night-riding-biker-gang-scary types; Clarence McQuiggle has arrived toting enough tacky souvenirs to offend and bully even the most tasteless angel from hell right out of you, with country music to nauseate the sappiest of you, and a twenty-year-old Buddhist biker chick on the back to utterly confuse the grievous tattoos off all of you.

Night fog from the sea had rolled ashore and the setting sun's amber rays had long since cast their farewell glow on our faces when Clarence finally cooled his various engines for the night. It was a neon, flashing red sign that lured Clarence off the road this time: "ALL YOU CAN EAT" proved as powerful a Pepto Bismol for seizing engines, it seemed, as "WELCOME TO...(anywhere, nowhere, population: 14)" and "SOUVENIRS FOR ALL." Those three signs, in their varied and enticing forms, are about all that ever did take Clarence off his road.

I felt wind-swept and groggy inside the restaurant but luckily its abrasively loud and crass interior awakened my numbed senses. Clarence delighted in the place and I could see he was truly in his element here. He really should have been an American. He didn't even wait for our overly-friendly waitress to present herself and give him his all-you-can-stuff-into-your-gut-and-pockets plate before he herded into line at the trough. That surprised me too because I'd ascertained by then that Clarence aspired to be a womanizer, and roadside waitresses always seem doomed to be the compliant targets for the Clarence McQuiggles of the world. Instead, he found someone's used plate on a vacated table and wiped it clean with his handkerchief.

I wished I hadn't seen him do that.

It was to be the first of several unforgettable moments on the momentous journey when it hit me, "Hey, who is this guy?" "What the hell am I doing this for?"

Between grazings, Clarence told me that he'd started out on his continental trip from Nova Scotia with his then ladyfriend (ladyfriend?) but she had tired of travel (read, tired of Clarence) somewhere outside of Portland, Maine one evening in a torrential downpour when Clarence insisted on making Boston that night.

"Yep. Gladys just threw her helmet into a big puddle, unstrapped her suitcase and by dang, she was a goner. Can't take a little wet."

Gladys was a wise woman.

I learned something else about Clarence that night, which if I'd given it any serious thought, I should have anticipated. He snored—not the expected, acceptable decibel level snore—but something far beyond that. There was no escaping it inside the hotel room even though I slept on the floor with a pillow and all my clothes over my ears, and the maximum distance away from the artillery fire. I had to trudge outside with my sleeping bag and sleep on a lawn chair in the hotel's back yard. Even then I could still hear the Maritime Marine Battleship thundering off shells in the distance.

Clarence's weakness for souvenirs was getting out of hand. After all, we were travelling on a motorcycle, not a tractor trailer, and although this vehicle, like Clarence, was of ample size, it did have its limits as to what it could carry. At the "WELCOME TO WASHINGTON STATE" sign picture-taking session, Clarence learned from a retired couple about a souvenir shop which sold redwood carvings just ahead, five miles off the highway. Clarence rarely ventured off the main highway—a point of contention between us—but for the ultimate in souvenir shops, Clarence would make an exception. Thirty minutes later, we motored down the highway for Seattle, country music blasting, 40 pounds heavier and a tad lopsided. Clarence had just purchased a genuine carved redwood four-and-a-half-foot totem pole. *Easy Rider* here we come.

As if the totem pole had given us wings, we found ourselves gusting through British Columbia's Okanagan Valley, passing all manner of traffic in our way. Clarence was still possessed. If I suggested we slow down for a while, or maybe even, god forbid, stop somewhere along the way at a lake, a small town, or a fruit stand, Clarence would bellow back to me, "Can't stop, gotta make time."

Make time? What exactly does that mean? Clarence was retired and had no appointments to be back for in Nova Scotia. What was the rush? Why had he even bothered to take a trip around the continent if he didn't want to see it? All he seemed to care about was getting back to Nova Scotia. He was missing everything along the way, thousands of miles worth of irretrievable moments, all just to GET THERE. I tried to convince him that somewhere is right here, now, along the way, but he never stopped to look, not even once. I realized then many of us live our lives this way, so focused on the future or a goal that we miss the journey of our lives along the way. Life slips away from us too quickly if we spend it on automatic pilot, lost in distraction, in unattended moments. But for now, seated behind the heavy hand of a motorman's fiendish fervor, I'd have to take his cue of getting my kicks out of speed and the open road. And really, that wasn't such a bad thing at all.

The Trans-Canada Highway, which I liked to call McQuiggle Highway, since that road was Clarence's religion, passes right through Glacier National Park just west of the B.C.-Alberta border and the park is a place of splendor and magnificence. The morning we sliced through there, hawks and eagles soared above us so high into the deep blue above that they seemed to disappear into another realm. The groaning upheaval of the Rockies lofting up into their nurturing clouds stirred my soul and breathed Life into me. I was trying to feel each moment, take it all in with all of my senses, notice every detail I might normally miss. I let the ecstasy of being alive, awake, and present take over my whole motored-out being. We whirled by a turquoise lake cradled inside a near-translucent glacier but Clarence refused to stop. Honestly, he refused to look! As loudly as possible I shouted this to the man: "Every moment stolen from the present is a moment lost forever. There's only NOW!" The words floated up into the mountain air somewhere and lingered, catching some hawk's ears perhaps, but not Clarence's. Tarmfoot, Nova Scotia lay ahead and by dang, Clarence McQuiggle was going to make time that day.

I shivered all the way through the Rockies because we forged through a blizzard unleashed from hell, and Clarence maintained a determined perversion to battle the blizzard and win. I thought some shelter from the elements and hot soup might be a preferable way to beat the nasty onslaught, but I'd learned by then that trying to persuade a tomorrow-bound maniac was futile. Besides, I was far too cold and exhausted to shout out my suggestion over the racket of storm and engine. Luckily, the aching tunes of studly lovesick wailers weren't part of the racket just then. Although the mountains stood cruel and austere that day, I thanked them for—whether in their compassion or good taste—they refused to allow country music radio waves to trespass through their valleys.

Somewhere out on the prairies of Saskatchewan late one golden afternoon, we came to a turning point of the journey. In a moment of clarity, I think I actually understood Clarence McQuiggle. We had pulled into a divey roadside restaurant called "Farmer's Co-op" and upon entering, Clarence nudged me to whisper, "Don't talk too loud in here. They're all gonna be commies."

"Commies? You must be kidding. Why? Because it's called a co-op?"

"Yep. This province is full of Reds."

That's it, I thought. I'm exasperated. I can't take him another second. But Clarence wasn't finished. Inside the restaurant, Clarence explained that the best president the United States had ever had was Richard Nixon because he had introduced Coke into China. That's when the turn-

> *Looking to find wildflowers and mushrooms, I bought myself a motorcycle when I was 35—a trail bike to explore the spiderweb of logging roads surrounding our North Woods Wisconsin summer home. Deep along those overgrown roads, I found abandoned houses instead—and abandoned lives. Depression-era loggers' homes suddenly and mysteriously left, some with dishes still on the table. You never know where a trail, or life, will lead.*
>
> —Paula McDonald,
> "Unexpected Trails"

ing point came. I could have screamed and walked away forever, towards freedom or an asylum perhaps. But then it came to me. Okay, I get it. This is Clarence McQuiggle. This is a lesson on the journey of life. Life is what you see in people's eyes. Accept, if not appreciate, the differences in people. I chose to laugh, do the "wise" thing, maybe because I had grown slightly wiser, or because we were at a dumpy roadside truck stop smelling of cows and greasy fries, somewhere between Nowheresville and 50 miles up the road from Hooterville, and the thought of being stuck there was actually even worse than the thought of indulging Clarence in more of his twisted political paranoias. Besides, I'd come to see this journey as something of a challenge by then. A Clarence Challenge. I couldn't just bail out; it would be too easy. This was the ultimate endurance test.

I've always thought the true beauty of the sunset comes not when the burning orange ball is falling into the lake, mountain, ocean, or prairie, but just after it has gone down and continues to shine its rays on the sky painting a luminous orangey-pink heaven when most of the world has turned its eyes away. But Clarence McQuiggle refused to watch any of the sunset. Not even an hour had passed from the time of our last speeding ticket, and Clarence was once again tearing across the Manitoba prairie at law-breaking speed. The sunset had cast the entire western sky a burning orange of such intensity I just had to tell Clarence about it.

"Nope. Can't look," he shouted back over his shoulder, "Wouldn't be as good as the sunset over the Bay of Fundy anyway."

We blasted onward towards Ontario, breezing past the lucky ones on the other side of the road, the ones driving into the sunset, the ones who would never have to discern the logic of a certain faceless fellow journeyer they had just passed on McQuiggle Highway.

Northern Ontario takes forever to drive across and since I happen to be from Ontario, Clarence concluded that the province's immensity was my fault. I think the long days of driving were starting to get to him so I thought I'd accept the blame for the size of my province. But his edginess continued all across the north shore of Lake Superior. The strapped-on collection of souvenirs all over the bike was really becoming annoying. Clarence was constantly re-arranging things. Somewhere between Sault Saint Marie and Sudbury, Clarence pulled over to the side of the road and stopped. I instinctively looked around for one of the "ALL U CAN EAT," "WELCOME TO..." or "SOUVENIR" signs but could see none of them. We were in the middle of nowhere and Clarence McQuiggle had stopped for no apparent reason. We were in the middle of nowhere when Clarence McQuiggle finally lost it: the totem pole I mean. He unloaded his stockpile of souvenirs amassed from across the two countries and proceeded to throw it all into the ditch.

"I can't take these goddamn things anymore. They're slowin' me down. They're falling off. I don't want 'em."

Clarence was having a fit, a temper tantrum, and I thought it best to keep quiet, try not to laugh, and let him do his thing. He was right to liberate the totem pole. I sometimes wonder whatever became of that Washington State genuine carved redwood totem pole that got turfed into the ditch up there in northern Ontario, so far away from its home. Quite possibly, it's still up there, enjoying a much-deserved rest after a three thousand-mile ramble with a runaway maritime marvel.

The further east we got and the closer to Nova Scotia, the more urgent it became for Clarence to GET THERE. We'd set off each morning at five-thirty or six after Clarence had consumed massive quantities of greasy breakfast food substitutes and the first of his sixteen diet pops of the day. We wouldn't stop until eleven or twelve at night, having ripped through eastern Canadian places of charm lost to those whose eyes are more enamoured with the asphalt of the highway.

Clarence seemed to have a strong dislike for Quebec and insisted on speaking English very loudly at gas stations in that province's villages where little English is spoken. By that time, I was well on my way to proficiency in embarrassment and I tried to compensate for Clarence's lack of social graces by smiling, rolling my eyes, and shaking my head behind Clarence's back as we roared off so that the bewildered gas station attendants, store owners, and anyone else around, would say to themselves, "Oh, she's not really with him; she's just getting a ride, poor thing."

On the outskirts of Quebec City one night, I very nearly fell off the bike because, out of exhaustion, I'd fallen asleep. When I jolted myself awake to see my favorite Canadian city approaching, I considered getting off right then and there. Ditching the whole scene. I could have just been killed! I'd be free if I got off. Forever. Why was I staying day after day on that bike with a fanatic? Not only was it frustrating, deafening (engine, country music, and snoring), often embarrassing, and generally absurd, now it was dangerous too. But somehow, somewhere, this journey had become a compulsion for me, an obsession even. As effortless as it should have been, I couldn't just get off. I could have said sayonara back in northern Ontario and simply headed south and gone home. Maybe Clarence's determination to get to Tarmfoot had blown back its irrational zeal onto me. All day long I'd see his shoulders hunched up, his head aimed into the wind bound for THERE—I guess it gave me a thrill. Not Clarence of course, but the ride itself—a twelve-day amusement park ride which I was shamelessly addicted to. If I'd spotted an advertisement for a motorcycle-mad passengers-anonymous support group, I'd have joined up immediately. Yes, I'm a Road Junkie. About eight days now. But how could I tear myself off the back seat? No time to chat about it. By dang, Tarmfoot, Nova Scotia, lay ahead and I was just dying to get there.

Clarence made a call home one afternoon at a pay phone outside a restaurant in New Brunswick, and it made me wonder about what he called his "people." I suppose it was all part of the curiosity I'd built up about Clarence, the compulsion to see this thing through to the end, make sense of it all, rather akin to being compelled to snatch a glance at a traffic accident's aftermath. The restaurant served lousy food although Clarence happily devoured three hamburgers before continuing his binge to gorge on the white lines of the highway. But his demon driving habits no longer bothered me. I felt so weary by then that Clarence being a road glutton had become a good thing. We were almost THERE and I think I could even smell fish, or fish factories

Clarence was swelled with pride and swagger on the sun-blazing afternoon we pulled up to the "WELCOME TO TARMFOOT" sign. He'd finally accomplished his feat of GETTING THERE, and as I peered through the viewfinder of his little camera to snap that last shot of him, I couldn't help but feel a rush of gladness for my friend. Through all the lunacy and conflict of two diametrically opposed humans gallivanting across the continent together, it had been kind of fun.

We rolled into Tarmfoot and for the first time on the entire preposterous jaunt, Clarence drove without breaking the speed limit. In fact, he moseyed. We held up traffic. Clarence honked the motorcycle's horn and waved at people on the street as if we were in a parade. He offered the "royal glaze" of not looking directly at anyone in particular, just a general gaze for the masses welcoming home their king. This homecoming affair embarrassed the heck out of me but what else could I do but pray to the god of random chance that I wouldn't know anyone in town?

I looked at the faces of the Tarmfootians strolling down the main street, smiling and waving at Clarence. Most of them seemed to know him, or at least, know of him. All of them gave me a thorough look-over and smiled as if they knew something I didn't. A young man shouted out, "Hey Clarence, how long did it take ya?"

"Eighteen days and a half," Clarence shouted back.

"Have a nice time Clarence?" called out a woman with a squeaky voice wearing a cotton print dress and rolled up hair. I wondered if she might be Gladys.

"Yep. Eighteen days and a half," was Clarence's proud reply.

A few more townspeople asked about Clarence's trip as we continued our crawl down Main Street. The men all asked how long it had taken; the women all asked if he'd had a nice time.

As I sat contemplating this difference between men and women I noticed the signs above the stores: "McQuiggle Furniture" was next to "McQuiggle Draperies" which was two doors down from "McQuiggle Hardware and Appliances." Across the street was "McQuiggle Sports Gear." On the corner was "Clarence's Own: Baked Goods and Assorted Snacks." My God. Clarence owned the whole town. Clarence was the Big Cheese of Tarmfoot.

"Clarence, are these all your businesses?" I asked, expecting him to reply, "Yep. Eighteen days and a half," since he seemed rather stuck on that particular phrase just then.

"Yep, sure are. Most of my ladyfriends run them for me now."

We pulled up to a corner store and Clarence bought a tootsie roll and the local newspaper. He opened up the paper to the local affairs section and said, "Good, they got the day right." He handed it to me to read.

TARMFOOT TELLINGS

Clarence McQuiggle is expected back today from his well-known, much-talked-about motorcycle caper which took him from Tarmfoot last month to Maine down to Florida, all across the southern United States to California, up to British Columbia, and back across Canada to his and our fair town. Word has it that Clarence has a traveling companion with him. Who will she be and how will she have survived travel with our Clarence? Welcome home, Clarence, and a warm welcome to Clarence's companion from all of us here in Tarmfoot.

I ended up staying a few days in that friendly little town of Tarmfoot before heading back home by way of the ferry to Maine. Clarence's house outside of town and right next to the ocean was far too large even for him and for all the souvenirs which didn't make it. Too bad. They would have fit into the decor of the place. Clarence gave me a room with shag carpet on the walls, a round bed, and a life-size, last-concert Elvis poster tacked to the door. Now I'll never have to worry that the decade of my formative childhood years is dead; the '70s are alive and sweating in the McQuiggle homestead.

Clarence and I watched the sunset every night over the Bay of Fundy, and I realized he was right about it being more beautiful than the sunset over the prairies. Not because it was more red, or any more spectacular, but because it was home, Clarence's home. Since my home was the Road at that time, all sunsets were beautiful to me, but in this also lay a loneliness and a longing for one place in this world where a sunset moved me more deeply than anywhere else. Although Clarence missed so much of the journey along the way, there was one thing he talked and cared about more than anything else: his town, his home. In Tarmfoot, he was a somebody, a rather comical somebody, but a somebody nonetheless. And that made him happy.

Maybe some things, some people, and places have to mean more to us than others. Maybe we all need to find our Tarmfoot whatever that may be—as long as it's something we can feel a part of and care for.

So I learned something from Clarence McQuiggle, something I'd never appreciated enough before: home and friends. But still to this day, I must draw the line at appreciating country music. I just ain't never had no hankerin' for it.

Laurie Gough is a writer, teacher, and traveler whose work has appeared in national newspapers, magazines, and numerous anthologies. Her book of travel adventures, Kite Strings of the Southern Cross, *won a ForeWord Book of the Year award and was a Thomas Cook/Daily Telegraph Travel Book Award finalist. She lives in Quebec.*

★

The greatest sadness of all is to come home to "normal" life with your little travel notebook full of a hundred addresses and realize, after a year back in the rut, you have written to almost no one. All those shining stars in the firmament you have touched with the intention of holding, you now find your grasp releasing and they are gone, existing only in your memory—and theirs. Each moment—travel teaches you—is divine: each moment on the road, each moment at home. Cherish it.

—Jan Haag, "Last Minute Terror"

PART FOUR

IN THE SHADOWS

DELIA OWENS

✶ ✶ ✶

Malaria Dreaming

Illness and fantasy strike in the Kalahari.

A VISE CRUSHED BOTH SIDES OF MY HEAD, AND A SHARP WEDGE pressed down from above, splitting my brain. The pain of resting my head on the pillow was unbearable. I tried to sit up, but a wave of nausea swept over me. Under the soft mesh of the mosquito net Mark slept restlessly beside me. Without moving my head I nudged him, "Mark... some pills...I must have malaria."

He felt my forehead, then eased from the bed, and brought me six bitter chloroquin tablets from our first-aid kit. I swallowed them with great difficulty. He carried me to a mattress on the floor of one of the smaller huts, which had no holes in its walls. There was no reason to take me to the mission clinic

Americans Delia and Mark Owens flew to Africa in 1974 with little more than the clothes on their back and $6,000. They bought a third-hand Land Rover and proceeded to journey deep into the Central Kalahari Desert in Botswana, where they set up a primitive research camp. They lived there for seven years conducting research on lions and brown hyenas. This remote area, one of the last and largest pristine areas on earth, provided dangerous and difficult conditions for observing animals that had never seen humans before. Lions, leopards, hyenas, and giraffes were frequent visitors. This area of the Kalahari is now closed to researchers and foreign visitors.

—MBB

353

in Maun, which had nothing better for malaria than chloroquin and where there was a good chance of picking up tuberculosis or something worse. In the rainy season Maun was rife with malaria. According to the hunters, "You either take the pills, sweat out the fever, and get better, or you die."

The hut was dank, dark. I was buried under heavy blankets of scratchy wool, but I was still stone-cold, my skin clammy. Mark lay next to me, trying to keep me from shivering, but I could feel no warmth. The blood in my head pounded against my skull, and a brilliant light from one tiny window stabbed at my eyes.

Then my body began to burn. With all my strength I shoved Mark away and threw back the covers. The sheets were damp and a putrid odor smothered me. For a long time my mind floated in darkness, and then there was a kind of peace. I saw home: live oaks and Spanish moss, the red-brick house where I grew up, and Fort Log, built with pine logs as a fortress against some imaginary neighborhood Indians. But when my thoughts tried to focus, I thrashed in the bed and cried out. Home was far away. *Clickety-clack, clickety-clack, you can't get off and you'll never get back. Clickety-clack.*

After a long time, the light from the hut's window grew softer and my mind began to clear. Tap-tap-tap-tap. We would stay in Africa somehow, and make it work. Tap-tap-tap. Mark was working on a borrowed typewriter set up on a tin trunk near my mattress. He came over to me. Clean sheets and warmth, a snug fresh feeling caressed me. His familiar smile, a kiss, hot soup, and cold, cold water welcomed me back. I tried to get up, but a firm hand gripped my shoulder and pushed me back...rest.

During the days that I had been delirious with fever, Mark had stayed at my side, writing proposals to conservation organizations all over the world, describing our progress and needs. When I was much better, he drove into Maun one morning to mail the stack of thick envelopes. I propped myself up on pillows and waited for him to come back. Though still a bit woozy, it felt good to sit up. I watched two scimitar-billed hoopoes flitting about in the fig trees just outside the window. An hour later I could hear the Land Rover growling its way back through the sand.

"Hi, Boo. Glad to see you sitting up," Mark said quietly. He sat on the edge of the bed. "Feeling better?"

"Yeah—I think we can get back to the desert soon." I smiled at him.

"Well, we can't rush it," he said. He walked to the small window.

"Didn't we get any mail, any news from home?" I asked.

"Uh...no." He went on staring blankly at the river beyond the trees.

"But isn't that a letter from Helen?" I had recognized one of my sister's personalized envelopes tucked in the back pocket of his cutoffs.

His hand shot to his hip. He turned and came to the bed, his face full of pain. "God, love, I didn't want to tell you until you were stronger. There's some bad news. It's your dad. He died of a heart attack about six weeks ago."

I sank numbly back in the bed. "My mother—what about my mother?" I heard myself ask. "And we don't even have the money to go home."

My father had been one of our staunchest supporters, writing letters of encouragement, sending addresses and reference books, not to mention the newspaper clippings about football games that piled up in our post box at Safari South over the months.

Mark lay down beside me. One of the hardest things to bear during our seven years in Africa was being away from home at such times. While we were gone, Mark's mother passed away, and his grandmother. And besides my father, I lost my grandmother. And I missed the marriage of my twin brother. We struggled with feelings of guilt because we were not at home to help our families through the difficult times, or to celebrate the good ones.

"If you want to go home, I'll get the money from somewhere, Boo," Mark told me.

"Let's make our project succeed, that's the best thing we can do," I whispered.

When I was finally strong enough to go into the village to see the doctor, he warned that I had not only malaria, but also hepatitis, mononucleosis, and anemia. "You must not try to go back to the Kalahari for at least a month," he said sternly in a thick Swedish accent, as he peered over his spectacles. "You must rest, or run the risk of a relapse. If that happened out there, you would be in serious trouble."

But I could rest in camp just as easily as in the dank hut at the river, and we had to do as much research as possible before our money was gone. So I didn't pass on the doctor's comments to Mark, and, instead, pretended to be feeling better than I really did. Three days later we were ready to leave for Deception.

On our way out of the village, our friends at Safari South, always ready to help in one way or another, loaned us a high-frequency, long-range radio. This meant that at noon every day, at least during the safari season, we could be in contact with the hunters in the field, or with someone in their Maun office. For the first time since our project began, we would be able to reach the outside world. But unless we received a grant soon, this would be our last trip to the Kalahari.

Back at camp we rationed our gasoline, food, and water more strictly than ever. Using only one point three gallons of gas each time we followed hyenas at night, and one gallon of water per day, we could last three months. By then we should have received word from our new grant applications. In the meantime we would get some solid data on lions and brown hyenas. At first I was too weak to stand the pounding in the truck, so I rested in camp while Mark followed the hyenas or lions by himself. But I slowly recovered, and for eight exhausting weeks we worked with mad enthusiasm, knowing we would soon have to leave Deception Valley.

"Zero, zero, nine, do you read me?" came the garbled voice of Phyllis Palmer on the radio.

"Roger, Phyllis, go ahead."

"Delia, Hans Veit, the director of the Okavango Wildlife Society, is in Maun. He would like to meet you to discuss a possible grant for your project. Can you come in? Over."

We looked at each other and rolled our eyes. It might turn out to be another van der Westhuizen story, but what choice did we have? "Roger, Phil. We'll be in touch as soon as we get in. Thanks."

In Maun, two days later, we were relieved to find that Hans Veit really was the director of the Okavango Wildlife Society and that a grant for our research was very likely. But we would have to go to Johannesburg for further discussions with the society's research committee before a final decision could be made.

Once in the city, we negotiated a grant with the society for two years of research in the Kalahari. The funds would allow us to get a better second-hand truck, a tent, and, most important, to make a round trip to the United States to see our families, consult with American researchers, and buy much-needed radio-tracking gear for the lions and brown hyenas. To be able to follow the predators consistently in the long dry season would mark a major turning point in our project.

But the first thing we did in Johannesburg was to walk to a bakery. Standing in front of glass cases filled with small pink-and-yellow iced cakes, chocolates bulging with nuts, cookies covered with cherries, and puffy cream pastries, Mark and I ordered two of everything in the shop. Carrying our stack of neat white boxes tied up with string, we walked to a green park and sat in the sun. After inhaling the sweet, warm aroma of the freshly baked goods, we took a bite from every one and finished off our favorites. Laughing and talking, our lips covered with powdered sugar, we lay on our backs to rest our aching stomachs.

Delia and Mark Owens are the authors of The Eye of the Elephant *and* Cry of the Kalahari, *from which this story was excerpted. They conducted research and conservation projects on endangered species in Africa for twenty-three years. The Owenses returned to the U.S. in 1997 to work on conservation in the northwest United States.*

*

Delia and Mark Owens, the authors of the controversial best seller, *Cry of the Kalahari,* were expelled from Botswana after its publication. Seven years later their Prohibited Immigrant status was reversed and they returned to the "moody dunes and ancient river valleys...to clean up our campsite, to remove every trace of our having lived there; to search for the lions we had radio collared before our deportation; and to say a proper good-bye to the Kalahari."

—MBB

* * *

Soroche

*Off-balance and far from home, the author struggles
to maintain her center of gravity.*

I HAD LANDED ON A MOON CRATER.

La Paz, Bolivia, was one great basin, all bumps and rocks and hills. And there was that other thing, that unearthly feel about it. At about 13,000 feet at the city's rim, it was also the air, cold and thin; it was the *soroche*—altitude sickness—that made you light-headed with mild hallucinations much of the time.

And it was the big bluish moon that rose above a snow-capped Mount Illimani towering at one end of the basin, dwarfing the city. It was the indigenous people—a few Quechua, with their high-boned faces, long and sad, but mostly Aymara, all sun-baked rosy roundness. It was the odd, tiny bowler hats the Aymara women wore off-center on their heads.

Two things happened the night I arrived: there was a solar eclipse, and I fainted in my hotel room. The *soroche* sent my heart racing and knocked me out cold for a few minutes. I awoke on the floor, wondering why I should stay in a land that had rejected me so outright from the very start. But I liked La Paz; I liked that it felt otherworldly, out of balance. Like anything could happen there.

I was in La Paz to write an analysis on the workings of its city hall, meant for study by graduate students at an American university. The study was to describe the Third World municipal government's efforts to contend with things like police corruption and inefficient bureaucracies. It didn't require descriptions of the intricate exchanges, spoken and unspoken, that occur between men and women in that society, about trysts between city hall men and lonely women writers from the States. But if it had, I'd have written this.

It was on La Paz Day that I met Ricardo—the *"16 de Julio,"* the day the city was founded and for which the main street in town was named. I had gotten up early and, throwing my rectangle of alpaca *mantila* around my shoulders, headed to the Plaza Murillo where a procession was assembling. I walked up cobblestones on a street that was so steep it had a hand rail, passing iron-grated windows and padlocked doors punctuated by circles of spit and the stench of old urine. I'd been in La Paz more than a week but I still panted from the altitude and the exertion, and stopped now and then when I felt faint.

The plaza was packed. People encircled the entire rim, held back by military police pointing rifles to the sky, keeping the

In La Paz, water boils at 189°F. The runway at the airport is a full two miles long; the altitude and resulting thin air means airplanes taking off and landing need every inch to gain power needed for liftoff. It is little wonder that soroche, *altitude sickness, is common among newcomers to La Paz. Symptoms include strong heart palpitations, shortness of breath, sleeplessness, and severe headache.*

Most La Paz hotels, even the smaller pensions, are prepared to deal with sickly arrivals. They keep oxygen tanks on the premises and offer patrons complimentary mate de coca—*that is, coca leaf tea, a common non-drug form of the coca plant. The beverage tastes comfortingly bland, not unlike dandelion tea, and is renown for curtailing the effects of high altitude.*

—MBB

crowd away from the plaza center and the cathedral doors at one end. I stood with the crowd; all eyes were on those doors. I too looked there, stood there, shifting my weight now and then, look-

ing around. I felt suddenly self-conscious and exposed; I was not
yet used to being the only light-haired person in a crowd. An indigenous woman in front of me hugged her child tightly then
handed him up to the man beside her. Up over his head the child
went, laughing, to straddle his neck and have a better view.

Of what? I finally asked the Aymara man next to me: *¿Para que
esperamos?*

Small black eyes surveyed me quickly, then: "The Virgin and the
president."

The man who'd answered my question looked back toward the
cathedral doors. The fact that his eyes did not linger on me—
something I'd learned to expect, along with catcalls and crude
comments, in other Latin American countries—took me by surprise. Then I remembered what someone in the States had told me
about indigenous Bolivian men: they have a great deal of innate
self-respect and *humilidad*—humility; they will not harass you in
any way.

Another quarter of an hour went by, and the church bells began
to ring, not altogether but one at a time, as if counting the hour.
As they rang, the crowd, impatient, began to clap.

The doors opened; out came two acolytes in white-and-black
robes. Out came a plaster Virgin borne on a pedestal by six men
in suits, holy pallbearers. The life-sized Virgin tilted from side to
side down the stairs, cradling in her arms a baby Jesus with unruly
brown locks. Two bishops in pointed caps followed her. Then
came Bolivia's president, smiling large white teeth, waving. He
looked happy, pleased to be the center of attention.

The city's mayor and the governor of the province flanked the
president, followed by ministers of state and the city council, all
wearing royal red sashes. Clearly there was no pretension to separate church from state here. The dignitaries had just finished Mass,
and this was the procession of the Virgin and the president.

I saw near the cathedral door some city hall professionals I'd
met on my first day of research. I started to move toward them, but
was suddenly shy. It was too late; one of them saw me and waved

me over. I made my way through the crowd and kissed the cheeks they offered, then stood with them to watch the parade.

We watched the figures, taut and small, growing larger as they came toward us; watched the Air Force then the Army file in front of us and halt, salute, and play a tune for the president. When the Navy marched by, people around me chuckled. I knew this was because Bolivia has no coast, that its port was lost in one of many defeats to its five neighboring countries, that time to Chile at the end of the last century. Only the elite city hall professionals laughed, as if the joke were on someone else. The indigenous faces nearby remained solemn and dignified.

At one point I noticed a tall man towering near the edge of our group, standing out among the crowd of compact men. His height and the *soroche* I still felt made me imagine him swaying slightly over the heads of the rest of us, like a somber (for he was expressionless), bigger-than-life helium balloon in a parade. Someone introduced him to me as Ricardo, a young administrator at city hall. He was handsome—pale, with hair black like seal skin. And his eyes, dark and long-lashed, reminded me of someone back home I missed.

That day he simply nodded to me, cool and disinterested. Two weeks from then he would ask me to have an affair.

It began with Ricardo stopping by my hotel lobby and calling my room. Soon it became a habit. I imagined his frame crammed into that small phone box downstairs. When I would tell him, no, you can't come up, he would say this: "Patience."

I had discovered Ricardo was married the first time we attended a city hall lunch together. Like many married men in Bolivia, he didn't wear a wedding band; still, in a low whisper he told me himself about his wife. Then he added that his marriage had nothing to do with "us." Couldn't we have an affair? I said no.

"Patience," he said.

He also made a point that day of telling me that his grandparents came from Spain, that he didn't have a drop of Indian blood in his veins. This was meant to impress me, but I remember thinking how he'd probably do better with a little of that indigenous *humilidad.*

A few weeks later, I met Ricardo for lunch to interview him for a particular part of my study. He was half an hour late. When he finally showed up, he rushed in and sat down beside me. He said he couldn't stay for the interview. But he had one important question for me: had I ever had a Latin lover? I looked at him in disbelief. He assured me that if I gave him a chance he'd be like no other lover I'd had.

I realized he would not leave the subject until I answered him. I stared for a moment at a calendar from the local brewery taped to the wall above his head. The impossibly blonde woman in a neon green bikini caressed the neck of a beer bottle, a backdrop of Mount Illimani towering straight up behind her. I told him no, I hadn't had a Latin lover. But that it did not make a difference. He was married, I said. And besides, I found short-term liaisons painful.

Even so, one day when I was feeling lonely and particularly isolated amid the swirling strangeness of the city, Ricardo appeared outside my door. I let him in. I was fresh from a shower, my hair was wet. I felt vulnerable and in need of comfort, and he had worn me down. He kissed my forehead. I told him I did not even know his last name. He wrote his name on a wide blank piece of paper. We kissed once before I pushed him away, ashamed, and suddenly, utterly sad.

He stood looking at me a moment. Then he said there was

blood on my forehead. I saw his mouth was bleeding, his front bottom gums.

I handed him mineral water for his bleeding mouth. As he rinsed and spat in the sink, I wiped my face with both hands, wiping off blood, suddenly tasting blood on my lips.

I had kissed a married man, and not even someone I loved but someone who was seducing me. Suddenly I felt a wave of loneliness, far more than before I'd let him in.

When I looked up, still wiping my face, he said, "It's gone now." He didn't explain the blood, but he shook his head—whether from shame or embarrassment or disappointment, I never knew. We avoided each other after that day.

Ricardo left, and in the mirror I saw there was still a smear of blood on my neck. I took the towel still wet from my shower and I wiped my neck clean. I felt relief, like one who'd made a narrow escape.

Many weeks later, I walked up that same hand-railed street to the plaza, bounding up more easily now, the *soroche* hardly winding me. There was to be yet another procession, this one strictly religious, a different dusty Virgin .

Looking around the crowd, I noticed another blonde, like me. Probably German, judging by her bandanna and backpack. She was alone, probably new here. I wondered if the *soroche* was getting to her.

It was then that I spotted Ricardo, a great helium head swaying above the crowd, marking a slow but steady path toward the woman. Mount Illimani, stark whiteness against a cloudless sky, towered high behind their heads. I watched as he edged in closer, reached out one long finger to tap her shoulder.

Lucy McCauley also contributed "What I Came For" to Part III.

*

I have been, and still am, a woman who has often found herself, through circumstance and fate, alone. Nothing terrible has ever happened to me.

I have had close calls, but I have never been raped or wounded or kid-napped or tortured. But I have been left and betrayed, bewildered and afraid....

When I see danger, I step away. When I think I can move forward, I move ahead, and when I think I can come closer, I do. Sometimes I am wrong, but often, if I pay attention, I am right, and these maps of my own instincts guide me as surely as any by Rand McNally would.

—Mary Morris, *Nothing to Declare: Memoirs of a Woman Traveling Alone*

MARY BETH SIMMONS

⋆ ⋆ ⋆

Lunch at Chaya's

A Peace Corps volunteer encounters cultural
misunderstanding in Cameroon.

HER REQUEST WAS ALMOST INAUDIBLE; WORDS EITHER WERE LOST in the sweep of my eraser cleaning the blackboard or were drowned by the noontime cries of students rushing home for a meal and *siesta*. When I asked her to repeat herself she looked embarrassed, and carefully began again, her eyes fixed to the burnt sienna dirt floor. "Miss, you can come to my house for a lunch time meal tomorrow?" Her words were clearly rehearsed; I imagined her rising early that morning to consult her French/English dictionary.

It is this shyness, this gentle manner of Chaya's, I think of now on the taxi ride to her home. A bottle of Johnnie Walker rests on the seat between my legs, and the biggest pineapple I could find in the market sits on the floor, bouncing wildly to the rhythms of the taxi traversing the rut-filled road. I had asked if there was something I should bring and she had said, "Nothing...oh, bring your French, my parents don't speak the English." But I bring gifts anyway, hoping they can act as stand-ins for my French which lacks grace and charm, essentials in any country when meeting new people, but especially crucial in Cameroonian protocol of introductions.

As the taxi nears her home I can see Chaya standing in her front yard, watching the road. She is dressed in a fine red blouse and black skirt. I look at my faded jeans, jeans that could use a good washing, and I am clearly underdressed. When I shake Chaya's hand and thank her for inviting me, she thanks me for coming and compliments my blue jeans. "They are so expensive in the market!" she says as she leads me into a small building next to her home.

Inside are cages stacked up against a wall, each one housing a fat white rabbit. Chaya looks at me. We are alone, so I say in English, "These are nice rabbits." She nods in agreement. As I wait for some clue as to why we're admiring these two dozen-or-so rabbits, I shift my weight from one foot to the other, and look from the rabbits to Chaya to the slippery-necked bottle of whiskey in my right hand and the sharp-edged leaves of the pineapple in my left. The rabbit stench—pellets, warm fur, nibbled-but-un-eaten greens—smacks me fully, and in a single moment it feels as though I'm wrapped completely in the heat of the little room. I begin to sweat. After another few minutes pass, ones in which I've watched Chaya feed and pet some of the rabbits, I finally emerge from the daze of empty observation, wipe a layer of sweat from my face with my forearm, and ask if we will be eating one of these rabbits for lunch. She laughs and playfully nudges me out the door into sunlight.

Once inside her house, she motions for me to sit on the couch. I look at the dining table, set for at least twelve people, and won-der why the place is so quiet, why I've seen no one but Chaya. When she disappears into another room, I study this one. The walls are a dirty sky blue that house cracks and chips and religious icons. On one wall is a ceramic Virgin Mary, on another a brass crucifix. Behind me is a life-size poster of Christ, which has a cal-endar that is eight years old. I set the pineapple and the booze on the table before me, waiting to offer them.

When Chaya emerges from a back room she carries a bottle of *Beaufort*, my favorite Cameroonian beer, and hands it to me. These beers are enormous, the size of a wine bottle back home, but in two long pulls on the bottle I manage to finish the beer. Partly anxious to rid my mouth of lingering rabbit house stink and partly unnerved by the sight of all those place settings, I nod when Chaya asks if I want another one.

Halfway through my third beer her father walks into the house. After shaking his hand and asking about his health, his business, his family, I hand him the Johnnie Walker. The life-size Jesus peers over my shoulder at the bottle; I look at Christian, Chaya's father, for reaction. He studies the label carefully, reading each word, feeling the raised gold letters. His rich dark eyes swim in a bloodshot pool, he is no stranger to liquor. He worships the stuff; I've seen men around the country take a bottle into their hands and caress it with pure passion. There is nothing desperate, nothing alcoholic in his hungry eyes devouring the label. He is admiring the work of the master distillers, appreciating Johnnie's jaunty stride, his distinguished top hat.

Chaya fetches two small glasses without being asked and Christian pours us each a hefty shot. *Sante!* (to your health!) we both exclaim as we clink our glasses. The burn of the whiskey punches my stomach when it lands, but it is not entirely unpleasant. The act of drinking is what seems important, even more important than the taste or effect. It is a shared adventure. We talk about his job at the electric company (it is boring, but pays well), what I think of the Cameroonian people (very, very nice), and how much I think it would cost to send Chaya to America for college (a lot).

Soon we are relaxed, the bottle is half-gone, I'm forgetting French words, can't remember how you say "rabbit," and with every shot of whiskey downed it seems another sibling enters the room. Chaya's three sisters and three brothers study me. The youngest has just recently pulled her two front teeth. She shows them to me and is quite proud. I want to ask her if the tooth fairy has visited but I'm not sure tooth fairies exist in Cameroon, nor am I sure I could properly explain the concept if I were asked. One of the sisters selects a *makossa* tape and turns the volume full blast, distorting the intricate rhythms of the drums, but still she backs away from the stereo moving her hips as if the beat of the music is quite clear. Perhaps I'm not listening closely enough. I'm still thinking about those rabbits.

Chaya is quiet, as ever, but smiles as she watches her siblings dance around the room. I tell her she should dance, too. She shakes her head, buries her chin in her neck, and peers up at me. Her oldest sister sees this exchange and comes to lift me from the couch. As we dance she asks if I have been to Canada and I tell her no. "I want to go to Canada!" she hollers over the garbled voice on the stereo. "Me too!" I shout back. But really I don't want to go to Canada at all. I want to dance before lunch with these strangers in this African living room and drink at midday and fall completely into the rhythms of their world. I find a comfort in their bizarre ritual to dance, and dance hard before they eat.

We're appreciative of one another's movements, mimicking aspects of each person's dance. We shake, applaud, laugh. Chaya's mother and a neighbor woman with her baby enter the room. I stop dancing so I can greet the women and give her mother the pineapple. She accepts the fruit and hugs me, taking my sweaty body into her arms, pressing me firmly against her big strong body. It is a welcome that speaks of family, acceptance. She pushes me back toward the dance, and we say little more to one another the rest of the afternoon.

Chaya hands me another beer. Her doting is sweet, but I have been a guest before in many African homes and never have I felt so celebrated. My suspicions rise, but I quickly drown them in gulps of beer. Besides, Chaya is a good kid, she wouldn't think in manipulative ways. She sits in the front row at school, she is polite. What does she want?

"Keep dancing," she tells me, before she shuffles off to one of the back rooms again.

When she reappears she's holding an ivory necklace. Its gaudiness makes it beautiful somehow. We're all looking at Chaya, watching her walk toward me, and things are slowing down. One of the brothers turns off the music, and Chaya's mother and father stand together across the room, arms around one another. It is a solemn moment.

I'm stunned when she drapes the necklace around my neck, touched and befuddled when she kisses each cheek. The family, all eight of them, applaud. The little one whoops with glee.

"I'm just your teacher, Chaya! Why the present?"

"No, no, you are friend, too. Good friend. My family love you."

It is a simple moment in memory. A brief journal entry from the day reminds me:

> I'll write of unexplainables. How today was simply mad and wonderful. Children in and out of the house, lots of food, beer, and whiskey. And the dancing! Spontaneous and celebratory! Celebrating for no particular reason. These are days I must remember in my life.

And of course I do remember it well, with or without the aid of my drunken, romantic prose. What I failed to scribble, and maybe it was a wise choice to neglect this, was what happened after the necklace was given to me. An overwhelming sense of guilt engulfed me, a terrible notion that I had simplified the day. To me the lunch date was a chance to be inside a Cameroonian home, an opportunity to test my doltish theory that life, no matter the hardships, was indeed richer in Africa. For Chaya, my presence in that house held the possibility that I could help her escape her world, that very world I was intoxicated with, and that she could return with me to the States some day.

Their pleas became more desperate as the day progressed. When Christian asked me early in the visit how much college in America might cost for Chaya, I had no idea he was asking me to help with the necessary funding. But at lunch, over a heaping plate of *endole* (various cooked greens and meat), it was clear the necklace I was wearing held larger implications than just a sign of friendship. They loved me, so I must love them back, too.

"If we could find the money for a plane ticket to America, could Chaya live with you and go to college?"

I laughed at the question, it seemed so absurd. But when I looked at Chaya's serious, downcast face, I could only think of how she loved my English class. Here was living proof that teachers could inspire, but I felt sick that this dream could not be realized, at least not with my help.

The more I spoke, the less they listened. My laughter had sealed Chaya's fate; she would not go to America. I spoke of my own education I hoped to further upon returning home, my paltry volunteer wages, but nothing could interest them. We all concentrated on our food until our plates were clean. I remember thinking at the time it was the best *endole* I had ever tasted, but I didn't tell Chaya's mother. I was afraid she would think I was merely saying it to make conversation, to win back her approval.

After lunch, Christian invited me back to the sitting area to finish the bottle of whiskey. One of the brothers switched on the television and its noise assaulted the room. I missed the music, the atmosphere before the meal. Now we were drinking to get a little drunk, to curb the edges of our dissatisfaction. I looked at Christian, who was no longer smiling, and I realized then what a magnificent smile he had. But he was drained now, exhausted with the production they had staged, and there was little energy to expend on idle chit-chat. The moment had passed; I had not come through.

After the final drops had passed our lips, I rose to leave. I grasped Christian's right hand with both of mine, thanking him repeatedly for a marvelous afternoon. He invited me back the following Tuesday, and I accepted his offer, thrilled by the thought I was not being discarded.

As Chaya walked me to the road she stopped and ran into the rabbit house. She emerged with one.

"What are you doing?" I asked.

"I want you to have this. He is biggest and my favorite."

I took the rabbit by the scruff of the neck and looked at his pink eyes.

"Thanks, Chaya. See you tomorrow at school."

"See you tomorrow, Miss."

Swinging the rabbit next to my side I headed down the road, looking for a taxi.

Mary Beth Simmons also contributed "Women at the Well" in Part I.

✷

The strong ethic of hospitality in many cultures demands that an invitation be extended, even from those who can ill afford to feed or take care of you. A popular guidebook explains that Fijian culture dictates people always invite a stranger into their home, whether or not they can afford to do so. The book recounts the story of a family whose child missed a term at school because they had spent her tuition money taking care of an uninvited guest who had stayed a month.

What do hosts get in return for your visit? The pleasure of sharing their home and town, their food and way of life. The entertainment of watching you and learning about your culture. Perhaps the fun of showing off their private foreigner to the neighbors. Try to cooperate in all activities, and accept invitations to visit their friends, attend church or temple, or drink tea when someone drops by.

Contribute something to the household during your stay. Hosts may be insulted by an offer of money; rarely will they be offended by willingness to work or a thoughtful gift. Subsistence farmers living in an almost cashless economy may need certain implements—tools or plastic buckets, for example.

Ask to accompany family members to the marketplace. They may forbid you to make purchases while you are with them (as well as try to buy anything that you ask about or admire). But if you observe what they buy, from whom, and at what prices, you can return on your own and purchase food to contribute to the household. Stock up on the more expensive, nonperishable items, like coffee, sugar, and canned milk.

—Thalia Zepatos, *Adventures in Good Company: The Complete Guide to Women's Tours and Outdoor Trips*

JENNIFER DUBOIS

✳

The Vomit Express

The author goes for a ride with the Upchuck family.

WHAT DO YOU GET WHEN YOU COMBINE CRAMPED BUSES, WIND-ing roads, fearless drivers, and motion sickness-prone locals? On a recent overland trip through western Indonesia I had a chance to find out.

The transportation experiences there are so harrowing it often takes Westerners several days to recuperate upon reaching a given destination. So, after a lazy week of relaxing at North Sumatra's Lake Toba—the world's largest crater lake—with a sigh, I bought a bus ticket to Sibolga, a port on the Indian Ocean. There I planned to catch a night boat to the primitive island of Nias.

Like most journeys in Sumatra, this one required several seg-ments, using a variety of modes of transportation. We left Samosir Island (within Lake Toba) on an open-deck boat bound for Parapat on the east shore. There we drank thick sweet coffee until a brightly colored minibus screeched to a halt outside. Our bags not-so-securely fastened to the roof, we set off at break-neck speed, though in relative comfort. For some reason this particular vehicle was carrying no more passengers than the number of seats would suggest.

About two hours into our journey, the inevitable transfer from minivan to bus began smoothly enough, with several empty seats to choose from. (Later we were confronted by the passengers whose places we had taken, returning from the restaurant where they had been eating lunch.) But as is the norm in Sumatra, once the bus is full it just keeps getting fuller.

The drawback to boarding any form of transport early enough to get a seat is that you end up not only cramped but cooked while waiting to depart. After ten minutes or so of sitting idle, pack on lap, skin adhered to plastic, oxygen supply dwindling, legs bent at sharp angles, the sweat starts to tickle as it rolls down flesh.

The bus was overflowing with adults, children, sacks of rice, and luggage. A tobacco-chewing granny expertly stuffed a wad between cheek and gum while pressed flat against a window. The already narrow aisle became impassable as cigarette-smoking teenagers took their seats, squatting back-to-back on wooden crates. Chattering school children perched side by side on the gear box.

We careened wildly up and down hairpin curves on roads that quickly turned to mud. We were high up in jungle territory, occasionally passing one-street settlements perched on a hillside.

Children lay sweating across their parents' laps, from time to time lurching upright to vomit into plastic bags held steady by mom or dad, which were then tossed out the window.

Every few minutes a chain reaction of shouts would carry to the front of the bus, where, oblivious to their meaning, we Westerners continued to swap travel tales. When the shouts were joined by frantic motions toward the ceiling, we glanced up and saw bundles of small plastic bags attached to hooks above the window. Without fully understanding, I grabbed a few and passed them back. When I heard the unmistakable sound of a child retching I began to get the picture. Oh well, I thought, at least barf bags are included in the price of the ticket.

At the final descent into Sibolga we were delayed due to road work for twenty minutes or so. We clamored off to stretch our crushed limbs, while the carsick kids plopped down on the grass and happily began gorging themselves on mangoes.

Soon the call came to board the bus for the final leg of the journey. We could see Sibolga and the Indian Ocean below as the roller coaster ride began again. Within five minutes the girl across the aisle was at it again, filling plastic bags with vomit as if she were on an assembly line. The smell mixed with that of ripe durian (a large spike-covered fruit whose sewer-like smell has prompted several Asian airlines to ban it), and was enough to push one over the edge.

Finally we stumbled off the bus in Sibolga, exhausted and relieved that the trip was over, breathing easier as the smell of vomit was replaced by that of the ocean. There was a moment of joy, of smiles on our faces, of a spring to our steps as we gazed toward the harbor...and the boat we were about to board for twelve hours with countless more motion sickness-prone locals in close quarters....

Jennifer DuBois is an award-winning journalist who lives in Seattle. She has co-authored three books in a series of alternative employment guides.

★

But it is not our comforts we remember—or that anyone else cares to remember for that matter. What is memorable is misery. It is our dismay, our disbelief, and the fact that we made it through. There is some perverse natural law which makes adversity lead to inspiration. I often wonder why I can't sit in a Paris café or in a nice Caribbean hotel and feel the travel writing muse. Somehow the lack of running water, the fear of disease, and the misery of a straw mat bring us closer to the brink and hence let us feel we are alive.

—Mary Morris, *I Should Have Stayed Home: The Worst Trips of Great Writers,* edited by Roger Rapoport and Marguerita Castanera

LAURIE GOUGH

✦ ✦ ✦

Heidi on the Edge

*A carefree hike in the mountains becomes a nightmare
that challenges innocence and faith.*

Sometimes the most dreadful things can happen in the most
beautiful places. It's always a shock. We wonder how things
could possibly go wrong amidst such godly splendor, in the
incorruptible air of mountain nirvanas innocent of the fallen
cities below. Later, we may realize that what we thought
dreadful was beautiful after all and lived up to its earthly do-
main because the grace of the earth itself swooped down to
remind us that we are not separate, like orphaned children, but
a melody in this grace carrying the earth's strength inside of
us. Then we can walk on, protected with this primal knowledge, to face any darkness on our way.

I WAS TRAVELING NORTH THROUGH ITALY AFTER HAVING SPENT
two months swimming in waves, waitressing in *tavernas* and reading books in the shade, camped on the Greek isle of Naxos. At 23
years old, one is allowed to do that kind of thing.

Even in temperate northern Italy, I was still hot. Greek heat, like
halcyon days spent in that country, stays lingering deep inside of
you and I craved cool alpine breezes on my skin to unearth that
heat. I'm a redhead and wilt readily.

That's how I found myself studying a map of the Italian-Swiss Alps one morning while I sat on a bench next to Lake Como, using my stored Greek heat to melt the dark Swiss chocolate in my mouth. I hoped to eat snow later that day. As for getting up to those chilly mountains I didn't yet have a plan.

So I was happy at first when two men in hiking boots asked me to check my map for trails into the mountains. My plan had just walked up to me on four tanned and muscular Italian legs. Good timing. Nice legs.

"*Ciao,*" I said to them, which pretty well covered the extent of my Italian. They both squinted their eyes in a confused kind of way as if I had just asked them to explain Fellini symbolism to me. I tried my French instead. "*Bonjour, comment ca va?*" They laughed and let loose a torrent of lexicon from one of those Romance languages. I was fairly sure it wasn't French because I didn't understand a single word of it and I do come from Canada. I smiled back as if I understood them completely and pointed at myself. "Laurie."

"Lau...urie, *ah si*, Laurie." Good they got that.

The especially good-looking one had a Renaissance grandeur to him with a strong and tall natural body, wavy brown hair like suede, and blue-green eyes that appeared to be ocean-fed. If he'd struck a pose of passive contemplation and been drenched in a bucket of white paint, he'd be taken for a Michelangelo statue. He pointed to himself and said, "Chico...Chico."

Then his friend smiled, pointed at himself in exact imitation and said, "Chico...Chico." Either they were both named Chico or the second one was really stupid.

It didn't matter much. Somehow we communicated that we all wanted to go hiking in the mountains that day. I discovered they were Italian but spoke a little French, a little English, and when that didn't work, I spoke broken Spanish to them which sounds rather Italian. It was good enough for me—they had a car.

Before setting off into the mountains, we stopped at a restaurant for cappuccino. I drank lots of the stuff because I figured I'd need all that caffeine to shoot itself through my leg muscles to keep pace with the Chicos. I could see they were born for the sole purpose of climbing mountains.

Then a strange thing happened. The second Chico stood up to go, leaving me and the Chico-Adonis face to face, alone. Things in the air changed then, unspoken things, things not part of any language. I wondered what to do next.

The atmosphere among the three of us had been light-hearted with the kind of laughter that accompanies foreigners who don't really understand anything about each other, but somehow bridge that cultural canyon through the hilarity of their apparent sameness. The idea of the three of us hiking together had held a serendipitous, spontaneous bravado to it, a casual jaunt, capricious and harmless. I had felt this even with the language barrier, a barrier which prevented us from learning detailed, possibly mundane facts about each others' lives but did not blockade an unspoken camaraderie. I felt like one of the players in a trio of wandering misfits wondering what to do on a sunny day. With Chico-2 quickly gone, I was at a loss. And Chico-1 across the table from me was no longer a comrade but a stranger.

I knew as I sat talking to him, watching his face over my coffee cup, that he was the most handsome man I'd ever seen up close. He was rugged and strong with life, and he laughed hard at my botched attempts to speak languages other than English. Those libido currents of electric intrigue that pass between strangers who find each other not quite believable silently charged themselves with intensity. We liked what we saw in each other because we saw what we wanted to see. Projection is easy: just fill in the blank spaces with your deep dreams.

I watched him closely, and he knew this, but I could not help noticing that something almost sinister would break through out of his eyes—not very often but enough for me to catch—and his handsomeness would melt into a crude brutality of bones under bronzed smooth skin. If it weren't for the language and cultural barriers I may have understood that look. I tried to pretend I hadn't seen any private darkness escaping from his eyes and deduced the glint to be some Italian male testosterone condition. I wanted to go hiking.

"Laurie, you and me. We go up in the mountains today to a different place, visit my aunt and uncle. They live up high in the mountain village, small. Beautiful, very beautiful place like you can't believe. Not far. Quiet, only the river and cowbells make the noise. People, they like you in this place."

"And snow? Will we get into the snow?"

He smiled and narrowed his eyes as if ascertaining whether snow meant a good or a bad thing to me. My expression betrayed me.

"Yes, a little snow I think. Really beautiful. You make the picture with the camera."

His eyes were aqua then and sparkled like the waves I'd watched from the beach in Greece. Any darkness stowawayed in those eyes had drowned in lighter shades of blue virtue.

Still, I was hesitant, of course. I'd been in the Mediterranean long enough to understand the warped single-mindedness of its men. Heck, I'd been on Planet Earth long enough. The Mediterranean doesn't hold a monopoly on sexism. But I also understood this: every so often one must wave off caution and be defiant of better judgment for the sanctity of Almighty Adventure, for survival of the soul. Maybe it's a symptom of age 23. Maybe it's a definition. In this case, my desire to go hiking into the mountains with a questionable Roman god exceeded my fear of danger. I've never been big on fear. Or danger. I knew this ascent to the Unknown may not be good for me but I also knew I would do it. I hung on like a cantankerous old fisherman holds his line, to the belief that this would be an innocent escapade between new friends. Because I wanted to believe it. Because gypsies dance and because I was 23 years old, people were good and life was whimsical.

So with a sudden impulse of recklessness and something not far from wild abandonment, I said to Chico, "*Andiamo!*" hoping that meant, "Let's hit the road," and didn't mean: please play the music with more animation.

Chico had to make a few stops along the way before the hike. I waited in his car for a whole half-hour outside of what I assumed to be his house. He returned carrying a backpack full of goods he explained his aunt needed in the mountains. I imagined his aunt to be a sweet woman of doughy abundance who would kiss me on both cheeks the way Europeans tend to do, stuff me with copious amounts of pasta, then ask me 246 questions in Italian and not hold it against me that I could only nod and smile back at her. Already I could taste the pasta and feel her vivacious amplitude press itself against my body. That's what I loved about Italy: zest.

We drove towards Lugano then parked the car by a raging river at a place where tall pines obscured the sunlight. I left my backpack locked in Chico's car, thinking I wouldn't need anything out of it for the afternoon hike. As we slammed the car doors and walked towards the trailhead, awkwardly smiling at each other, a thought struck me: we all live in our own heads. This person and I hardly exist to each other. We're each a living embodiment of each others' imaginations based on our separate lives up until now. Who I am in his eyes may be based on an American television show he once watched. Likewise, the Chico in my head and this real Chico don't even know each other. I followed him up the rocky path, sincerely hoping he'd never caught an episode of *I Dream of Jeannie*.

The beauty of the place nearly knocked me over. Green relieved every part of my being after the desert and arid sparseness of Greece. The trail followed alongside a stream which ran full and noisily, crowding out our voices. Not that Chico and I had that much to say to each other. We mostly smiled a lot. The sun behaved the way I like it to, warming my skin without scorching. Finally the cool breezes I sought were doing their job and they felt heavenly. The world was a happy place inside my head that afternoon.

We walked for a long time without stopping. Hours passed and the sun made its way down to its gentler place in the sky where it offers the world that pink subdued time of day. Ahead of us stood nothing but mountains—massive, grey, and imposing. The trail gradually disappeared the higher we went although Chico seemed to know exactly where we were going as we trudged through boulder fields, thick shrubs, and the stream itself, at times. I began to wonder when we'd arrive at the village. Remote and high as we were in the wild heart of this lone-wolf place, I began to wonder if there was a village.

It became dark and Chico's smiles had gone the way of the trail, and the sun. It was as if his layers of charm kept shedding the higher we climbed. We'd become strangers.

I was thirsty so I cupped my hands into the stream to drink. "Here," he said. "Drink this." His manner was gruff and irritable as he handed me a canteen. I took a drink of what I discovered was red wine.

Eventually he stopped in front of me and I could see a flicker of light ahead of us although I couldn't make out what it was. He shouted something, a sharp call, as if someone he knew was near. Another man answered as a door slammed. "Come," Chico said to me. Anger shot through me because he ordered me like that and because I could do nothing but follow his orders.

We entered a little hovel of a home containing a wooden table in the center, a single chair, a tiny bed covered with a sparse grey wool blanket, and a wooden counter cluttered with dirty cooking things. The feeble light given off from the oil lamp on the table wasn't even tempting enough for moths. An odor of recently fried fish barely made its escape out of an old pan to overrule the ranker, mustier smell of the cabin itself. An oldness hung about the place, an oldness depriving and aging even the place's inhabitant. I could see that the old man living there couldn't fight it, wouldn't even try, and fate would have him bound to that shack long past the time when his body began to crumble in on itself, decay, and freeze. Really, he and the shack were part of the same thing.

The old man never looked me in the eyes. I wasn't a person to him. He and Chico talked in Italian, clearly about me. At one point, Chico held up a piece of my hair to show the old man, as if I were a prize horse. Then the old man poured Chico a glass of red wine, which Chico guzzled, and we turned to go. Even though

I hated the place, and the old man, I wanted to stay there rather than continue to walk farther up into the night.

Another two hours must have passed and still we walked. The cooling breezes had given way to cold breezes and I wasn't dressed for their harshness. The caffeine had long since abandoned me and my body ached with exhaustion. Caffeine still residing in my body wouldn't have made sense anyway because I was a different person than that silly girl who had gulped cupfuls of cappuccino with two handsome Italians that morning. She no longer existed.

I knew that I couldn't just take off somewhere and hide from him because I'd be so cold, having left my clothes and sleeping bag in his car. Also I'd be lost. How could I find my way back to his car the next day when we'd come so far in the dark and had left the trail so far behind? We'd crossed over and followed so many different streams that any one stream couldn't lead me back. I had to follow him.

The night wore on, seemingly with no end to it as if the world had decided forever to remain dark. I felt like I was on a treadmill going nowhere, walking upwards into a perpetual present. I had no way of knowing how long or how far we'd continue like this.

Thankfully, the moon eventually rose more than half-full over the mountains so I no longer stumbled over rocks in the dark as I scrambled to keep pace with the monster. Tree leaves and boulders reflected back the moon's light as did the water in the rapids. I slowed down to watch the moon glide through the pine trees as we moved along. Chico yanked my arm and yelled at me, "Go more fast!" A peculiar dark look had come out of his chest through his eyes which were no longer aqua but black. No moonlight reflected itself in those eyes and I knew that Chico no longer existed either.

The curious thing was that I couldn't quite believe any of it was happening to me, so I wasn't particularly scared. We were in this beautiful place lit up by the moon, far away from where anything truly bad could ever happen; it made no sense to me that everything wouldn't be all right in a place like this and I wouldn't let it make sense. I walked faster but continued to watch for the moon.

At last we came to a clearing. I could smell food cooking and wood smoke in the air. Not far off I heard the familiar hollow clanging of cowbells. Lights shone behind glass windows and I could make out a cabin in front of us. More than anything, the clatter of the cowbells came as the greatest relief. Again, the feeling came over me of being safe under the reign of what is natural and innocent in this world. Big and dumb alpine cows made me think of Swiss cheese, Swiss chocolate, Heidi, and all things wholesome, and I couldn't associate that with anything sinister. Then again, I live from my own head.

I followed Chico into the cabin. This was no inhospitable decaying shack like the old man's, but a home well cared for. Almost everything was made of pine and the place had that Swiss Alps homey freshness to it. I wasn't surprised to see a woman there, stirring something in a large pot over a wood cook stove. I wondered what she would be cooking so late in the night. She wasn't an especially old woman, but she barely looked up when Chico and I arrived, as if she'd lived too many years already and life didn't hold anything of much interest left to

Look closely at her.

She crosses a city street, juggling her briefcase and her sack of groceries. Or she walks down a dirt road, balancing a basket on her head. Or she hurries toward her locked car, pulling a small child along with her. Or she trudges home from the fields, the baby strapped to her back.

Suddenly there are footsteps behind her. Heavy, rapid. A man's footsteps. She knows this immediately, just as she knows that she must not look around. She quickens her pace in time to the quickening of her pulse. She is afraid. He could be a rapist. He could be a soldier, a harasser, a robber, a killer. He could be none of these. He could be a man in a hurry. He could be a man merely walking at his normal pace. But she fears him. She fears him because he is a man. She has reason to fear.

She does not feel the same way— on city street or dirt road, in parking lot or field—if she hears a woman's footsteps behind her.

It is the footstep of a man she fears. This moment she shares with every human being who is female.

This is the democratization of fear.

—Robin Morgan, *The Demon Lover: On the Sexuality of Terrorism* see. Her husband pulled back two chairs, motioning for us to sit down, and although he didn't smile, it was the first act of kindness shown towards me in what felt like a distant forgotten time. I remembered being human again.

The woman served hot tomato vegetable soup which I devoured while the three of them sat at the far end of the table from me and rattled off their Italian. Again they looked me over as if all that existed of me were my extremities—my red hair, my skin, my legs, and arms. My secret from them was that these things weren't really me at all; I knew that in this, somehow, also lay my protection.

Finally it was the husband who spoke to me. "You Chico's wife," he said flatly, accusingly.

"No," I answered, although I don't think it had been a question. I looked to the woman for help, for some sort of universal motherly warmth, for understanding. I found none of these things. She seemed to hate me as much as the two men. Apparently the feminist movement hadn't made its way up there yet.

Well, gee thanks for the soup. Delicious. I'll be toddling off now. I'll visit again some day when another low-life scum-sucking dirt bag excuse for a man asks me out on a little afternoon hike with him. Nice meeting you all. Ta-ta.

If only.

The three of them didn't know how to take me. Their discussion in Italian continued, even got a little heated, yet they never took their eyes off me as they spoke. They didn't have to make it so obvious. Very impolite, I thought. I suspected they weren't discussing the possible ramifications of German reunification but they could have at least pretended.

Remember: No one can make you feel inferior without your consent.

—Eleanor Roosevelt, *Readings from the Hurricane Island Outward Bound School*

I hate being excluded. This was worse than being chosen last for the baseball team. I tried staring back at them, quizzically, so they might know how it feels to be a freak on a stage or a caged animal.

Then Chico stood up. "Come."

"Where?"

"Come."

The husband walked to the door and held it open for us, stone-faced, gesturing with a sweeping move of his arm for us to get lost. This mountain village hospitality overwhelmed me. And he was my favourite of the three.

Back out in the cold night I gazed up into the sky, jealous of and dazzled by the stars I saw up there, so distant, so untouched by and oblivious to the Italian Alps. I found it incredible that they'd still be up there. My world was falling away, it was a different place entirely than it had been that morning, and still the Big Dipper dipped along the same as ever. I had to stay strong, keep myself intact. But this was becoming difficult. Never had I been so thoroughly spent, so drained of myself.

We didn't have to walk far before reaching another cabin. This one felt empty and cold inside. Chico lit an oil lamp and started to make a fire in the wood stove. I could see a series of bunk beds, stern little hard cots covered tightly in grey wool blankets of the type I'd seen at the old man's shack, so long ago. Why hadn't I demanded to stay there? Could I have? The limits, the rules in this bizarre game, weren't clear to me.

The sight of the tiny beds came as a relief; austere as they were, they were single. I didn't know what was happening inside Chico's head, but I was so completely ready to drop, only deep sleep mattered to me. With determination, his presence could be blocked out of my awareness. A numbness throughout every part of me had frozen any lingering fear and anger. Only a vague tiredness in my leg muscles remained to faintly remind me I still existed.

I collapsed on top of the nearest bottom bunk bed, too weary to try to figure out what "goodnight" could be in Italian. I didn't care. I couldn't even summon the effort to take off my shoes. On top of the hard cot, I tried to pretend this was normal, not a moment to become unhinged. Everything would be fine. After making the fire, he'd fall onto his own cot, and in mutual exhaustion we'd both become unconscious, slip away back into our own safe and separate worlds. I shut my eyes against the weightiness and confusion of it all, longing to escape into sleep. The next morning I'd get away on my own. I'd get away and reclaim myself.

The fire's warmth steadily took over the place and Chico blew out the oil lamp. My body clenched itself into an adrenaline factory of nerves thriving off impulses as I listened in the quiet for every rustle. First his voice, angry and hard, came out of the darkness: Italian, talking to himself. Then the careless and noisy throwing off of his clothes—the heavy leather boots, kicked off in different directions, the wool coat dropping to the floor, the zipper of his jeans unzipping too close to my ears. "Move." It was almost a shout but not quite and I didn't move.

"Move," he said again. On my back, I rolled my knees up to my chest to kick. I knew he was strong with life but so am I.

And so began a fight of wills that continued far too long into a night that insisted on perpetuating itself. A fight between two heads that had overtaken the bodies they were placed on. For the first time, we faced each other as the people we were. I called up every part of myself that I thought had deserted me that day. He won in the end, his body stronger than my will. A feeble winning. I didn't have anything left in me to fight with; nothing remained for him to take over.

When it was finally over, I lay on the cot staring up into the blackness with an anger surging through me like I'd never known. Sleep no longer offered itself as a temporary rescue. I needed to get his car keys out of the pocket of his jeans so I could try to find my way down the mountain on my own at first light, get my backpack out of his car, and get away, north to Switzerland. I groped around in the dark as silently as possible to discover that his jeans were under his head, being used as a pillow. Too empty to cry and to defeated to move, I let sleep take me away from there.

The next morning, I realized that Chico had no intention of going back down the mountain. Not that day or any day soon to come. He had enough supplies in his backpack to last us a long time. Us. Somehow, he had the idea that he and I would stay up there together, that we'd be like husband and wife. Somehow, I would submit to this.

I'd heard of things like this happening before, maybe in the Middle Ages, maybe in the white slave trade. But not now, not to me.

If anything, Chico's demon charm had grown even more unbearable. His hatred for me seemed as deep as mine for him. So deep ran my loathing of him, I couldn't look him in the eye, nor would he look at me. Rather than try to understand it, I had to concentrate on getting away. Outside in the bright morning, I gazed around at the snow-peaked mountains on all sides of me, and I knew I had no idea how to find my way back down. It was as if the previous night's dark madness had displaced me into a snowy medieval kingdom not a part of this world.

I started walking. The husband and wife who had fed me the soup in disdain would be of no help, but surely others would. A few more cabins were close by; I could smell the wood smoke. Maybe somebody could give me a map. At least point me in the right direction? I came across an old man who was chopping wood in front of his house. I smiled, said "*Ciao*," but he grunted at me and continued with his chopping. What was wrong with these people? Another elderly couple who were tending to their goats proved to be equally enchanting. Was the word "whore" written across my forehead? Had the darkness inside Chico passed itself onto me? Had they never read *How To Win Friends and Be Kind to Strangers?*

I'd have to do this on my own. I walked along beside the stream through the little valley, leaving the village and the clanging of cowbells in the distance behind me, I broke down and cried. There didn't seem to be any way out of this. I wondered how I could have been so stupid to get myself into such a situation. What could I have been thinking? It occurred to me that what is safe and nice and known in this world has never been enough for me. I always have to tread too closely to that line beyond which nothing makes sense anymore, nothing is known absolutely. I live for that line; it's what gives my life substance. I have to push it out to a farther edge, to the brink of myself. This time I'd pushed the line too far. Maybe crossed over it.

I sat down on a big rock by the edge of the stream. The sun had just reached high enough in the sky to topple itself over the closest mountain and pour its warmth and light onto me and the rock. Nothing but excruciating beauty surrounded me. Beside cold and gushing water, I sat in a green mountain valley out of a picture book. Small white alpine flowers grew in silence beside my rock, and stretched out into a mossy patch of green underneath the trees to the foot of the snowy mountains. Just as quietly, overhead, white-feathered birds glided their wings along the air. Never had I recalled being a part of such a heaven. Never had I found myself in such a hell.

Yet hell could not exist in such a place. It wasn't welcome.

I didn't know what to do. Tears kept welling up in my eyes, blurring my view of the stream. It seemed I had few options. None in fact. I'd reached a void, an alarming impasse of hope. This had eased itself upon me too calmly and I could almost have been lost in its lull, like the last moment before giving in to drowning. The water suddenly feels good, they say, welcoming, no longer a force to fight. Just slip into the gap of passivity. Silent resignation and never heard from again.

That's when the magnitude, the majesty of the place began to take over me. Hell Not Welcome Here. Here was sacred, a watering hole for the gods, a life force.

The best remedy for those who are afraid, lonely, or unhappy is to go outside, somewhere where they can be quiet, alone with the heavens, nature, and God. Because only then does one feel that all is as it should be and that God wishes to see people happy, amidst the simple beauty of nature. As long as this exists, and it certainly always will, I know that then there will always be comfort for every sorrow, whatever the circumstances may be.

—Anne Frank, *Anne Frank: The Diary of a Young Girl*

My tears dried and a rush of happiness washed over me as if the sun, the mountains, and the stream all conspired to be a surrogate mother and assure me that everything would be all right; I was of their world. I took in their strength, as I had none left of my own.

I walked back towards the village, towards Chico. I found him chopping wood in front of the cabin. He didn't even look up at me even though I stood squarely in front of the chopping block. I had myself back when I said, "Chico, I want us to go down the mountain now." He stopped chopping.

We stared into each others' eyes and saw the world: rage, tumbling havoc, passion, shadowy understatements, and conviction. What a larger story these same ocean eyes spoke than they had the morning before over my coffee cup. But he was human after all, responding to the earth's calling, and he nodded his head in resignation. "*Sí*, we go down."

At the bottom of the mountains that night, I was too tired to set up my tent so I lay on top of it instead in my sleeping bag and watched the sky. I tried to figure out if Chico had actually been evil or just a man doing what some men do. Either way, he was nothing to me and barely existed anymore.

Still, I felt broken. Broken because a little of who I was before this happened had died. Broken because a little of the world had died too. But then I saw a shooting star spread itself across the whole sky and I remembered the stream and the mountains and how they'd saved me, had been on my side. And I knew that nothing could ever shake my foundation, destroy me, because whatever sublime wisdom lies behind the soul of the Universe is also part of me. As I fell asleep, something I once read somewhere came back to me: there is always beauty at the moment when a ray from eternity strikes upon our gross natures. We should revere every illumination, every transfiguring terror. May God give each of us his criminal and his sin to awaken us. But there must be other kinds of illumination, from far purer terrors, out of which a deed goes up like a star.

Laurie Gough also contributed "Travels with Chester" in Part III.

★

(To be said by a healer)

> In the name of God and all His angels, I cast
> out the demon left in you by this evil.
> I say unto you, the force of darkness, be gone
> from this beloved child.
> Through the power of God within us, I order
> you gone, nevermore to return or to cast your
> wicked energies in the direction of this
> precious child of God.

—Marianne Williamson, *Illuminata: Thoughts, Prayers, Rites of Passage*

★ ✳ ★

Taken for a Ride

Listen to your instincts.

I WAS ON MY DREAM VACATION. THE SIGHTS WERE NEW AND exciting. I was busy taking it all in. But I had a foreboding that we shouldn't be with Joel.

It was summer. I had joined a friend, Vicki, and her friend, Sarah, in London, for what we'd planned to be our college education grand tour. When Vicki said they'd met a guy named Joel in the bookstore at Oxford University, accompanied him to Stratford-on-Avon, and accepted his invitation to drive to Paris, I immediately responded, "No, I don't want to go by car."

Several people had cautioned, "European drivers are crazy. Roads are circuitous. It's better to take the train."

Vicki overrode my objection. "It's so much fun to be able to stop whenever you want." The trip was supposed to be fun. No one expected to have to make a life or death decision. So I didn't say any more.

They'd bought concert tickets with Joel for the evening; but, exhausted from being up all night on the flight from New York, I begged off.

Joel picked them up; he was a slight young man who slouched and shrugged nervously, and he repelled me. His eyes avoided mine. I shrank back. An alarm went off in my brain: don't drive with him! However, jet-lagged, I ignored my inner voice, crawled into bed and slept.

We didn't see him the next day; I was glad. Arrangements were made by phone to try to link up the day after in Dover. I assumed Dover would be a large city, we'd never meet, and I dismissed him from thought.

Late the following afternoon, we arrived in Dover. We exited the train station, and right at the bottom of the steps was a red MG. My companions exclaimed, "It must be Joel's." I stiffened. Dread filled me while they hurried over, peered inside. They scribbled a note, shoved it under a wiper blade. My impulse was to snatch the note and destroy it.

It *was* his car and we joined him for dinner. When he took us back to our hostel, he drove much too quickly down a steep hill. As he tried to steer on the unfamiliar left side of the road, his hands shook. He knew none of the curves, or where streets intersected. After he'd dropped us at the hostel, I spoke up, "He's a lousy driver. I don't want to drive with him."

"He hasn't been driving long. I'm sure he'll be fine," said Vicki. How come she didn't feel the concern I did? He gave me the creeps. I had to keep shoving my feelings aside.

We took the morning ferry across the English Channel to Calais, France. In a field outside the town, we shared a picnic lunch of bread, paté, and wine.

I asked Joel to teach me to drive his car. I had never driven a car with a shift. Every time I stepped on the clutch, the engine stalled.

On an empty country road, stalling wasn't hazardous. But I was scared to get into traffic, so I relinquished the wheel to Joel. I sat in the front passenger seat that afternoon.

Used to driving a much larger car, I didn't like so little distance between me and the car ahead. The following day I made sure to sit in back.

We left Rouen after breakfast. We chose a road that wound through beautiful meadows and woods. It was being resurfaced. If it was too torn up, we all agreed we'd go back and take the high-way. After a few minutes, we'd passed the face-lifted area, and then continued on the scenic route.

Soon Joel was tailgating the car ahead. In the lane to the right, a second car rode neck and neck beside it. Joel swerved into the oncoming traffic's lane to pass. The car in the right lane sped up and changed lanes into the spot Joel was aiming for. Now he had two cars to pass. Suddenly, the oncoming cars loomed threaten-ingly close.

Sarah, sitting beside Joel, sobbed hysterically.

"Cover your face, Sarah," I shouted.

Joel floored the gas, and, through a miracle, passed both cars and squeezed back onto our side of the road just in time.

"Please slow down," Sarah pleaded.

"Were in no hurry," Vicki yelled.

"Shut up, I know what I'm doing," he said through clenched teeth.

In the distance, a train sped across the fields. I wished we were on it.

A couple of hours into the journey we passed a roadside fruit stand; doubled back for a snack. Since Sarah spoke French, she and Joel went to buy the produce.

I said to Vicki, "I don't like the way he drives; I won't go with him after we get to Paris." She finally agreed.

While we ate peaches, Joel reached under the driver's seat, and pulled out the bottle of wine we'd all shared the previous day dur-ing our picnic lunch. He gulped down the wine. I was on the verge of asking him not to drink, but the bottle was empty.

Back on the road, Joel drove faster. The little car rattled. His hands shook on the steering wheel. A nervous chill raced through me. Trying to calm myself I rationalized, nothing will happen; we'll be in Paris soon. I started to read a Paris travel brochure.

In the middle of my prayers to slow down, Sarah's voice shrieked, "Why are you passing on the right? You can't see. There's construction ahead."

Screams ripped the air. The brochure dropped from my hand.

We were about to crash into a wooden barricade. It happened so fast, I froze. Joel spun the steering wheel hard. Too hard. We shot across the road, out of control.

Facing us was an approaching gasoline truck. Suspended in shock, my thoughts raced. Drop to the floor? If the seat jumps back, I'll be crushed. How will we get to Paris now? Dear Mom and Dad, We had a little accident...

I woke up four weeks later, and they were by my bed. They told me what had happened. Sarah died instantly. Joel lost an arm and a leg. Vicki's legs were broken; one will never bend. My right arm and hip broke in so many places I'm constantly in pain.

My inner voice is a part of me now, and when it speaks, I listen.

Ronnie Golden loves travel, but not by car, although she drives to her office where she is a freelance writer. She is also a gourmet cook, bargain shopper, and she is passionate about opera, cats, and ice cream. She lives in Studio City, California.

★

Opening up to the pain of death, our own or that of someone we love, is one of the most mysterious blessings of life. Nothing focuses us more clearly on what matters, helps us drop our defenses more quickly or gives us more compassion for human suffering.

—Marianne Williamson, *Illuminata: Thoughts, Prayers, Rites of Passage*

KAREN CHENEY

⋆ ⋆ ⋆

Contraband Carrier

*Innocents get more than they bargained for
on a Colombian cargo ship.*

WE JOKED LIGHTHEARTEDLY ABOUT THE BENEVOLENCE OF THE travel gods, but it wasn't until we were safely inside Colombia that I began to truly believe in their existence. For what are the odds—given chance alone—that two young North American women could survive entering a country like Colombia illegally in a cargo ship carrying contraband goods? Our survival had to be due to the divine intervention of our favorite gods.

We found the cargo ship at the Caribbean end of the Panama Canal in Colón, the kind of run-down city that kept my grandmother up at night worrying about me. And her worries weren't exactly unfounded. Colón was the only city during all of our travels that made me long for the safe, be it dull, familiarity of North American suburbia. The streets were busy, but as strangers, an eerie silence seemed to glide along with us that compelled me to whistle nervously, taking furtive glances behind with each step. Sticking out like a pair of missionaries, we hustled through town and to the docks to begin our search for a ship.

I had no special desire to take a trip in a cargo ship. There are daily flights over Panama's Darien jungle to Colombia, but a force stronger than my own volition—my wallet—dictated the terms of travel, and because I really wanted to see Colombia, I complied. After bouncing all the way across Mexico and Central America in public buses packed to three times their legal capacity, my friend and I considered ourselves veterans of budget travel who could outlive any discomforts.

Finding the ship was surprisingly easy. We didn't have to ask more than a handful of sailors before being directed to the *Benybell*, captained by a shrewd fellow known as "the compass." The greatest challenge for us was trying to make sense of the most rapid, slurred Spanish we had ever heard. The first mate, Juan, spoke a more comprehensible version of Spanish, so we made him our liaison while we negotiated travel terms. After about an hour of serious wrangling, we reached the reasonable rate of $30 for the three-day passage and meals.

The *Benybell* was a small, but cheerfully clean ship with the captain's quarters and the navigation room up top, and two sleeping cabins, a bathroom, and the galley below. Mani, the ship's cook, prepared a festive meal of coconut rice, beans, and fried bananas in the galley that evening, and we all celebrated enthusiastically before taking off. Unfortunately, my enthusiasm found itself blown across the Caribbean very quickly.

Weaving and grasping the wall like a drunk, I made my way to the stablest spot in the ship, under a covered area on the deck directly over the engine room. I felt like I was riding a wild bull in the rodeo back home—only without the joy of falling off. He would rear up, crash down, swing about madly, and then pace around just long enough for me to relax before the next startling jolt.

While my travel companion, Linda, eventually acquired a pair of wobbly, yet seaworthy legs, I remained in a permanently horizontal position curled up between two boxes of cargo. From this angle, I observed the tedium of daily life—taking shifts on the deck, catching the occasional television program the ship picked up, and eating Mani's enormous plates of rice, beans, and fried bananas. Those smells could still turn me green months later!

The captain's repeated concerns about running into patrol boats began to puzzle us. Just what were we carrying in those hundreds of boxes of cargo? We shrugged off our uncertainties, however, and assumed that the captain didn't want the coastal patrol to discover that he was carrying passengers. Since he wasn't certified to carry passengers, we had sworn not to reveal the ship's identity at customs.

At night the warmth of the engine penetrated my thin cushion while I watched the dark, grey sea, lit up in flashes of white foam, rush over the top of the railings. The three or four times that the comforting hum of the engine ceased and nothing but the dark night and the roar of the sea surrounded me, I did grow panicky. Each time it stopped I was sure that mine was the ill-fated destiny of being lost at sea, but soon the hum would vibrate below me again.

It was dark when we finally docked three days later, so in spite of our eagerness to feel that beloved, firm earth, we continued to sleep. At five o'clock slits of sun shot through the cracks between my cargo boxes and I heard shouts and noises outside. After climbing through the dark belly of the boat onto the deck, the sun momentarily blinded me. When the scene before me began to clear, a wave of queasy disorientation made me grope for support, as I tried to determine the reality of the sight below the boat.

Hundreds of small Indian men, stooped under the weight of large boxes of cargo, which they were depositing in a fleet of trucks, swarmed beneath the ship. Women in long, billowy dresses, their heads covered and their faces painted black for protection from the relentless sun, stood gazing at the activity. In an attempt to fit this picture into what I had imagined I'd see upon entering Colombia, my glance searched the horizon for green mountains richly covered with coffee plants. Other than a few lonely shacks, beyond all the bustle near the ship, nothing but a vast desert opened up like a hot, disdainful yawn.

Where was the port town? Where was the customs office? Where was the place we had planned to take a shower and eat a meal of anything besides rice, beans, and fried bananas? With a look of incredulity, Linda asked, "Are we in some kind of Indiana Jones movie?"

During the six hours it took to move the cargo from the boat to the trucks, we finally assembled all the facts into a startlingly vivid understanding of our situation. The use of code names, the evasion of patrol ships, and docking in a hidden port on the Guajira desert in northeastern Colombia were all precautions necessary for an illegal ship smuggling contraband clothing. Even more unnerving was that our only means of transportation across the desert was to join a caravan of contraband trucks. Immediately, we began devising stories that would clear us of any implication once caught.

I hung my head and admitted a rather reckless lack of foresight. Yet our naïve, venturesome attitudes allowed us to forego the comforts and safety of a tour package and to investigate a pocket of Colombia where the country makes no effort to maintain the thin veneer of law and order that exists in the tourist areas.

The desert patrol did stop our trucks, but the police—a fine example of the anti-tattletale system—gladly accepted our roll of extra Christmas money, and we continued on our way. The anti-tattletale system bases its rationale on the theory that tattletales don't exist in a system where everyone benefits from illegality. Its tentacles reach the general public, who benefit from the plethora of contraband goods (Pioneer stereos, Benetton jeans, Oscar de la Renta luggage, etc.) sold at tax-free rates at the market in Maicao, and to the Colombian customs officers at the Venezuelan border who, after a brief ritual of wagging their fingers at us, accepted a few bills to stamp our passports for proof of legal entry into the country.

The days we spent on the Guajira desert certainly didn't prepare us for the modern country we proceeded to visit. Just a day's travel from Maicao, the elegant beachside resort of Santa Marta vaunts First World luxuries we never expected to encounter: modern highrise apartments surrounded by wide, well-groomed sidewalks, people dressed in the latest European fashions, and air-conditioned buses equipped with TVs and VCRs. With well-worn clothes and packs, we looked like we belonged in a parade celebrating frontier days.

We might not have questioned Colombia's deceptively effective camouflage of law and order if we hadn't spent those enlightening days on the Guajira desert. Safe at home, it seems worth it to take risks when travelling, but it might be wise to light a few candles to the travel gods before setting off.

Karen Cheney is a staff writer for Money *and* Retire with Money *magazines, where she is learning how to fund her next voyage, this time around as a paid passenger on the QE2.*

★

The unexpectedness of life, waiting round every corner, catches even wise women unawares. To avoid corners altogether is, after all, to refuse to live.
    —Freya Stark, *The Journey's Echo: Selections from Freya Stark*

TERRY STROTHER

* * *

Terry and the Monkey

Forced to take a closer look at local life, the author
takes a step toward enlightenment.

IT SEEMS I WAS NOT MEANT TO LEAVE INDONESIA JUST YET. THE past three days have been very hectic here. It all started with a leisurely swim in a small fishing town on the south coast of Java. We were walking back through a beautiful nature reserve when a group of monkeys came scampering through. One calmly walked up, grabbed my leg with both hands, and turning its head to the side like a little vampire or a rat, sunk its fangs into my leg. With an absolutely evil look in its quite human-looking eyes, it held my sarong, glaring up at me and chattering. I slowly backed away and told my companion, Tad, I'd been bitten. It all happened so quickly I don't think he knew, or I really, because the desire to deny it was so strong. We had been told by a doctor in New Zealand to be particularly careful with animals in Indonesia because of rabies. He admonished us for not having been vaccinated and warned us ominously how painful the remedy is. All of this was going through my mind; bits and pieces of what he'd said. In slow motion, the little vampire scene began playing out over and over as we stared at my leg with tremendous concentration, hoping to stare the wound back together.

The following hours crept by like days. Tad went in search of information, a phone, anything useful. I sat in the doctor's waiting room at the local "hospital." In the outer room maybe twenty people sat, squatted, lay in a five-by-seven-foot space with their handprinted queue number, waiting to see a man at a desk in another small room. They spoke in hushed tones and eventually left, all seeming to clutch the same small bottle of pills regardless of their affliction. Because I was bleeding, I was first ushered into yet a third room, the "operating room," but only after all present removed our shoes at the door, which seemed a rather nice touch though certainly pointless considering that this room was every bit as filthy as the other two. I sat on the operating table on the blood-encrusted sheet as the attendant shuffled through various jars of crude and antique-looking instruments, trying to decide on an appropriate course of action. After I politely (I hoped) rejected a few options that seemed rather hasty, if not downright dangerous, he shrugged, washed out the cut and shuffled me back to the waiting room. I was, of course, terrified. And I felt ridiculous. Others around me were sporting much more serious afflictions, yet everyone smiled, spoke kindly and calmly to one another, shaking hands with everyone (including me) who entered. Everyone smiled. No matter what. So...I smiled. And tried to respond in kind to the young woman who wanted to practice her sketchy English and who, of course, wanted to know my address, occupation, marital status, why I did not have children, how I liked Indonesia.

I knew most of the expected answers by now but it was difficult to concentrate. I couldn't take my eyes off one of my fellow waiters: a small child, perhaps two years old, held in the cloth sling that all parents here use to tote around their children. He was lying in his father's lap, looking up at his smiling face with big, sad, somewhat-glazed eyes. Lying ever so still. Most of his body was an oozing, glistening mass of rawness with bits of charred flesh, like meat left on the barbecue a bit too close to the coals. Surely he was dying. Surely everyone including his parents knew this. Yet all continued to smile and chat and ask how did I like *gado-gado?*

Occasionally someone would get up and go speak with the parents, smiling of course, and rather absent-mindedly stroke the child's unburned face gently. And as the hours crept by, I can't begin to explain why, but it all began to make perfect sense to me. The smiling, the gentleness, the hand shaking, the socializing. I felt very much a part of some mutual understanding of the need for gentleness in the room, in the world, but mostly in the face of helplessness and fear. Like a big "of course" it just settled into my body.

By the time I did get to see the doctor, I didn't even find it odd to go through all the same questions as in the waiting room before: eventually, almost beside the point, why did I happen to be here. His English and my Bahasa Indonesian were both too lacking to go very far, but I did manage to understand that he did not have the rabies serum (no refrigeration) and I would have to go to the nearest large city in hopes of finding some.

At this point, Tad burst through the door. His movements, his loud hurried voice, his urgency was such a contrast to the past few hours. I was startled and stared at him blankly. As he pulled me toward the door, I hurriedly said my goodbyes and politenesses. Tad looked at me as if I were in shock or crazy. In a waiting jeep was a German doctor whom Tad had literally dragged away from his dinner and who had come to rescue me from what every Westerner fears in Indonesia: unsterilized needles. He gave me all the disposable needles in his possession and gravely told me to leave for Bandung (six hours away) as soon as possible.

Tad left in search again, this time for transport, and I waited, this time alone. It was harder waiting alone. I had thought it would be easier. I was frightened and feverish and my wound throbbed ominously. I stared at it, imagining scenes from *Old Yeller*, imagining invading rabies creeping slowly up my leg. I was tired and it was late. But each time I shut my eyes I was engulfed by a sea of monkeys grabbing at me with tiny hands. Pulling, clutching, ripping, and gobbling, fangs flashing, eyes glowing, and everywhere—the hands. I would silently scream and open my eyes and purposefully give myself a pep talk full of grown-up logic. But it was useless. A new archetype had entered solidly into my repertoire of haunts and private demons. The stuff nightmares are made of.

Tad returned after midnight with tickets secured for the ride to Bandung at 6 a.m. Poor Tad, I don't think he slept at all for nearly 36 hours between his anxiety and my nightmares. I remember feeling glad it was me instead of him because it seemed easier to be in the center of this fear than on the outside; a spectator of sorts.

We found the Bandung rabies clinic. Although I felt immediately comfortable with the doctor and with the quality of care, it took a bit of convincing for Tad. Time was also a factor. I managed to get most of my questions answered and more important to me, I felt in good hands with Stephen S. (as his name tag read), the doctor. He was a gentle, soft-spoken man with no trace of ego invested in his occupation. His calm, happy manner colored his environment and rubbed off on those around him. There was one unsettling moment when his assistant walked toward me with the largest, most unsavory needle I'd ever seen (Tad later told me my face went white), but it was for the dog behind me who didn't seem to mind. The medical profession here is necessarily unspecialized and animals and people alike waited together to see the doctor.

Monsoon season in Java is solidly underway. Even when it's not raining I breathe wetness. The worst part was not the shots, but the new nightmare images that took up residence in my psyche, touching a deep chord in me. As though some unacknowledged fear living inside me finally had found the perfect symbol, the vehicle for expression, in the tiny hands of the monkey. Serving as an antidote to this fear is the overall experience of this country and the calmness it leaves in me. The Balinese tending the rice fields…the man who wrapped packages outside the post office in Yogyakarta, sewing cloth around the boxes with such care…the way the Javanese laugh when confronted with calamity…. Their desire to help is so much more natural and easy, even with the language difference, than my ability to express thanks. It is the gentleness, spirituality, and beauty of the people that will stay with me forever.

Terry Strother is a university administrator who lives in New York City with her husband and two-year-old daughter. This story, which won first place in the Travelers' Tales Writing Contest, is her first published work.

✳

Four principal elements make up *priyayi* (Javanese) etiquette:

1) The ability to recognize and honor age and rank...

2) The ability to avoid shocking and offending others...

3) The ability to conceal one's real feelings.

4) The ability to exercise an almost catatonic self-control, because jerkiness and unpredictablity are signs of a lack of inner refinement.... Loud voices, flamboyant behavior, bragging, roars of laughter, wails of sorrow are all considered ill-mannered. Passion or anger is expected only of children, wild animals, peasants, the retarded, and foreigners. The Javanese keep it all inside; you only see the placid exterior and the seemingly calm smile.

—Bill Dalton, *Indonesia Handbook*

PART FIVE

THE LAST WORD

ANN JONES

★ ＊ ★

The Next Destination

The idea and inspiration for the next adventure
often springs from unlikely sources.

EVERY TRAVELER KEEPS IN MIND THE NEXT DESTINATION. YOU
don't dwell on it, of course, for that could only distract you and
make you unhappy with where you are. But you know it's there,
in some corner of your mind, nagging from time to time like the
memory of a thing misplaced. It's a journey to come.

You may not even know how it got into your head—a scrap of
conversation overheard on a train perhaps, or an odd name
glimpsed on a map when you were looking up something else. You
only know that some day you're going to go *there*.

Homebodies don't understand this itch. Common terms—
words like *wanderlust* and *footloose*—define the urge to travel as if it
were some mental or physical aberration, thus encouraging stay-
at-homes to regard travel as vaguely pathological. Someone is always telling me, in the high-minded tone people take when
they've hit upon the occasion to utter a truism: "You can't run
away from yourself." (Is there a traveler who has been spared that
line?) I've always thought it a peculiar remark, for "yourself" is certainly the one person every traveler always takes along. (It's the
stay-at-home who gets left behind.) But people who don't travel
seem to take great comfort in repeating it nonetheless. In fact, like

407

all the devoted travelers I know, I'm always running *to*, not away; though the particular destination is often not so easy to explain.

I'll admit I wanted to go to Udaipur to see the "Nawab's Palace" because I'd watched *The Jewel in the Crown* on Masterpiece Theater. And Casablanca because of the movie. And Bangkok because I'd been given, as a child, a beautiful Thai ring. And Fiji and Singapore just for the sound of the names. Never mind that nowadays Fiji is a fancy resort and Singapore a shopping center. Never mind that Casablanca and Bangkok are big, dirty cities, or that the Nawab's magical floating Palace, the last time I saw it, was a hotel beached high and dry by drought, in the midst of a dry lake bed strewn with trash. I had all the pleasures of imagining each place beforehand, and—because the real place was nothing like what I imagined—the interest of discovering the real thing when I got there.

But you ask, "Doesn't this lead to disappointment?"

Not a bit. Because I never expect a place to be as I imagined it. (What a let down if it were!) And by the time I'm actually fighting traffic or travel restrictions or voracious insects in Sophia or Murmansk or Progresso, my imagination has been ambushed by someplace else—the next destination.

You can't avoid it. Set off on a trip—anywhere—and the next thing you know, someone will mention the name of a place you've never heard of. That's all it takes. You come upon the name again. You ask a question or two, pick up some insignificant fact—just enough to brush the imagination—and you're hooked.

A few months ago, on a flight from Jakarta to Denpasar, I sat next to an Indonesian man who was terribly excited. He couldn't stop smiling. He had been studying for a year in Jakarta—some kind of an advanced course in fishery management—and now he was flying back to his home: a beautiful place, cleaner and quieter than Jakarta, with kindlier people and no air pollution. He kept looking at his watch, trying to make the plane go faster. He was friendly too, in the courteous way of Indonesians, and hospitable. "I hope you visit my house," he said, writing down the address, "next time you come to Biak."

"Biak?" I looked at what he had written in my notebook. Biak it was. Not Bali, where this flight would land, but another Indonesian island, a smaller one, near Iran Jaya—which is to say near what used to be called New Guinea when I studied geography. Having figured out roughly where it was, I asked what it was like; but he was far too enthusiastic to be specific. I learned only that it is a wonderful place vastly unlike Jakarta—which anyone who has been to Jakarta will recognize as a big point in Biak's favor.

The plane landed in Denpasar. We shook hands. He headed for his connecting flight, and I headed for the beach. Weeks later I boarded another plane in Denpasar: a Garuda flight bound for Los Angeles. "Do we stop in Honolulu?" I asked the flight attendant as she handed me a pillow. "Yes," she said. "But first Biak." I won't say that bells rang, but I did feel a flash of curiosity, and then a pang of disappointment as I realized that we would arrive in Biak after dark, too late to get a look at the "wonderful place."

In fact it was the middle of the night when we laid over in Biak—for fuel, I think—and almost all the passengers left the plane to stretch. The airport was tiny—just one high-ceilinged room with a couple rows of plastic chairs and a balcony with three or four small stands selling snacks and post cards and back issues of *Time* and *Asia Week*. And souvenirs of Biak. What souvenirs! Rattan bracelets. "String" bags intricately woven from bark. Carved wooden combs. Necklaces of cowrie shells. And *horim*—penis sheaths—the primary item of local male haberdashery: long, skinny, paper-thin gourds, elaborately painted, to be worn on the penis and held upright by a string looped around the waist. A band began to play—four men in feathers and not much else, playing with a fine gusto on conga drums and something like guitars. Biak knew how to welcome tourists and help them spend their last *rupiah*. Travelers too, I'll bet.

I bought some postcards; and as I write, two pictures hang over my desk. One shows a row of five muscular black men, naked but for their *horim* and what appear to be long, dark tassels worn like neckties. One man, whose penis sheath reaches almost to his chin, wears a red skull cap. In front of the man is a human mummy. (I know that's what it is because it says so on the back of the post-card.) The mummy squats in a wooden lawn chair with its knees drawn up beside its ears and its hands clutching its feet. Its skin is fire-blackened. Although it seems to be wearing a necklace and some sort of feathery helmet, it looks like a large, angular bat.

The other photo shows two women standing in front of a thatched hut. They wear only short, dark brown skirts and their wiry black hair hangs to their elbows. Their breasts are pendulous, their bare legs gray with mud. They hold out their hands to show that most of their fingers have been cut off at the second joint. (Amputation is a common funerary practice, I learn from the back of this postcard; in Biak a woman says goodbye all at once to a dead male relative and another of her precious commemorative finger joints.) The taller woman looks very, very angry—though perhaps I am only projecting how I would feel if someone cut off my finger in memory of my Uncle Marvin. I don't know anything about these Biakans, you see. So I have to make it up.

I don't even know whether these are old photos, from bygone days. Or were they shot at some international tourist hotel: publicity stills for the floor show of colorful folk dances? If I had been allowed to leave the airport and hike into town, would I have seen such people—naked, digitless—strolling about? Any guidebook on Indonesia could answer these questions for me, but I don't really want to know. In a weak moment I looked up Biak in the *Lonely Planet Survival Kit* for Indonesia, and the first thing it said was this: "It's a more-or-less nothing town, just somewhere on the way to somewhere else." I stopped reading. Stuff like that is death to the imagination.

Soon enough I'll find out for myself. But in my mind Biak is already something. Something wonderful. Something like the next destination.

Ann Jones is an award-winning travel writer and photographer. She also writes on women, violence, and criminal justice. Her books on this topic in-clude: Women Who Kill, When Love Goes Wrong, *and* Next Time She'll be Dead. *She lives in New York City and in South Hadley, Massachusetts, with her cats and her horse, the incomparable Sailor.*

Books for Further Reading

I hope *A Woman's World* has inspired you to read on. A good place to start is the books from which I've made selections, and I have listed them below along with other books that I have found valuable. Many of the general guidebooks are also worth reading, and the best have annotated bibliographies or sections on recommended books and maps.

Aebi, Tania with Bernadette Brennan. *Maiden Voyage.* New York: Simon & Schuster, Inc., 1989.

Allison, Stacy. *Beyond the Limits: A Woman's Triumph on Everest.* New York: Little, Brown & Company, 1993.

Alpine, Lisa, et al. *Wild Writing Women: Stories of World Travel.* Old Saybrook, Conn.: Globe Pequot, 2002.

Atwood, Margaret. *Good Bones and Simple Murders.* New York: Doubleday, 1994.

Baranay, Inez. *The Saddest Pleasure.* Sydney, Australia: Collins Publishers Australia, 1989.

Bird, Isabella. *Unbeaten Tracks in Japan.* San Francisco: Travelers' Tales, 2000.

Birkett, Sara Wheele. *Amazonian: The Penguin Book of Women's New Travel Writing.* New York: Penguin Books, 2002.

Bolen, Jean Shinoda. *Crossing to Avalon: A Woman's Midlife Pilgrimage.* New York: HarperCollins Publishers, Inc., 1994.

Coffey, Maria. *A Boat in Our Baggage: Around the World with a Kayak.* London: Little, Brown & Company, 1994.

Conlon, Faith (ed.), et al. *A Woman Alone: Travel Tales from Around the Globe.* Seattle: Seal Press, 2001.

Coskran, Kathleen. *An Inn Near Kyoto: Writing by American Women Abroad.* Moorehead, Minn.: New Rivers Press, 1998.

Coskran, Kathleen (ed.), et al. *Tanzania on Tuesday: Writing by American*

411

Women Abroad. Moorehead, Minn.: New Rivers Press, 1997.

Cressy-Marcks, Violet. *Up the Amazon*. London: Hodder & Stoughton, 1932.

da Silva, Rachel. *Leading Out: Women Climbers Reaching for the Top*. Seattle: Seal Press, 1992.

David-Neel, Alexandra. *Magic & Mystery in Tibet*. London: Souvenir Press, Ltd, 1967.

Davidson, Cathy N. *36 Views of Mount Fuji: On Finding Myself in Japan*. New York: Penguin, 1993.

Davidson, Robyn. *Tracks*. New York: Random House, Inc., 1980.

Davidson, Robyn. *Traveling Light*. Sydney, Australia: HarperCollins Publishers, 1989.

Davidson, Robyn. Photographed by Rick Smolan. *From Alice to Ocean: Alone Across the Outback*. New York: Addison-Wesley Publishing Company in association with Against All Odds Productions, 1992.

de Beauvoir, Simone. *The Blood of Others*. New York: Pantheon, 1948.

De Tessan, Christina. *Expat: Women's True Tales of Life Abroad*. Seattle: Seal Press, 2002.

Dillard, Annie. *Teaching a Stone to Talk: Expeditions and Encounters*. New York: HarperCollins, 1999.

Dykstra, Monique. *Alone in the Appalachians: A City Girl's Trek from Maine to Gaspesie*. Vancouver: Raincoast Books, 2002.

Ehrlich, Gretel. *Islands, The Universe, Home*. New York: Viking Penguin, 1991.

Ehrlich, Gretel. *A Match to the Heart: One Woman's Story of Being Struck by Lightning*. New York: Random House, Inc., 1994.

Estés, Clarissa Pinkola. *The Gift of Story: A Wise Tale About What is Enough*. New York: Random House, Inc., 1993.

Estés, Clarissa Pinkola. *Women Who Run With the Wolves: Myths and Stories of the Wild Woman Archetype*. New York: Ballantine, 1992.

Fonseca, Isabel. *Bury Me Standing: The Gypsies and Their Journey*. New York: Vintage, 1996.

Frank, Anne. *Anne Frank: The Diary of a Young Girl*. New York: Doubleday, 1967.

Gallagher, Winifred. *The Power of Place: How Our Surroundings Shape Our Thoughts, Emotions, and Actions*. New York: Simon & Schuster, Inc., 1993.

Gelman, Rita Goldman. *Tales of a Female Nomad: Living at Large in the World*. New York: Three Rivers Press, 2002.

Goode, Jennie. *Drive: Women's True Stories from the Open Road*. Seattle: Seal Press, 2002.

Gosnell, Mariana. *Zero Three Bravo: Solo Across America in a Small Plane*. New York: Simon & Schuster, Inc., 1993.

Gougaud, Henri and Collette Gouvion. *Egypt Observed*. New York: W. H. Smith Publishers, Inc., 1980.

Gough, Laurie. *Kite Strings of the Southern Cross: A Woman's Travel Odyssey*. San Francisco: Travelers' Tales, 2000.

Gould, Jean. *Hot Flashes from Abroad: Women's Travel Tales and Adventures* (2nd ed.). Seattle: Seal Press, 2001.

Harrison, Barbara Grizutti. *Italian Days*. New York: Ticknor & Fields, 1989.

Hickman, Katie. *Dreams of the Peaceful Dragon: A Journey into Bhutan*. London: Hodder & Stoughton, 1989.

Hickman, Katie. *A Trip to the Light Fantastic: Travels with a Mexican Circus*. London: HarperCollins Publishers, Ltd. UK, 1993

Hoffman, Eva. *Exit Into History: A Journey Through the New Eastern Europe*. New York: Viking Penguin, 1993.

Hopkirk, Peter. *Trespassers on the Roof of the World: The Race for Lhasa*. Oxford: Oxford University Press, 1982.

James, Kelly. *Dancing with the Witchdoctor: One Woman's Stories of Mystery and Adventure in Africa*. New York: HarperPerennial, 2002.

Jansz, Natania and Miranda Davies. *Rough Guide Women Travel*. London: Rough Guides Ltd., 1999.

Jansz, Natania and Miranda Davies. *More Women Travel - Adventures and advice from more than 60 countries - A Rough Guide Special*. London: Rough Guides Ltd., 1995.

Johnson, Diane. *Natural Opium: Some Travelers' Tales*. New York: Alfred A. Knopf, Inc., 1992.

Johnston, Tracy. *Shooting the Boh: A Woman's Voyage Down the Wildest River in Borneo*. New York: Random House, Inc., 1992.

Kennedy, Geraldine. *From the Center of the Earth: Stories Out of the Peace Corps*. Santa Monica, California: Clover Park Press, 1991.

Kiley, Deborah Scaling and Meg Noonan. *Albatross: The True Story of A Woman's Survival at Sea*. New York: Houghton Mifflin Company, 1994.

Kurtz, Irma. *The Great American Bus Ride: An Intrepid Woman's Cross Country Adenture*. New York: Simon & Schuster, Inc., 1993.

Lee, Elaine. *Black Woman's Book of Travel and Adventure*. Portland: Eighth

Mountain Press, 1997.

Lindbergh, Anne Morrow. *Gift From the Sea*. New York: Random House, Inc., London: Chatto and Windus, 1953.

McCauley, Lucy (ed.). *Women in the Wild: True Stories of Adventure and Connection*. San Francisco: Travelers' Tales, 1998.

McCauley, Lucy (ed.), et al. *A Woman's Path: Women's Best Spiritual Writing*. San Francisco: Travelers' Tales, 2003.

McDaniel, Judith. *Sanctuary: A Journey*. New York: Firebrand Books, 1987.

Melchett, Sonia. *Passionate Quests: Five Modern Women Travellers*. Winchester, Massachusetts: Faber & Faber, Inc., 1992.

Miller, Luree. *On Top of the World: Five Women Explorers in Tibet*. Seattle: The Mountaineers, 1984.

Minatoya, Lydia. *Talking to High Monks in the Snow: An Asian American Odyssey*. New York: HarperCollins Publishers, 1992.

Morgan, Robin. *The Demon Lover: On the Sexuality of Terrorism*. New York: W. W. Norton & Co., 1989.

Morris, Mary. *The Illustrated Virago Book of Women Travellers*. London: Little Brown UK, 2002.

Morris, Mary. *Nothing to Declare: Memoirs of a Woman Traveling Alone*. New York: Houghton Mifflin Company, 1988.

Morris, Mary and Larry O'Connor. *Maiden Voyages: Writings of Women Travelers*. New York: Vintage Departures, 1993.

Morrow, Susan Brind. T*he Names of Things: Life, Language and the Beginnings in the Egyptian Desert*. New York: Broadway, 1998.

Murphy, Dervla. *Full Tilt.: Ireland to India with a Bicycle*. Woodstock, New York: Overlook Press, 1965.

Murphy, Dervla. *Eight Feet in the Andes*. Woodstock, New York: Overlook Press, 1986.

Murphy, Dervla. *Muddling Through in Madagascar*. Woodstock, New York: Overlook Press, 1989.

Murphy, Dervla. *Cameroon with Egbert*. Woodstock, New York: Overlook Press, 1991.

Murphy, Dervla. *Transylvania and Beyond*. London: John Murray Publishers, Ltd., 1992.

Olds, Elizabeth Fagg. *Women of the Four Winds*. Boston: Houghton Mifflin Company, 1985.

Olschak, Blanche C. *Bhutan: Land of Hidden Treasures*. New York: Stein & Day Publishers, 1971.

Owens, Mark and Delia. *Cry of the Kalihari*. New York: Houghton Mifflin Company, 1984.

Owens, Mark and Delia. *The Eye of the Elephant: An Epic Adventure in the African Wilderness*. New York: Houghton Mifflin Company, 1992.

Polk, Milbry and Mary Tiegreen. *Women of Discovery: A Celebration of Intrepid Women Who Explored the World*. New York: Clarkson Potter, 2001.

Rapoport, Roger and Marguerita Castanera. *I Should Have Stayed Home: The Worst Trips of Great Writers*. Berkeley, California: Book Passage Press, 1994.

Robinson, Jane. *Unsuitable for Ladies: An Anthology of Women Travellers*. Oxford: Oxford University Press, 1994.

Rogers, Susan Fox. *Another Wilderness: New Outdoor Writing About Women*. Seattle: Seal Press, 1994.

Russell, Mary. *The Blessings of a Good Thick Skirt: Women Travelers and Their World*. New York: HarperCollins Publishers, Inc., 1986.

Schnedler, Marcia. *The Seasoned Traveler*. Castine, Maine: Country Roads Press, 1992.

Slung, Michele and Reeve Lindbergh. *Living with Cannibals and Other Women's Adventures*. Washington, DC: National Geographic Society, 2001.

Smith, Sidonie. *Moving Lives: Twentieth-Century Women's Travel Writing*. Minnesota: University of Minnesota Press, 2001.

Sprengnether, Madelon & C. W. Truesdale. *The House on Via Gombito: Writing by North American Women Abroad*. Minneapolis: New Rivers Press, 1991.

Stark, Freya. *The Journey's Echo: Selections from Freya Stark*. New York: Harcourt, Brace & World, Inc., 1963.

Steinbach, Alice. *Without Reservations: The Travels of an Independent Woman*. New York: Random House, 2002.

Swenson, Karen. *The Landlady in Bangkok*. Port Townsend, Washington: Copper Canyon Press, 1994.

Thayer, Helen. *Polar Dream: The Heroic Saga of the First Solo Journey by a Woman and Her Dog to the Pole*. New York: Simon & Schuster, Inc., 1993.

Walker, Barbara G. *The Woman's Dictionary of Symbols & Sacred Objects*. New York: Harper & Row Publishers, 1988.

Wheeler, Maureen. *Travels with Children - a travel survival kit.*
    Hawthorne, Victoria, Australia: Lonely Planet Publications, 1990.

Wheeler, Sara. *Terra Incognita: Travels in Antarctica.* New York: Modern
    Library, 1999.

Williams, Terry Tempest. *Refuge: An Unnatural History of Family and
    Place.* New York: Vintage, 1992.

Williamson, Marianne. *Illuminata: Thoughts, Prayers, Rites of Passage.*
    New York: Random House, Inc., 1994.

Zepatos, Thalia. *Adventures in Good Company: The Complete Guide to
    Women's Tours and Outdoor Trips.* Portland, Oregon: The Eighth
    Mountain Press, 1994.

Zepatos, Thalia. *A Journey of One's Own: Uncommon Advice for the
    Independent Woman Traveler.* Portland, Oregon: The Eighth
    Mountain Press, 1992.

Zeppa, Jamie. *Beyond the Sky and the Earth: A Journey into Bhutan.* New
    York: Riverhead Books, 2000.

Index of Contributors

Acknowledgments

Many people have influenced me and my work on this book—courageous friends, singular strangers, and most importantly my mother, who always believed in me and thus taught me to believe in myself. Thanks to Dad, as well as Mom, for taking us on long car trips across the USA, giving us roots and wings, and exposing us to the world beyond Ohio.

I have been inspired, advised, encouraged, and soothed by my patient, supportive husband, Gary Sheppard. I have been tolerated and forgiven my absences in mind and body by my heart's great joy, my daughters Julieclaire and Annalyse. Simply, sincerely, thank you.

Some time ago, on a journey over the Himalayas from Tibet to Nepal, I developed a friendship with two wonderfully crazy, entrepreneurial writers, James O'Reilly and Larry Habegger, the editors of the Travelers' Tales series. Under a tropical moon on the shores of the Pacific in Mexico six years later, we began and ended the evening, as we had so often before, sharing travelers' stories. During our chats we decided to work together on an anthology about contemporary women travelers. Heartfelt thanks to James and Larry, friends as well as the series editors. A special thanks to their loved ones Wenda O'Reilly and Paula McCabe for bearing with us and giving their invaluable feminine points of view. My gratitude to Susan Brady who kept us all organized, on time, and fed during crucial meetings. Additional appreciation to Krista Holmstrom and Kathy Meengs.

Finally, my deepest appreciation to all the women who are included in this book, for giving us new stories to live by and strengthening our resolve and courage to step out the door.

permission of Alfred A. Knopf, Inc. and H. Brann Literary Agency. Copyright © 1992 by Diane Johnson.

"Women at the Well" and "Lunch at Chayas" by Mary Beth Simmons reprinted by permission of the author. Copyright © 1995 by Mary Beth Simmons.

"Boh Knows Hormones" by Tracy Johnston excerpted from *Shooting the Boh: A Woman's Voyage Down the Wildest River in Borneo* by Tracy Johnston. Copyright © 1992 by Tracy Johnston. Reprinted by permission of Vintage Books, a division of Random House, Inc. and International Creative Management, Inc.

"Quickening: Chartres Cathedral" by Jean Shinoda Bolen, M.D. excerpted from *Crossing to Avalon: A Woman's Midlife Pilgrimage* by Jean Shinoda Bolen, M.D. Copyright © 1994 by Jean Shinoda Bolen. Reprinted by permission of HarperCollins Publishers, Inc.

"Across the Steppes on a Horse with No Name" by Lynn Ferrin originally appeared in the March 15, 1987 issue of *Great Escapes* (Sunday magazine, *San Francisco Examiner*). Reprinted by permission of the author. Copyright © 1987 by Lynn Ferrin.

"Surfing is Better than Sex" by Thalia Zepatos excerpted from *Adventures in Good Company: The Complete Guide to Women's Tours and Outdoor Trips* by Thalia Zapatos. Reprinted by permission of The Eighth Mountain Press, Portland, Oregon. Copyright © 1994 by Thalia Anastasia Zepatos.

"Same Place Every Year" by Catherine Watson originally appeared in the *Minneapolis Star Tribune*. Reprinted by permission of the *Minneapolis Star Tribune*. Copyright © 1994 by the *Star Tribune*.

"Mirror of the Holocaust" by Maria Streshinsky originally appeared in the December 12, 1993 issue of the *San Francisco Examiner*. Reprinted by permission of the author. Copyright © 1993 by Maria Streshinsky.

"Oh Rome!" by Barbara Grizzuti Harrison excerpted from *Italian Days* by Barbara Grizzuti Harrison. Reprinted by permission of Grove/Atlantic, Inc. Copyright © 1989 by Barbara Grizzuti Harrison.

"Granny Shoots the Rapids" by Ruth Bond reprinted by permission of the author. Copyright © 1987 by Ruth Bond.

Additional Credits (arranged alphabetically by title)

Selections from "A Cautious Enjoyment" by Sara Wetherall excerpted from *Women Travel: A Rough Guide Special* edited by Natania Jansz and Miranda Davies with Alisa Joyce and Jane Parkin. New edition published as *More Women Travel - Adventures and advice from more than 60 countries - A Rough Guide Special* edited by Miranda Davies and Natania Jansz. Reprinted by permission of the Rough Guides, Ltd. Copyright © 1990 by Miranda Davies and Natania Jansz.

Selection from *Crossing to Avalon: A Woman's Midlife Pilgrimage* by Jean Shinoda Bolen, M.D. Copyright © 1994 by Jean Shinoda Bolen. Reprinted by permission of HarperCollins Publishers, Inc.

Selection from *The Demon Lover: On the Sexuality of Terrorism* by Robin Morgan reprinted by permission of W. W. Norton & Company, Inc. and Edite Kroll Literary Agency. Copyright © 1989 by Robin Morgan.

Selection from *Dreams of the Peaceful Dragon: A Journey into Bhutan* by Katie Hickman reprinted by permission of Victor Gollancz, Ltd. Copyright © 1987 by Katie Hickman.

Selection from "An Eastern Westerner in China" by Adrienne Su excerpted from *More Women Travel - Adventures and advice from more than 60 countries - A Rough Guide Special* edited by Miranda Davies and Natania Jansz. Reprinted by permission of the Rough Guides, Ltd. Copyright © 1995 by Miranda Davies and Natania Jansz.

Selection from *Egypt Observed* by Henri Gougaud and Collette Gouvion, translated by Stephen Hardman and published by Kaye and Ward. Reprinted by permission of Reed Consumer Books. Text copyright © 1980 by Hachette, translation copyright © 1980 by Kaye & Ward.

Selection from "European Journal" by Libby Lubin reprinted from the April 1991 issue of *European Travel & Life*. Copyright © 1991 by Libby Lubin.

Selection from "Finding a Place in Kyoto" by Riki Therivel excerpted from *More Women Travel - Adventures and advice from more than 60 countries - A Rough Guide Special* edited by Miranda Davies and Natania Jansz. Reprinted by permission of the Rough Guides, Ltd. Copyright © 1995 by Miranda Davies and Natania Jansz.

reprinted by permission of Book Passage Press. Copyright ©
1994 by Book Passage Press.

Selection from "I Touched a Whale" by Paula McDonald reprinted
by permission of author. Copyright © 1995 by Paula
McDonald.

Selections from *Illuminata: Thoughts, Prayers, Rites of Passage* by
Marianne Williamson. Copyright © 1994 by Marianne
Williamson. Reprinted by permission of Random House, Inc.

Selection from *Indonesia Handbook* by Bill Dalton reprinted by permission of Moon Publications. Copyright © 1991 by Bill
Dalton.

Selection from *Italian Days* by Barbara Grizzuti Harrison reprinted
by permission of Grove/Atlantic, Inc. Copyright © 1989 by
Barbara Grizzuti Harrison.

Selections from *A Journey of One's Own: Uncommon Advice for the
Independent Woman Traveler* by Thalia Zepatos reprinted by per-
mission of The Eighth Mountain Press. Copyright © 1992 by
Thalia Anastasia Zepatos.

Selection from "Journey of Remembrance" by Betty Ann Webster
reprinted by permisison of the author. Copyright © 1995 by
Betty Ann Webster.

Selections from *The Journey's Echo: Selections from Freya Stark* by Freya
Stark reprinted by permission of John Murray (Publishers)
Ltd. Copyright © 1963 by Freya Stark.

Selection from "The Joys of Solo Travel" by Kimberly Brown published with permission from the author. Copyright © 2001 by
Kimberly Brown.

Selection from "Kenya on Horseback" by Ann Jones originally appeared in *Town & Country*. Reprinted by permission of the
author. Copyright © 1994 by Ann Jones.

Selections from *The Landlady in Bangkok* by Karen Swenson
reprinted by permission of Copper Canyon Press (P.O.B. 271,
Port Townsend, Washington), and the author. Copyright ©
1994 by Karen Swenson.

Selections from "Last Minute Terror" by Jan Haag reprinted by permission of the author. Copyright © 1995 by Jan Haag.

Selection from "Like Readers of Romance Novels, Some Women
Wish to be Taken Away" by Mary Morris reprinted from the
May 7, 1987 issue of *The New York Times*. Copyright © 1987
by The New York Times Company. Reprinted by permission.

Selection from "The Scuba Solution" by Claire Walter reprinted by permission of the author. Copyright © 1995 by Claire Walter.

Selection from *The Seasoned Traveler* by Marcia Schnedler reprinted by permission of Country Roads Press. Copyright © 1992 by Marcia Schnedler.

Selections from "Spirit Walk" by Karen Monk excerpted from *Another Wilderness: New Outdoor Writing About Women* edited by Susan Fox Rogers. Reprinted by permission of Seal Press. Copyright © 1994 by Karen Monk.

Selection from *A Sportswoman in India* (1900) by Isabel Savory published by Oxford University Press.

Selection from *Springs of Oriental Wisdom* published by Marcel Schuman Company, Inc. Copyright © Leobuchbandlang, Germany.

Selection from "Take That!" by Katy Koontz reprinted by permision of author. Copyright © 1995 by Katy Koontz.

Selections from *Tracks* by Robyn Davidson copyright © 1980 by Robyn Davidson. Reprinted by permission of Pantheon Books, a division of Random House, Inc. and Rogers Coleridge & White, Ltd.

Selection from "Travel Diary" by Paula McDonald reprinted by permission of the author. Copyright © 1995 by Paula McDonald.

Selection from *Travels with Children - a travel survival kit* by Maureen Wheeler reprinted by permission of Lonely Planet Publications. Copyright © 1990 by Maureen Wheeler.

Selection from "Two Qualities Make a Good Angler" by Mark Jenkins reprinted from the November 1994 issue of *Condé Nast Traveler*. Reprinted by permission of *Condé Nast Traveler*. Copyright © 1994 by *Condé Nast Traveler*.

Selection from "Unexpected Trails" by Paula McDonald reprinted by permission of author. Copyright © 1995 by Paula McDonald.

Selection from *Unprotected Females in Norway* written in 1857 by Emily Lowe published by Oxford University Press.

Selection from *Up the Amazon* by Violet Cressy-Marcks reprinted by permission of Hodder Headline Plc. Copyright © 1932 by Hodder & Stoughton.

Selection from "Up the Volcano" by Lucy McCauley reprinted by permission of the author. Copyright © 1995 by Lucy McCauley.

About the Editor

Marybeth Bond is well known in the world of travel. She is the award-winning author/editor of five women's travel books in the Travelers' Tales series, was the travel expert for CBS Evening Magazine, and was also a featured guest on *The Oprah Winfrey Show*. Her travel articles have been published worldwide in magazines such as *Islands* and *Shape*, and newspapers such as the *San Francisco Examiner* and *Kuala Lumpur Star*. She is also the travel columnist for a Northern California newspaper. She has appeared on more than 250 television and radio shows and her Travelers' Tales book, *Gutsy Women: Travel Tips and Wisdom for the Road*, was featured on the *Today* show and *The Oprah Winfrey Show*.

She has been a marketing executive for Xerox and Honeywell, spokesperson for Fortune 500 companies, travel editor/expert for ivillage.com and Outside Radio, consultant for international tour operators, and frequent guest on CNN, Oxygen, NPR, and "Ask the Experts" (Reader's Digest).

Marybeth has hiked, cycled, climbed, dived, and kayaked her way through six continents and more than seventy countries around the world, from the depths of the Flores Sea to the summit of Mt. Kilimanjaro. She has trekked in the Himalayas and ridden camels across the Thar and Sahara Deserts. At age thirty, she left her corporate job in the computer industry, put all her possessions in storage, bought a one-way ticket to Bangkok, and took off. She continued to travel for two years around the world solo, and on that journey met her future husband in Kathmandu. In the past two decades she has traveled with her daughters and husband from Lombok to Luxor, Zanzibar to Killarny.

Marybeth is a member of the Society of American Travel Writers and was an advisor for Northwestern University's Medill School of Journalism. She lives in Northern California with her husband, two children, and a dog.

TRAVELERS' TALES

THE SOUL OF TRAVEL

Footsteps Series

THE FIRE NEVER DIES
One Man's Raucous Romp Down the Road of Food, Passion, and Adventure
By Richard Sterling
ISBN 1-885-211-70-8
$14.95

"Sterling's writing is like spit-fire, foursquare and jazzy with crackle...."
—*Kirkus Reviews*

LAST TROUT IN VENICE
The Far-Flung Escapades of an Accidental Adventurer
By Doug Lansky
ISBN 1-885-211-63-5
$14.95

"Traveling with Doug Lansky might result in a considerably shortened life expectancy...but what a way to go." —Tony Wheeler, Lonely Planet Publications

ONE YEAR OFF
Leaving It All Behind for a Round-the-World Journey with Our Children
By David Elliot Cohen
ISBN 1-885-211-65-1
$14.95

A once-in-a-lifetime adventure generously shared.

THE WAY OF THE WANDERER
Discover Your True Self Through Travel
By David Yeadon
ISBN 1-885-211-60-0
$14.95

Experience transformation through travel with this delightful, illustrated collection by award-winning author David Yeadon.

TAKE ME WITH YOU
A Round-the-World Journey to Invite a Stranger Home
By Brad Newsham
ISBN 1-885-211-51-1
$24.00 (cloth)

"Newsham is an ideal guide. His journey, at heart, is into humanity." —Pico Iyer, author of *Video Night in Kathmandu*

KITE STRINGS OF THE SOUTHERN CROSS
A Woman's Travel Odyssey
By Laurie Gough
ISBN 1-885-211-54-6
$14.95

—★ ★ ★—

ForeWord Silver Medal Winner
— *Travel Book of the Year*

THE SWORD OF HEAVEN
A Five Continent Odyssey to Save the World
By Mikkel Aaland
ISBN 1-885-211-44-9
$24.00 (cloth)

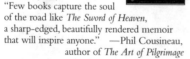

"Few books capture the soul of the road like *The Sword of Heaven*, a sharp-edged, beautifully rendered memoir that will inspire anyone." —Phil Cousineau, author of *The Art of Pilgrimage*

STORM
A Motorcycle Journey of Love, Endurance, and Transformation
By Allen Noren
ISBN 1-885-211-45-7
$24.00 (cloth)

—★ ★ ★—

ForeWord Gold Medal Winner
— *Travel Book of the Year*

Travelers' Tales Classics

COAST TO COAST
A Journey Across 1950s America
By Jan Morris
ISBN 1-885-211-79-1
$16.95

After reporting on the first Everest ascent in 1953, Morris spent a year journeying by car, train, ship, and aircraft across the United States. In her brilliant prose, Morris records with exuberance and curiosity a time of innocence in the U.S.

TRADER HORN
A Young Man's Astounding Adventures in 19th Century Equatorial Africa
By Alfred Aloysius Horn
ISBN 1-885-211-81-3
$16.95

Here is the stuff of legends —tale of thrills and danger, wild beasts, serpents, and savages. An unforgettable and vivid portrait of a vanished late-19th century Africa.

THE ROYAL ROAD TO ROMANCE
By Richard Halliburton
ISBN 1-885-211-53-8
$14.95

"Laughing at hardships, dreaming of beauty, ardent for adventure, Halliburton has managed to sing into the pages of this glorious book his own exultant spirit of youth and freedom."
—*Chicago Post*

UNBEATEN TRACKS IN JAPAN
By Isabella L. Bird
ISBN 1-885-211-57-0
$14.95

Isabella Bird was one of the most adventurous women travelers of the 19th century with journeys to Tibet, Canada, Korea, Turkey, Hawaii, and Japan. A fascinating read for anyone interested in women's travel, spirituality, and Asian culture.

THE RIVERS RAN EAST
By Leonard Clark
ISBN 1-885-211-66-X
$16.95

Clark is the original Indiana Jones, relaying a breathtaking account of his search for the legendary El Dorado gold in the Amazon.

Travel Humor

NOT SO FUNNY WHEN IT HAPPENED
The Best of Travel Humor and Misadventure
Edited by Tim Cahill
ISBN 1-885-211-55-4
$12.95

Laugh with Bill Bryson, Dave Barry, Anne Lamott, Adair Lara, and many more.

THERE'S NO TOILET PAPER...ON THE ROAD LESS TRAVELED
The Best of Travel Humor and Misadventure
Edited by Doug Lansky
ISBN 1-885-211-27-9
$12.95

★ ★ —

Humor Book of the Year
—Independent Publisher's Book Award

— ★ ★ —

ForeWord Gold Medal Winner— Humor Book of the Year

LAST TROUT IN VENICE
The Far-Flung Escapades of an Accidental Adventurer
By Doug Lansky
ISBN 1-885-211-63-5
$14.95

"Traveling with Doug Lansky might result in a considerably shortened life expectancy...but what a way to go."
—Tony Wheeler, Lonely Planet Publications

Women's Travel

A WOMAN'S PASSION FOR TRAVEL
More True Stories from A Woman's World
Edited by Marybeth Bond
& Pamela Michael
ISBN 1-885-211-36-8
$17.95

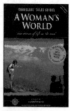

"A diverse and gripping
series of stories!" —Arlene Blum, author of
Annapurna: A Woman's Place

A WOMAN'S WORLD
**True Stories of
Life on the Road**
Edited by Marybeth Bond
Introduction by
Dervla Murphy
ISBN 1-885-211-06-6
$17.95

— ★ ★ ★ —

*Winner of the Lowell Thomas
Award for Best Travel Book—
Society of American Travel Writers*

WOMEN IN THE WILD
**True Stories of
Adventure and
Connection**
Edited by Lucy McCauley
ISBN 1-885-211-21-X
$17.95

"A spiritual, moving, and
totally female book to take you
around the world and back." —*Mademoiselle*

A MOTHER'S WORLD
Journeys of the Heart
Edited by Marybeth Bond
& Pamela Michael
ISBN 1-885-211-26-0
$14.95

"These stories remind us
that motherhood is one
of the great unifying forces
in the world" —*San Francisco Examiner*

Food

ADVENTURES IN WINE
**True Stories of
Vineyards and Vintages
around the World**
Edited by Thom Elkjer
ISBN 1-885-211-80-5
$17.95

Humanity, community, and
brotherhood comprise the marvelous virtues of
the wine world. This collection toasts the
warmth and wonders of this large, extended
family in stories by travelers who are wine
novices and experts alike.

FOOD (Updated)
A Taste of the Road
Edited by Richard Sterling
Introduction by Margo True
ISBN 1-885-211-77-5
$18.95

— ★ ★ ★ —

*Silver Medal Winner of the
Lowell Thomas Award for
Best Travel Book—Society
of American Travel Writers*

HER FORK IN THE ROAD
**Women Celebrate Food
and Travel**
Edited by Lisa Bach
ISBN 1-885-211-71-6
$16.95

A savory sampling of stories
by some of the best writers
in and out of the food and travel fields.

THE ADVENTURE OF FOOD
**True Stories of
Eating Everything**
Edited by Richard Sterling
ISBN 1-885-211-37-6
$17.95

"These stories are bound to
whet appetites for more
than food."

—*Publishers Weekly*

Spiritual Travel

THE SPIRITUAL GIFTS OF TRAVEL
The Best of Travelers' Tales
Edited by James O'Reilly and Sean O'Reilly
ISBN 1-885-211-69-4
$16.95

A collection of favorite stories of transformation on the road from our award-winning Travelers' Tales series that shows the myriad ways travel indelibly alters our inner landscapes.

THE WAY OF THE WANDERER
Discover Your True Self Through Travel
By David Yeadon
ISBN 1-885-211-60-0
$14.95

Experience transformation through travel with this delightful, illustrated collection by award-winning author David Yeadon.

PILGRIMAGE
Adventures of the Spirit
Edited by Sean O'Reilly & James O'Reilly
Introduction by Phil Cousineau
ISBN 1-885-211-56-2
$16.95

— ★ ★ ★ —

ForeWord Silver Medal Winner — Travel Book of the Year

A WOMAN'S PATH
Women's Best Spiritual Travel Writing
Edited by Lucy McCauley, Amy G. Carlson & Jennifer Leo
ISBN 1-885-211-48-1
$16.95

"A sensitive exploration of women's lives that have been unexpectedly and spiritually touched by travel experiences.... Highly recommended."
— *Library Journal*

THE ROAD WITHIN
True Stories of Transformation and the Soul
Edited by Sean O'Reilly, James O'Reilly & Tim O'Reilly
ISBN 1-885-211-19-8
$17.95

— ★ ★ ★ —

Best Spiritual Book — Independent Publisher's Book Award

THE ULTIMATE JOURNEY
Inspiring Stories of Living and Dying
James O'Reilly, Sean O'Reilly & Richard Sterling
ISBN 1-885-211-38-4
$17.95

"A glorious collection of writings about the ultimate adventure. A book to keep by one's bedside—and close to one's heart." —Philip Zaleski, editor, *The Best Spiritual Writing series*

Adventure

TESTOSTERONE PLANET
True Stories from a Man's World
Edited by Sean O'Reilly, Larry Habegger & James O'Reilly
ISBN 1-885-211-43-0
$17.95

Thrills and laughter with some of today's best writers: Sebastian Junger, Tim Cahill, Bill Bryson, and Jon Krakauer.

DANGER!
True Stories of Trouble and Survival
Edited by James O'Reilly, Larry Habegger & Sean O'Reilly
ISBN 1-885-211-32-5
$17.95

"Exciting...for those who enjoy living on the edge or prefer to read the survival stories of others, this is a good pick."
— *Library Journal*

Special Interest

365 TRAVEL
A Daily Book of Journeys, Meditations, and Adventures
Edited by Lisa Bach
ISBN 1-885-211-67-8
$14.95
An illuminating collection of travel wisdom and adventures that reminds us all of the lessons we learn while on the road.

THE GIFT OF RIVERS
True Stories of Life on the Water
Edited by Pamela Michael
Introduction by Robert Hass
ISBN 1-885-211-42-2
$14.95
"*The Gift of Rivers* is a soulful compendium of wonderful stories that illuminate, educate, inspire, and delight."
—David Brower, Chairman of Earth Island Institute

FAMILY TRAVEL
The Farther You Go, the Closer You Get
Edited by Laura Manske
ISBN 1-885-211-33-3
$17.95
"This is family travel at its finest." —*Working Mother*

LOVE & ROMANCE
True Stories of Passion on the Road
Edited by Judith Babcock Wylie
ISBN 1-885-211-18-X
$17.95
"A wonderful book to read by a crackling fire."
—*Romantic Traveling*

THE GIFT OF BIRDS
True Encounters with Avian Spirits
Edited by Larry Habegger & Amy G. Carlson
ISBN 1-885-211-41-4
$17.95
"These are all wonderful, entertaining stories offering a *bird's-eye view!* of our avian friends."
—*Booklist*

A DOG'S WORLD
True Stories of Man's Best Friend on the Road
Edited by Christine Hunsicker
ISBN 1-885-211-23-6
$12.95
This extraordinary collection includes stories by John Steinbeck, Helen Thayer, James Herriot, Pico Iyer, and many others.

THE GIFT OF TRAVEL
The Best of Travelers' Tales
Edited by Larry Habegger, James O'Reilly & Sean O'Reilly
ISBN 1-885-211-25-2
$14.95
"Like gourmet chefs in a French market, the editors of Travelers' Tales pick, sift, and prod their way through the weighty shelves of contemporary travel writing, creaming off the very best."
—William Dalrymple, author of *City of Djinns*

Travel Advice

SHITTING PRETTY
How to Stay Clean and Healthy While Traveling
By Dr. Jane Wilson-Howarth
ISBN 1-885-211-47-3
$12.95

A light-hearted book about a serious subject for millions of travelers—staying healthy on the road—written by international health expert, Dr. Jane Wilson-Howarth.

THE FEARLESS SHOPPER
How to Get the Best Deals on the Planet
By Kathy Borrus
ISBN 1-885-211-39-2
$14.95

"Anyone who reads *The Fearless Shopper* will come away a smarter, more responsible shopper and a more curious, culturally attuned traveler."
—Jo Mancuso, *The Shopologist*

GUTSY WOMEN
More Travel Tips and Wisdom for the Road
By Marybeth Bond
ISBN 1-885-211-61-9
$12.95

Second Edition—Packed with funny, instructive, and inspiring advice for women heading out to see the world.

SAFETY AND SECURITY FOR WOMEN WHO TRAVEL
By Sheila Swan & Peter Laufer
ISBN 1-885-211-29-5
$12.95

A must for every woman traveler!

THE FEARLESS DINER
Travel Tips and Wisdom for Eating around the World
By Richard Sterling
ISBN 1-885-211-22-8
$7.95

Combines practical advice on foodstuffs, habits, and etiquette, with hilarious accounts of others' eating adventures.

THE PENNY PINCHER'S PASSPORT TO LUXURY TRAVEL
The Art of Cultivating Preferred Customer Status
By Joel L. Widzer
ISBN 1-885-211-31-7
$12.95

Proven techniques on how to travel first class at discount prices, even if you're not a frequent flyer.

GUTSY MAMAS
Travel Tips and Wisdom for Mothers on the Road
By Marybeth Bond
ISBN 1-885-211-20-1
$7.95

A delightful guide for mothers traveling with their children—or without them!

Destination Titles:
True Stories of Life on the Road

AMERICA
Edited by Fred Setterberg
ISBN 1-885-211-28-7
$19.95

AMERICAN SOUTHWEST
Edited by Sean O'Reilly
& James O'Reilly
ISBN 1-885-211-58-9
$17.95

AUSTRALIA
Edited by Larry Habegger
ISBN 1-885-211-40-6
$17.95

BRAZIL
Edited by Annette Haddad
& Scott Doggett
Introduction by Alex
Shoumatoff
ISBN 1-885-211-11-2
$17.95

CENTRAL AMERICA
Edited by Larry Habegger
& Natanya Pearlman
ISBN 1-885-211-74-0
$17.95

CUBA
Edited by Tom Miller
ISBN 1-885-211-62-7
$17.95

FRANCE (Updated)
Edited by James O'Reilly,
Larry Habegger &
Sean O'Reilly
ISBN 1-885-211-73-2
$18.95

GRAND CANYON
Edited by Sean O'Reilly,
James O'Reilly &
Larry Habegger
ISBN 1-885-211-34-1
$17.95

GREECE
Edited by Larry Habegger,
Sean O'Reilly &
Brian Alexander
ISBN 1-885-211-52-X
$17.95

HAWAI'I
Edited by Rick &
Marcie Carroll
ISBN 1-885-211-35-X
$17.95

HONG KONG
Edited by James O'Reilly,
Larry Habegger &
Sean O'Reilly
ISBN 1-885-211-03-1
$17.95

INDIA
Edited by James O'Reilly
& Larry Habegger
ISBN 1-885-211-01-5
$17.95

IRELAND

Edited by James O'Reilly,
Larry Habegger &
Sean O'Reilly
ISBN 1-885-211-46-5
$17.95

SAN FRANCISCO

Edited by James O'Reilly,
Larry Habegger &
Sean O'Reilly
ISBN 1-885-211-08-2
$17.95

ITALY (Updated)

Edited by Anne Calcagno
Introduction by Jan Morris
ISBN 1-885-211-72-4
$18.95

SPAIN (Updated)

Edited by Lucy McCauley
ISBN 1-885-211-78-3
$19.95

JAPAN

Edited by Donald W. George
& Amy G. Carlson
ISBN 1-885-211-04-X
$17.95

THAILAND (Updated)

Edited by James O'Reilly
& Larry Habegger
ISBN 1-885-211-75-9
$18.95

MEXICO (Updated)

Edited by James O'Reilly
& Larry Habegger
ISBN 1-885-211-59-7
$17.95

TIBET

Edited by James O'Reilly,
Larry Habegger, & Kim
Morris
ISBN 1-885-211-76-7
$18.95

NEPAL

Edited by Rajendra
S. Khadka
ISBN 1-885-211-14-7
$17.95

TUSCANY

Edited by James O'Reilly, &
Tara Austen Weaver
ISBN 1-885-211-68-6
$16.95

PARIS

Edited by James O'Reilly,
Larry Habegger &
Sean O'Reilly
ISBN 1-885-211-10-4
$17.95